Amnesty International and F
in Postwar Britain, 1945–19'.

M000290371

In this definitive new account of the emergence of human rights activism in postwar Britain, Tom Buchanan shows how disparate individuals, organisations and causes gradually came to acquire a common identity as 'human rights activists'. This was a slow process whereby a coalition of activists, working on causes ranging from anti-fascism, anti-apartheid and decolonisation to civil liberties and the peace movement, began to come together under the banner of human rights. The launch of Amnesty International in 1961 and its landmark winning of the Nobel Peace Prize in 1977 provided a model and inspiration to many new activist movements in 'the field of human rights', and helped to effect major changes in terms of public and political attitudes towards human rights issues across the globe.

Tom Buchanan is Professor of Modern British and European History at the University of Oxford. He is the author of *The Spanish Civil War and the British Labour Movement* (1991), *Britain and the Spanish Civil War* (1997) and *The Impact of the Spanish Civil War on Britain: War, Loss and Memory* (2007). He has also published *Europe's Troubled Peace, 1945 to the Present* (2006, second edition 2012), and *East Wind: China and the British Left, 1925–1976* (2012). His most recent publication is a co-edited book on the centenary of the Balkan Wars titled *War in the Balkans: Conflict and Diplomacy before World War I* (2015).

Human Rights in History

Edited by

Stefan-Ludwig Hoffmann, University of California, Berkeley

Samuel Moyn, Yale University, Connecticut

This series showcases new scholarship exploring the backgrounds of human rights today. With an open-ended chronology and international perspective, the series seeks works attentive to the surprises and contingencies in the historical origins and legacies of human rights ideals and interventions. Books in the series will focus not only on the intellectual antecedents and foundations of human rights, but also on the incorporation of the concept by movements, nation-states, international governance, and transnational law.

A full list of titles in the series can be found at:
www.cambridge.org/human-rights-history

Amnesty International and Human Rights Activism in Postwar Britain, 1945–1977

Tom Buchanan

University of Oxford

CAMBRIDGE
UNIVERSITY PRESS

University Printing House, Cambridge CB2 8BS, United Kingdom

One Liberty Plaza, 20th Floor, New York, NY 10006, USA

477 Williamstown Road, Port Melbourne, VIC 3207, Australia

314–321, 3rd Floor, Plot 3, Splendor Forum, Jasola District Centre,
New Delhi – 110025, India

79 Anson Road, #06–04/06, Singapore 079906

Cambridge University Press is part of the University of Cambridge.

It furthers the University's mission by disseminating knowledge in the pursuit of
education, learning, and research at the highest international levels of excellence.

www.cambridge.org
Information on this title: www.cambridge.org/9781107127517
DOI: 10.1017/9781316422397

First published 2020

Printed in the United Kingdom by TJ International Ltd, Padstow Cornwall

A catalogue record for this publication is available from the British Library.

The use of 70 (seventy) words from PERSECUTION 1961 written by Peter
Benenson (Penguin Books, 1961.) Copyright © Peter Benenson, 1961.
Reproduced by permission of Penguin Books Ltd.

ISBN 978-1-107-12751-7 Hardback
ISBN 978-1-107-56655-2 Paperback

For Bertha, Roy, Doris and Harry

I have been sitting at this desk since 5 am enjoying this supreme pleasure, quiet undisturbed work before anyone else is up. There's nothing like it. I wonder how I managed all those years when I worked into the night, instead of enjoying the best part of the day, the dawn.

Patrick Duncan (Algeria) to Peter Benenson (London), undated,
October 1965

Contents

Preface and Acknowledgements

Although I began to work on this book in earnest in 2012, my interest in the history of Amnesty International stretches back to 1996, when I was invited to speak at a conference on 'Spain in an International Context, 1936–1959'. It was while researching my paper, on British anti-Franco campaigns in the decades after the Spanish Civil War,[1] that I realised that there was more than one organisation in the early 1960s using the name 'Amnesty' to campaign on behalf of political prisoners. Indeed, a group calling for an amnesty for prisoners in Spain preceded Amnesty International by almost two years. This piqued my interest in Amnesty International, an organisation that I had been aware of (although never actively involved in) since the late 1970s. In 1997 I received permission to look at Amnesty's archives – at that point still held at its headquarters in London, now at the International Institute of Social History, Amsterdam. This rich and, until then, largely unconsulted source formed the basis for my first two articles on this subject, one on how Amnesty International was formed, and the second on the crisis that gripped the organisation in 1966–67.[2]

Over the years my interests have widened significantly to embrace the British 'human rights movement' more broadly conceived, albeit with Amnesty still very much at the centre of the story. In the intervening period the history of human rights has taken off as a major new field of study, with its own journals, a burgeoning literature and scholarly debates. However, while making a contribution to this exciting new field, this book is still essentially about the activism that first attracted my interest. More specifically it explores how individuals and organisations slowly came to perceive themselves as forming part of a broader movement that could be defined by a shared concern for human rights. Interestingly, this distinction – between the emergence of a legal and institutional framework of human rights, and activism which may or may not have been understood at the time as being in support of human rights – is not just a question of historical interpretation, but was a discussion that British activists were consciously engaged in at the time. In 1979–80, members of the British Section of Amnesty International debated what kind of educational policy they should pursue. According to one view, Amnesty derived its moral authority from a pre-existing system of human rights to which it was subordinate: its task, therefore, was to launch a programme of 'Human Rights Education'. However, another group argued that human rights did not 'precede' Amnesty, and only acquired 'reality and force' through the 'ceaseless vigilance' of Amnesty and similar organisations. From this perspective Amnesty should avoid assuming a general educational role, and its work in schools must only use material that was 'within earshot of its proper activity and concerns'.[3]

My decision to focus on organisations and grass-roots activists, in line with the second of these perspectives, has, therefore, shaped the parameters of this book, whether geographical, temporal or conceptual. First, the book deals primarily with activism within Britain and Northern Ireland. While Amnesty and many other organisations became wholly or partially internationalised during this period, the emphasis here is primarily on how the 'international' and the 'British' elements interrelated. The growth of Amnesty sections in other countries – which is now the subject of a number of scholarly studies – is not addressed in any detail. Secondly, although opening with a brief account of the 1930s, the book deals essentially with the three and a half decades after the end of World War II. Two dates suggest chronological boundaries for the project: the signing of the Universal Declaration of Human Rights on 10 December 1948 and the award of the Nobel Peace Prize to Amnesty International on 10 October 1977. Both events have undoubtedly gained greater significance with the benefit of hindsight. The UN Declaration gave later activists a 'Charter' around which they could unite, while the Nobel Prize gave an international seal of approval to a new kind of human rights activism. It was not the first time that an organisation had won the prize, but it was the first time that it had been awarded to an activist-driven one. Thirdly, the book is not about the growth of international law and institutions, subjects that already have a substantial literature devoted to them, but rather about causes, networks and individuals. The book is not, therefore, about legal and philosophical conceptions of human rights, but rather about the small, interconnected circles of activists, shaped by shared beliefs, education, friendships and even wartime experiences, who came to see their activities as part of the struggle for 'human rights'.

In many regards, therefore, this is a group portrait and it may seem invidious to single out the role of any individual. However, the emergence of British human rights activism cannot be understood without understanding the personalities and motivations of individuals, their immediate circles and the wider movements that they inspired. Accordingly, I have sought to ensure that somewhat neglected figures, such as the Rev. Michael Scott and the Quaker activists Eric Baker and Eileen Fletcher, are given due credit. But the individual whose career truly unites the somewhat disparate threads of the following chapters is Peter Benenson, the lawyer who emerged through the struggles against political imprisonment of the 1940s and 1950s to found Amnesty International in May 1961. The world of modern human rights campaigning was born in that moment. As his close colleague Eric Baker recalled in 1975, despite the many men and women who worked tirelessly to get Amnesty off the ground, it was Benenson's ideas, energy and enthusiasm that were the essential ingredients of its success.[4] He made a vivid impression on those who worked with him at this time: for instance, newspaper editor Charles Foley, who was defended by Benenson in Cyprus in 1957, described him as having a 'warm heart for lost causes' and as being 'irrepressibly cheerful', with a 'thrusting style' in court.[5] Particularly apposite are the comments of Peggy Crane, who worked closely with Benenson in the opening phase of Amnesty. She recalled his 'touch of genius' which enabled him to convince the early volunteers to join him in 'creating something of importance, [something] of History': an account all the more compelling because she so clearly perceived his weaknesses as an administrator.[6] During the years between 1961 and his troubled departure from Amnesty in 1967, Benenson – Crane's 'evangelist with a divine spark' – was at the height of his powers. In telling the fuller story of the emergence of human rights activism, therefore, this book has at its core the shaping of Benenson's ideas about activism in the 1940s and 1950s, their articulation through Amnesty International in the 1960s and their fulfilment (and evolution) in the 1970s.

*

Throughout my research I have been fortunate to receive advice, support and encouragement from Tricia Feeney, who came to work for Amnesty in the 1970s. At an early stage I was able to interview Peter Benenson in Oxford, as well as two other prominent early figures in Amnesty – Lord Archer (Peter Archer) and Louis Blom-Cooper – at Westminster. I also met Richard Reoch, Amnesty's former press officer, at this time. While working on my article on the Amnesty crisis of 1966–67, I interviewed Polly Toynbee and corresponded with Aidan Foster-Carter, Peter Calvocoressi, Ben Whitaker, Anthony Marreco and Phillip Knightley (then of the *Sunday Times*). Peter Calvocoressi very kindly sent me his own copy of the report that he had drafted in 1967, on the condition – which I have fulfilled – that I eventually deposit it with Amnesty. Following Peter Benenson's death in 2005 I was asked to write his entry for the *Oxford Dictionary of National Biography*. As a consequence, I met Benenson's daughter, Natasha, who kindly allowed me to consult her father's private papers. I also looked at a quantity of his private papers that the family had deposited at Amnesty's headquarters. I must express my thanks to the Amnesty staff for their help during the two periods that I spent researching at Amnesty's headquarters. I must also thank Sophie Halpern who kindly gave additional information about the papers of her late husband, Jack Halpern.

As this project has developed over the last twenty years, I have been helped by many friends and colleagues. I am deeply grateful to all of those listed above, and must also thank Eric Poinsot, Andrew Shacknove, Paul Hoffman, David Lewis, Mikael R. Madsen, Heather Faulkner, Philip Boobyer, Holger Nehring, Sebastian Gehrig, Steven Jensen, Mark Cornwall, Dagmar Hajkova, Meirian Jump, Rob Lemkin, Paul Betts and Natalia Benjamin. At a late stage in my research Michael Yudkin kindly shared his recollections of campaigning on behalf of Jews in the Soviet Union during the 1970s and 1980s. Martin Conway has been a tremendous source of support throughout. The series of seminars on political justice and human rights that we jointly organised in Oxford during Michaelmas term 1997 gave me the incentive to turn my initial encounter with Amnesty into a research paper. A draft of this book has been read by Natasha Benenson and Greg Marsh, and I am extremely grateful for their comments and corrections, especially on the history of the Benenson family. I am also grateful for the comments of David Grylls and Tricia Feeney, who both read the manuscript closely, and for the comments of the anonymous reader. Of course, all mistakes of fact and interpretation are my own.

I have given seminar papers on my research at the University of Oxford (1998 and 2016); the LSE (1998); the University of York (1999); The Hague, Europaeum conference (2008); Manchester University (2012); the University of Northumbria (2013); and the University of Padua (2015). I developed my interest in human rights activism through participation in the series of joint Oxford–Berlin seminars on the theme of 'Europeanization', funded by the AHRC and DFG and organised by Martin Conway and Kiran Klaus Patel (2005–8). I also contributed to the DANGO conference at the University of Birmingham, organised by Nick Crowson, Matthew Hilton and James McKay (2008). My participation in the Global Anti-Apartheid conference (Oxford, 2016), organised by Anna Konieczna, encouraged me to look more deeply at Amnesty's links to southern Africa.

Researching and writing this book would not have been possible without a number of terms of sabbatical leave from the University of Oxford. I must record my gratitude to Professor Jonathan Michie and Professor Angus Hawkins at OUDCE, and in particular to all those who helped to provide cover in my absence: Dr Christine Jackson, Annette Mayer, Dr Michael Redley, Sheila Tremlett and Dr Suan Sheridan Breakwell. I undertook research visits with assistance from the Research Funds of both OUDCE and the History Faculty.

For permission to quote from archive sources I would like to thank: Natasha Benenson; Inspire Nottinghamshire Archives; the Board of Deputies of British Jews; Lambeth Palace Library; Borthwick Institute, University of York; J. B. Priestley Library, University of Bradford; Lucy Astor; the LSE Library; Georgia Glover for David Higham Associates; Penguin Random House; and the ITV archive. With the kind assistance of Emily Burgoyne at Regent's Park College, every effort has been made to establish the copyright ownership for the Ernest Payne and David Russell papers.

As ever, I am deeply grateful to my wife Julia, for her constant support and understanding throughout the period in which I have worked on this project. Finally, I would like to thank my parents, Angus and Brenda Buchanan, who were closely involved in the religious, political and social world of the late 1940s and 1950s, and happily shared their reminiscences of many of the individuals mentioned in this book. Their recollections of meeting Michael Scott on Iona in 1954 were an inspiration as I struggled to understand this brilliant, elusive man. This book is dedicated to the memory of their parents, my grandparents.

Abbreviations

AI	Amnesty International
AIR	Amnesty International Review
ANC	African National Congress
BAZO	British Anti-Zionist Organisation
BUF	British Union of Fascists
CARD	Campaign Against Racial Discrimination
CAT	Campaign for the Abolition of Torture
CCHR	Chile Committee for Human Rights
CEWC	Council for Education in World Citizenship
CHRR	Centre for Human Rights and Responsibilities
CMS	Church Missionary Society
COPAI	Confederation of Peoples Against Imperialism
CPGB	Communist Party of Great Britain
CSC	Chile Solidarity Campaign
DAF	Defence and Aid Fund
FSC	Friends' Service Council
HRAS	Human Rights Advisory Service
IADL	International Association of Democratic Lawyers
IBA	International Brigades Association
ICJ	International Commission of Jurists
ICRC	International Committee of the Red Cross
IEC	International Executive Committee (Amnesty International)
ILD	International Labour Defence
IRC	International Rescue Committee
IYHR	UN International Year for Human Rights
JDC	Jewish Defence Committee
KCL	King's College London
LNU	League of Nations Union
LOCP	League of Coloured Peoples
LSE	London School of Economics and Political Science
MCF	Movement for Colonial Freedom

MML	Marx Memorial Library
MRA	Moral Re-Armament
MRC	Modern Records Centre, University of Warwick
MRG	Minority Rights Group
MCF	Movement for Colonial Freedom
NCCI	National Committee for Commonwealth Immigrants
NCCL	National Council for Civil Liberties
NCSS	National Council of Social Service
NICRA	Northern Ireland Civil Rights Association
NLS	National Library of Scotland
NPC	National Peace Council
ODNB	*Oxford Dictionary of National Biography*
PTA	Prevention of Terrorism Act
SCESWUN	Standing Conference on the Economic and Social Work of the UN
SDDFC	Spanish Democrats Defence Fund Committee
SLL	Society of Labour Lawyers
SOAS	School of Oriental and African Studies
SRLA&WF	Southern Rhodesia Legal Aid and Welfare Fund
TNA	The National Archives, Kew, London
TUC	Trades Union Congress
UDI	Unilateral Declaration of Independence
UN	United Nations
UNA	United Nations Association of Great Britain and Northern Ireland
UNESCO	United Nations Educational, Scientific and Cultural Organization
WCML	Working Class Movement Library, Salford
WJC	World Jewish Council
WSI	Writers and Scholars International

Introduction

A Community of Conscience

This vast Community of Conscience, as it should rightly be called, today embraces the whole world, though many who belong to it do not openly admit it. Wherever people go out of their way to help the helpless, it is their conscience which drives them. Whenever people protest against injustice, it is their conscience which inspires them. Whoever says: give that person another chance is waving the standard of the Community of Conscience.
(Peter Benenson, founder of Amnesty International, speaking in June 1976)[1]

*

We encounter human rights at every turn in modern Britain. They are built into the law and international agreements, argued over by politicians, are empowering to once marginal and oppressed social groups, taught in schools and universities, and vilified by sections of the media. And yet, only a few decades ago human rights were the preserve of a small group of campaigners, motivated by idealism but aware of the weakness of their position, their main enemy not political hostility but public indifference. In fact, human rights activism only emerged in Britain as a collective endeavour between the conclusion of World War II and the late 1970s. By the end of this period 'the human rights activist' was a recognisable entity: the term was shorthand for a campaigner – possibly employed as such, but more likely a volunteer – engaged on one of the many fronts which, collectively, had become known as the struggle for human rights.[2] There was, of course, a long tradition in Britain, stretching back at least to the anti-slavery movement of the late eighteenth century, of campaigning on behalf of those deprived of their rights. More recently, in the interwar years some anti-fascists had chosen to mobilise under the banner of 'human rights', although it was far more common at the time to refer to the defence of 'civil liberties'.[3] What was new during these postwar decades, however, was that disparate individuals, organisations and causes gradually came to acquire a common identity, even if many of those who were now being described as 'human rights activists', or as

1

participating in 'human rights organisations', would only latterly have thought of themselves in such terms.

By the 1970s the outlines of a human rights movement in Britain were becoming clear. The number of voluntary organisations taking a specific interest in human rights issues, domestic and international, was large and rapidly increasing.[4] These organisations were winning the attention of government, news media, the public, and international institutions. They increasingly made common cause, or shared ideas, experiences and personnel through informal networks. One, Amnesty International, had to some extent transcended its national origins (albeit still based in London and, until 1980, under British leadership), while others lay at the centre of their own international networks. Even greater success and recognition beckoned by the end of the decade. However, it must be borne in mind that such activism was still most commonly described in the 1970s – as it had been for many years – as work *'in the field of human rights'*. This was a loose and somewhat amorphous association, whereby activists pursued their own campaigns under the umbrella of human rights. A campaign for human rights per se was very rarely attempted, and never undertaken successfully.[5] Even by the end of the 1970s, therefore, the human rights movement was still, in essence, the sum of its parts. Human rights activism shaded off into many other related areas, such as peace campaigning or the alleviation of global poverty. An analysis of the membership of the Human Rights Network (an informal grouping of voluntary organisations), for instance, indicates that, of 80 groups listed in 1977, only about a quarter were explicitly or solely concerned with human rights issues: of the remainder, 14 were religious bodies, 7 were explicitly connected to the Jewish community and 6 campaigned for the advancement of women.[6] At the local level, moreover, human rights lay at the centre of other interlocking circles of activism. In 1977 the Bristol branch of the National Council for Civil Liberties (NCCL) referred to its 'close links and overlapping membership' with groups such as Justice, Amnesty International, the local Trades Council, the Child Poverty Action Group and Radical Alternatives to Prison.[7]

It is only in recent years that historians have begun to address the social and political history of human rights activism, and this book provides the first detailed account of how it emerged in postwar Britain. The book takes up Stephen Hopgood's comment, in his 2006 study of Amnesty International, that there was a 'void ... where work on the culture of human rights ought to be found'. How, he asked, could scholars in fields such as international relations and political philosophy 'talk so confidently about the meaning of human rights norms when so little was known about the social origins of those norms ... and *what motivates those who make them their life's work*.[8] It also responds to a point made by Professor Andrew Blane after he and Priscilla Ellsworth had completed a pioneering oral history of the first generation of Amnesty activists. In delivering the tapes and transcripts to Amnesty's offices in 1983, Blane referred to the need for a 'substantive history of the A[mnesty] I[international] movement within the context of the human rights awakening'.[9] This is what this book seeks to provide. Amnesty, as the largest and most influential human rights organisation in Britain, inevitably commands central attention, but its success cannot be understood outside the context of the many other organisations which also – in different ways – campaigned for human rights.

The rise of human rights organisations forms part of the wider phenomenon of the rise of the NGO (non-governmental organisation), a term originally coined to describe the non-state actors invited to serve as consultants during the drafting of the UN Charter in 1945. The transformative role of NGOs – defined in one recent study as those elements of the voluntary sector which sought to exert sociopolitical influence – in postwar Britain is only belatedly receiving the historical recognition that it deserves.[10] Above all, historians have started to look beyond the histories of individual organisations to wider patterns of voluntary activity, including the many interactions and synergies at both the national and international level. For instance, the great stimulus to human rights activism provided by the formation of Amnesty International in 1961 not only followed closely on the formation of two other highly influential voluntary organisations – the Campaign for Nuclear Disarmament (CND) in 1957 and the Anti-Apartheid Movement in 1959 – but also involved many of the same people. These and countless other voluntary organisations dramatically reshaped postwar politics.[11] However, the current connotations of NGOs as bureaucratic, expert-driven institutions offering a professional career path provide little help in understanding the emergence of human rights activism. Such connotations would apply to none of the organisations specifically interested in human rights during their formative phase, many of which either had very small full-time staffs or, in some cases, made a virtue of their lack of professionalism. Moreover, although human rights activism depended on many varieties of expertise it was never simply an extension of any single profession. Many lawyers were involved in establishing human rights organisations, but their legal skills were only one element in their activism, just as the many clergymen who participated did not do so as clerics alone. Amnesty, for instance, was associated with many lawyers but did not have a designated legal officer until the appointment of Nigel Rodley in 1973.

Peter Benenson's idea of a 'Community of Conscience', cited at the start of this chapter, offers a different perspective. While imperfect as a definition of human rights activism, it does combine a sense of the looseness of the endeavour with its inherent internationalism, while also employing one of the concepts that meant the most to activists at the time. Taking their cue from the preamble to the Universal Declaration of Human Rights (UDHR) of 1948, which stated that disregard for human rights had 'resulted in barbarous acts which have *outraged the conscience of mankind*', activists' language was steeped in references to conscience. The best-known example is Amnesty's use of the term 'Prisoners of Conscience' for the prisoners that its groups adopted, but the usage goes far beyond that. Amnesty's first chairman Lionel Elvin spoke about how the organisation wished to become the 'ombudsman of the imprisoned conscience everywhere', and 5000 copies of a journal entitled *World Conscience* were distributed by Amnesty to 25 countries in 1963 to mark the fifteenth anniversary of the UDHR; indeed, if Amnesty's members had not believed that such a collective conscience existed, Amnesty's task would have been impossible.[12] None paid more regard to conscience than the Quakers (members of the Society of Friends), for whom it represented the guiding 'inner light' or 'light within'. John Fletcher, a Quaker who visited jailed conscientious objectors during World War I recalled how during these conversations he reached the conclusion that conscience was 'the ear through which we heard the voice of God, or the eye through which we saw Him'. And conscience was not just to be heard, but to be obeyed: on recently listening to Trevor Huddleston and Michael Scott preach about apartheid, Fletcher noted that conscience 'will not let any of us rest until we do the will of God and let his people go free'.[13] Fletcher spent much time in private study of the writings of the American Quaker John Woolman and of Lord Acton, both of whom had much to say about conscience, and this degree of scholarly reflection was admittedly unusual amongst non-Quakers. Even so, most human rights activists implicitly acknowledged the importance of conscience when defining what they did and what motivated them in terms of simple morality. A survey of Amnesty's British members in 1977 found that a very low proportion specified 'human rights' as their reason for joining the organisation, as opposed to more general concerns over injustice and oppression.[14] Ten years earlier, the US trade union leader Victor Reuther, invited by Amnesty International to give its human rights day lecture, said that he had heard his hosts described as 'that outfit over there in London which is against evil': he defined evil as 'that which threatens the quality of man ... poverty, injustice, humiliation, torture, [and] infringement upon man's freedom'.[15] Peter Benenson put it in similar terms when he told Patrick Duncan, a leading South African opponent of apartheid, that, although the two men no longer agreed over the supreme importance of non-violence, 'your militarism and my pacifism are opposite sides of the same coin, which is a firm determination, cast in bronze, th[at] evil shall not be allowed to triumph'.[16]

Activists

Activists lie at the heart of this book: from the handful of inspirational leaders who founded new organisations and watched them grow (or, indeed, fade away) to the large numbers of volunteers who gave their time and energy to organise meetings, write letters and raise funds. What united them was their dedication to a cause, although they may well have come to it by very different routes. Human rights activism was, if nothing else, about activity, and activists showed little interest in discussing human rights in the abstract. The 'great debate' over a new Declaration of the Rights of Man, initiated by H. G. Wells in the spring of 1940, is the one exception to that rule, but took place in the unusual circumstances of wartime.[17] A survey of the branches of the United Nations Association in 1973 found that members were generally not interested in 'just general talks about human rights but prefer particular topics, eg [sic] human rights in armed conflicts'. The report's author noted with some envy that groups like Amnesty were 'newsworthy because they specialise in particular types of denials of human rights'.[18] This lack of interest in theory was both a strength and a weakness. Activists were unlikely to be deterred by the failures of the fragile arrangements to protect human rights in the postwar world and, indeed, drew fresh inspiration from the repeated assaults on individual freedoms. Yet there was also a danger that the activist might become an unguided missile, that action might precede thought: a sentiment evoked by this revealing account of an exchange between the influential Italian social activist Danilo Dolci and British peace campaigner Peter Cadogan in 1963:

Met Danilo Dolci in Perugia ... We talked about all sorts of things, and then he said, quite out of the blue, that he proposed to spend next January in Africa – West or Central and he asked me which I thought would be more likely. I immediately said – Central – and that is where he is likely to go. I was not very clear about just what he intended to do – presumably he would look for a big problem and try to get to the bottom of it with a view to saying and perhaps doing something useful.[19]

Until the 1970s, when a more managerial type of leader emerged, leadership was necessarily creative, personal and inspirational. With a few exceptions, notably the long-established Anti-Slavery Society, new causes demanded new responses in the postwar world. This required leaders who could perceive the need for a campaign (Dolci's 'big problem'), and then inspire others to join them in addressing it. Leaders such as the Rev. Michael Scott, Peter Benenson and Canon John Collins were wholly devoted to the causes that they adopted and launched multiple commit-tees. They worked exceptionally hard but were often highly demanding and difficult to work with. They fitted uneasily into bureaucratic structures, or sought to mould them around themselves to the exclusion of others. In the early days of the Minority Rights Group, for instance, David Astor (who was providing the funds) made clear that – whoever held the title Honorary Secretary – Michael Scott had to be the 'political chief'.[20] The relationship between the individual leader and the organisation remained proble-matic, and Scott's attitude appears to have been akin to David Low's famous 1940 cartoon of the defiant British Tommy: organisation was important, but, if necessary, 'Very well, alone'. In 1951 Scott wrote that 'maybe it is wrong to rely too much on organisations and we should just go on ploughing the next furrow in the belief that it is all part of a larger pattern'.[21] Many years later, when he befriended Peter Benenson, Scott was still following the same troubled line of thought. Benenson – who had recently parted company with Amnesty in difficult circumstances – agreed that there must still be organisations: 'we can't just sit on isolated sea-girt rocks waving to each other. But the corollary that we should take the initiative in organising them doesn't follow automatically'.[22]

Throughout this period leadership was largely a male preserve, with women tending to play secondary roles, although there were significant exceptions. Elizabeth Allen led the NCCL for almost twenty years after 1941, albeit with a low public profile, and the NCCL was later led by Patricia Hewitt (1974–83). However, strong, challenging women gener-ally provoked a very different reaction from inspirational men. Senior Quakers did not know what to make of Eileen Fletcher, who led a campaign against the maltreatment of 'Mau Mau' detainees in Kenya. One was reduced to sending a ditty to a colleague: 'I also hope that Eileen Fletcher / Won't suddenly leap out and get yer!'[23] During the founding of Amnesty, women played a crucial role in starting up the local groups, but only two – the barrister Hilary Cartwright and administrator Peggy Crane – took a prominent central role in the campaign. Both suffered from tacit institutional obstacles to women holding the most senior roles, above all a prevailing belief that the administration should be controlled by a man.[24] When he was still at the NCCL, Amnesty's future Secretary General Martin Ennals once accused Amnesty of sex discrimination in refusing to give an application by one of his female colleagues proper consideration.[25] Sylvia Scaffardi (nee Crowther-Smith), who had founded the NCCL with her partner Ronald Kidd, and provided essential administrative support during its early years, felt that she was invisible to the 'young barristers' who dominated the organisation and who never did the 'donkey work'. She noted that she was not even asked to speak at committee meetings until Elizabeth Allen took over.[26] Conversely, some women who made a significant contribution deliberately avoided any public recognition. For instance, the wealthy South African Quaker Clara Urquhart held a position of considerable responsibility in Amnesty in the early 1960s, by dint of her friendship with Peter Benenson, but did so very much on her own terms – one of which was that she would have no formal office and would only work directly through Benenson and a handful of other leading figures.[27]

Leaders were often closely supported by individuals of private means such as David Astor and Victor Gollancz: men who shared their concerns, but maybe not their dedication to a single cause. Astor, with his family wealth and extensive connections in politics and the press, had a hand in almost every significant organisation mentioned in this book, whether providing pump-priming money or publicity. He was loyal to Michael Scott – almost to a fault – and realised that the brittle cleric needed constant support. Astor's own campaigning tended to be restricted to quiet conversations with government ministers or occasional articles in the press. By comparison, Gollancz was a highly effective speaker and campaigner in own right, his political persona hardened in the anti-fascist struggles of the 1930s and the shock of the Nazi–Soviet Pact. He launched his own campaigns as well as helping to launch others (such as Collins' Christian Action). Peggy Duff, one of the best-known campaigners of the postwar decades, noted that Gollancz taught her most of what she knew.[28] However, Gollancz's personal resources also put him in a position to facilitate new campaigns. In 1965 he noted that 'we normally have at least two [rooms] vacant … it was these rooms that the [Left Book] Club used (as they were used later by the "Save Europe Now" campaign, the "War on Want" campaign, the anti-capital punishment campaign, etc. etc.)'.[29] He was also quite willing to put an end to campaigns when required, commenting in 1952 that he was against the 'proliferation of societies' and had made it a strict rule to 'see that they were closed down (often in face of considerable opposition) as soon as they had done their job'.[30] Gollancz could be ferocious in debate, but this was tempered by bonds of friendship and generosity. In 1962, for instance, he knew that he should withdraw his support from John Collins after the wayward canon had acted in an arbitrary manner once too often, but somehow never found the right occasion to tell him.[31] By the 1970s this particular kind of proprietorial relationship was beginning to give way to the more impersonal pursuit of funding from British and US foundations, and, latterly, from the European Community.

Another tier of activists can be identified as those who were closely involved in a campaign and utterly dedicated to its success, while – like Clara Urquhart – for a variety of reasons not seeking a leadership position. Eric Baker was willing to play the role of lieutenant and intellectual foil to Peter Benenson in Amnesty, although following Benenson's departure he emerged as a leader in his own right. Another Quaker, John Fletcher, was quick to understand the inspirational qualities of both Michael Scott and Eileen Fletcher (no relation) and threw himself into organising campaigns on their behalf. Mary Benson took over John Fletcher's role with Scott, and was described as Scott's 'secretary', although their relationship was complicated by her unrequited love for him.[32] Many of the women initially involved in Amnesty, such as Christel Marsh and Marlys Deeds, voluntarily took on innovative and challenging administrative tasks. Marsh, for instance, created Amnesty's research archive from scratch, while Deeds organised the newly formed local groups, which were highly enthusiastic but desperate for support and direction.

What of those employed to manage or to work for human rights organisations? It was only in the late 1950s that we see the emergence of a small but fast-growing group of individuals who would make their career in human-rights and related organisations. Martin Ennals, for instance, had previously worked for the NCCL and the National Committee for Commonwealth Immigrants before joining Amnesty in 1968. Although described as 'cautious, sober and undramatic', this does not quite do justice to a man whose early career was watched with interest by both the Communist Party and MI5, and who had a posthumous prize for 'Human Rights Defenders' named in his honour.[33] Moreover, whereas prior to the 1960s most organisations would have only had a small staff, principally concerned with administration, press relations and advertising, Amnesty created a completely new stratum of paid employees who were both researchers and advocates. Amnesty had initially tapped into an existing pool of expertise in academia and journalism, but increasingly developed its own 'in-house' regional experts. Under Zbynek Zeman and Stephanie Grant in the early 1970s Amnesty's research staff became by far the largest group of paid employees at Amnesty's London headquarters. These researchers were inspired by the movement's ideals but also brought their own expertise. Tricia Feeney, for instance, joined Amnesty, still in her words 'young and impressionable', after completing a Master's in Latin American Studies. At the age of twenty-five she participated in a perilous mission to

Argentina at the height of the 'Dirty War', where she recalled that she 'felt fear for the first time'.[34] Amnesty's researchers came eventually to embody the organisation and to act as 'keepers of the flame', with strong views about its direction and well-being.[35] As a result, there was always the implicit danger of a gap between the salaried staff and the volunteer members. A complaint by Ivan Morris (of the US Amnesty Section) that Zeman saw the voluntary groups as a 'necessary nuisance' who merely provided the funding for his researchers, is indicative of that gap.[36] Amnesty's British Section experienced similar tensions when Cosmas Desmond, the Catholic priest and anti-apartheid activist who was appointed Director in 1979, was forced out after failing to reconcile the interests of staff and volunteers.[37]

The largest body of activists – voluntary grass-roots members – have left the least historical trace of all. Of course, many human rights groups did not follow Amnesty's lead in seeking to build a large and active membership base. Throughout the twentieth century, for instance, the Anti-Slavery Society survived happily with less than 1000 members, safe in the knowledge that its strength lay in its reputation and the extraordinary personal and familial connections, stretching back over a century, at its core. The membership of Justice was composed almost entirely of barristers and solicitors. The NCCL expanded rapidly during the 1960s and at its peak in 1972 had more individual members (5400) than Amnesty's British Section, but it could never decide what purpose they should serve.[38] Only Amnesty viewed the activism of its members as an integral part of its work. The ideal – not always realised – was that Head Office staff collected and sieved information before 'funnelling it through to the Groups. The two arms of Amnesty thus work as one, investigating, communicating, campaigning.'[39] A further complication is that in many cases human rights organisations have left few formal archives, and those that survive tend to record the decisions of leaders rather than the identities or actions of grass-roots members. Fortunately, in the case of Amnesty the oral history project to mark the organisation's twentieth anniversary conducted nineteen lengthy interviews, not only with Amnesty's founders and better-known members but also with some of those who helped to set up the first local groups. This material provides invaluable insight into a period in the organisation's history for which few formal records survive – indeed, most that do survive from the earliest phase were acquired in the process of compiling the oral history. Moreover, Amnesty's various bulletins are a source of information about ordinary members, as is the biographical material released by candidates for elected posts. For instance, the list of five candidates for a place on the Executive Committee of Amnesty's British Section in 1973 gives an interesting snapshot of a white-collar world: they were a former General Secretary of International Voluntary Service, a Professor of Statistics (and former anarchist), an Articled Solicitor's Clerk, a designer who ran his own company and a computer programmer for IBM.[40]

Activist Environments

Few activists were involved in just a single campaign or organisation, and most were part of larger communities based on faith, humanitarianism or internationalist idealism. Such communities had a broad range of interests, but all, in different ways, felt a special affinity with human rights. Perhaps the most obvious example amongst secular organisations is the United Nations Association (UNA), which bore the principal responsibility for promoting the UN's commitment to human rights (as enshrined in both the UN Charter and the Universal Declaration) within Britain.[41] Hence, the UNA provided the natural organisational base for both the UN's Human Rights Year in 1968 and the Human Rights Network in the mid-1970s. The association enjoyed cross-party support, as well as backing from religious denominations, trade unions and professional organisations, and its main task was to educate the public in the activities and ideals of the UN. It avoided public controversy but occasionally made significant interventions when British policy appeared to contravene UN principles (such as during the Suez crisis in 1956). The UNA was the lineal successor of the League of Nations Union (LNU), established in 1919, and its upper echelons contained all of the surviving 'old League champions' such as Lord Robert Cecil, Gilbert Murray and Philip Noel-Baker.[42] What it did not inherit, however, was the LNU's membership and branches, many of which had languished during World War II. At its peak the LNU had more than 400,000 paid-up members and some 3000 branches: the UNA started in the autumn of 1945 with 265 branches and 46,600 members. Although it expanded rapidly in the later 1940s, to a peak of around 85,000 members, many pacifists resigned over its support for the UN intervention in the Korean War (1950–53). By 1955 membership was down to 62,000, and by the mid-1970s it stood at a mere 25,000.[43]

The UNA's focus on human rights was, at best, intermittent given the UN's vast range of other activities and responsibilities. However, it provided a vital link to the UN's central institutions as the convenor of the Standing Conference on the Economic and Social Work of the United Nations (SCESWUN). This brought together all the British NGOs which formed part of international organisations with Consultative

Status 'A' at the UN's Economic and Social Council (ECOSOC), and, therefore, had the right to suggest agenda items; SCESWUN acted as a clearing house for discussing such proposals. It also made representations to the British government on issues of joint concern, such as the rights of refugees or the lack of progress towards a covenant on human rights. The organisation was composed of four separate working groups on human rights, economic development and technical assistance, refugees, and the status of women (which in 1960 nominated Margaret Thatcher as a delegate to its corresponding UN committee). The Human Rights Working Group, chaired by the distinguished Jewish lawyer and scholar Norman Bentwich, was, until 1968, the only body in Britain which specifically brought together non-governmental organisations around the issue of human rights. However, given that only organisations with consultative status qualified, none of the member organisations – until the Anti-Slavery Society joined SCESWUN in 1957 – were specifically concerned with human rights.[44] Another important aspect of the UNA's international work was through its involvement in the World Federation of United Nations Associations (WFUNA) which, as early as 1946, had set up a Commission of Human Rights with a very active European subcommittee to discuss the pending Universal Declaration.[45]

Amongst faith-based groups the Quakers exercised a disproportionately large influence over the development of human rights activism, just as they did over humanitarian and peace campaigning more generally, given that their numbers in Britain hovered around the 20,000 mark throughout this period. Their influence owed much to the dedication of individual Quaker activists such as John Fletcher and Eric Baker, as well as the financial support provided by wealthy Quaker families such as the Rowntrees and Cadburys through their philanthropic trusts. However, the very history and structure of the Society of Friends was also conducive for social and political activism. The Quakers had experienced persecution in the seventeenth century, and discrimination until the nineteenth, and one of their first formal institutions was a 'Meeting for Sufferings'. By the twentieth century this meeting had evolved into a regular opportunity for Friends to present a 'concern' – to which they had been drawn by conscience – and thereby seek the support of their fellows. The most formative experience for British Quakers in the twentieth century was World War I, when most opposed military service. Some chose to serve in the Friends' Ambulance Unit, but about 1000 opted for imprisonment as conscientious objectors. These events helped to orient the Quakers towards an engaged, pacifist internationalism, a process that had started with the rise of the Quaker missions to Africa and China in the late nineteenth century. The Friends' Service Council, which was set up in 1927 to combine mission work with international work for peace, soon became the most significant of the Friends' numerous committees.

In the years after 1945 Quaker support proved invaluable for building any successful campaign around human rights issues.[46] However, the Quakers could also be awkward allies. Their democratic, consensual methods of decision-making might also appear cautious and conservative; their attempts to build bridges with the communist world did not endear them to Cold War anti-communist liberals; and their willingness to work alongside the colonial authorities in Kenya in the 'rehabilitation' of Mau Mau rebels appears questionable with hindsight. Quakers, after all, opposed state violence, but had no principled objection to working with the state. When *The War Resister* published an account of Eileen Fletcher's efforts to reintegrate 'hard-core' Mau Mau prisoners, the editor acknowledged that some readers would 'wince' at the idea of working for the government in a detention centre.[47] Above all, whatever their individual political views, the Quakers were a religious movement, and this continued to inform their actions. Eric Baker successfully mobilised Quakers behind Amnesty's Campaign for the Abolition of Torture in the early 1970s but remained convinced that this was at heart a profoundly 'spiritual' campaign. Urgent Action notices issued by the campaign not only identified practical steps for Quakers to take to alleviate suffering, but also gave them the information that allowed them to pray for both the torturers and the tortured.[48]

Another religious group which exercised an influence disproportionate to its size was the Iona Community.[49] The community was founded in 1938 by Rev. George MacLeod, an inspirational minister of the Church of Scotland who had fought in World War I and – as a consequence – became a dedicated pacifist. MacLeod had been a highly successful parish priest in Govan during the worst of the Great Depression, and there he had combined religious revival with very practical schemes for community self-organisation. At the height of his success in Govan he resigned, to take a group of young, male priests and craftsmen to the Hebridean island of Iona with the intention of completing the rebuilding of the medieval abbey dedicated to Saint Columba, while also building an ecumenical, internationalist and pacifist religious community. The community flourished in the postwar era, with many coming as members (women were eventually admitted to full membership in 1969) or attending annual summer schools. In the 1950s the Community (which had its headquarters in Glasgow) was closely involved in War on Want, and developed a special relationship with central Africa, where many members served as missionaries. Both MacLeod (as an influential figure in the Church of

Scotland, elected Moderator of the General Assembly in 1957) and the Community played an important role in galvanising opposition to the Central African Federation and campaigning for racial equality in the region. While not party political – despite what critics might say – the community's ethos was overtly engaged and activist: 'the Christian's place is in political action'.[50] As with the UNA, human rights were merely one of many themes to emerge from this fascinating experiment, but MacLeod was an enthusiastic supporter of Amnesty. In May 1968 when acting as a 'Spiritual Adviser' on an 'Inter-Church Travel' cruise to the Mediterranean he used Amnesty documents to denounce an unscheduled meeting with the Metropolitan of Athens, whom he regarded as the appointee of the Greek Colonels.[51] Another direct link to human rights activism was the appointment of Keith Dowding, a member of the Iona Community in 1950, as the field officer of the United Kingdom's UN Human Rights Year Committee in 1968. Dowding was an Australian priest from near Perth, as well as a left-wing politician and well-travelled internationalist who, after his stay on the island told MacLeod that he had discovered a 'real coherence of political campaigning and preaching'.[52]

In 1958 Maurice Edelman, chairman of the Foreign Affairs Committee of the Anglo-Jewish Association, wrote that: 'we Jews have a special interest in human rights and must, if necessary, take the lead in reminding the public of its importance'.[53] Five years later Barnett Janner, President of the Board of Deputies, in welcoming the fifteenth anniversary of the Universal Declaration noted that it was 'of the greatest concern to us not only as Jews, but also as members of the human family'.[54] Such views hardly need elaboration: Jews had suffered centuries of persecution, followed by the interwar failure of international agreements for the protection of minority rights, the tragedy of the Holocaust and the revival of anti-Semitism in the postwar world. For many Jews, such as Hersch Lauterpacht, the Cambridge Professor of International Law who published an International Bill of the Rights of Man in 1945, an enforceable regime of universal human rights offered the best protection for Jews and other minorities in the postwar world.[55] Accordingly, the Jewish community in Britain (which stood at 420,000 in 1951, declining to some 330,000 by the 1980s) played a significant role in campaigns for human rights, both at an individual and a collective level. Jewish organisations were, for instance, very well represented on the SCESWUN Human Rights Working Group.[56] The Board of Deputies participated in the NCCL's conference on international human rights in 1947, and twenty-one years later marked the UN's Human Rights Year with a conference on Race Relations.[57] In both cases, the Board understood that the Jewish community's own interests overlapped with – and could be secured by – a universalist approach.

Over time, however, frictions entered these relationships, above all due to the creation of the state of Israel in 1948 and its crushing victory over the Arab states in the 'Six-Day War' of 1967. Israel's dramatic success in 1967 – which resulted in its occupation of the West Bank, Gaza and other Arab territory – united and enthused the Jewish community. However, it put it at odds with the UN General Assembly (which passed a controversial resolution in 1975 equating Zionism with racism) and the increasingly pro-Palestinian British left. Human rights organisations began to appear somewhat less welcoming after Amnesty criticised Israel over its treatment of Arab prisoners in the occupied territories in 1970. When the American section of Amnesty dissociated itself from this report, the *Times* noted that nine out of seventeen of the section's executive committee were Jewish: it added gratuitously that Amnesty's founder Peter Benenson (who had by now stepped down) was 'Russian Jewish by origin, English by practice and Catholic by conversion'.[58] From the mid-1960s onwards, Jewish concern over human rights was largely focused on the plight of Jews in the Soviet Union, many of whom sought the right to emigrate. The Board's Soviet Jewry Action Committee offered leadership in this work, but numerous other groups emerged which felt that the Board was not acting with sufficient conviction.[59] In all, these activities formed an important component of the human rights campaigning of the 1970s, but also marked something of a change of emphasis from the Jewish organisations' emphasis on universalism in the late 1940s.

Inspirations and Antecedents

In August 1974 Eric Baker addressed the Quakers' Yearly Meeting in York about the campaign for the abolition of torture. He began by evoking John Woolman, the North American Friend who had dedicated his life to the struggle against slavery and who had died in the city some 200 years earlier: 'Today Friends are presented with a similar challenge, the spread of torture. May not the Society once more be called to give a lead to other Christians in the struggle against this modern epidemic of evil.'[60] For many Quakers, the campaign against torture was not only a direct successor to the struggle against slavery, but an opportunity to reignite the 'fire' of those pioneering days, as indicated by the use of the term 'abolition'. This was typical of the way in which human rights activists have consistently looked to past struggles and exemplary lives, not only as an inspiration, but also as a way of coping with the frustrations and disappointments of their work. Peter Benenson's hero, for instance, was the

German pastor Dietrich Bonhoeffer, murdered by the Nazis in 1944, a man that he hailed as the 'archetypal prisoner of conscience'.[61] But can the campaigns of the past also offer a template for future actions? Peter Archer, a politician and lawyer closely involved in the early years of Amnesty, certainly thought so when he described the anti-slavery campaigns as 'the prototype' of all subsequent unofficial action.[62] In fact, human rights activism as it developed in Britain has claimed at least four principal sources: the tradition of 'English' rights and freedoms; a method of campaigning forged in the struggle for the abolition of slavery; humanitarianism; and internationalism, especially international solidarity with the politically oppressed.

In Britain the Universal Declaration of Human Rights (1948) – for all its debts to the Declaration of Independence by the thirteen colonies (1776) and the French Declaration of the Rights of Man and the Citizen (1789) – resonated more powerfully with the far older Magna Carta. Despite its legal anachronism, this treaty between King John and his barons, signed in Runnymede meadow in 1215, had evolved over the centuries into a 'symbolic shorthand for liberty', cherished by advocates of individual liberties from Sir Edward Coke to the Chartists and the suffragettes.[63] It was this tradition (equally powerful in North America) that Eleanor Roosevelt embraced when she presented the Universal Declaration of Human Rights as a document that 'may well become the international Magna Carta of all men everywhere'.[64] In 1951 UNESCO's journal ran a feature on 'Documents of Freedom', which identified Magna Carta as 'one of the earliest documents of man's struggle for freedom and human rights ... the basis for those political and personal freedoms which are now part of the English tradition'.[65] During the UN's Human Rights Year the Universal Declaration – the centrepiece of the campaign – was frequently styled the 'universal Magna Carta'.[66] We can see evidence of Magna Carta's enduring influence in a public meeting called in 1965 by the Lincoln Amnesty International group to mark its 750th anniversary: the speaker was Professor James Holt, author of a well-known study of the charter.[67] Likewise, Magna Carta lived on in the name of the Runnymede Trust, a pressure group for racial equality established in 1968, and, twenty years later, in the 'Charter 88' campaign for a written constitution.[68]

Magna Carta could easily be used for diplomatic one-upmanship, such as when the British representative to the UN's Human Rights Year planning committee, while warning other states against making propaganda, added that 'the rights of the individual is a cause for which my countrymen have struggled ever since 1215'.[69] More significantly, however, a distinctly English tradition of individual freedoms still shaped the thinking of politicians of both left and right on questions of human rights in the postwar era. For instance, Winston Churchill, in his 'Iron Curtain' speech of 5 March 1946 proclaimed 'the great principles of freedom and the rights of man which are the joint inheritance of the English-speaking world and which through Magna Carta, the Bill of Rights, the Habeas Corpus, trial by jury, and the English common law find their most famous expression in the American Declaration of Independence'.[70] He was one of the principal advocates of the Convention for the Protection of Human Rights and Fundamental Freedoms (1950, better known as the European Convention on Human Rights) which sought to protect these freedoms within non-communist Western Europe. Likewise, while the left might prefer rights won by the 'strong arms and keen brains'[71] of the common people to those conceded by reluctant monarchs, it also based its thinking on the idea of the free-born Englishman. The first major declaration by the NCCL in 1935 called for a 'determined stand to retain those rights for which generations of Englishmen have fought', and warned against erosion of access to traditional sites of popular protest on 'our village greens and the open spaces of our towns'.[72] The NCCL's founder Ronald Kidd looked to habeas corpus (1679) as the cornerstone of modern freedoms, and saw British liberties as consistently under threat, whether from reactionary judges or the arbitrary tendencies of the state. In the 1970s, suspicion of giving undue power to judges still held the Labour movement back from readily endorsing a Bill of Rights.[73]

If the Universal Declaration – presented as Magna Carta reimagined for the modern era – was the iconic text for postwar human rights activists, the struggle for the abolition of the slave trade (and later of slavery itself) remained the fount of all modern campaigning. It has rightly been argued that many of the techniques of human rights campaigning were first developed during the late 1780s and early 1790s: from mass petitions, the formation of local committees and the forging of transatlantic corresponding networks, to the consumer boycott and the use of eye-catching symbols (such as Josiah Wedgwood's famous 'Am I not a brother and a man?' medallion) to convey the message to a wider audience.[74] The campaign's success rested on a combination of Thomas Clarkson's relentless organising, Quaker networks and funding, and William Wilberforce's persistence in Parliament, the equivalents of which still have their place in modern activism. However, there were also lessons for later campaigners to absorb. First, there was the question of the balance between pragmatism and principle: the initial focus, after all, was on abolishing the slave trade rather than slavery itself. The first goal was achieved in 1807, but slavery was not banned within the British Empire until 1833, and only at the cost of high levels of compensation for slave owners. Secondly, while abolitionists attracted impressive levels of support, campaigning alone was not enough to force change. Other factors played a vital part, such as the impact of the Napoleonic Wars and the slave revolts in the West Indies, or parliamentary reform in the early 1830s. Thirdly, abolition – like Magna Carta – granted Britain an odour of sanctity and self-congratulation: ending slavery was often seen as a mark of Britain's civilisation – something which was still evident in the centenary celebrations in 1933[75] – and Britain's gift to the world. Little attention was paid to the plight of the former slaves, or to the ways in which slavery had underpinned Britain's economic success. Abolitionists were also open to the criticism that they pursued a moral cause abroad while neglecting immoralities at home: the poet Robert Bridges referred to the 'cross-eyed . . . pride of our world-wide crusade against Nigerian slavery', which ignored the plight of the London poor.[76]

The most direct lineal connection with modern activism was the remarkable survival of the Anti-Slavery Society (founded in 1839 as the British and Foreign Anti-Slavery Society and later passing through numerous changes of name). The Society had committed itself to 'the universal extinction of slavery and the slave-trade' by 'moral, religious and pacific means'. As Joseph Sturge told an early meeting, while slavery was no longer a 'national crime' within the British Empire, 'Christian love and Christian zeal were not to be circumscribed by national boundaries'.[77] It is precisely this universalism which entitles the Society to be thought of as the progenitor of British campaigning for international human rights: indeed, when it finally incorporated the phrase 'and for the Protection of Human Rights' into its title in 1955 the chairman noted that it had been 'interested in human rights [as a committee] from 1823 and as a Society from 1839'.[78] However, for all of its pacific intentions the Society came to accept that the slave trade in East Africa and the Red Sea could only be crushed by working closely with the British state, especially the Royal Navy.[79] Moreover, while many members remained sceptical of the virtues of force, they fully believed in the civilising effects of European colonialism. Little had changed in this regard by the 1930s, when leading members of the Society such as Lady Simon supported the invasion of Abyssinia by fascist Italy, valuing an (apparent) victory over slavery more highly than the destruction of an independent African state.[80] Well into the twentieth century, and even past the imperial meridian of the 1940s, British humanitarian movements continued to be profoundly influenced by assumptions about the essential benevolence of empire, as a means to promote the interests of less developed peoples.[81]

Sir John Harris, who led the Anti-Slavery Society from 1910 until his death in 1940, had started his career as a missionary in the Congo and had helped E. D. Morel to found the Congo Reform Association, which campaigned against the brutally exploitative colonial regime of King Leopold of Belgium. Following World War I Harris carved out an influential role for the Society at the League of Nations in Geneva and made an important contribution to the 1926 Convention to Suppress the Slave Trade and Slavery. Under Harris, therefore, the Anti-Slavery Society was one of the first non-governmental organisations to use its expertise and moral standing to exercise influence at the League. This kind of relationship would become increasingly important under the United Nations after 1945, even though the UN initially rather downplayed the struggle against slavery.[82] During the postwar years Harris's successors, C. W. W. Greenidge (secretary 1942–56), Thomas Fox-Pitt (1956–63) and Patrick Montgomery (1963–80), all former colonial administrators or members of the armed forces, maintained the formidable reputation for lobbying that Harris had established. At the same time, however, the Society's brand of activism was conservative, paternalistic and, crucially, relied more on expertise and reputation than on a mass membership. This increasingly set it apart from the new human rights organisations that began to emerge in the postwar era. When Tony Benn introduced a Human Rights Bill into Parliament in 1958, to mark the tenth anniversary of the Universal Declaration, the Anti-Slavery Society refused to join twenty other voluntary organisations in backing it. Norman Bentwich told his colleagues on the executive committee that to refuse to support Benn's bill mocked their professed goals, and he resigned in disgust when he failed to convince them.[83] In 1964 Peter Benenson cited the Society as an example of how 'movements can be conducted with absolute propriety and devotion and yet fall by the wayside of history'.[84]

Human rights campaigning was also strongly related to (and arguably a branch of) humanitarianism, the impulse, originating in the later eighteenth century and gaining organisational form in the mid-nineteenth, that emphasised bonds of common humanity over divisions of religion, ethnicity and statehood. Since the formation of the Red Cross in the 1860s, humanitarianism (carried out principally by voluntary organisations, although at times in tandem with states) had manifested itself in different ways: assistance for soldiers and civilians in wartime and its aftermath, relief for the victims of natural emergencies, and, increasingly since 1945, as aid and development for what would become known as the 'Third World'. In the process, humanitarianism had come to be defined by principles of impartiality, political neutrality and independence from government.[85] Some highly significant humanitarian organisations originated in Britain, notably Save the Children (1919) and the Oxford Committee for Famine Relief/Oxfam (1942), both of which went on to acquire a global remit. Oxfam did much to reinvent humanitarian campaigning in the late 1940s when Cecil Jackson-Cole wedded fundraising and advertising principles derived from business to the kudos of a committee made up of leading academics and clergymen.[86]

There was considerable interplay between humanitarian work and emergent human rights activism. Oxfam played a significant role in Amnesty's early days, as the two organisations shared some premises and – to an extent – expertise in the field in southern Africa. From Amnesty's perspective the distinction between human rights and humanitarianism was often initially blurred. David Astor, for instance, located Amnesty in the 'strong tradition [in Britain] of trying to rescue people', while Stephanie Grant noted that in the mid-1960s there was no such thing as 'human rights work' and Amnesty was known as an 'adoption organisation [for political prisoners]'.[87] These congruencies aside, however, human rights activism was generally distinguished from humanitarianism by its more overt political focus (which often precluded charitable status) and its specific grounding in the language of rights, which most humanitarian organisations did not adopt until the 1990s.[88] Some organisations, however, stood on the cusp of humanitarianism and human rights campaigning, notably Third World First (which started in 1970 as a movement to persuade students to donate a percentage of their grants to help the developing world). Another example was War on Want, which in the 1960s became a campaign to challenge the roots of global poverty by supporting 'organised groups of the poor struggling for self-reliance, power and dignity'. In both cases, by the late 1970s these organisations were giving prominence to human rights issues – for instance, the first edition of War on Want's avowedly 'radical' new journal in 1978 posed the question 'Human Rights: Who's Paying for Our Freedom?'[89]

Humanitarianism, in turn, overlapped with a final historical root, internationalism. Some steps had been taken towards international governance in the later nineteenth century, as the great powers sought to take the edge off their imperial rivalries, create stability through the protection of religious and ethnic minorities, and regulate the suffering caused by war (at least between 'civilised' states). In the process, significant new concepts were introduced into international relations, albeit without effective mechanisms for monitoring and enforcement. The Treaty of Berlin (1878), for instance, stipulated that the civil and political rights of all religious groups should be upheld in an independent Romania, while the Berlin Conference of 1884–85 (which opened the way to the partition of Africa) committed the powers to end the slave trade and care for the 'moral and material well-being' of native tribes under their rule. The Hague Peace Conferences of 1899 and

1907 codified the laws of war, although no provision was made at this point for the protection of civilians. After World War I this limited international cooperation was revived and given fresh momentum by the Treaty of Versailles and the establishment of the League of Nations in 1919. Hence, the Polish Minorities Treaty (or 'Little Versailles') enshrined specific human rights for minorities in the restored Poland – while not imposing similar arrangements on established states and empires.[90] During the 1920s the League promoted a variety of rights, in particular those of children, those facing the threat of slavery and trafficked women (the so-called 'White Slaves'). In these areas the League moved ahead through a combination of formal international declarations, new mechanisms for monitoring and reporting transgressions, and working closely with non-governmental organisations. This was, indeed, the beginnings of an 'international society', but it was a fragile edifice, unable to withstand the waves of hyper-nationalism that followed the Great Depression in the 1930s.[91] Poland's decision to renounce its despised minorities' treaty in 1934 was indicative of the collapse of international supervision.

If intergovernmental and institutional action was one hallmark of this post-World War I internationalism, non-governmental actors also believed that they had a crucial role to play, whether in providing expertise in areas such as anti-slavery and women's rights or in placing moral pressure on politicians. For a generation convinced that the Great War had been caused by secret diplomacy, the solution lay in greater transparency which would empower an informed and activist public. As Lord Cecil, leader of the LNU, argued in 1919: 'in a democratic age, everything depends on public opinion. This means that the public must have an opinion on international affairs, and that its opinion must be right'.[92] Another commentator argued that 'the driving power (if any) behind the League of Nations will be organised public opinion, expressed through the League of Nations Union and analogous societies'.[93] From here it was not a great distance to the proposition that, if only the public was properly informed, a 'world conscience' would become the supreme arbiter in international relations. The journalist Sir Philip Gibbs, for instance, discerned in World War I's aftermath 'the faint stirrings, at least, of a world conscience which presently may lead to action ... a welling up of generous ardent idealism ...'.[94] Belief in this ideal was expressed – with ever-waning confidence – into the mid-1930s, but it resurfaced in the 1960s when Amnesty International regularly appealed to the 'world conscience'.

In practical terms, the form of internationalism that fed most directly into human rights activism was international political solidarity on behalf of those imprisoned for their religious and political views. There was a long history of such sympathy in Britain – from Gladstone's impassioned attacks on the treatment of political prisoners in the Kingdom of Naples in 1851 to the widespread agitation in support of the anarchist educator Francisco Ferrer, executed by the Spanish authorities in 1909 as a scapegoat for the 'Tragic Week' disturbances in Barcelona. In the twentieth century this kind of campaigning was increasingly identified with the left, although by no means exclusively so – Catholics, for instance, campaigned vociferously against the imprisonment of Catholic bishops and clerics during the early years of the Cold War. This kind of campaigning was transformed during the interwar years by the rise of international communism, as well as by new means of communication and international travel. During the two decades after World War I some *causes célèbres* reached a truly global audience, such as the cases of Sacco and Vanzetti (1921–27), the Scottsboro boys (1931–37), the Meerut trial (1929–33), and victims of Nazi terror such as Carl von Ossietzky. Such cases were often taken up by the communist-led International Labour Defence (ILD), which had a British section, although it would be wrong to see these campaigns necessarily as mere communist fronts. Campaigners always had to balance the positive resources and political energies that communist involvement would bring against the negative political costs, and sometimes preferred to keep their distance. It is certainly true, however, that when communists attempted to run international campaigns without support from non-communist liberals and social democrats they tended to fail, as was the case with the campaign around the imprisonment of the agent known as 'Hilaire Noulens' and his wife in Shanghai in 1931.[95]

The greatest synergy was achieved during 1933–39 when the Communist International adopted a new strategy of building broad anti-fascist alliances known as the 'Popular Front' (or 'People's Front'). The Popular Front era was a heyday of international solidarity, when communism's greater inclusivity coincided potently with the anti-fascist energies of non-communist politicians and intellectuals in an era dominated by the rise of fascist dictatorships, international aggression and the Spanish Civil War. Many postwar advocates of human rights had their first taste of activism during the desperate – often doomed – struggles of the 1930s. Frederick Elwyn Jones (later a Labour Lord Chancellor) went to Vienna in 1935 to secure an amnesty for prisoners following the suppression of the Austrian socialist movement in February 1934. Norman Marsh (who became an eminent international lawyer, active in both the International Commission of Jurists and Amnesty) made a series of visits to Nazi Germany to write articles for the *Guardian*. Here he met his wife Christel (Amnesty's first 'Librarian') who came to Britain in

June 1939 after falling under Gestapo investigation. Peter Benenson was powerfully affected by the Spanish Civil War while still at Eton, and set up a scheme to 'adopt' Spanish and, subsequently, German Jewish refugee children: he would later say, apropos of Amnesty, that the Spanish conflict was 'where it all started'.[96] Marlys Deeds, the sister of a young man rescued by Benenson, also came to Britain from Germany and later helped to organise Amnesty's first local groups.[97] Michael Scott flung open his East London parish church to feed Hunger Marchers, and subsequently became an organiser for the Communist Party.[98]

Anti-fascist unity ended badly, with the Nazi–Soviet Pact of August 1939 and Stalin's instruction to communists not to take sides after war broke out with Germany in September 1939. However, it did not end as badly in Britain as in the United States, where the leading champion of civil liberties, Roger Baldwin, broke with the communists and expelled them from the American Civil Liberties Union in 1940.[99] Although Britain was affected by the anti-communist hysteria of the early Cold War years (and the NCCL was shunned by many non-communists for its close links to the Communist Party) its influence was far less destructive than McCarthyism in the USA. Solidarity movements remained a potent force in the postwar era and were increasingly receptive to ideas about human rights. They developed in parallel with the human rights movement, with areas of mutual attraction, accommodation and repulsion.[100]

Parameters

When presenting the Universal Declaration of Human Rights in 1948, Eleanor Roosevelt expressed the hope that the news would 'seep in' even when governments were 'not so anxious for it', and that it might even filter through to the Russian people by means of a 'curious grapevine'. It seems unlikely, as some have argued, that she was thinking here of the role of the NGOs, at least as they were currently constituted.[101] Instead, her comment brings to mind an often-cited quotation by the American philosopher William James, which was also a personal favourite of Amnesty's Eric Baker:

I am against bigness and greatness in all their forms, and with the invisible molecular moral forces that work from individual to individual, stealing in through the crannies of the world like so many soft rootlets, or like the capillary oozing of water, and yet rending the hardest monuments of man's pride, if you give them time.[102]

It is easy to understand why James's paean to the osmotic power of 'the eternal forces of truth', destined to triumph in the long run, would appeal to a human rights activist of the postwar decades. Throughout the period covered by this book the Cold War largely prevented the emergence of international consensus, state power remained supreme (even in the democracies) and, by the late 1970s, authoritarian rule was only clearly on the retreat in southern Europe. For human rights activists the task appeared daunting and the weapons at their disposal were meagre. To write a letter on behalf of a political prisoner seemed like an act of faith: to secure the release of such a prisoner was a major victory, and even more so to press successfully for a new international agreement, although that in turn simply raised the question of how it would be enforced.

Understandably, given the odds stacked against activists, recent historical debates have focused on the question of when – if at all – human rights became a meaningful factor in international politics. In his influential book *The Last Utopia* Samuel Moyn has led the way in emphasising the importance of the 1970s, a decade in which the Carter presidency placed human rights – rhetorically at least – at the centre of its foreign policy and Amnesty International won the Nobel Peace Prize. More recently Stefan-Ludwig Hoffman has argued that human rights only became a 'basic concept' in international affairs after the end of the Cold War – for instance, the Kosovo war in 1999 was the first military intervention to be justified in the name of human rights.[103] Powerful arguments can be marshalled for both interpretations, and the merits of the case for the 1970s will be examined in greater depth below. More telling, however, is Hoffman's challenge to the very idea of a history of human rights 'that does not begin in our own present', and his warning against telling the story 'myopically as the breakthrough to our notions of individual human rights'. There is no question that historians of human rights activism must take this point extremely seriously: the danger of imposing a hindsight view of human rights activism on the past is very real, as this risks smoothing away the considerable differences that existed between different campaigns and organisations, as well as other potential trajectories and the paths not taken. At the same time, however, one must also acknowledge that from the late 1940s onwards such a trajectory *did* exist and that the momentum was towards the emergence of the new identity of the human rights activist. We cannot ignore, for instance, the fact that when Archbishop Joost de Blank died in 1968, his brass-lettered gravestone in Westminster Abbey commemorated him not as an ardent critic of apartheid – which is how he is best remembered – but as an 'indomitable fighter for human rights'.[104]

Accordingly, the argument presented below will be that there was a gradual coming together of ideas and methods of campaigning, shaped by political and religious idealism, inspirational leadership, and interaction with the political and social changes of the postwar decades. The emergence of human rights activism did not happen steadily or inevitably: instead, there were moments of rapid acceleration, such as the formation of what would become Amnesty International in 1961 or the UN's Year for Human Rights in 1968. Ironically, one crucial moment which did not produce rapid acceleration was the signing of the Universal Declaration of Human Rights in 1948. Yet, although the Declaration's impact was limited in the short term, looking back from, say, 1968 we can appreciate its profound significance to human rights activists. From this vantage point there was evidently a growing awareness that the Declaration was a foundational document which offered activists a clear and succinct statement of the rights that they sought to defend. Much the same can be said for the impact of World War II as a whole. Historians are rightly sceptical about drawing direct connections between the war and the emergence of human rights as a force in the modern world – after all, the full dimensions of the Holocaust were not yet understood at the war's end, and governments of every political shade felt confident that a new charter of human rights would not affect how they conducted their affairs.[105] However, the war's longer-term impacts were manifold and slow-burning, and over time activists came to attribute ever more – not less – influence to them. In so far as human rights activists articulated a historical narrative of what motivated them, by the 1960s and 1970s few would look any further back than Nazism and World War II.

The war and the Universal Declaration, therefore, broadly constitute this book's starting point. Clearly, elements of what might be called human rights activism existed long before this period. However, during the interwar years references to 'human rights' within British political discourse were infrequent. During the 1930s the term was adopted by some anti-Nazi groups, principally to indicate that they were not campaigning for the rights of Jews alone.[106] It was also sometimes used to describe the more basic entitlements of native peoples denied civil rights by colonial rule.[107] It is only with the events of the 1940s, from the debate initiated by H. G. Wells in 1940 to the signing of the Universal Declaration in 1948, that ideas of human rights began to shape political action, even if there were many false starts. As early as 1948, however, we can find Catholics using the exact phrase 'human rights campaign', a term likewise used by members of the UNA in 1951, even if the aims of these initiatives were very different.[108] More importantly, it is in the 1950s that we see human rights beginning to influence the demands of campaigning organisations in fields such as anti-colonialism or solidarity with the victims of dictatorships (of both right and left). The Universal Declaration, then, provided a crucial – and increasingly valued – reference point for activists. For instance, the fact that the Universal Declaration made no reference to sexuality and gender relations did not automatically discredit it in the eyes of activists in the 1970s.[109]

The book concludes with the award of the Nobel Peace Prize to Amnesty International in 1977, an event of tremendous symbolic value which not only recognised the remarkable success of Amnesty itself, but also offered legitimation to human rights activism more broadly. The Nobel Prize marked, therefore, a coming of age for human rights activism as it had developed in Britain since the end of World War II. A further reason for concluding in the late 1970s is that the election victory of Margaret Thatcher in May 1979, followed by that of Ronald Reagan in November 1980, represents a sea change in British and world politics, characterised by the renewed Cold War and an assault on many of the social, political and economic assumptions of the postwar era. In Britain the focus of activists was now far more on the defence of domestic freedoms that had previously been taken for granted, culminating in the Charter 88 movement. Human rights organisations flourished in the more conflictual domestic arena, but the increasing importance of lawyers *as lawyers* during this period, coinciding with the new opportunities offered by the European Court of Human Rights and the EEC, gave this period a very different character. It is during the 1980s that the 'human rights lawyer' joined the 'human rights activist' as a recognisable entity.[110] This was rather different from the blanket condemnation of lawyers – only a few years previously – by the departing head of the NCCL as incompetent, 'cautious ... uncreative, idle and status-mad'.[111]

For much of the period covering 1945–77 the development of human rights activism was dominated by small, interlocking clusters of friends and fellow professionals from the law, politics and the media. Their ideas and relationships have also, inevitably, shaped the aspects of human rights which receive most attention in this book. If the primary focus is on international political rights, rather than on the full range of social and economic rights, this is because this was where these individuals and groups chose to direct their energies, to the exclusion of many other areas. For instance, for the Catholic expert on international relations John Eppstein, writing at the time of the Universal Declaration, the right to migrate and travel freely was one of the most important human rights, threatened by the 'whole horrid apparatus' of passports and visas.[112] However, the issue was only intermittently taken up, generally in the context of asylum. Likewise, although lawyers played a vital role in human rights activism, the book does not attempt to discuss the development of human rights law in postwar Britain. This is partly because aspects of this subject have already been thoroughly studied elsewhere[113] but, more importantly because lawyers involved in human rights activism were often disenchanted with the conservatism of the legal profession or were seeking to complement what they could achieve through more conventional legal and political structures. Peter Benenson wrote in 1963 that Amnesty 'carefully eschews law, and concentrates on humanity', while Ben Whitaker, who had a hand in many human rights organisations, wrote in 1962 that he was happy to form a local Amnesty group but was more and more 'dissatisfied with the unconstructiveness of being a barrister'.[114] Peter Archer, a future Solicitor General, perhaps surprisingly told the House of Commons in 1973 that there was more to human rights than ratifying international covenants: 'the cutting edge of human rights arises in grim prisons and dismal ghettoes, in areas of squalor and famine . . . .'[115]

The book opens with a brief discussion of the formation of the NCCL in 1934,[116] and this raises one final, introductory question: how do 'human rights' relate to 'civil liberties'? For some activists this was only a semantic distinction. In 1947 the Belgian Baron van den Branden de Reeth told the NCCL's international conference on human rights that: 'Whether we call them "democratic liberties", "human rights" or "Civil liberties", as you do in England, it is all very much the same. These terms are practically synonymous'.[117] (One could add the term 'civil rights' to this list, given its adoption by the Catholic minority in Northern Ireland in the late 1960s.) It is certainly true that the distinction began to narrow and, indeed, in 1980 the NCCL toyed with changing its name to 'Rights'.[118] It eventually adopted the title 'Liberty' ('defending civil liberties, promoting human rights') in 1989 and has since promoted itself as a human rights organisation. In 2007 the then-Director Shami Chakrabarti claimed to see no distinction between civil liberties and human rights and warned that partisans of left or right might use civil liberties 'as a means of protecting just citizens or people they like . . . .'[119]

Even so, these were not mere synonyms. Indeed, the Director of the NCCL, Tony Smythe, acknowledged as much in 1972, while noting the legal and jurisdictional inadequacy of both: 'Civil liberty has no hard legal meaning and the term is only part synonymous with the human rights described in the broadest terms in the UN's Universal Declaration, which only in the watered-down formulation contained in the European Convention on Human Rights are marginally binding on Britain'.[120] The concept of civil liberties was steeped in the 'English' tradition of individual freedoms, defined by resistance to a constantly threatening and encroaching state. The NCCL acted as an important bridge between civil liberties and human rights, notably by organising an international conference on human rights in 1947, but during much of the period covered in this book it carried too much political baggage to cross that bridge itself. The NCCL was strongly associated with the political left and saw itself as standing up to the repressive actions of governments, the courts and the police. At a meeting of local NCCL representatives in 1969 more than one expressed concern that the organisation was unable to promote itself effectively so long as it was known above all for being 'anti-police'.[121] During the postwar decades, therefore, the divisions between the civil liberties movement (as represented primarily by the NCCL) and human rights campaigns were real, and they were both theoretical and sociopolitical. If civil liberties activists were more likely to be located in left-wing political parties and trade unions and sought to address abuses within the national (and, until the early 1960s, imperial) sphere, human rights activists were less driven by political ideology, more at home in religious and non-political associational cultures, and moved easily between national and international theatres.

1 Dawn: 1934–1950

1.1 Civil Liberties and the State: 1934–1941

The Council for Civil Liberties (the word 'National' was only added a few months later) met for the first time on 22 February 1934.[1] The choice of venue – the vestry hall of St Martin-in-the-Fields, just off Trafalgar Square – was no accident. Under the Reverend Dick Sheppard (vicar from 1914 to 1927), St Martin's had become a haven for London's homeless and a gathering point for pacifists and internationalists, while Sheppard's pioneering use of theatre and radio placed his church firmly in the public eye. Sheppard famously had 'no use for religion which does not transform the world and save human beings from misery'.[2] By 1934, therefore, St Martin's was already well established as a centre for dissent and social engagement, a reputation that was nurtured by Sheppard's successors – indeed, in 1961 it was to be the site of a number of formative moments in the early life of Amnesty International.[3] The issues discussed at that first meeting of the National Council for Civil Liberties, or NCCL, bore testimony to a prevailing sense of social and political crisis in the wake of the Great Depression: this was a political landscape shaped by more than 2 million unemployed, the Conservative-dominated National Government's unprecedented majority in Parliament following the 1931 election and the rise of Sir Oswald Mosley's British Union of Fascists (BUF). The meeting's agenda ranged from the arrival in London of the latest Hunger March, alleged threats to free speech and assembly and 'Police provocation and irregularities', to a report by the campaigning journalist Claud Cockburn on 'Fascist tendencies in Britain'.[4] The threat of 'fascism' overhung the meeting, and as far as the NCCL's founder Ronald Kidd was concerned, emanated just as much from the government and police as it did from Mosley and his Blackshirts. In a private message to International Labour Defence (ILD) immediately prior to the meeting he noted that the NCCL would be a 'propagandist body of intellectuals [whose aim was] *to fight against official Fascist or semi-Fascist abuses*'.[5]

If the NCCL was a product of the crisis of the early 1930s, it arose, more specifically, from an exchange between Kidd and the writer A. P. Herbert in *The Weekend Review* about the police harassment of demonstrators. Kidd, a bookseller and theatre stage manager with no apparent political affiliations, claimed to have witnessed the actions of police agents provocateurs during the closing stages of the 1932 Hunger March.[6] His response was to organise a 'vigilance committee' to defend 'hard-won rights'[7] against the encroachments of the state. Kidd's plan was for impartial observers to monitor police behaviour in the expectation that – as educated people of substance, such as writers and lawyers – their complaints could not be easily ignored. The initial objective was to protect that year's Hunger Marchers as they gathered in Hyde Park on 25 February, three days after the NCCL's inaugural meeting. This time the demonstration passed off peacefully, although it is not clear what part the presence of luminaries such as H. G. Wells played in this.[8] The NCCL soon diversified away from simply monitoring protests, important as this work remained. Its first major campaign was against the Incitement to Disaffection Act of 1934 (popularly known as the 'Sedition Bill'), which sought to ban political agitation that targeted members of the armed forces. Kidd was not alone in regarding some aspects of the bill, such as the introduction of a General Search Warrant (which he saw as a 'reversal of English legal usage') as an unacceptable encroachment on 'citizens' rights'.[9] The NCCL played a significant role not only in organising protest meetings against the bill, but also in providing legal advice to sympathetic MPs, such as the Liberal parliamentarian Dingle Foot.[10] The significant amendments that were imposed by parliamentary opposition during the bill's passage into law were understandably claimed as both victory and vindication for the new organisation.[11]

More of a departure was the NCCL's decision to launch an inquiry in 1935 into the unique governance arrangements in Northern Ireland. Following the partition of Ireland in 1922 and the creation of a devolved government and parliament in six counties of Ulster, the temporary Special Powers Act of 1922 had become a permanent means for the repression of the Catholic/Nationalist minority in the North in favour of the Protestant/Unionist majority. This was a topic that had been largely ignored by politicians in mainland Britain since the Troubles of 1918–21, and the NCCL's decision to investigate was partly due to the influence of the Northern-Irish-born barrister and left-wing politician Geoffrey Bing.[12] However, the inquiry also provides further evidence of how broadly the NCCL interpreted the threat of fascism, as Kidd's glib comment that fascism was being 'tried out on the dog' in Northern Ireland, and that Ulster had a form of 'dictatorship' with parallels to

Nazism, indicated.[13] Although the commission failed to bring about any reforms at the time, the published report proved to be a valuable documentary record and stood the NCCL in good stead when tensions between the two communities once more became acute in the mid-1960s.[14]

The NCCL was avowedly 'non-political' and Kidd was consistently at pains to make clear that he was not a member of the Communist Party.[15] Even so, the organisation was dogged by allegations that it was under communist control and it is important to gain an understanding of what lay behind this, not only because the accusation of communist influence was so widely believed within official circles, but also because it influenced the relationship between the NCCL and non-communist organisations well into the 1960s. Like so many progressive institutions during the 1930s, the NCCL was shaped by the politics of the 'Popular Front'. In the mid-1930s the Soviet Union, deeply concerned about the rise of Nazi Germany, abandoned the extreme factionalism which had characterised international communism in the late 1920s and early 1930s in favour of a more open and inclusive politics. Communists now sought to forge the widest possible alliances against the rise of fascism and were willing to cooperate with almost anyone so long as they were anti-fascist. In Britain they worked through new organisations such as the Left Book Club (established by the publisher Victor Gollancz in May 1936), the International Peace Campaign and a myriad of committees supporting the Spanish Republic during the Civil War. Many liberals felt comfortable working alongside communists in such organisations, and in the case of the NCCL this applied to the writer E. M. Forster and his successor as NCCL President, the radical journalist Henry Nevinson. However, the presence of liberal intellectuals such as Forster (who remained loyal to the NCCL through numerous vicissitudes until he resigned his membership in 1948) should not conceal the internal dynamics at play. As Kevin Morgan has argued, the political openness of the Popular Front era required the Communist Party to engage in 'far more negotiated and conditional relationships' than had been the case when it had worked through organisations directly controlled by its members.[16] Accordingly, the debate over whether Kidd and his partner Sylvia Crowther-Smith were Communist Party members, for which there is no conclusive evidence, should not distract from the fact that there are at least three good reasons for believing that there was a strong alignment and close working relationship between the two organisations.[17]

Firstly, the NCCL's policies never significantly departed from those of the Communist Party throughout this period. While Kidd's precise meaning in a private message of 19 February 1934 – which stated that the NCCL would be 'keen to keep the correct party line' – remains open to interpretation,[18] the pattern of alignment between the two organisations is beyond doubt. This caused few tensions when the communist and non-communist left was united against fascism in the 1930s. However, it became a pressing issue during periods of abrupt change in Communist Party policy such as the early phase of World War II, when the Communist Party of Great Britain (CPGB) decided to oppose the war and then, following the invasion of the Soviet Union in June 1941, swung back sharply to support the war effort. Many who had travelled willingly with the communists during 1935–39, such as Gollancz, turned sharply against them after their volte-face in the autumn of 1939, and some would never trust them again. The NCCL, however, closely followed every twist and turn in CPGB policy.

Secondly, the NCCL's analysis of British politics was very much in line with that of the Communist Party, in both tone and content. Hence, Kidd, a self-styled 'Gladstonian Radical'[19] in his upbringing, saw the Sedition Bill of 1934 as merely a further example of the unwelcome long-term shift in the balance of power between the individual and the state since the start of World War I. This had begun with legislation such as the Official Secrets Act (1911) and the Northern Ireland Special Powers Act (1922) and would continue with the Public Order Act (1936) and the Prevention of Violence Act (passed in 1939 following an IRA bombing campaign in mainland Britain). Such views were not unusual or noteworthy: what made them so was Kidd's insistence on where this trend would lead. In 1936 he warned of a state of 'incipient fascism' in Britain and predicted that within three years a crisis would occur that would precipitate 'conscription or a state of semi-fascism'.[20] Likewise, in a book published in 1940 he argued that Britain might well be under a 'virtually Fascist state' by the end of the war.[21] These dark forebodings were shared by others who moved in the same circles. W. H. Thompson, a radical lawyer and pillar of the NCCL, argued in 1938 that the British people faced the imposition of a totalitarian regime 'while we sleep',[22] and Frederick Elwyn Jones, another lawyer who was at this point close to the communists, argued in 1938 that the National Government wanted to reduce Parliament to a 'species of Fascist Grand Council'.[23] Such language was closely in line with the communist argument that the Conservative-dominated National Government (1931–40) was not just sympathetic to fascism, but was itself fascistic, and represented a threat to civil liberties akin to that posed by the European dictatorships.[24]

Thirdly, a group of communist or fellow-travelling lawyers formed a crucial point of connection between the CPGB and the NCCL, an influence that was magnified by the NCCL's reliance on their expertise for legal advice and representation. Many of these lawyers were also members of both the Haldane Society and the Communist Party's own 'secret lawyers' group', a group that British intelligence viewed 'with considerable suspicion' as it was 'made up of men of education and intellectual power'.[25] The party had publicly set up a legal panel of barristers and solicitors in April 1931 with a view to offering defence against police harassment, and this contained many of the lawyers later prominent in the NCCL. The panel appears to have lapsed at the end of 1933, and Special Branch was convinced that it had been absorbed into the NCCL once the Communist Party realised that it would achieve 'much better results' through a non-party organisation.[26] Another potential rival to the NCCL, the communist-led International Defence League, was also dissolved in 1934. Intelligence records show that these lawyers continued to meet as a secret Communist Party caucus or 'fraction' within the NCCL, a very typical tool of influence during the Popular Front period, whereby political coalitions could be guided by small numbers of communist activists.[27] John Platts-Mills, then a young barrister from New Zealand, concedes in his memoirs that 'interested Haldane [Society] lawyers' would meet prior to meetings of the NCCL's executive committee to 'discuss the agenda'. He adds that W. H. Thompson put a stop to these meetings to avoid antagonising liberal allies, but many continuing references to the existence of a communist fraction in British intelligence reports indicate that if this was the case it was merely a cosmetic concession.[28]

One particularly important figure who operated in the shadowy area between the law, civil liberties and the politics of the left was D. N. Pritt, a fellow-travelling barrister and MP, elected to represent Hammersmith North in 1935 and expelled from the Labour Party in 1940 for his support for the Soviet invasion of Finland. Pritt exercised considerable influence within the NCCL – hence the comment in 1946 from one admirer that 'I know what you say goes with [the NCCL]'.[29] He was a much sought-after advocate in civil liberties cases in the 1930s, and after World War II gained an international reputation for his defence of Asian and African nationalists, such as Jomo Kenyatta. He had come to prominence in the London-based Reichstag Fire Trial Commission in 1933, which placed the actions of the Nazi regime under quasi-judicial scrutiny. His reputation as a notorious fellow-traveller was confirmed by his decision to attend one of the Moscow show trials of Stalin's rivals in 1936. On his return he declared the grotesque proceedings to be legally sound: no prisoners were ill-treated or refused legal aid, and the trial was not 'unfair'.[30] As John Saville has written, Pritt exemplified one of the major paradoxes of the British left: he was a lifelong defender of the Soviet Union, but 'his personal history, as a defender of justice ... was quite unassailable'.[31] Like Kidd, Pritt always denied that he was a Communist Party member, and as a Labour MP he was clearly in a separate category from other lawyers involved with the NCCL such as Dudley Collard (who also reported back enthusiastically from the Moscow trials a few months after Pritt and declared that the fanatical Prosecutor Vyshinsky had behaved with 'utmost politeness' towards the accused).[32] However, it is clear from copies of Pritt's correspondence with Angela Tuckett, the NCCL legal officer during the period 1940–42 and an intimate friend of his at this time, that he had decided to join the Communist Party after the German invasion of the Soviet Union – 'if', as he put it, 'I can be admitted' – even as he continued to scoff at the idea in public. According to one letter he craved the 'warmth and the responsibility, the fellowship *and* the duty' of party membership after ploughing a lonely furrow in the Labour Party. It seems likely, however, that the CPGB preferred Pritt not to join the party for tactical reasons.[33]

By 1939 the NCCL had grown to some 3000 members and 700 affiliated organisations, including many trade unions.[34] However, the wartime years proved very difficult, not least because of the illness and premature death of Ronald Kidd in 1942. Had he lived, his natural libertarianism and apparent growing discomfort with the communist influence[35] might have helped the NCCL to steer a somewhat more independent course in the remaining years of the war. He was greatly missed by Forster, who gave Kidd's funeral address, and his legacy was hotly, if respectfully, debated in the years to come. He was replaced by Elizabeth Acland Allen, who had formerly worked for the International Peace Campaign and was said to be endorsed by the Communist Party, who led the NCCL until 1960. During the years 1939–41 the NCCL was severely critical of the sweeping defence regulations introduced during the war and the threat which they presented to civil liberties. Moreover, it was willing to defend all those detained without trial under Regulation 18b, including fascists. This emphasis on maintaining traditional civil liberties, such as the freedom of the press, exposed the NCCL to the allegation that it did not understand the nature and magnitude of the challenge facing the British state, and was, in effect, undermining the war effort. Its campaign against the wartime limitations on workers' rights antagonised the trade unions, who felt that the NCCL was trespassing on their territory. Likewise, a conference in February 1941 on civil liberties in the colonies, organised in association with the left-wing Indian nationalist Krishna Menon, which branded British colonial practices as 'fascist', was deemed untimely by many supporters. As the government became less tolerant of criticism – notably with the banning of the communist

Daily Worker in January 1941 – the NCCL became increasingly important to the Communist Party as a means of defending its interests. Accordingly, it came under intensified attack over these links. The Labour intellectual Harold Laski resigned from the NCCL Council over this issue in May 1941, and Alfred Wall, former Secretary of the London Trades Council, mounted a damaging and very public attack on the NCCL at the Labour Party conference, where he stated that 'for the last few months' it had been 'almost mainly' under Communist control.[36]

The NCCL was to an extent saved from further attack when 'history took a hand'[37] only a few weeks later. The German invasion of the Soviet Union on 22 June 1941, and the CPGB's immediate change of policy on supporting the war, allowed the NCCL to adopt more mainstream positions for the remainder of the conflict. Hence, once the Soviet Union had been drawn into the war the NCCL decided to call only for the amendment, rather than the repeal, of Regulation 18b.[38] Even a follow-up conference on colonial liberties in July 1944 was now just one of numerous similar initiatives in the latter stages of the war.[39] However, the damage had been done, and the image of the NCCL was to a large degree fixed in the minds of the non-communist and liberal left by this time. Two comments by informed observers support this point: in late 1944 the writer Rose Macaulay spoke of the NCCL having been under communist influence for at least eight years, while in 1950 Violet Bonham Carter described it as an organisation that even before its 'capture' by the CPGB had been only interested in 'patches of Civil Liberty' and was unwilling to face up to violations by the left.[40] In the words of one historian of the organisation, the NCCL's 'years of ostracism' (which he dated as lasting until the end of the 1950s) had begun.[41]

1.2   Wartime

The outbreak of war in September 1939, and the relative military inactivity following the fall of Poland little more than a month later, created a fertile environment for discussions about peace aims: above all, the question of how enduring security could be established on a basis of individual rights and freedoms. On 5 February 1940 the writer H. G. Wells launched a 'Great Debate' over his 'New Declaration of the Rights of Man' in the Labour-supporting *Daily Herald* newspaper.[42] Wells's ambition, previously stated in his letter to *The Times* of 25 October 1939, was to establish a universal minimum of human rights which would form the foundation of the postwar settlement. His proposed 10 articles for a Declaration of Human Rights were published in stages, and – translated into 10 languages – were sent to 300 newspapers in 48 countries with a view to promoting a worldwide discussion.[43] Within Britain, the articles elicited responses from religious, political and academic leaders, as well as contributions from the 'common man' and woman, digests of which were prepared by Wells' associate, the journalist Ritchie Calder. These comments were then discussed by a drafting committee under the Chairmanship of Lord Sankey (the former Lord Chancellor) who took the chair when Wells' partisan attacks on Prime Minister Neville Chamberlain threatened the collapse of the whole enterprise. A final revised version was published in April 1940, by which point the war had intensified – and taken a turn for the worse.

Wells made no secret that his ten points represented a 'liberal socialist' world view, and that they did not simply address the current war, but also the increase in state power that had been gathering pace over the last century. This latter development was not in itself unwelcome to Wells, as he believed that civilisation faced a choice between 'political and economic collectivisation and disaster'. His goal was to make collectivisation 'workable', and to preserve liberty within a socialist state.[44] The declaration he proposed contained some surprisingly illiberal points, and Ronald Kidd, for instance, objected that the proposed period of detention without charge or trial was more severe than the law currently allowed in Britain. The Declaration also attracted criticism for being wholly secular – a charge that Wells rebuffed by claiming that there were far too many different creeds in the world to take them all into account. Even so, many otherwise sympathetic religious leaders argued that the Declaration fell short in failing to acknowledge that no new order based on rights could succeed without a foundation in religious faith. Harold Moody, President of the League of Coloured Peoples (LOCP), responded that 'if you leave God out, man has no rights except the supposed right to be selfish and exploit his brother man'.[45] Here Wells's vision clashed with an increasingly influential discourse that saw human rights as being derived from the divinely inspired human 'personality'.[46] As one Catholic priest wrote in response to the draft Declaration, there was no such thing as 'natural rights', but only the rights endowed by God on the human personality. Otherwise, rights would be merely 'the common agreement of mankind at a particular time', and could just as easily be taken away as agreed.[47] Meanwhile, Mahatma Gandhi cabled to inform Wells that he had 'begun at the wrong end ... Begin with a Charter of Duties of Man ... and I promise the rights will follow as spring follows winter'.[48]

Although Wells was adamant that the Declaration was intended as 'a project for a liberal and hopeful world order ... and not the prospectus of a millennium',[49] it gave no indication of how these rights were to be secured in the short term. As Professor Selig Brodetsky, President of the

Board of Deputies, pointed out, how would it have helped Jews and democrats in Germany after 1933?[50] Nor did the Declaration stimulate activism amongst its supporters. Kingsley Martin, editor of the *New Statesman*, took part in the well-attended public meeting at Central Hall, Westminster which marked the end of the 'Great Debate', but at its close stepped out into the blackout disappointed: 'everybody ought to have been signed up with a job to do, and been told exactly how to fight for their freedom'.[51] The Declaration's only recorded political success was the endorsement that it received – albeit heavily glossed – from the National Council of the Peace Pledge Union in July 1941.[52] In many ways, therefore, the 'Sankey Declaration' (as it became known, although in reality the authorship remained essentially with Wells) was an oddity of the 'phoney war' period. It was soon overtaken by events, when the military debacle in Norway in April (which immediately led to restrictions on newspaper capacity[53]) was followed soon afterwards by the victorious German offensive in Western Europe. As Labour's Clement Attlee commented in February, it was a good time to formulate peace aims while the country awaited the 'full fury of war':[54] but when the crisis came there was no more time for discussing a 'Wellsian fantasy'.[55] Once the immediate threat of invasion had receded after Dunkirk in June 1940, thinking about the future would eventually turn to more practical visions of social progress, such as the Beveridge Report's recommendations for a welfare state.

A second, and more significant, stimulus for wartime discussion of human rights was provided by the leaders of Britain and the United States prior to the latter's formal entry into the war in December 1941. On 6 January 1941 President Roosevelt made his famous 'Four Freedoms' speech to Congress, identifying them as freedom of speech, freedom of worship, freedom from want and freedom from fear. Tellingly, he made clear that these would be universal rights: 'Freedom means the supremacy of human rights everywhere'. These simple and resonant words were swiftly seized upon in Britain, and in July 1941 were adopted wholesale in a speech by Attlee, now Deputy Prime Minister.[56] However, the impact of Roosevelt's speech should be assessed alongside the joint statement agreed between him and Churchill on 14 August 1941 at Placentia Bay, Canada. (The statement was immediately christened the 'Atlantic Charter' by journalists, and this is the somewhat misleading term by which the declaration is now known.) In November 1941 H. G. Wells fumed that 'nobody attended' any longer to his own declaration, while the Atlantic Charter – 'a woolly document full of holes' – excited 'continuing fuss'.[57]

The Atlantic Charter was drafted by US diplomats and was somewhat sprung on Churchill who, reliant on American aid and desiring America's entry into the war, was only able to take the edges off some of its articles.[58] The document offered a very broad outline of Allied war aims and principles, including a commitment not to seek territorial aggrandisement, and to provide equal access to economic resources. Article Three, arguably the most discussed, committed the Allies to restoring sovereign rights and self-government to those 'forcibly deprived of them'. This was preceded by an ambiguously worded statement: 'Third, they respect the right of all peoples to choose the form of government under which they will live'.[59] Accordingly, the Charter raised immediate and unrealisable hopes in the colonial world that the end of imperial rule was at hand, reinforced by Attlee's comment to a gathering of West African students on 16 August that the freedoms for which the war was being fought would not be denied to 'any of the races of mankind'. This interpretation was immediately slapped down by Churchill on his return from Canada, when he told Parliament that Article Three applied 'primarily' to states under Nazi occupation, and that the 'progressive evolution of self-governing institutions' in the British Empire was a wholly separate process.[60]

However, the wording could not be undone, and long continued to provide inspiration. As late as 1943 Arthur Shearly Cripps, an Anglican missionary and leading advocate of African rights in Southern Rhodesia, still envisaged that Britain would – like the biblical David – deliver Africa from colonial rule: the Charter's articles were 'eight priceless pebbles for your sling!'[61] Although it is correct that the Atlantic Charter was not in itself a human rights instrument,[62] the document – and perhaps more importantly the sense that freedoms had been tantalisingly offered then rescinded – undoubtedly contributed to the growth of human rights activism during and after the war. Leslie Hale, a Labour politician and leading campaigner for colonial freedom, told Parliament in 1953 that, with the Atlantic Charter, 'which suggested man's advance to a newer and higher conception of the dignity of mankind, most of us then found a new inspiration in political life and new hope for the future'.[63] The impact in the colonial world (and amongst African Americans) is well recorded.[64] Within Britain, the Atlantic Charter inspired activists to work on further documents intended to extend its freedoms to the colonies. A conference organised by the Fabian Colonial Bureau in February 1943 discussed a 'Charter for the Colonial Peoples', and in 1944 Harold Moody's LOCP devised a 'Charter for Coloured Peoples' which contained a commitment to equal economic, legal and political rights for all.[65]

While the anti-colonial reading of the Atlantic Charter proved influential, the text was open to an even wider range of interpretations and its impacts were difficult to foretell. For instance, William Douglas-Home, a British officer and critic of the conduct and purpose of the war, secured some 2000 votes standing as an 'Atlantic Charter' candidate in the Clay Cross by-election of 1944. His idiosyncratic interpretation of the Charter was that it committed the Allies to not pursue unconditional surrender.[66] The Charter also inspired diverse cultural interpretations. In 1943 the Artists International Association, a leading anti-fascist organisation, commissioned well-known artists to interpret 'the Four Freedoms as defined in the Atlantic Charter'. The exhibition, sponsored by the *News Chronicle* and the Ministry of Information, was held in the bombed-out site of the John Lewis store in Oxford Street. One painting, *The Land of Ears* by Carel Weight, which depicted the fear of talking openly under Nazi rule, attracted special interest.[67] However, for the left, Allied policy towards liberated countries emerging from Nazi occupation proved just as disappointing as the failure to deliver colonial freedom. For instance, in December 1944 the NCCL passed a resolution calling for Belgium, Italy and Greece to be allowed to exercise democratic control 'in accordance with the Atlantic Charter',[68] and the Charter was cited in Communist Party speakers' notes calling for self-determination for Greece.[69] Meanwhile, in Catholic and Conservative circles there was mounting concern that the war would end with Poland and the Baltic States firmly under Soviet control. The Duchess of Atholl placed this issue at the heart of her 'League for European Freedom', having initially planned to call it the 'Atlantic Charter Association'.[70] The Charter's impact, therefore, proved remarkably enduring, and as late as 1962 a Greek political prisoner was still longing for the freedoms that it had promised.[71] In this sense the 'woolly' Atlantic Charter proved far more inspirational than the Declaration of the United Nations, signed by twenty-six states in January 1942, which specifically mentioned a commitment to human rights in its preamble.

During the final years of the war, civil liberties activism was less prominent in Britain, primarily because the NCCL had become more discerning in its challenges to government. Indeed, it took a noticeably illiberal position on some issues, such as opposing the release of Oswald Mosley from detention in 1943 (again, in line with Communist Party policy). In 1944 the NCCL refused to defend striking Tyneside apprentices, as well as a young man who was facing jail for refusing, on conscientious grounds, to serve as a fire-watcher. In the latter case the NCCL decided that it could not take up the case of someone 'who has admittedly broken the law' (something which had not previously been a consideration). When this decision was criticised, the reply was intemperate – the NCCL was an 'educative, propagandist and advisory organisation', and would only take up those cases which would rally public support: it could not act as a 'Poor Person's Lawyer'.[72] This case divided the NCCL Executive Committee and brought together a coalition of pacifist, religious and left-wing critics. The Peace Pledge Union disaffiliated from the NCCL and set up a Civil Liberties Vigilance Committee to rally groups such as the Independent Labour Party and the Anglican Pacifist Fellowship, although the new body failed to flourish and eventually merged with the Anarchists' Freedom Defence Committee. Even so, NCCL insiders like Angela Tuckett and D. N. Pritt were wrong to dismiss the Vigilance Committee as simply the work of a 'hostile caucus' of Trotskyists and pacifists, determined to destroy their organisation. It represented an important constituency that would only partially be reclaimed during the Cold War. As one concerned correspondent wrote in 1946: 'What has happened to the NCCL during the war years? Where is that forward looking liberal spirit . . .?'[73]

Not all pacifists distanced themselves from the NCCL during the war. One significant figure who managed to combine the worlds of the NCCL and pacifism was John Fletcher, a long-time member of the Society of Friends and a highly experienced peace campaigner who joined the NCCL Executive Committee in 1942. Fletcher, who had been in Australia at the start of World War I, returned to Britain in 1915 and joined the No Conscription Fellowship. He acted as a Quaker 'chaplain' for jailed Conscientious Objectors during and after World War II. He was also a strong supporter of the missionary Albert Schweitzer, whose support committee in Britain he ran, and he achieved prominence towards the end of his life as a campaigner for racial equality in both Britain and Africa. While for admirers he was 'the last of the real Quakers' and a 'congenital rebel',[74] he was denounced by one magistrate in 1948 as an 'evil thing' for encouraging young men to go to prison for refusing to do national service.[75] Fletcher brought the voice of conscience to NCCL discussions,[76] and was joined by another pacifist, the barrister and future Lord Chancellor Gerald Gardiner, who had recently served in the Friends' Ambulance Unit.

One issue that encapsulated the dilemmas facing the NCCL in the latter stages of the war and the early postwar years was its campaign for a ban on fascism and anti-Semitism. Both had staged a disturbing revival in Britain, especially in parts of London, and the situation was anxiously monitored by the Board of Deputies and its Jewish Defence Committee (JDC). In October 1943 they noted that anti-Semitism was on the rise after the heavy air raids had ceased and was worryingly present in the factories. When the journalist and future Labour MP Tom Driberg took up the issue he was subjected to a barrage of abusive mail.[77] In 1947 the Board and the NCCL agreed to make common cause against fascism and anti-Semitism, and the JDC pledged a grant of £600 to organise the campaign.[78] But this relationship was not without tensions. The Board was wary of commissioning an NCCL touring exhibition on anti-Semitism in 1943, warning against 'getting into the habit of creating increased Jew-consciousness in many areas where it never existed before . . .'.[79] When the NCCL proposed a ban on all fascist demonstrations, the Board preferred a ban on the use of loudspeakers, which would have affected communist rallies as well. (Elizabeth Allen protested that only the fascists 'abused' their loudspeakers by using them to drown out their opponents.[80]) When the NCCL's annual meeting voted in March 1944 in favour of 'restrictive legislation' against fascism during wartime, pacifists unsuccessfully sought to replace this with a pledge to uphold all freedoms.[81] In 1946 a subcommittee of the NCCL endorsed D. N. Pritt's draft bill to prevent fascist activity and propaganda. John Fletcher alone voted against, arguing that denying civil liberties to one single party was 'too high a price to pay for the destruction of Fascism'. Robert Pollard, a lawyer and recent Labour candidate, resigned, having committed himself to upholding civil liberties in the 1945 election, and claimed that Ronald Kidd would no longer recognise the organisation that he had founded.[82]

1.3   Human Rights in the Postwar World

With the end of World War II, ideas about human rights began to play a more important role in British political discourse, albeit in a still limited form. The Labour Party's manifesto for the 1945 election, for instance, was couched in terms of 'freedoms' rather than human rights. Even so, the concept of a universal standard of behaviour for governments was gaining ground through the United Nations (UN) Charter adopted at the organisation's founding conference in San Francisco in June 1945. (Article 55 enjoined all member states to observe and promote human rights.) The conference established a Commission on Human Rights which, after extensive negotiations, produced the UN Declaration, agreed *nem. con.* by member states on 10 December 1948. The Declaration, which was devised by an international drafting committee headed by Eleanor Roosevelt and including experts from China, Lebanon and the Philippines, combined traditional political freedoms with – for the first time in a major international document – economic and social rights.[83] The document has become so well known that it is important to note that it was a mere declaration, lacking the force of an international treaty. It did not stipulate how the rights laid out by its authors should be guaranteed, and this was left to a subsequent legal covenant (or, in the event, two covenants) which would then require ratification. Indeed, as Harold Laski wrote at the time, referring to the ill-fated international agreement of 1928 to renounce war as an instrument of policy, the danger was that the Declaration would be merely a new Kellogg–Briand Pact, and just as likely to be ignored by its signatories.[84] The Cambridge legal scholar Hersch Lauterpacht, a prominent advocate of an international charter during World War II, wrote gloomily in 1949 that the Declaration offered lawyers the dread prospect of rights without legal remedies.[85]

One glimmer of hope for Lauterpacht was the possibility of swifter progress on a narrower front, rather than a universal commitment of only nominal worth. The 1950 European Convention on Human Rights (ECHR) largely fulfilled this goal, but only by limiting itself to the democratic states of Western Europe and by offering a far smaller menu of – essentially political – rights to be protected. The Convention, which grew out of the postwar movement for European unity and was the first fruit of the newly established Council of Europe, was largely driven by centre-right European politicians such as the former Resistance activist Pierre-Henri Teitgen and David Maxwell Fyfe, lead British prosecutor at the International Military Tribunal at Nuremberg (1945–46) and future Lord Chancellor. Britain's Labour government was sceptical about the project, with some ministers fearing that the state's ability to intervene in the economy might be impaired, while others were concerned about the impact on the colonies. As Marco Duranti has compellingly argued,[86] the ECHR was essentially a conservative project intended to secure against the possibility of future totalitarian governments of right or left, rather than to extend rights – and certainly not to extend rights to the European colonial empires. Moreover, there was no right of individual petition until the mid-1960s. The Convention attracted little interest in Britain, and the Labour Party International Secretary Denis Healey reported on it in the same breath as agreements on fishing.[87] Maxwell Fyfe told the United Europe Movement in 1951 that 'people in Britain are completely uninterested in human rights, because, of course, they have not seen them go like some of the other fifteen nations who have adopted the Convention'.[88] Even so, the ECHR rapidly developed a legal and administrative capacity during the 1950s, through its court and commission, and became an increasingly assertive actor in international relations.[89]

The UN's avowed commitment to human rights created an important new international focus for campaigners in what was already being termed the 'field of Human Rights'.[90] During the interwar years organisations such as the Anti-Slavery Society had established a base in Geneva and used their expertise and contacts to influence policymakers at the League of Nations.[91] Likewise, Jewish organisations were well placed to lobby international institutions. Now this practice was replicated in New York and, with the advent of the European Court, Strasbourg. Privileged advisory status became highly desirable for British organisations either acting alone or working through international bodies, and partners in the United States also became more important. The emergence of new independent states from colonial rule also began to transform the work of campaigners. The Rev. Michael Scott, an unwelcome figure in New York due to his previous communist connections, was only able to take his campaign on behalf of the native peoples of South West Africa to the UN because he was adopted as part of the Indian delegation.

The European Convention was shaped by the intensification of tensions associated with the Cold War in the later 1940s, and these pressures also had a profound effect on British campaigning organisations. For instance, the Haldane Society was widely thought to have fallen under communist control during the war, to the frustration of lawyers such as Gerald Gardiner, who regarded this development – despite his personal regard for D. N. Pritt and others – as damaging to its credibility.[92] Eventually, a new Society of Labour Lawyers (SLL) was established in 1949, excluding not only CPGB members but also fellow travellers such as the Labour MP Geoffrey Bing.[93] A similar split occurred on an international level when the International Association of Democratic Lawyers (IADL) sided openly with the communists in the Cold War – notably over the Korean War (1950–53). A more Western-oriented International Commission of Jurists (ICJ) was established in 1953, and prominent British participants included Sir Hartley Shawcross (a Labour MP, and another Nuremberg counsel) and the Oxford Law don Norman Marsh. The ICJ took as its mantra 'the rule of law', although, as Peter Benenson noted in a moment of exasperation in 1963, this was a platitude and 'virtually meaningless'.[94]

The Cold War also had a powerful impact on the NCCL, accentuating its isolation by putting further strain on links with liberals and the non-communist left. The Council's refusal to take up the case of the 'Soviet brides' – Russian women who had married British men during the war and now wished to join them – exposed the NCCL to allegations not only of political bias, but also of a lack of humanity.[95] The resignation in May 1948 of E. M. Forster, who had stood by the NCCL during the debates with the pacifists in 1944 on the grounds that it still did 'much more good than harm',[96] was another painful blow. In his public resignation letter Forster stated that he had resigned because a recent NCCL emergency resolution censuring the government's proposed 'purge' of communist and fascist civil servants was a political act, unacceptable in a non-political body. Tellingly, he alluded warmly to its heyday under Ronald Kidd, while expressing sympathy with only 'some' of the NCCL's more recent work.[97] In private correspondence with John Fletcher he gave a fuller account of his concerns. While he was aware from a recent visit to the United States of the dangers of a 'witch-mania', he felt that the British government had acted 'reasonably' in moving certain individuals who might face divided loyalty in a conflict with Russia and who therefore represented a danger. He could not agree with Fletcher that the remedy was 'worse than the disease'.[98]

Despite these serious setbacks, the NCCL was alert to the changes in the postwar order and made a serious attempt to engage with – if not wholly to embrace – the new recognition that was being accorded to human rights. It convened two conferences in 1946 and 1947 (one domestic and the other international) in response to the UN Commission on Human Rights' appeal for discussion of the forthcoming declaration. The November 1947 international conference brought together a wide range of delegates, primarily from within Europe, but also from the United States and South Africa. Angela Tuckett later claimed to be disappointed with the attendance, which she partly blamed on a rail strike in France,[99] but in fact it was a signal achievement to bring together sixty-nine delegates (of whom thirty were women) from fifteen countries and four British colonies. Delegates divided into four commissions to discuss racial discrimination, sex discrimination, anti-Semitism and the freedom of the press. It was an eclectic and unpredictable gathering. For instance, the delegate from the South African Institute of International Relations offered staggeringly patronising stereotypes of the black majority ('a very cheerful people') and stated that the Jews' unpopularity in South Africa was 'their own fault'.[100] The American delegate Ira Latimer, from the Chicago Civil Liberties Committee, was later said to have spent most time on canvassing support for Henry Wallace's third party-presidential candidature.[101]

The conference was undoubtedly a pioneering endeavour: the first gathering of non-governmental organisations in Britain devoted to the subject of human rights. But it was also deeply flawed. This was partly because of an evident insularity and complacency on the part of the hosts, whereby Britain was consistently hailed as the world leader in the fight for human rights. For Elizabeth Allen, 'freedom's long trail' began in Britain with Magna Carta, and the NCCL offered a model for other countries to follow. Her approach was similar to that of Prime Minister Clement Attlee, who would argue in 1949 that Britain and its Commonwealth approached 'more nearly to reaching these ideals [embodied in the UN Declaration] than any other country in the world'.[102] More importantly, by 1947 Cold War tensions were already evident, and the conference hardly represented an ideal of universality. There was sustained criticism of the European empires, but none whatsoever of the emergent communist regimes in Central and Eastern Europe, which were engaged in vicious struggles for power with non-communists under the eye of the occupying Red Army. A paper by the Polish delegate, for instance, made clear that any tolerance for traitors, Quislings and other 'criminal elements' would be 'suicidal for democracy itself'.[103] Following the conference a preparatory committee was set up to plan a further meeting in Prague, the city where the Czech communists would seize power in February 1948. In 1950 these plans were finally shelved when the Czech League for the Rights of Man decided that the 'fight for Human Rights should be united with the fight for Peace'[104] (at the time of the worldwide Communist Peace Campaign). It is easy, therefore, to see these conferences as Cold War follies or, at best, far ahead of their time. Indeed, the lawyer Neil Lawson was quoted as saying that the conferences were '10 years too early'.[105] In reality, however, the NCCL was not the right vehicle – it was too firmly on the left and too Anglocentric – to forge a worthwhile consensus around human rights.

1.4   Towards Human Rights Activism?

The NCCL's conferences of 1946/1947 show how the left was intrigued by the opportunities created by the Universal Declaration but struggled to fit universalist values into its existing ideology and practices. The left was by no means alone in this: all non-governmental organisations brought their own agenda to the new politics of human rights, and this appears to support Samuel Moyn's comment that during the 1940s human rights 'inspired no movement'.[106] However, there are some interesting cases, especially amongst lay Christian movements, whereby serious attempts were made to integrate human rights into activism at this time. This was not so much a rapid and immediately successful embrace of human rights as a process of exploring their potential from a wide range of ideological standpoints.

As the Catholic writer John Eppstein argued in 1947, Christian organisations benefited from the development of 'personalist' thought as an alternative to both liberal individualism and the totalitarianism of right and left.[107] Personalism had first gained currency amongst French intellectuals such as Jacques Maritain and Emmanuel Mounier in the 1930s and offered a basis for Pius XII to embrace human rights during World

War II, notably in his allocution of Christmas 1942. Personalism privileged the individual and family over the state, but also emphasised that the individual – by virtue of possessing a divinely inspired personality – was committed to duties and moral responsibilities. Personalism was not so well developed in Britain – indeed, one authority wrote in 1948 that it was 'only three years old'.[108] However, the concept was becoming better known, partly due to the considerable interest in the writings of the Russian émigré Nicholas Berdayev, above all his book *Freedom and Slavery* (1947), which was cited increasingly widely at this time. To take one example, the Jesuit priest Thomas Corbishley, who would take a keen interest in human rights throughout his career, wrote in 1942 that no human 'person' is of greater weight than another, and no human being may interfere with the development of the personality of another: 'such is the basis of the rights of man'.[109] But personalism was by no means restricted to Catholic circles, and one also encounters it in sources as diverse as a speech by the Liberal leader Archibald Sinclair at an NCCL conference in 1939;[110] in the writings and speeches of Victor Gollancz, notably his book *Our Threatened Values* (1946); in the 1945 election address of the lawyer and Labour candidate Robert Pollard; and in many pacifist publications. What personalism provided – and what to an extent the NCCL had lacked – was a strong intellectual basis for adopting human rights as a basis for action, just as thinking about the Universal Declaration began to crystallise in the postwar years.

The most significant Catholic lay organisation to emerge during the war was the Sword of the Spirit, which had been inspired by Archbishop Hinsley during the crisis after Dunkirk. Hinsley understood that the Catholic Church had been identified with support for authoritarian Catholic rulers such as Franco and Salazar in the 1930s, and – without renouncing these associations – he was determined not only to prove its patriotism, but also to offer spiritual leadership in the war. Leading figures in the movement included the prominent Catholic intellectual Christopher Dawson, the educationalist A. C. F. Beales, and both Peter Benenson's aunt (Manya Harari) and his cousin, Mira Benenson.[111] A parallel Anglican movement, Religion and Life, was also established, and while not wholly ecumenical, the high level of cooperation achieved between Catholics, the Church of England and the Free Churches (including the formation of many local Christian councils) was pioneering. The movement lost momentum after Hinsley's death in 1943: many years later Oliver Tomkins, Anglican Bishop of Bristol, sadly recalled 'the brief swallow-like flight of Cardinal Hinsley which promised the arrival of an ecumenical summer that never arrived for twenty years'.[112] In 1944 Hinsley's more conservative successor, Archbishop Griffin, vetoed a draft joint declaration on religious freedom when his theological advisers objected to any 'natural and civic right' to such a claim. Even so, the Sword of the Spirit survived into the postwar world, strengthened by former servicemen and women, who formed a new 'cell' structure.

The Sword of the Spirit (which had a strong Polish branch within Britain) was deeply apprehensive about the prospect of the postwar Soviet domination of Central and Eastern Europe, which it regarded as the betrayal of the Atlantic Charter. The trials of leading clerics by the new communist regimes – notably that of Yugoslavia's Archbishop Stepinac in 1946 and of the Hungarian Cardinal Mindszenty in February 1949 – provided it with clear evidence of religious persecution. The Mindszenty trial, coming so soon after the signing of the Universal Declaration, was widely presented in the West as a violation of human rights, and has been regarded as a prime early example of a human rights cause.[113] Of course, the intensity of their campaign on behalf of Mindszenty laid Catholics open to the charge of hypocrisy, given that they ignored the plight of left-wing prisoners of Catholic authoritarian states such as Spain and Portugal. Accordingly, Cardinal Griffin was deeply grateful when Anglicans offered their support (despite their reservations about Mindszenty's record as an anti-Semite and supporter of Admiral Horthy's interwar dictatorship). In turn, Griffin offered reciprocal support for imprisoned Protestants.

The Sword of the Spirit ran an extensive 'human rights campaign' (probably the first occasion on which this specific term was used in Britain) throughout the period 1948–49 alongside the Catholic Social Guild, and this included a large rally in London in October 1948.[114] The campaign was not only concerned with Mindszenty, and in fact was more interested in discussing, and (through the British government) amending, the forthcoming Universal Declaration of Human Rights. Above all, while broadly content with the Declaration's draft articles, Catholics wanted to see four changes: reference to God as the source of all rights; a statement of the prior position of the family over the state; a clearer reference to the right to own property; and a statement of the right of religious associations to own land. The campaign was pursued vigorously through local meetings, leaflets, lobbying of MPs and a delegation to the Foreign Office. A parallel campaign was being run within the Anglican Church and the British Council of Churches for the promotion of religious freedoms in the Declaration of Human Rights. The crucial difference, however, is that this was essentially restricted to high-level discussions, while the Catholic campaign alone sought to involve the laity.

There are, therefore, some similarities between the lay Catholics and the NCCL in their engagement with human rights in the late 1940s. In both cases activists saw new opportunities in the Universal Declaration; both approached it on their own terms and with a view to promoting their own interests. Some Sword of the Spirit groups, for instance, took the opportunity to campaign against birth control clinics in the name of human rights.[115] In the case of the Catholics, however, buoyed by a powerful sense of grievance over the treatment of their co-religionists in Eastern Europe, and sustained by secure intellectual foundations, activism around issues of human rights did become possible in the later 1940s in a way that eluded the NCCL. However, it is also notable that neither case led to full-blown human rights activism during the 1950s. The NCCL became principally identified at this time with campaigning over civil liberties issues related to mental health, while the Sword of the Spirit focused increasingly on development in Africa and eventually merged with the Catholic Institute for International Relations.

While the Sword of the Spirit's campaign was the most specific mobilisation around the question of human rights in the late 1940s, there are a number of other cases that show how activists from different traditions were coming to take an interest in human rights at this time. The first case concerns the Reverend John Collins, who went on to play a leading role in the anti-apartheid movement, the Campaign for Nuclear Disarmament and the campaign for the abolition of the death penalty. Collins served during World War II as a chaplain for the RAF, latterly at Bomber Command. However, his most formative experience was at RAF Yatesbury, where he had created a lay Christian community, the Fellowship of the Transfiguration. Following the end of the war Collins returned to Oriel College, Oxford, as chaplain and, in 1946 – closely supported by his wife Diana – launched a movement for Christian Action at a meeting attended by some 3000 people in the Town Hall. The movement was intended to encourage Christians to act in the public sphere and had no specific objectives. Collins, who had close relations with Victor Gollancz and the Labour politician Sir Stafford Cripps, initially focused his attention on reconciliation with Germany, and one major early initiative, following Collins' visit to the British zone of occupation, was to arrange for the Berlin Philharmonic Orchestra to play in Britain. The Oxford meeting was very much shaped by Gollancz's moral outrage at Britain's failure to respond adequately to the humanitarian crisis in Germany. Collins was also on the fringes of the movement for European unity, influenced by his association with the former Foreign Secretary and leading lay Anglican Lord Halifax. In April 1948 he organised a meeting at the Albert Hall in support of Western Union and he attended the Hague Congress in May, although he later came to rather regret the former episode.[116] His career was transformed by his decision to leave Oxford in 1949 to become a canon at St Paul's Cathedral. This not only gave him a much higher profile within the church, and a pulpit for him and those who shared his campaigning passions, but also provided a new home at Amen Court, near the cathedral, with the space and security to pursue his activism. Significantly, he turned down the opportunity to become General Secretary of the British Council of Churches, preferring to continue his work with Christian Action whose administrator, Freda Nuell, moved with him to London.

Until this point human rights do not seem to have played a discernible part in Collins' thinking. However, his encounter in 1949 with Michael Scott, recently returned from the UN, as well as his reading of Alan Paton's *Cry, the Beloved Country* (1948), challenged him to turn his attention to Africa. At a meeting in early 1949 the Council of Christian Action committed the organisation to working to defend human rights and liberty 'as set out' in the Universal Declaration, although this came second to a new obligation to comfort the lonely. However, the story was more complex than this, as Collins had originally sought support not for the defence of human rights, but rather for a campaign on 'the coloured problem', with special reference to Scott's work in South West Africa. This had been opposed by Lord Halifax on the grounds that it was not an appropriate task for Christian Action, and Collins conceded that his work in this area would therefore have to be carried out on a personal basis. The situation was saved by the intervention of Sir Kenneth Grubb, a leading Anglican layman prominent in the World Council of Churches, who proposed that Christian Action should actively support the defence of human rights and religious liberty. Collins accepted this formulation but clearly regarded it primarily as granting him the latitude to support Scott. Indeed, a short book by Diana Collins written at the time made clear that 'under this heading [of the defence of human rights and liberty] will come any work which we may be able to do to help Mr Michael Scott to establish the human rights of the native tribes of South-West Africa'.[117] Ironically, Scott and Collins would clash repeatedly over both South Africa and nuclear disarmament in the ensuing decades, but Collins had recognised Scott's inspirational powers and given a valuable early boost to his campaign.

A second example relates to the peace movement. As we have seen, pacifists were very open to personalist ideas. For instance, in defining what it stood for in 1940, the Peace Pledge Union stated that its first principle was to attach 'supreme value to the human person and the integrity of the individual'.[118] However, in the postwar years the absence of any reference to a right to conscientious objection in the human rights documents of the period presented a major obstacle to the peace movement's deeper engagement. This was a particularly pressing issue in Britain following the reintroduction of conscription (or 'National Service') in 1948. In March 1947 Herbert Runham Brown of the War Resisters' International argued in a letter to the UN Human Rights Commission that 'any World Charter of the Rights of Man must include the right of refusing military service in obedience to conscience'. The struggle for the freedom of conscience was, he argued, the defining cause of the twentieth century, just as the struggle for religious freedom had defined the seventeenth.[119] This petitioning continued well into the 1950s and disappointment over such a central issue left the peace movement surprisingly sceptical about the value of the UN Declaration.[120]

One final case was more in the nature of an experiment conducted by UNESCO, the UN Educational, Scientific and Cultural Organization. In early 1952 UNESCO commissioned parallel surveys in three European university cities of comparable size – Cambridge, Uppsala and Grenoble – to establish how far the public knew of (and understood) the UN Declaration on Human Rights. Five hundred half-hour interviews were conducted in each city, followed by intensive local campaigns to raise public awareness. In the case of Cambridge, which had a 1000-strong UNA group, this self-styled 'human rights campaign' took the form of articles in the local press, a shop-window exhibition, a letter to every schoolchild and a public meeting addressed by the African-American Nobel laureate Ralph Bunche. Two months later a further round of interviews was carried out. The results were fascinating and showed interesting disparities between the three cities. In Cambridge, for instance, a very high proportion made no response when asked to identify specific rights (43 per cent), while those who did referred to standard 'civil liberties' such as the right to free speech and personal freedoms. There was general support for the proposition that all human beings were born free and equal in dignity (78 per cent). In practical terms, this was expressed in support for access to education regardless of wealth and gender: however, in Cambridge a striking 42 per cent agreed with the statement that 'the white race is certainly superior to and more efficient than other races', far higher than the figure in Uppsala and Grenoble.[121] UNESCO pronounced the results as 'satisfactory', not only because the second round of interviews indicated a mild increase in public awareness, but also because the survey had identified support for some of the 'new' social and economic rights included in the UN Declaration (such as the right to education or state subsidy for cultural activities). However, the campaign does not appear to have been followed up or replicated elsewhere, and the next serious attempt to raise public awareness about the rights embodied in the UN Declaration had to wait until 1968.

1.5   Michael Scott: Towards the Human Rights Activist

It is difficult to overestimate the impact of Michael Scott on progressive Christian opinion in the late 1940s and early 1950s. This austere cleric – previously largely unknown in Britain – burst on the scene on his return from the UN in December 1949. He was featured in an influential profile in David Astor's *Observer*, which noted that his 'strikingly handsome face has something of the saint about it and something of the rebel'.[122] He was frequently referred to as a moral arbiter: the 'guardian of the white man's conscience in Africa'.[123] *Peace News* noted that Scott was one of those 'outstanding men' in every generation who 'personify and symbolise the vital issues of their time'.[124] Although others, including Astor, were already coming to see the importance of South Africa following the election victory of D. F. Malan's National Party and the beginnings of the apartheid regime in 1948, Scott injected a new moral earnestness into these concerns, combined with an ineffable star quality.

Scott was the son of a vicar and had spent time in South Africa as a young man in the 1920s. During the early 1930s, working as the vicar of an East End parish he had been profoundly affected by the impact of the Depression and was drawn to the Communist Party, for whom he briefly worked as an industrial organiser. In 1935, with party approval,[125] he went to India as chaplain for the Bishop of Bombay. Behind the scenes he worked with the civil servant Michael Carritt – the self-styled 'mole in the crown' – to act as a liaison between the CPGB and the Indian communists. On his return to Britain in 1939, and having learnt to fly, Scott enlisted in the RAF, not – like Collins – as a chaplain, but as a pilot. When ill health resulted in his discharge, in 1943 Scott returned to South Africa as a priest, again with the approval of the CPGB, which saw him as a valuable asset for the South African Communist Party. Here he became involved in African nationalist politics and established the short-lived but influential 'Campaign for Right and Justice'. Scott blamed its failure on the manoeuvrings of the Communist Party[126] and for the rest of his career – although remaining on the left – was deeply suspicious of the communists. While not concealing his communist past he successfully downplayed it, and in 1976 Roger Baldwin, a key ally in the United States, expressed surprise at finding so much communism hidden in Scott's past – a case, as he put it, of 'the red cap on the cross'.[127]

Scott forged his reputation with four significant interventions. First, in what has been termed the 'dividing line' in his life,[128] he went to Durban in 1946 during the campaign of passive resistance by Indians against the Asiatic Land Tenure and Indian Representation Act. Scott stood alongside the Indian protestors when they were assaulted by whites and was subsequently jailed for three months. The experience not only converted Scott to the principle of non-violent protest, but also reinforced a powerful personal link with India that lasted until the mid-1960s. Secondly, he went to serve in a township known as 'Tobruk' on the edge of Johannesburg, enduring uncomplainingly not only the poor conditions but also threats of violence from local gangsters. Thirdly, if further proof of his physical courage were needed, in 1947 he confronted an angry meeting of white farmers while investigating alleged 'slave' conditions amongst black labourers in the Transvaal town of Bethel.[129] Fourthly, in 1949 he was introduced to the plight of the exiled Hereros, the tribe driven from their lands by German colonial forces in 1904. He visited those Hereros living in Bechuanaland and was deeply impressed by the quiet Christian dignity of their paramount chief, Frederick Mahareru. He also visited the Hereros within South West Africa, and Scott would always thereafter close his speeches and sermons on their plight with the prayer of their Chief Hosea Kutako, delivered movingly to an open-air gathering:

O Lord, help us who roam about. Help us who have been placed in Africa and have no dwelling place of our own. Give us back a dwelling place.[130]

The moment was propitious, as South Africa, which had been given authority over South West Africa in 1919 as a League of Nations mandate, was now seeking to annex the vast territory. Scott was commissioned by the Hereros to go to the UN to speak on their behalf. Despite efforts by both the British and the American governments to stop him, Scott eventually arrived in New York with Indian support. After several transatlantic visits, he was finally called to speak at the UN's Fourth Committee (by twenty-five votes to fifteen) on 26 November 1949 and his speech made international news. According to the *News Chronicle*, this 'gaunt man with the burning eyes' succeeded in turning the debate from 'arid legal disputation into a moral assize'.[131]

Scott's stock was never higher than on his return to Britain (initially en route to the World Pacifist Congress in Gandhi's home of Seagram). He attracted a small group of loyal supporters: the Quaker activist John Fletcher, Esther Muirhead (who had links to the India League) and South African clergyman George Norton. Together these three formed a self-appointed 'Michael Scott Committee' and issued the *Michael Scott Newsletter*. They were later joined by another South African, Mary Benson, who had been working in the film industry and had become fascinated with Scott after reading the *Observer* profile. She became his closest ally and confidante for the next seven years, although her own intense feelings for Scott (and hopes for marriage) were never to be reciprocated.[132] Scott received support from a range of organisations such as the NCCL (which had petitioned Eleanor Roosevelt for his admission to the United States) and the India League. However, Fletcher's committee, conscious of Scott's delicate health, fiercely patrolled access to him. Indeed, the Communist Party believed that 'the Quakers had got hold of him, and they were keeping him thoroughly wrapped up'.[133]

The other crucial contact that Scott forged at this time was with David Astor, a member of the wealthy Astor family, whose immense portfolio included ownership of the *Observer*. Under Astor's combined control and editorship (1948–75) the *Observer* was emerging after the war as the definitive voice of engaged, internationally minded liberalism. He surrounded himself with highly intelligent, freethinking writers, many of whom had arrived as exiles from oppression in Europe. The *Observer* was opposed to Soviet communism, but also believed that rapid reform was needed in the colonial world to forestall communism, and – influenced by writers such as Colin Legum – it took a highly principled stance against apartheid. Like Scott, Astor was a diffident man, but he was committed to using his wealth to pump prime movements for reform, becoming arguably the greatest individual facilitator of social and political activism in the two decades after World War II.[134] His contributions to Scott's work were manifold. On a personal level he gave Scott a generous annuity[135] and often provided him with somewhere to recuperate during his frequent periods of ill health. (Scott suffered from Crohn's Disease, and underwent numerous operations.) On one occasion he even offered Scott the family shooting lodge on Jura for convalescence, the same island where a few years previously Astor had sent his friend George Orwell to complete *Nineteen Eighty-Four*.[136] Just as importantly, Astor gave Scott access to high-level contacts in government and politics, and offered him a vision for how to develop his work in Britain more effectively. Both Astor and Mary Benson believed that the close attention of Fletcher and his allies ('the chronically oppositional and crankish, and a fringe of near fellow-travellers'[137]) was holding Scott back. Astor worked assiduously in 1950–51 to wean Scott away from his followers and to create a new structure within which he could operate.

In May 1950 Scott spoke on 'Christ and the Colour Problem' at St Paul's, and in June his supporters organised a conference on the 'Human Crisis in Africa'. In a session on 'democracy and human rights' Scott demanded that the Universal Declaration of Human Rights must be imposed in Africa and warned that communism would succeed if the colonial powers failed to deliver. Out of this grew a new 'Africa Relations Council' involving, amongst others, the National Peace Council and The

Friends, under the administration of Esther Muirhead. However, the new organisation failed to flourish, and in April 1952 Astor helped Scott to form the more enduring Africa Bureau. This not only provided Scott with a 'vehicle' but also fulfilled Astor's ambition for a 'central body of liberal bi-partisan opinion'.[138] The Bureau's executive committee was drawn from the ranks of Astor's contacts in the political and business elite: these were influential people, such as Lord Hemingford, and they were more restrained than Scott's previous allies had been. Scott had hoped that the Bureau would support his work on his return to South Africa, but in 1951 he was declared a 'prohibited migrant' to both the Union of South Africa and South West Africa, and he never returned. Muirhead, who felt that she had been sidelined, departed for India and worked more productively in Bangalore for War on Want in the late 1950s.[139]

Scott was remarkably successful in troubling the conscience of British Christians. According to the Iona Community he had 'stabbed us awake',[140] while Fletcher told a sceptical South African friend that Scott had 'stirred us to action'.[141] Paradoxically, Scott appeared to lack many of the attributes needed to promote his cause. Cyril Dunn (*Observer* journalist and Scott's initial biographer) argued that he was strangely averse to the press. Indeed, he was offended by his face being used by the Union of Democratic Control on the cover of the one of its pamphlets.[142] He was also known to be a very poor public speaker. However, Scott's saintly demeanour and appearance concealed a resilient and canny activist who was adept at using many different media. For example, he made his own film about life in the South African townships, which he showed to sympathetic MPs and with which he toured in 1949.[143] Interest in Scott was further boosted by the publication of a book by his South African friend Freda Troup (based on the notes that he had left with her) which wove elements of Scott's life into the story of his campaign on behalf of the Hereros.[144] Typically, the ascetic Scott ploughed the profits from the book into funding an African Protectorates Trust which offered scholarships for poor African students.[145]

Scott was a deeply complex man, driven by a passion for justice, but shy and often strangely uncaring to those close to him. In 1961 Trevor Huddleston, seeking to deter him from accepting the Bishopric of Nyasaland, hinted at this when he told him that 'you are a prophet ... rather than a pastor'.[146] Tom Driberg wrote that 'he is emptied of self. He lives his cause. He can talk of little else'.[147] Margery Perham, the doyenne of British experts on colonial Africa and a cautious supporter of Scott's work, told him in 1954 that 'you go straight ahead without bothering whether people on the side lines agree or not'.[148] This purblind attitude would steadily reduce his effectiveness over the years, as his later enthusiasms found less and less resonance with the public. However, in the early 1950s he had made the problems of southern Africa the great moral and political issue of the day. He would later be remembered as a 'human rights activist', but, while he regularly invoked the Universal Declaration in his campaigning, he did not make human rights central to it. Instead, his work at this time combined at least three separate threads: a belief in non-violence; a precocious understanding that the new mechanisms of the UN, backed up by international links with activists such as Roger Baldwin of the American Civil Liberties Union (ACLU), and recourse to international law, could be used to work in favour of the oppressed and disinherited; and a very practical approach (inspired by his reading of Lewis Mumford) to the salvation of Africa through vast schemes of economic development. While it would be wrong, therefore, to see Scott as the first British icon of human rights, there is a good case for seeing him as the brightest light in the new world of possibilities created by the Universal Declaration.

2   Africa, Decolonisation and Human Rights in the 1950s

In the summer of 1950 Michael Scott and a small group of journalists and academics gathered at David Astor's house in Sutton Courtney, near Oxford. Their discussions and drafts, knocked into shape by Mary Benson, were published in 1951 as the influential book *Attitude to Africa*, the 'manifesto of the liberal Africanist'.[1] In his contribution, Scott noted that '[i]n the British Commonwealth and in the United Nations we have become much preoccupied with questions of fundamental human rights. But it is in the realm of belief, of values and faith and consequently of practise, that these rights of men have yet to be realised. They cannot remain abstractions ... '.[2] As Scott understood, a gulf still existed between the hopes generated by the signing of the Universal Declaration of Human Rights and the ability of activists to monitor and enforce the rights that it proclaimed. Even so, the ripples created by the Declaration continued to spread during the 1950s. In 1952 the newly created organisation Racial Unity gave pride of place to Article 1 of the Universal Declaration in its foundation document. Likewise, in 1955 the venerable Anti-Slavery Society added – after considerable internal debate – the suffix 'and for the protection of human rights' to its name.[3] However, changing a name proved far easier than setting up a new organisation specifically devoted to human rights. In 1955, for instance, Peter Benenson's attempt to launch a cross-party British League for Human Rights, dedicated to upholding the European Convention, failed to take off.[4] Accordingly, while activists continued to engage with questions of human rights, they did so using language that was moral just as much as legal. The two most significant areas in response to which they developed this work during the 1950s – the rise of African nationalism, and political imprisonment – form the basis of Chapters 2 and 3.

2.1   African Challenges and British Responses

The decade was neatly bracketed by Michael Scott's intervention at the UN in 1949 at one end and the dramatic events of 1960 at the other.

55

The year 1960 – the so-called 'year of Africa' – encompassed British Prime Minister Harold Macmillan's 'winds of change' speech in Cape Town on 3 February, the massacre of sixty-nine black South African protestors in Sharpeville on 21 March, and the sudden rush to independent statehood by former colonies across Africa. In the intervening decade a succession of controversies over issues such as the Mau Mau rebellion in Kenya and the Central African Federation absorbed the attentions of both government and Parliament in Britain and stimulated new campaigning organisations, notably the Movement for Colonial Freedom (MCF).[5] Local committees dedicated to African affairs were also established in major cities such as Sheffield, Manchester and Hull.[6] Many other organisations shifted their focus to Africa, or set up bespoke committees. Under the leadership of Basil Davidson, for instance, the Union of Democratic Control became almost exclusively concerned with Africa.[7] Likewise, Thomas Fox-Pitt brought his experience from twenty years as a colonial civil servant in Northern Rhodesia to his stewardship of the Anti-Slavery Society in the period 1956–62.[8] Both the Labour and Communist parties set up Africa Committees, while the Society of Friends and Christian Action set up Race Relations committees. (Tellingly, in the former case this was a new name for the long-standing Slavery Committee.) In the early 1950s the term 'race relations' was generally used to refer to racial tensions in the colonial world, and specifically Africa, at a time when racial minorities within Britain were widely regarded as either too small, or too limited to specific locations and groups (such as students), to constitute a major domestic issue. In 1950 the head of the Congress of Peoples against Imperialism (COPAI) could still write that race prejudice was a problem for South Africa but not in Britain, and that 'we hardly notice the "black man" sitting next to us in the bus'.[9] Such complacent attitudes arguably did not change until the Notting Hill riots of August–September 1958, when attacks by white youths on black immigrants in West London demanded a political response.

There is plentiful evidence to demonstrate the prominence of Africa as an issue within British politics and culture during this period. When the Council for Education in World Citizenship (CEWC), an offshoot of the UNA, ran Christmas lectures in 1953–54 on 'The Challenge of Africa', students opted overwhelmingly to join discussion groups on racial issues. Indeed, by 1957 schools were telling the Council that 'pupils are tired of hearing about Africa'.[10] In 1959 one member of the Africa Bureau who participated in the CND march from Aldermaston to London noted that 'we talked rather more about how impossible Govt. policy was on Africa than about anything to do with bombs'.[11] In 1957 Trevor Huddleston, recently returned from South Africa, commented after speaking to a rally of 2000 people in Bradford that: 'It is astonishing how many people in this country still will come to hear about Africa'.[12] Africa was also a major issue in Scotland, where a Scottish Council for African Questions was set up in 1953, having developed out of the opposition to the Central African Federation. According to Freda White of the Scottish UNA in 1953, Scotland was 'afire' over Central Africa: why 'fight two wars against racialism in Europe if one then establishes it under the British Crown in Africa'?[13] In 1956 Mary Benson noted that 'there is a very great interest in Africa [in Scotland], especially in the University towns'.[14] In 1960 the Labour Party organised its own 'Africa Year' in order that its activists could gain a fuller understanding of 'the facts of African life' during the continent's 'year of destiny', as rapid decolonisation coincided with mounting pressure for sanctions against South Africa. Although attendance was uneven, regional meetings regularly drew up to 100 members to hear the party's experts such as Leslie Hale and Dingle Foot.[15]

It was not only liberals, the left and religious groups that took a keen interest in Africa. Michael Scott's Africa Bureau attracted an eclectic mixture of politicians, opinion-formers and businessmen. One former Foreign Office official who joined the Bureau in the early 1960s described it as a combination of Scott's 'hair shirt' and 'the ex-intelligence, rich, tough, old-fashioned Imperialist with a moral conscience'. These were 'anti-communist Whigs' who wanted to 'remedy injustice but not to advance communism'.[16] The same to some extent applied to the organisation 'Capricorn Africa', which was established by the ex-soldier and businessman David Stirling in 1949.[17] The 'Capricorn Contract' rejected the 'barren doctrine of racial nationalism' in favour of racial equality and a cautious transition towards an orderly self-governing Africa. Stirling not only derived support from moderate white settlers in East Central Africa and British businessmen, but also the trade union leader David Rhydderch, barrister Tony McNulty (later Secretary of the European Commission of Human Rights, 1959–76) and liberal journalist Vernon Bartlett. Understandably, Capricorn's message of patriotic 'human unity under God' was treated with suspicion by African nationalists, and its influence was in decline by the late 1950s.[18] A third case was Frank Buchman's Moral Re-Armament (MRA) movement, which became involved in late colonial conflicts both within the British Empire (Kenya and Cyprus) and without (Algeria and Vietnam). The MRA movement promoted racial harmony and the peaceful resolution of conflicts, but its anti-communist politics and dubious theology won it many critics. For John Collins, for instance, it was a 'racket' that was doing 'great harm, not only to the causes for which we stand in Africa, but also, and from my point of view more tragically, to the cause of Christianity'.[19] The organisation had the distinction of being condemned by both the Communist Party and the Catholic Church.[20]

Why did Africa attract so much interest in Britain, and why did morality form such an important element of its appeal? One obvious answer is that, while Britain continued to control the fate of its still vast and complex colonial empire, the problems of Africa remained the responsibility of British voters and taxpayers. As one prominent critic of British policy in Kenya put it: 'It is *our* money that is being spent on these brutal and repressive measures. What are we going to do about it?'[21] Kenya aside, the most controversial government initiative of the period was the proposed Central African Federation – first discussed under Attlee's Labour government and enacted under the Conservatives – which was seen by opponents as simply entrenching the white minority rule of Southern Rhodesia across the other federal territories of Northern Rhodesia and Nyasaland (later Zambia and Malawi). The federation therefore appeared to represent a negation of Britain's imperial duty, and a distancing between Britain (where many professed that there was no 'colour bar') and the white settlers. Even in South Africa, where apartheid-era governments were steadily moving towards cutting all formal links with the British Crown, Britain retained substantial strategic and economic interests which it was careful to protect. Issues such as the sale of arms to South Africa and the maintenance of a naval base under the 1955 Simonstown agreement generated increasing unease in Britain, as did the consequences of appeasing South Africa in neighbouring areas still under British rule. For instance, during the Seretse Khama affair (1950–56) British governments of both major parties prevented the heir of the Bangwato chiefdom of Bechuanaland from coming into his inheritance due to South Africa's displeasure at his marriage to a white woman, Ruth Williams.[22]

However, what gave Africa special prominence was the belief that so much was at stake there. The fate of Africa still hung in the balance, and the joyful (if exaggerated) hopes surrounding Ghana's independence in 1957 were offset by the evidence elsewhere of white minorities consolidating their power. Mishandling of the situation could be catastrophic for both Africans and the metropolitan powers. Peter Benenson warned in 1959 that repressive policies in Kenya might extinguish 'the flame of faith in democracy, already flickering in Britain' just as the abuses in Algeria had undermined the French Fourth Republic.[23] Fenner Brockway warned of a 'disastrous race conflict' in Africa if decolonisation were mismanaged, while Scott's 'manifesto' in 1951 claimed that Britain could face its 'worst moral defeat or win our greatest moral victory' over Africa.[24] Trevor Huddleston wrote in 1959 that Africa was the 'key to Peace in the next 20 years'.[25]

The responsibilities of the present were framed by powerful historical influences, whether through the missionary tradition, white settlement or indeed colonial service. Some of the leading critics of empire had colonial backgrounds, such as Fox-Pitt and Thomas Hodgkin (who had served in Palestine in the 1930s). This historical framing tended to support a positive reading of Britain's record, and the enduring concept of an 'imperial mission'. Hence, the Scottish Council for African Questions defined its first aim as to 'strengthen and further the best traditions of Britain's policy in relation to Africa, especially with regard to the moral and legal obligation to safeguard the rights of all communities against domination by any minority or majority'.[26] Its chairman privately looked forward in 1953 to the 'continued fulfilment of all Britain's moral responsibilities to the Africans': at the same time he worried over whether they should seek a declaration by India's Prime Minister Nehru, denouncing the proposed terms of Central African Federation as a 'flagrant denial . . . of basic human rights', fearing that it would merely antagonise the whites.[27] The rapid, and largely unexpected, transition to full independence of many African countries from the later 1950s onwards, therefore, brought out generational differences amongst Africa's supporters in Britain. Many senior progressives, brought up in a more paternalistic and gradualist tradition, found it difficult to accept that African states were ready for self-government and preferred a longer period of transition. In 1952 C. W. W. Greenidge, an influential campaigner against slavery, strongly opposed the plans for Central African Federation, principally on the grounds that most blacks were 'intellectually too backward' to stand up to the white minority. The only solution was not for African self-government, but for Britain to continue with its 'trusteeship . . . until they are more advanced'.[28] He also saw the partition of South West Africa as a wholly acceptable solution to South Africa's aim to absorb the whole territory.[29] When the Anti-Slavery Society refused to support Tony Benn's Human Rights Bill in 1958, the chairman won the day by warning of the dangers of advertising these rights to 'immature' and 'primitive' peoples.[30] Even Barbara Castle, on the left of the Labour Party, conceded in 1958 that the Africans were still at the same level of development as the Ancient Britons, and like them would benefit from having 'a higher standard of civilisation brought to them from outside by other races'.[31]

These issues are further illustrated by the case of Racial Unity, which was set up in 1952 by Mary Attlee, sister of the former Prime Minister, who had recently returned to Britain after some forty years as a missionary in South Africa. In 1927 she had decided to 'throw in [her] lot with the Bantus [black Africans] and the coloured people',[32] and set up a Community Centre and Day Nursery in the still racially mixed Cape Town suburb of Claremont. On her return to Britain in 1948 she was appalled by the ignorance that she encountered about racial questions. Her own frame of reference remained resolutely African – as she told Michael Scott, 'you and I specially think of Africa naturally'.[33] The new organisation did some pioneering survey work on racial minorities in Britain in the mid-1950s, having merged with the 'Racial Relations Group', a small educational organisation previously associated with the Institute of Sociology. It also took practical steps to promote better race relations through the work of its branches.[34] The great prominence given to Article One of the Universal Declaration in the organisation's founding documents shows an awareness of how an emphasis on human rights might offer a way forward. But the focus was still essentially on the immorality of racial discrimination. The organisation's first report reminded supporters that the organisation was 'founded on Christian principles' and must 'manifest a moral integrity' on the great African questions of the day.[35] Secretary Colin Turnbull wrote that 'we are not politicians ... our policy [is] to attempt to discern the moral rights and wrongs of any given issue...'.[36] A speech given by Mary Attlee at the Royal Empire Society in April 1947, before her decision to leave South Africa, gives interesting texture to her views. She had been 'constantly disgusted and saddened' by the racial attitudes of the whites in South Africa. However, 'the British Empire, to my mind, has a wonderful vocation, and the answer to all these problems and difficulties is to be found in Christ and only in Christ'. If only Europeans would be true to what they learned from Christ, 'all would be right'.[37] Therefore, like so many of the organisations of this period, Racial Unity stood on a cusp between long-established imperial and humanitarian traditions and the wholehearted embrace of a discourse of human rights.

To some extent the moral tone taken over African issues also reflected the remarkably high profile of three Anglican priests, Michael Scott, John Collins and Trevor Huddleston, who not only shaped the debate over Africa but also played a central role in campaigning.[38] Although both Collins and Scott took up many other causes – in the case of Collins the campaign for the abolition of the death penalty and for nuclear disarmament, and for Scott a brand of disarmament that favoured direct action across national borders – both men remained intensely involved with African affairs during the 1950s. Yet by the middle of the decade they were both a known quantity, and the return to Britain of Huddleston, after twelve years of missionary work in South Africa, buoyed by the success of his recent book *Naught for Your Comfort*, re-energised the struggle against apartheid. Strangely, the three men very rarely succeeded in working together for any length of time, and when Huddleston returned to Britain it required elaborate choreography to even create a joint platform for Scott's and Collins's followers.[39] The contrast between the three is striking. Scott (the driven activist) and Collins (the consummate organiser) both seemed to relish politics more than Huddleston, who appeared as the 'priest drawn reluctantly into politics'.[40] But Huddleston combined an intensity of feeling over apartheid with a keen appreciation of how to use the power of the press and television. At least Collins had the insight to acknowledge that 'many of us, I fear, are like prima donnas', while David Astor, who had some hand in the matter, once noted that both Christian Action and the Africa Bureau were 'largely the creation of a single individual'.[41] Collins and Scott were profoundly different in temperament, and clashed repeatedly, not least over the Seretse Khama case. Most on the left in Britain sympathised with Seretse and regarded his uncle Tshekedi Khama as the villain of the piece. However, Scott, Astor and Mary Benson forged a strong and enduring relationship with Tshekedi, who Scott had first met in 1946, and whom they admired as a strong and effective ruler. From Astor's perspective, public opinion in Britain was 'chiefly emotional' and could 'waste itself making heroes of Seretse and [his wife] Ruth'.[42]

Such 'moral' voices flourished during the period that straddled the decline of colonialism and the rise of assertive African nationalist movements, and there was still an important role for individuals who went out from Britain as academics and experts. Michael Scott wrote in 1952 about how 'something of the old pioneer readiness to explore new paths in distant lands' survived in Britain. 'In the changing Africa of today these paths are fraught with great dangers but can also lead to immense possibilities'.[43] Scott was here referring to Guy and Molly Clutton-Brock, whose work he supported through the African Development Trust. The Clutton-Brocks, who had served as community workers in Bethnal Green and had no previous experience of Africa, took on the running of St Faith's Mission Farm, Southern Rhodesia, in 1949. They sought to establish a true partnership with Africans, thereby serving as a model to both European and African communities. The farm became – in the words of one admirer – an 'adventure in democratic, co-operative, inter-racial community life'.[44] Likewise, Terence Ranger went to Salisbury (Harare) in 1957 as a lecturer in history fresh from completing his doctorate on the first Earl of Cork, a seventeenth-century grandee. Once in Southern Rhodesia, however, he not only discovered his vocation as a historian of Africa, but also – until his deportation in 1963 – as an active supporter of African nationalism. He and his wife Shelagh threw themselves into campaigning on behalf of the families of detainees and against the colour bar.[45] However, even in activist circles an unselfconscious paternalism lingered on. In 1955 *Peace News* ran a series on 'pioneers of the New Africa' in which all the features were on whites, such as Scott and the Clutton-Brocks, rather than Africans themselves. In 1959 it was still necessary for George MacLeod to tell the Church of Scotland assembly that 'someone must speak for the Africans'.[46]

Evaluating the role of human rights in anti-colonial campaigns, Samuel Moyn has written that actors on the left in Britain 'did not invoke the new human rights in their activities, and once the [MCF] crystallised in 1954, it did not, either'.[47] The plentiful evidence to the contrary hardly supports such a categorical dismissal, especially when one considers that Fenner Brockway was being hailed as a 'champion of human rights' as early as 1952.[48] It should also be noted that in its 1955 policy statement the MCF gave as its 'first principle the right of all peoples to self-government and self-determination and to the enjoyment of all the rights embodied in the Universal Declaration of Human Rights'.[49] However, it is certainly true that human rights were only invoked intermittently, and in general terms rather than in response to specific conflicts (as we shall see in the case of Mau Mau). It is also true that during the 1950s the Universal Declaration was often invoked interchangeably with the Atlantic Charter or even the 'Four Freedoms', again suggesting an aspirational rather than a systematic usage. As in the immediate postwar years, the value of human rights as a campaigning tool was still being tested by activists, and – especially once the first African states became independent – the question of their universality became an important issue.

The politician who most fully embraced human rights during this period was the so-called 'MP for Africa'[50] Fenner Brockway, Secretary of the Independent Labour Party (ILP) during the 1930s and Labour MP for Eton and Slough from 1950 to 1964. Brockway, who was born in 1888 in India to a missionary family, had a fine pedigree as an anti-colonial campaigner. He had been a delegate at the founding of the League Against Imperialism in 1927 and had set up the ILP's British Centre Against Imperialism in 1937. He knew most of the leading African and Asian nationalists personally, as many of them, such as Jomo Kenyatta, had not only spent time in Britain during the 1930s but also had moved – like the ILP – in the political space between the Labour and Communist parties. During the 1950s Brockway travelled extensively in the colonial world and played a key role in forging the MCF. This gave him a remarkable breadth of experience, and Thomas Fox-Pitt marvelled at his ability to 'work up a subject or country that is coming into political importance'.[51] In Parliament he was an advocate for extending human rights to the colonies, and first introduced a bill to this effect in 1952. He also defended immigration from within the Commonwealth and in the 1959 election noted that resentment at housing for immigrants was a significant factor in his reduced vote in Slough.[52] In the late 1950s and early 1960s he introduced repeated private members' bills for legislation to ban racial discrimination. As Stephen Howe has noted, his sincerity was never in doubt and allowed him to overcome the many organisational rivalries of the period. Brockway told Michael Scott in 1952 that he had no intention of being sectarian: 'our only concern is the good of Africa'.[53] His weakness was his unwillingness to believe that African leaders – often long-standing friends – were capable of abuses of power after independence.[54] When Brockway turned seventy in 1957, and Nehru and Nkrumah both sent him birthday greetings, Tony Benn (then known as Anthony Wedgwood Benn) hailed him as 'one of the greatest men of his time'.[55] Others were not so complimentary: the communists (who regarded Africa as a 'burning topic among the British people') lamented the fact that African nationalists might be drawn to Brockway rather than to them, and muttered darkly about the 'Brockway problem'.[56]

Brockway was the most prominent of a group of Labour MPs committed to Africa. Leslie Hale was probably his closest ally and travelled with him extensively in Africa. Harold Wilson, who had resigned from the Attlee government in 1951, became chair of the Labour Party Africa Committee,[57] and was closely involved with Victor Gollancz in the campaign against poverty that eventually became War on Want. Barbara Castle had caught Roger Baldwin's eye for having done a 'fine job for human rights at Lake Success' during her stint as an alternate delegate at the UN General Assembly in 1949–50.[58] She went on to make brave and often controversial interventions during the crises in Kenya and Cyprus, when she was willing to criticise the actions of British troops. She also attended the Treason Trial in South Africa. John Stonehouse, later disgraced twice over (first as a bankrupt who faked his own death in 1974, and second when unmasked as a Czechoslovak agent) was a highly regarded authority on African affairs when elected to Parliament in 1959. He had met Brockway while a student at the LSE and was inspired to spend two years in Uganda and Kenya as an agricultural development worker during 1952–54.[59]

After Brockway, however, the Labour politician who took the keenest interest in human rights was Tony Benn, at this point a young moderniser who had spent time studying the political system in the United States. Benn was prone to quote from the US Declaration of Independence at meetings on human rights and attempted to write the Universal Declaration of Human Rights into Clause 4 of the Labour Party constitution in 1960.[60] He also introduced a private member's bill in December 1957, calling for advisory commissions on human rights to be set up in all British dependent territories and protectorates. In an associated article he presented the second half of the twentieth century as defined by a global 'battle for Human Rights', whether over the colour bar in the USA and Africa, the suppression of the Hungarian uprising or even phone-tapping in Britain.[61]

2.2   Kenya, Mau Mau and Eileen Fletcher's 'Concern'

The Mau Mau uprising of 1952 swiftly turned into Britain's most sustained and violent late-colonial conflict. The principal support for the rebellion was amongst the 1.4 million Kikuyu, the ethnic group that had suffered most from the intrusion of white settlement into Kenya's best farming land. Many had been forced by land shortages to live in the colony's capital, Nairobi. During the late 1940s great numbers of Kikuyu had pledged themselves by oath to support a secretive movement for the defence of their rights that became known as Mau Mau. Although the rebel guerrilla groups in the mountains had largely been defeated by the end of 1954, the struggle to break Kikuyu political resistance took far longer. A State of Emergency lasted until 1960, at least in part to justify the British government's continued derogation from the European Convention on Human Rights (which had been invoked initially in May 1954). The Mau Mau oaths and associated ceremonies, alongside the ferocity of the attacks on white settlers, allowed the rebellion to be presented in savage, atavistic terms in Britain. The imbalance in casualties is, therefore, startling. Only some 30 settlers were killed during the conflict, whereas 1000 rebels were hanged, at least 11,500 were killed by the authorities (and undoubtedly many more), and many thousands were detained in camps without trial. As with all anti-colonial struggles, the rebellion was also fought out between elements within African society. Almost 100 loyalists were murdered by Mau Mau supporters in the infamous Lari massacre of March 1953, while some of the worst abuses were perpetrated by the African loyalist Home Guard.

The rebellion was inchoate and lacked a clearly defined leadership or public identity – even the origin of the phrase 'Mau Mau' is still disputed. The authorities were keen to cast Jomo Kenyatta, leader of the Kenyan African Union (KAU) as the rebellion's mastermind, and in 1953 he and other KAU leaders were tried at Kapenguria. Although the defence barrister D. N. Pritt shredded the prosecution case (for which he was made a Kikuyu elder) Kenyatta was sentenced to prolonged imprisonment, much of which he served in isolation. The trial of Kenyatta was accompanied by a campaign of remarkable brutality – approved at the highest level within the British government and colonial administration – to break Kikuyu resistance. In the eyes of liberal colonial officials such as Thomas Askwith, this was a programme intended to screen out the 'hard-core' rebels from the rest, and to rehabilitate those who could be weaned away from Mau Mau so that they could be released into the reserves. The reality, however, was a sustained, violent assault on the detainees. Some information about this was revealed at the time by whistle-blowers from within the colonial administration, but the damage was largely contained until news broke of the so-called 'Hola massacre' in 1959. Controversy was reignited in 2005 when Caroline Elkins and David Anderson both published books containing powerful new research that exposed what one of them would term Britain's 'Gulag' and the other Britain's 'dirty war'. These books were based on the surviving colonial documents (most having been apparently destroyed at the end of British rule in 1963), supported by private papers and interviews with Kikuyu survivors. Their conclusions – if not Elkins' projections of Kikuyu casualties – were vindicated by the remarkable revelation in 2011 that some 1500 files had been kept in secret at a government facility, Hanslope Park in Buckinghamshire. These documents, which were only disclosed when Kikuyu survivors brought a case of torture against the British government, not only provided far more detail about British colonial practices in Kenya, but also helped to establish a chain of decision-making.[62]

Although the documents kept at Hanslope Park have provided invaluable new evidence, they still raise two further questions. First, why did the allegations made at the time – albeit often limited in nature and difficult to prove – fail to make greater political impact in Britain, and, secondly, why did they not become the focus for a campaign that utilised the language of human rights? Fabian Klose has argued that in Britain 'an organized protest movement against military operations in Kenya never formed', while Jan Eckel refers to the 'noncampaign on Kenya' as illustrating 'the yawning gap that opens between international human rights politics in the 1950s and 1970s'.[63] Neither view is completely accurate in the British case where, as we shall see, the allegations by Eileen Fletcher did give rise to a lively, if short-lived, campaign in the summer and autumn of 1956.

Many factors worked against support for Mau Mau in Britain. One was the ferocious and one-sided depiction of the rebels in the press as barbaric, bestial and lacking a worthwhile political programme.[64] The detainees – especially women and children – might well inspire sympathy, but this was unlikely to extend to the rebels themselves. The forerunner of the

MCF, COPAI, sought to mobilise the 'substantial body of opinion in this country which, *while deploring the violence of Mau Mau*, understands the grievous social, economic and political disabilities under which Kenya Africans live'.[65] Interviewed many years afterwards, Barbara Castle recalled that Mau Mau atrocities created difficulties for campaigners: 'anybody who raised the case of human rights among Africans was considered to be at best [naïve] at worst aiding and abetting violence'.[66] Moreover, as Klose has argued, the rebels lacked the sophistication of the National Liberation Front (FLN) in Algeria in establishing a foreign presence and winning international support (above all, at the UN, which was becoming increasingly important due to the creation of many new, postcolonial states). Although some Kenyan nationalists such as Joseph Murumbi and Peter Koinange were based in Britain during the conflict and worked closely with the MCF (Murumbi was even joint secretary), they had to keep their distance from the rebels.[67] Even Fenner Brockway, a habitual supporter of African nationalists who had visited Kenya in 1950 and 1952, regarded Mau Mau as a 'reversion to a primitive barbaric mentality' and fundamentally at odds with 'civilised' Western ethics. He was suspicious of Kenyatta, who was evasive about his role in Mau Mau and was already showing signs of dangerous 'egoism'. The two men fell out over Kenyatta's defence of female genital mutilation.[68]

These concerns complicated, but by no means silenced, dissent over the abuses taking place in Kenya, as the following cases indicate. Colonel Arthur Young, who had been seconded to reorganise the Kenyan police after similar service in Malaya, resigned in December 1954 when he failed to receive the support of the Governor, Sir Evelyn Baring, for his reforms.[69] Canon Bewes of the Church Missionary Society (CMS) was so concerned about reports from the field that he visited Kenya in 1953 and subsequently gave a press conference to publicise his criticisms. And the Irish barrister Peter Evans, who had assisted Pritt at Kenyatta's trial, collected witness statements after a prisoner in the hands of a sergeant in the Kenya Regiment was killed during interrogation. However, these challenges were all contained. Colonel Young pulled no punches about the 'rule of fear' (as opposed to 'impartial justice') in Kenya in his resignation letter, but it was not published. Although he did meet Michael Scott and Barbara Castle in private on his return, he remained a senior serving officer and was unwilling to make a public intervention.[70] The pressure from the CMS resulted in a meeting between the Archbishop of Canterbury, Geoffrey Fisher and Governor Baring in December 1953. However, Fisher accepted that Baring, a 'very keen and devoted Christian', was doing the 'utmost to cope' with abuses, and he recommended that no further public action be taken. Crucially, the Archbishop of Mombasa, Leonard Beecher, also urged Fisher to leave any issues of 'brutality and lawlessness' to the churches in Kenya.[71] Meanwhile, Peter Evans was promptly deported from Kenya, ostensibly for exceeding his visitor's permit. He went on to write some highly critical articles from India, where he spent the next three months, and eventually a book.[72]

The most powerful intervention was that of Eileen Fletcher, a Quaker who served the government of Kenya as a rehabilitation officer working with female prisoners for sixteen months from December 1954. On her return to Britain Fletcher wrote three articles for *Peace News* in May 1956, later published as a pamphlet by the MCF, which gave detailed evidence of the routinely brutal and inhumane conditions in the camps. Most shockingly, she claimed that some of the prisoners, even those serving life sentences, were still children, some as young as eleven.[73] Unlike the other critics, she was also willing to undertake a campaign in support of her allegations, which was organised by Michael Scott's former lieutenant John Fletcher. This campaign generated intense interest, principally amongst fellow Friends and in the peace movement. Over the next six months she addressed more than eighty meetings across Britain, on behalf of twenty-one different organisations, and received hundreds of letters of support. Fletcher's emphasis on the suffering of women and children, her ability to speak from close personal experience, her resilience and determination and her lack of association with communism, all combined to make her a dangerous adversary for the Colonial Office. Alan Lennox-Boyd, the Colonial Secretary, sought to undermine her credibility (calling her a 'liar' in Parliament), and explained away her allegations about the age of the detainees as a slip of the bureaucratic pen. However, her campaign was also highly divisive within the Society of Friends, and to understand the limitations of her challenge it is necessary to look at her own background.

By the time of the Kenyan Emergency Fletcher was already in her fifties, having trained as a social scientist. She was an Anglican who had joined the Society of Friends in 1939 and, as a conscientious objector, had resigned from her civil service post during World War II. Later in the war she had worked in camps for Polish refugees in East Africa. On her return to Britain in 1946 she organised a conference on East Africa at Friends' House, where she took the position that Britain was not so much giving the empire away as providing a latchkey and a house to 'children growing up'.[74] In 1953 the Friends (through the Friends Service Council/FSC) responded to an appeal from the government of Kenya for religious groups in Britain to become involved in the 'rehabilitation' of Mau Mau detainees in the camps. Accordingly, in December 1954 a group of four Quakers and their children set off for Kenya by boat. Eileen Fletcher had applied unsuccessfully to join this team and had then been employed directly by the Kenyan government. Ironically, after her air fare had been paid by a benefactor, she had already been in post for some time before the FSC team arrived in Mombasa. The publication of her allegations shocked the Quaker volunteers, who were still in the field, and one of them (supported by the Secretary of the Christian Council of Kenya) ill-advisedly wrote to the press to accuse her of peddling 'odd scraps of gossip'. She also caused alarm amongst senior Friends in Britain – a group that she characterised as a 'small hierarchy' of conservative males. They feared that the standing of the FSC ('the Queen of all our committees') might be damaged, as would the Quakers' progressive reputation on issues of race relations. Many concerns were privately expressed about her intemperate, un-Quakerly behaviour, as 'l'affaire Fletcher' threatened to drive a wedge between activists in the local Quaker Meetings and the influential committee chairs in Friends' House.[75]

Although there was clearly an important element of exasperation at being challenged by an articulate and highly forceful woman, some Friends were also genuinely perplexed about Fletcher's motivation. One team member in Kenya even accused her of seeking 'revenge' for grievances against her employer. It is true that in July 1955 she wrote to her department head about how to reorganise the work at Kamiti camp, demanding back-payment, transport and a senior post commensurate with her qualifications if she were to remain.[76] She had expressed no concern about abuses when she left Kenya and less than two months before her hard-hitting articles were published in *Peace News* had written privately to tell the head of the FSC that her work was 'not only extremely interesting but very worthwhile'.[77] Even more strangely, she had written an article in a liberal Southern Rhodesian journal in which she enthused about the rewarding work that she had done amongst the women detainees.[78] There is no indication of why she changed her focus so abruptly, although she did later confess that she had deliberately excluded any positive, 'heart-warming' incidents from her articles in *Peace News* as 'my concern was to get injustices put right'.[79] However, while her actions may have struck colleagues as erratic and individualist, two points need to be emphasised. First, her behaviour had been quite correct. As John Fletcher well knew, expressing a 'concern' was the established procedure within the Society of Friends for placing a matter of conscience before fellow Quakers, and urging them to reflect and respond.[80] In the same way, years later, Eric Baker's 'concern' would grow into the Campaign for the Abolition of Torture. Secondly, Fletcher was clearly convinced that she had been guided in her work in the camps by her deep Christian beliefs. The conclusion that she drew from her work was that 'if we only leave things to God he will clear away the difficulties and show us the way forward'.[81] Her faith also informed her belief that Mau Mau was evil. As she told a private meeting of the Anti-Slavery Society's executive, in her work with the 'hard-core' female detainees 'the teaching which she had invented herself was based on a series of fables based on "Pilgrim's Progress"' so that 'Christian's burden of sin was represented by Mau Mau'.[82] After the controversy had died down it was the positive moments of genuine reconciliation in her work that she chose to recall.[83]

Throughout the controversy, Fletcher maintained a distinction between the flawed practices of colonial officials in the camps on one hand, and the benign potential of the rehabilitation programme on the other. In neither case, however, did she use a language of human rights for the detainees, and it was left to others to do so. In June 1956 Fletcher stole the headlines at an MCF rally in London on 'Human Rights in the colonies', when she took the opportunity to defend herself against government accusations that she had given misleading information about the youngest prisoners. Kenya dominated the entire meeting,[84] but it had been planned months before Fletcher's revelations and had originally been intended to address a far wider range of human rights abuses. Surviving correspondence gives an indication of what the organisers originally had in mind. As early as March Brockway had asked Thomas Fox-Pitt of the Anti-Slavery Society for 'material about death sentences, floggings, manacled prisoners, unjust imprisonments etc. You must have a lot of this'.[85] Brockway also managed to involve Victor Gollancz, whose current focus was the campaign against the death penalty in Britain, by telling him that the meeting would call for abolition of capital punishment to be extended to the colonies, along with 'floggings, manacling of prisoners and other inhumanities'.[86] A year later, when Fletcher spoke at an NCCL meeting on 'Civil Liberties in Kenya', Elizabeth Allen wrote to thank her for a moving speech: 'You made clear to many the necessity of some change in policy if the African people are to live like human beings and enjoy the rights which the Universal Declaration of Human Rights has promised to all people'. However, in the absence of a full report of the meeting it is unclear whether this was the gloss which Allen was placing on Fletcher's 'really moving description of a tragic situation'.[87]

By 1957 Fletcher's campaign over Kenya had run out of steam, and she was working to help Hungarian refugees. However, she claimed vindication in March 1959 when it was revealed that eleven 'hard-core' Mau Mau prisoners had been beaten to death at Hola Camp. The 'Hola massacre' was greeted with outrage in Parliament, where the usual suspects on the Labour left were now joined by Enoch Powell, recently resigned from Harold Macmillan's Conservative government. Powell famously couched his comments in the language of universality: 'We cannot say, "We will have African standards in Africa, Asian standards in Asia and perhaps British standards here at home"'.[88] However, the end of the Emergency was now in sight – as, indeed, was the end of British rule in Kenya – and the massacre failed to generate a lasting impact. No senior officials lost their jobs, and Eileen Fletcher was not called to give evidence to the subsequent Commission of Inquiry, as she would have wished. She remained a somewhat awkward and independent-minded Friend until her death, which went almost unnoticed, in 1976.[89] Unlike those of Captain Law, her claims were not repeated in Peter Benenson's book *Gangrene* (1959), a pioneering comparison between the colonial policies of Britain and France. And unlike another critic of British policy in Kenya, Peter Evans, she does not appear to have been in contact with Amnesty International in the 1960s.[90]

*

There is one intriguing footnote to the Fletcher case to consider. In October 1928 the Liverpool Association for the Welfare of Half-Caste Children commissioned Muriel E. Fletcher, a former student of the Liverpool University School of Social Science, to carry out research into 'the colour problem in Liverpool and other ports'. The report, published in 1930 and dubbed 'the Fletcher Report' concluded that, while mixed-race children were 'only slightly' below average in intelligence and social aptitude, the presence of coloured families in Britain presented a 'a special problem from both a moral and an economic point of view'.[91] The pastor of the Liverpool African and West Indian Mission, where much of the research had been carried out, was appalled, and accused Fletcher of abusing his trust. He said that some of the women and children who had been interviewed 'said that they could never trust a white person again'.[92] The report has since been pilloried as an example of deeply flawed and misguided research, influenced by the fashionable eugenic theories of the day. What no scholar appears to have realised is that the Muriel E. Fletcher of the 1930 report was one and the same person as M. Eileen Fletcher, the heroine of 1956. It is tempting to surmise that her calls for justice for the Kenyan detainees represented some form of expiation for a previous error, but the limited evidence available does not support this supposition. Her closest ally, John Fletcher, clearly knew Eileen from this time, having taken over the Liverpool Association's welfare work in the 1930s. In 1956 he wrote that 'I first heard of Eileen Fletcher in 1930, when she was making a survey in Liverpool on the conditions of the coloured families living there ... I have admired her ability as a trained investigator into social conditions ... '.[93] The relations between the two Fletchers were affectionate and based on high personal regard (she always addressed him as 'Head of the Class'), and there is no indication that he disapproved of her 1930 report.[94] At the very least, the strange case of Muriel Eileen Fletcher shows that we can take nothing for granted in the racial politics of the mid-twentieth century.

2.3   South Africa

By contrast with Mau Mau, the struggle against white minority rule in South Africa was frequently and readily presented in Britain as a deeply moral cause and an affront to fundamental human rights. The tenor of the campaign can be clearly seen in two public interventions some ten years apart. The first was a sermon by Canon Collins at St Paul's in September 1952, during a major campaign of passive resistance in South Africa. Collins, who took for his text Galatians 3:28, 'Ye are all one in Christ Jesus', was unequivocal: 'Any racial discrimination, any avoidable denial of human rights, any vestige of colour prejudice, any one of these is a vile infringement of the law of love: it is a sin'. Christians, he went on, must oppose it at home and abroad, but it was in South Africa that 'this problem is best seen for what it is'. Referring to the current campaign he concluded that 'laws which deny to men their most basic human rights are evil', and if all other democratic means failed, there was no alternative to revolution or passive resistance.[95] The second was a speech by Harold Wilson, recently elected leader of the Labour Party, in March 1963 at a rally to mark the third anniversary of the Sharpeville massacre. Wilson pledged the next Labour government to ban arms sales to South Africa and to introduce legislation against racial intolerance within Britain. Departing from the notes provided by Labour's International Department he went on to argue there was a 'moral issue' at stake. 'One of the formative influences in my life was a sermon I heard preached at a scout service by a colleague, now a leading Nonconformist Minister. He took as his text "He hath made of one blood all nations of men for to dwell on all the face of the earth" [Acts 17:126]. That is the faith in which we stand'. Returning to the theme a few weeks later, he defended outside intervention against an 'odious' South African regime that was making 'slaves' of the black majority. 'What are the United Nations Charter and the Declaration of Human Rights if they are not a reaffirmation of the principle that "no man is an island"'.[96]

These two texts were striking, but hardly unique. The themes developed here, such as the insistence that apartheid was not just wrong but sinful, and that there was a right and duty for the outside world to intervene (sanctioned by the Declaration of Human Rights), marked out South Africa from other major late colonial conflicts. Rather like the Spanish Civil War in the 1930s, for many the struggle against apartheid had come to symbolise a conflict between the forces of good and evil. In his 1952 sermon Collins had stated that they could not – 'as was done by so many of us at the time of the Nazi tyrannies' – pretend not to know what was happening in South Africa. 'Neutrality' he added in language straight from the 1930s, 'is no longer possible'.[97] How had this situation arisen? After all, like that of Spain, the South African situation was hardly without its complexities for the outside observer, such as whether (*pace* Collins) the question of when violent resistance might be justified, the deep divisions that opened in the African nationalist movement in the later 1950s, or, indeed, the tensions between the black majority and other groups discriminated against under apartheid (such as the Indian and Coloured communities).

One factor was undoubtedly the character of apartheid, and of its most ardent supporters, as it was currently understood in Britain. The idea that apartheid represented a unique departure in the politics of South Africa made it an easier political target, even though the adoption of 'apartheid' measures there after the May 1948 election concealed substantial continuities with the segregationist policies of the preceding decades, with their roots in British rule.[98] Likewise, the fact that apartheid was driven forward by radical Afrikaaners (who in many cases had sympathised with Germany during World War II) accentuated an apparent identification with Nazism.

Secondly, the moderate manner in which the struggle against apartheid was conducted during the 1950s was also significant. As Christian Action noted in 1953: 'There is, throughout the whole of Africa, a growing resistance to white domination, *but in South Africa this resistance is taking a course which we can wholeheartedly support and endorse*'. This campaign of passive resistance in South Africa offered 'a vindication of the Christian way of life for Africa': the alternative was 'a triumph of Mau-Mau-ism'.[99] The Freedom Charter, adopted by the African National Congress (ANC) and its allies at the 'Congress of the People' in June 1955, was a resolute (but peaceful) set of demands for democracy, racial equality and 'equal human rights' for all.[100] The ANC President Chief Albert Luthuli, who was awarded the Nobel Peace Prize in 1960, was treated with particular reverence. Peter Benenson, recalling the mass arrests of ANC leaders in the autumn of 1956, commented that 'the importance of the accused, including Chief Luthuli, seemed to me to make it vital that the [o]bserver sent [from Britain] should be someone of considerable stature, not a junior like myself'. When a recorded message from Luthuli was played to a meeting in Britain it was heard with 'hushed' silence.[101] The moderate leadership of Luthuli was taken as a guarantee that the ANC would not pursue a violent path so long as he was President.[102] If support remained solid in Britain when a younger, more radical generation led by Nelson Mandela and Oliver Tambo adopted armed resistance after the Sharpeville massacre, this was largely due to the belief that all other peaceful avenues were now closed.

A third important factor was the religious character of the debate. Apartheid was strongly supported within the Dutch Reformed Church but opposed by most other religious groupings. Therefore, the debate over apartheid was also conducted within and between churches, and leading religious figures in both Britain and South Africa could not easily stay aloof. Criticism came not only from radical clerics, such as Collins and Huddleston, but also from the most senior levels in the Anglican Church. Joost de Blank – Dutch-born but raised and educated in Britain – was a highly combative and outspoken critic of apartheid while serving as Archbishop of Cape Town in 1957–63.[103] Ambrose Reeves, Bishop of Johannesburg in the period 1949–61, was more cautious in his criticism until Sharpeville, after which he left South Africa to spread word of the massacre, and was deported on his return. In Britain he became a focal point for opposition to apartheid and chaired the informal 'South Africa Circle' of concerned voluntary organisations.[104] Raymond Raynes, Huddleston's predecessor as Provincial in South Africa and later his religious superior, denounced apartheid as 'the most damnable of modern heresies'.[105]

Amongst the clerical opponents of apartheid, Michael Scott remained an inspirational figure during the 1950s. As one admirer put it, 'like many other people in England I was introduced to the facts of modern South Africa' by his work.[106] However, Scott's Africa Bureau was increasingly focused on helping African nations approaching statehood, and the South African cause was primarily taken forward, in very different ways, by Collins and Huddleston. Both played a crucial role in shaping the emergent Anti-Apartheid Movement (AAM): Collins by creating a mechanism to fund and support defendants on trial in South Africa, and Huddleston through his passionate advocacy of cultural and consumer boycotts.

In the early 1950s Christian Action had continued to pursue many different initiatives, of which supporting Scott's work in southern Africa was only one. However, Collins later recalled that Alan Paton's *Cry, the Beloved Country* (1948) had already convinced him that South Africa was a 'burning issue'.[107] His first major intervention came in response to the

ANC campaign of passive resistance, the 'Defiance Campaign against Unjust Laws', launched in June 1952. Protestors courted arrest by burning their hated pass books, which controlled freedom of movement within South Africa, and in October Christian Action established a fund to support prisoners' families, which raised some £2500. Collins created a small committee of white liberals, chaired by a reluctant Paton, to allocate the funds in South Africa, having determined that only such a group could avoid confiscation of the funds and make sure that they did not fall into 'the wrong hands'.[108] Despite these precautions, however, Collins' initiative proved controversial. Some senior politicians, notably Lord Halifax, withdrew their support from Christian Action, and both the Church of England and the Catholic Church distanced themselves.[109] Moreover, the South African Quakers, who were conservative on political and racial issues, discouraged support for the fund on the grounds that the money would be used to support the Defiance campaign rather than the families, and that the campaigners might turn to violence (a view which the Society of Friends respectfully ignored).[110]

Collins' commitment to the struggle against apartheid was reinforced when he made his only visit to South Africa in 1954. On his return he described it as a 'pleasant mad-house', in which every human relationship was infected with racialism.[111] However, it was the mass arrest of ANC leaders and their allies in December 1956, and the rambling 'Treason Trial' which ensued (1956–61), that truly determined the course of Collins' future activism in this area. Christian Action immediately established a fund (which became the Defence and Aid Fund/DAF) to pay for the defendants' legal costs, support their families and ensure that the 'conscience of the world' was 'kept fully alive' to the situation.[112] This time, fundraising was matched by a mobilisation of the legal profession to monitor the trial and offer support to the defence. The visit to the preliminary hearings in South Africa by Gerald Gardiner, a highly respected and politically active 'silk' (Queen's Counsel), did much to galvanise support amongst his fellow lawyers, and a substantial number attended a meeting on his return. The Treason Trial confirmed that the very legalism with which the South African government sought to ensnare its opponents was also its principal weakness. Although South Africa's laws were highly partial, a rule of law still existed and could be challenged by determined, well-funded opponents. This aspect, which formed one of the bases for Peter Benenson's organisation 'Justice', will be examined further in Chapter 3. Collins' fund, meanwhile, was exceptionally successful and raised some £100,000 in the first three years. By the end of 1959 Christian Action was protesting that it was 'swamped' by the amount raised and needed more administrative support.[113] However, the very success of the fund – alongside the suspicion that Collins was too close to the ANC and to the communists – created its own problems, as it reignited Collins' rivalry with Scott.[114]

Huddleston, a member of the Community of the Resurrection based at Mirfield in Yorkshire, represented a very different brand of activism. He rose to prominence on his recall to Britain in 1956 after twelve years working as a missionary in South Africa, the first six in Sophiatown, a ramshackle but intensely vibrant black community on the edge of Johannesburg. Huddleston did not initially take a strong stance on the politics of South Africa, and later apologised for not having given Scott more support during his travails in 'Tobruk'.[115] However, his anger against the South African government crystallised around his staunch opposition to two new apartheid initiatives. First, Sophiatown was threatened (and eventually demolished) under the Western Areas Removal Scheme, ostensibly a slum clearance project that would relocate the black residents to more distant new townships such as Soweto. Secondly, the Bantu Education Act of 1953 offered a state-run education for all black children, but at a lower educational level than that offered to whites. This was perceived as a threat to the existing system of education provided by the Mission schools which, while poorly resourced and patchy in coverage, did offer a small number of able black students the opportunity to enter the middle class through professions such as the law. In September 1953 Huddleston told Mary Benson that the Act was 'the most vicious attack on all that the Church stands for in regard to human rights . . . it is a denial of all that we mean by civilisation'.[116] The Act made a powerful impression in Britain – even the conservative Archbishop Fisher strongly criticised it – and presented the authorities in charge of the existing schools with an agonising dilemma. Huddleston eventually took the decision to close the Community's school at St Peter's, Rosettenville. His increasing politicisation brought him to participate in the Congress of the People in June 1955, where he was accorded – alongside only Luthuli and Y. M. Dadoo – the ANC's highest honour, the 'Isitwalandwe' medal.

By the autumn of 1953 Huddleston had already decided that only external pressure could influence the South African government. In his letter to Mary Benson, Huddleston called for a sustained campaign in Britain, including a boycott of South African goods, 'especially Wines and citrus fruit', and a withdrawal of investments. On his return to Britain the struggle for a boycott intensified, and in June 1956 Huddleston and Scott met prominent members of the actors' union Equity, many of whose members performed in South Africa.[117] A formal campaign was launched in June 1959 under the auspices of the London-based Committee of African Organisations: this evolved into the South African Boycott Committee, and, in turn, the Anti-Apartheid Movement. Both have been discussed in detail elsewhere,[118] but two points should be noted. First, support for the boycott, and even more so the response to the Sharpeville massacre in March 1960, showed how far a concern for human rights had come to define solidarity with the majority in South Africa. The Labour Party, for instance, was not only quick to support the boycott, but also couched its support in terms of the defence of human rights.[119] Secondly, the boycott brought to prominence two brothers, David and Martin Ennals, who would play significant roles in future campaigns. David, the older of the two (a third brother, John, played a leading role in the UNA) combined being International Secretary of the Labour Party with organising the boycott campaign. His place would later be taken by Martin, 'tall, bespectacled, suede-booted' and fresh from working for UNESCO, who was immediately spotted as a 'first class organiser'.[120] Martin Ennals eventually rose to direct both the NCCL and Amnesty International.

When the boycott was launched, one question that the organisers anticipated was why South Africa should be singled out ahead of other countries that also pursued 'objectionable' policies. The suggested answer – that Britain had a unique historical responsibility towards South Africa as well as current concerns about a Commonwealth member state – did not provide a wholly convincing reply.[121] Likewise, the Labour Party's argument that a consumer boycott of South Africa did not represent 'interference' in other countries' internal affairs – '[t]his could as well be said of Hungary or Tibet or wherever there is a denial of human rights' – rather begged the question of why, therefore, other boycotts were not being proposed.[122] Arguably, the factors that allowed British activists to see the issues in South Africa with such clarity impeded activism around lesser-known or more complex questions, even in Africa. In 1961 Michael Scott asked why 'the conscience of the whole world' was aroused by Sharpeville, but the 'wickedness and folly' of Portugal, a NATO ally, in its colony Angola was left unchallenged?[123] The same may well have been said about the bitter colonial conflict in Algeria in the late 1950s and early 1960s. The widespread abuses by French forces in their struggle against the FLN were hardly a secret at the time, but raised relatively little interest in Britain.[124] While activists had succeeded in presenting the struggle against apartheid as a question of human rights, they were still not giving voice to the universality of those rights. This would become a pressing issue with the rush to decolonisation after 1957.

2.4   Ghana and the Problems of Decolonisation

Ghana's independence on 6 March 1957 was a moment of high promise: the new state was a bright star in the firmament of Africa, represented as such in the flag of South Africa's Pan Africanist Congress. Kwame Nkrumah, the first Prime Minister, and (from 1960) President, of independent Ghana was a well-known and popular figure in British anticolonial circles, having lived and studied in Britain during the 1940s. Michael Scott attended the celebrations and in a radio broadcast from Accra compared the situation there – where 'human rights [were] being extended' – with the ever-greater restrictions on freedom in South Africa.[125] However, the promise did not last long and from the outset Nkrumah was determined to enhance the powers of the government against tribal, ethnic and political enemies (real or imagined). As early as September 1957 there was an emergency meeting of Justice, the recently founded organisation of British lawyers, to express concern about the deportation of two Muslim leaders by ministerial order, and to declare support for the Ghana Bar Council.[126] By March 1959, Justice had identified a 'trend towards Government dictatorship'. Likewise, in August 1961, barely two months after its establishment, Amnesty's house journal ran an article which lamented 'the great shadow cast by 200 detainees' in Ghana, 'a muzzled press', and party control 'in the Soviet pattern'. The author, the academic Adam Curle, had recently left University College Ghana due to alleged interference with academic freedom.[127] The lawyer Louis Blom-Cooper conducted one of the earliest Amnesty overseas missions, in January 1962, in an unsuccessful attempt to secure the release of Nkrumah's rival, Dr Joseph Danquah, from detention.[128] Although there were concerns about the authoritarian traits of other African leaders, notably Hastings Banda, who led Malawi to independence in 1964,[129] Nkrumah's case was clearly of greater international significance.

Nkrumah's conduct opened a division between those activists from a legal background, who saw the rule of law as absolute, and left-wing anti-colonial campaigners, such as Fenner Brockway and Tom Driberg, who initially sought to explain away Nkrumah's lapses. In 1958, for instance, Brockway argued that Nkrumah's stern action was justified against an opposition that showed 'violence of spirit' – and, in any case, the Ghanaian government was not guilty of doing anything that was not already being done in the British colonies.[130] Driberg, who wrote to Nkrumah by his title 'Osagyefo' ('redeemer'), remained convinced that it was better for Ghana to move 'rapidly towards Socialism, even if it is tinged with Marxism', than to endure postcolonial economic exploitation.[131] It was the government's introduction of preventive detention that finally convinced many on the left to speak out. In November 1963 a group of Labour politicians with impeccable anti-colonial credentials – including Brockway, Barbara Castle, Dingle Foot and former Colonial Secretary Arthur Creech-Jones – wrote a joint letter to Nkrumah as personal friends who had all protested when 'human rights were invaded in African Colonial Territories'. Open-ended detention without trial, they argued, not only offended the principle of human freedom, but was also flung back at them whenever they protested against abuses in South Africa, Southern Rhodesia and the Portuguese colonies.[132] The letter was delivered personally, via a circuitous route involving Peter Benenson and Roger Baldwin, to Ghana's ambassador in New York.[133] Even so, despite their disappointment with the pattern of events in Ghana, it was difficult for these politicians to burn their bridges completely. Dingle Foot, who as a lawyer had first defended nationalist politicians in the former Gold Coast in the late 1940s, wrote to congratulate Nkrumah on surviving an assassination attempt in January 1964, while also providing a glowing tribute to his critic Danquah, who died in detention a year later.[134]

Left-wing support for Nkrumah was taken to an extreme by Geoffrey Bing, who served as his Attorney General (1957–61) and was a personal adviser until Nkrumah's overthrow by *coup d'état* in February 1966. Bing, a barrister closely associated with the Communist Party, had been a stalwart of the NCCL during the later 1930s and had, at times, deputised for Ronald Kidd. After wartime military service dominated by MI5's attempts to keep him away from any conceivable position of authority,[135] he was surprisingly elected as Labour MP for Hornchurch in 1945. He met Nkrumah in 1947 and revived his friendship when he started a legal practice in the Gold Coast in 1950. Bing lost his seat in the 1955 election and settled in Ghana. As Attorney General he gained notoriety as an unprincipled enforcer of Nkrumah's will. In the words of one obituarist, whatever was needed, 'the elaborate legalism of Bing's mind would find a way', while the *Daily Mail* wrote that 'he could draft a law which made black white and not even a paint box could prove it false'.[136] Tom Sargant, the secretary of Justice, privately described Bing as 'the arch-destroyer of civil liberty'[137] – a strange fate for such a strong advocate of civil liberties in Britain (and more specifically of his native Northern Ireland) in the 1930s. Following Nkrumah's overthrow Bing was beaten up and briefly imprisoned, and on his return wrote a memoir intended to restore his shattered legal reputation.[138] It was an uphill struggle, as an Amnesty book review castigated Bing as an 'apologist' for Nkrumah, and said that his defence of preventive detention required 'suspension of logic'.[139] Perhaps his main achievement as Attorney General was to make Ghana a home for political refugees from South Africa. Indeed, his second wife Eileen was dubbed 'the Pimpernel wife' when she made a secret mission to Bechuanaland, funded by Collins' Christian Action, to organise an airlift to Accra.[140]

Nkrumah's Ghana raised two issues that would continue to trouble advocates of human rights well into the 1960s. The first was the question of the one-party state, which – in the postcolonial context – was often seen as a legitimate developmental stage during the formation and consolidation of independent African states. In January 1961 Antony Allott, an authority on African Law at the School of Oriental and African Studies (SOAS), attended a major conference on 'the rule of law' in Lagos, organised by the International Commission of Jurists. He reported that there had been considerable criticism of Ghana's preventive detention by fellow Africans at the conference, and that the Ghanaian delegate's suggestion that Africa should pursue its own '"purely African" legal system and ideology' found little public favour. He also noted with satisfaction that at least the former British colonies were all building fundamental human rights into their constitutions. However, he expressed surprise that 'the major problem of Africa, whether the new states require a period of authoritarian rule and a limitation of individual rights so as to establish the political and economic basis of their society', was barely mentioned.[141] Others were less restrained. In 1963 a group of Birmingham University students organised a conference for Amnesty International on the provocative topic 'Is the one-party state inevitable for Africa?', while in the same year Arthur Creech-Jones objected forcefully to positive comments about single-party government in the Africa Bureau's draft annual report: 'I am utterly opposed ... it is not democratic'.[142] Peter Benenson, also in 1963, wrote that for at least the next decade almost all countries in Africa and Asia would be ruled by one-party government: 'it is a fact that newly developing countries do not find that the conventional type of European multi-party democracy meets their situation'. Although the essential 'rottenness' of such a regime would eventually destroy it, he went on, the resilience of the dictatorships in Spain and Portugal suggested that such an arrangement could last for many years. The real question was whether these states would eventually progress to a parliamentary democracy, and what – in the short term – could be done to help dissidents and ethnic or religious minorities that often faced persecution.[143]

This question of how the rights of minorities could be protected against the centralising and intolerant tendencies of the postcolonial state was the second major issue raised by decolonisation. There was, of course, one significant complication, in that criticisms emanating from the former colonial power could so easily be dismissed as patronising or even neo-colonial: indeed, in June 1964 Nkrumah would label Amnesty as 'imperialist'.[144] However, Michael Scott was untroubled by such considerations, and took a keen interest in the plight of the Naga people who occupied the remote border region between India and Burma. When he met Indian Foreign Minister Krishna Menon in June 1960 his concerns were angrily rejected, and Scott later complained to Brockway that 'few of the habitual defenders of subject peoples are willing to offend New Delhi by showing any interest in the Naga cause'.[145] Three months later Scott published an article in *The Observer* in which he noted that the creation of postcolonial states had not only increased the pressures on minorities but also reduced the ability of the United Nations to intervene on their behalf. He called for a new international Convention to protect minorities' interests and argued that Britain had enough 'moral capital' to take a lead.[146] Eventually this concern resulted in Scott's last major campaign, the Minority Rights Group, but the prolonged periods that he spent in the Naga country in the mid-1960s ensured a lengthy gestation and there were several false starts. In January 1962 he proposed a 'Council for Human Rights' that would 'enable minority groups and numerically small peoples to appeal to the conscience of humanity' for protection and the right to self-determination. A scrawled note at the top indicated that Scott sought a balance of cases based on ethnicity and politics, a similar principle to the one that Peter Benenson had applied in his recent Amnesty appeal: 'Black – Ghana; Yellow – Tibet; Brown – Naga; – Red – Hungary etc'.[147] The project was announced a few months later as an 'International Committee for the Study of Group Rights', and, once funding had been secured, the Minority Rights Group. However, this would only take off in the late 1960s (see Chapter 8).

3   Political Imprisonment and Human Rights, 1945–1964

3.1   Political Prisoners: Known and Unknown

In 1953 the Institute of Contemporary Arts in London launched an international sculpture competition in honour of 'all those who have given their lives or their liberty to the cause of human freedom'. The challenge – to represent the 'Unknown Political Prisoner' – was won by the British artist Reg Butler, ahead of a distinguished field that included Barbara Hepworth, Theodore Roszak and F. E. McWilliam.[1] However, the maquette of the winning design, which was described as 'like an iron cage on a stick', with 'very small and highly stylized figures' looking upward from the base, was vandalised almost as soon as it went on display at the Tate Gallery. The culprit, a stateless young artist called Laslo Szilvassy who had escaped from Hungary in 1948, claimed to be acting for both aesthetic and political reasons. He justified his actions in a note: 'Those unknown political prisoners have been and still are human beings. To reduce them – the memory of the dead and the suffering of the living – into scrap metal is just as much a crime as it was to reduce them into ashes or scrap. It is an absolute lack of human-ism'. Happily for Szilvassy the judge, acknowledging that he had 'undoubtedly suffered much', gave him a conditional discharge and ordered him to pay £10.10s costs.

The competition and the subsequent attack provoked something of a debate in cultural circles, and Butler did not help matters when he conceded that the maquette, valued at £1000, was merely a 'shilling's worth of wire ... [bent] about in a certain way'. Szilvassy's barrister argued that the design was an 'inept, witless contraption, futile as a contribution to those who had suffered under the whip and concentra-tion camp'. Butler told a broadcast discussion that he was very aware of the need to present both 'the awareness of the tragedy and the resolution of it'.[2] But who were the 'unknown political prisoners', and how would a sense of identification with small, by-standing figures at the base of the sculpture help to resolve their suffering? These issues went beyond the cultural sphere, and yet, strangely, the discussion took place without overt reference to the Cold War context. In fact, it is now known that the £4500 prize money came from US sources fronting for the CIA, and the only offer of a home for the winning design (which was never realised) was in West Berlin, where it was proposed that it should face the large Soviet war memorial in Treptower Park.[3] If nothing else, the controversy demonstrated the difficulty of addressing the universality of political imprisonment at the peak of the Cold War – something which Peter Benenson would finally achieve with his campaign for the 'Forgotten Prisoners' in 1961.

Political imprisonment played a critical role in the popularisation of human rights in Britain. The commemoration of 'Human Rights Day' on 10 December, the date on which the Universal Declaration had been signed, had languished during the 1950s. The day was generally ignored by the British government, which saw it as the responsibility of organisations such as the United Nations Association, while the UNA in turn saw it as less important than United Nations Day on 24 October. In 1957 there was a sharp debate within the Board of Deputies and other Jewish organisations about whether a special effort should be made to honour the forthcoming tenth anniversary of the Universal Declaration. Norman Bentwich, the eminent lawyer and academic, declared that in the current climate, and especially with so little progress on the human rights covenants, such a celebration would be hypocritical.[4] He preferred concrete legal advances to empty celebrations. It was, again, only in 1961, when Amnesty began to celebrate Human Rights Day with a remarkable talent for eye-catching publicity, that the date became better known in Britain. But if the new concern for political imprisonment saved Human Rights Day from neglect, it also marked a potentially unhealthy over-identification of human rights with the rights of political prisoners, at the expense of other political rights, let alone social and economic rights.

The major obstacle to a universalist approach during the 1950s was the sheer divisiveness of the Cold War. Certain organisations (typically on the left) existed to campaign on behalf of prisoners of right-wing, authoritarian regimes in Europe, or of colonial administrations, while other organisations (typically Catholic or conservative) campaigned for the release of prisoners of Marxist regimes. This was what Peter Benenson would later describe as 'the self-defeating character of like's concern with like'.[5] These campaigns could be vibrant, at least in the short term, as in the case of the agitation over Cardinal Mindszenty, but they lacked a broader perspective. As a member of the Iona Community noted in the late 1940s, 'if we are going to talk about Mindszenty (as I believe we should) our voices will not ring firm unless we are also prepared to talk about the blemish on Personal Rights that is at another level the mark of our witness in some of [Britain's] colonies and in the USA'.[6] The Labour MP Reginald Sorenson made a similar point in 1957 when asked to sign a petition for the release of Greek communist prisoners: he supported political prisoners irrespective of their views, he replied, but would communists be 'as ready to do this in their own form of democracy'? His own conception of democracy involved a belief in '"Human Rights" and in personal liberty that is unacceptable to other interpretations of democracy, and perhaps to some whose release from imprisonment and detention I desire'.[7]

The Cold War impinged directly on the organisations seeking to address political imprisonment, as in almost every case a communist-aligned committee would have a non-communist (liberal or social democratic) rival. The split in British lawyers' organisations had occurred in the late 1940s when the Society of Labour Lawyers (SLL) broke away from the Haldane Society. Likewise, in the international sphere the older International Association of Democratic Lawyers (IADL) was challenged after 1953 by the Hague-based International Commission of Jurists (ICJ). The ICJ had a strong British input during its formative years when the lawyer and Oxford academic Norman Marsh was Secretary-General (1956–58). The Haldane Society was loyal to the IADL until the Hungarian uprising of 1956, when a special meeting voted to condemn both the Anglo-French operation in Suez and the Soviet intervention in Hungary, and to make enquiries with the Hungarian Embassy about the abduction of Prime Minister Imre Nagy.[8] Thereafter the society became increasingly exasperated by the IADL's 'one-sided approach' to international law and citizens' rights and decided that it could 'no longer be a party' to them.[9] Peter Benenson's relationship with the Haldane Society was complex as he had resigned from it in 1952 but continued to brief it about his work on behalf of Spanish prisoners.[10] In 1956 he excluded the society from the launch of his new organisation Justice – as he deemed it incapable of working against political oppression in both South Africa and Hungary – but in 1958 he was again engaged in 'friendly discussion' with a view to developing informal cooperation between the Haldane Society and the SLL.[11]

Aside from the campaigns arising from anti-colonial struggles described in Chapter 2, the left was principally concerned with abuses of human rights in Spain, Portugal and Greece, which had their roots in the ideological and social conflicts of the 1930s and 1940s. In the case of Spain, the left – alongside much liberal and non-Catholic Christian opinion – had sided with the Republic against Franco's Nationalist rebels during the Civil War of 1936–39. Although both sides had been guilty of atrocities during the Civil War, Franco's victory meant that his highly repressive regime lasted – with fluctuating degrees of violent coercion – until the dictator's death in 1975. External opposition to the Franco regime only revived on a substantial scale after the end of World War II, when the regime became more vulnerable to criticism and was initially denied entry to most postwar international institutions. Well into the 1950s the mainstay of support for Spanish political prisoners in Britain was the communist-dominated International Brigade Association (IBA), an organisation for British veterans of the conflict, which made protests to the Spanish government, arranged for qualified legal observers (including Peter Benenson) to attend political trials and sent aid to prisoners' families.[12] Conversely, repression in Spain evoked little sympathy in Catholic circles – for instance, when A. C. F. Beales of The Sword of the Spirit attended a Catholic Conference on Human Rights in San Sebastian in 1948 he was fully aware that the venue might seem 'ironic'. However, he noted that Negroes in the USA also had grievances, and that even in Britain some groups were not allowed to broadcast on the radio. 'The shoe pinches all countries', he concluded, and only the Netherlands and Eire could hold such a conference with a completely clear conscience.[13] The memory of the Spanish Civil War, and the more than 500 British lives lost in the conflict, gave Spain an enduring significance in Britain – indeed, as late as 1968 Cardinal Heenan complained that the tendency to investigate injustice in Spain 'rather than anywhere else ... seems to be a common English trait'.[14] (For Heenan, of course, 'anywhere else' meant the communist world.) However, ease of access was also an issue. When Saul Rose, the Labour Party's International Secretary, asked the SLL why they were 'only interested in Spain', they replied that they 'would very much like to go eastwards'. Rose had to concede that this would be 'more difficult [than] going to Spain'.[15]

The Estado Novo (New State) of Portuguese dictator Antonio Salazar had been established in the 1920s, although – not having emerged from a civil war – was not built on such a high level of repressive violence as Franco's Spain. Moreover, as a neutral state that gave significant help to the Allies during World War II, Portugal was never such a pariah state. Portugal was a founder member of NATO in 1949, but did not join the United Nations until 1955, and did not initially sign either the Universal Declaration or the European Convention on Human Rights. Unlike Spain, moreover, which had lost most of its empire by 1898, Portugal retained very substantial imperial possessions in Africa (notably Angola, Mozambique and Guinea Bissau) and India (Goa). Serious British interest in Portuguese human rights abuses only crystallised in the later 1950s, when internal opposition to the regime became manifest, and typically centred on the repression of the emerging anti-colonial movements in Africa.

The Greek situation was the most complex of the three, as the British government had played a crucial role in curbing the ambitions of the communist-dominated resistance after the end of the German occupation in late 1944, and in ensuring the return of a conservative, monarchist regime at the end of the war. The bitter civil war of 1946–49 pitted the communist guerrillas against government forces armed and supported by Britain's Labour government and (under the Truman Doctrine of March 1947) the United States. Despite the right-wing victory in the Civil War, the mass imprisonment of former enemies continued until the early 1960s. Many – especially those held on the island of Makronisos – faced very harsh conditions. Some prisoners had formerly been detained under the Nazi occupation, and, indeed, before that under the prewar dictatorship of General Metaxas. A League for Democracy in Greece (LDG) was launched in the autumn of 1945, chaired by the novelist Compton McKenzie, who had served with British intelligence in Greece during World War I. Initially the League was a broad front of communists, liberals and the Labour left, although it became more firmly aligned with the communists as the Cold War intensified. It was run by three energetic and determined women: Diana Pym, Marion Pascoe (who later married the rebel General Stefanos Sarafis) and Betty Ambatielos, who had married the Greek seamen's union leader Tony Ambatielos. Betty's tireless campaigning ensured that her husband, who endured imprisonment – sometimes under sentence of death – between 1948 and 1964 and again during the Colonel's dictatorship, became the best-known Greek political prisoner within the British labour movement. Indeed, Betty Ambatielos took part in the launch of Amnesty in May 1961, and her husband was featured in Peter Benenson's article on 'The Forgotten Prisoners' (although left out of his subsequent book *Persecution 1961* because his left-wing politics would have upset the delicate political balance). The League carefully collected information on the Greek prisoners, and – despite some disagreements between the two organisations – this was a vital source for Amnesty in its early days. However, the League's leaders lacked sympathy for prisoners of a different political and religious background. For instance, when one supporter, Colonel A. W. Sheppard, wrote a pamphlet about the Mindszenty trial, Diana Pym commented that at least this was a 'real trial [based] on evidence', whereas the recent Greek trials were based 'on convictions, pure and simple'.[16]

In the later 1950s the 'unknown' political prisoners began to be identifiable faces and names: indeed, in certain cases they began to enjoy celebrity status. The left-wing activist Manolis Glezos, who had first become famous for tearing down the Swastika from the Acropolis in May 1941, became an international *cause célèbre* while under sentence of death for espionage in the late 1950s. There was also something of a vogue for memoirs by former prisoners. For instance, both Edith Bone and Paul Ignotus, writers of Hungarian origin who had returned to their native country in 1949, only to be jailed as alleged spies, wrote influential accounts of their experiences in prison after their release in 1956.[17] Prisoners also became the focus of sustained national and international campaigns for their release: the most prominent cases were Glezos, the Spanish poet Marcos Ana and the distinguished Hungarian writer Tibor Dery, who was jailed for nine years in 1957, after a trial in camera, for his part in the 1956 uprising.[18] All three later visited Britain, although, unlike the others, Dery refused to speak to the press. By the end of the decade the image of the political prisoner had changed from the faceless victims of Reg Butler's abstract design to identifiable, active participants in their own struggles. Moreover, the success of the Tibor Dery committees demonstrated that repressive regimes were becoming more responsive to mobilisations of international opinion.[19]

3.2   Peter Benenson and the Formation of Justice

Peter Benenson had become interested in the Spanish Civil War as a pupil at Eton, where he set up a committee in solidarity with the Republic.[20] After his undergraduate studies at Balliol College, Oxford were cut short by the coming of World War II, he served in intelligence at Bletchley Park, the secret centre for British code-breaking. In his only specific reference to this period he stated that he had worked for MI8 (signals intelligence).[21] He studied for the Bar and in the late 1940s began to visit political trials in Spain as an observer for organisations including the Trades Union Congress (TUC) and the IBA (which at this point was being run by the Irish International Brigade veteran Alec Digges). Therefore, his political activism was nurtured above all by his engagement with the plight of the Spanish political prisoners. Many years later Benenson reminisced that 'gradually [in Spain] I learned the technique by which an Observer could make his weight felt'.[22] Indeed, when Gerald Gardiner travelled to South Africa to attend the Treason Trial in December 1956 on behalf of the newly formed Justice, Benenson distilled what he had learnt from his experiences into three pages of typed notes for Gardiner to read on the flight. The lessons included the need to cater to both the legal and the political aspects of the defence; to take care in hiring a defence team and avoid those with a 'red' taint; to talk to 'responsible' political and religious figures; and to work with the press to provide 'human interest' stories. There was no need to sit through the whole of the proceedings, Benenson added: time was limited and a 'ceremonial appearance' at the beginning would suffice, allowing the remainder of the trial to be followed by reading the transcripts while Gardiner got his finger on the 'political pulse'.[23] Although it has been claimed that Benenson's future strategy in Amnesty was learnt from the communist Alec Digges at the IBA, and that Amnesty International was therefore a product of Cold War communism, the evidence shows that what influenced him most were the very practical (and highly transferable) skills learnt on the ground in Spain.[24]

Benenson was born in 1921 to a Jewish family. His father Harold Solomon was a senior British army officer who suffered crippling injuries in a riding accident in 1923 and died in 1930. His mother Flora Benenson, the daughter of a Russian banker who escaped to the United States after the revolution, established the renowned staff welfare services for the Marks & Spencer stores, and is best remembered for furnishing MI5 with the information that precipitated the downfall of the Soviet spy Kim Philby in 1962.[25] She was a passionate Zionist, an enthusiasm that Peter Benenson – who became increasingly critical of Israel's treatment of the Palestinians – did not share. At the request of Flora's father her son kept alive the family surname, and he was known during the 1940s as Peter Solomon-Benenson. Benenson's background and education was, therefore, a privileged one, and the links that he forged at Eton and Balliol College, Oxford, as well as his own family's extensive contacts, were an important thread throughout his life. For instance, one of Benenson's closest friends and associates during the 1950s was the liberal Conservative Sir Ian Gilmour (Eton and Balliol). The two men set up legal chambers together in 1953, and Gilmour was the owner/editor of *The Spectator* (for which Benenson often wrote at this time). However, as we shall see, these influential connections also made Benenson unduly optimistic about the readiness of 'the establishment', as it was becoming known in the mid-1950s, to support his campaigns.[26]

Benenson was a man of remarkable energy and alongside building his legal career, dabbling in journalism, writing children's novels, supporting political prisoners in Spain and raising a family, he also sought election to parliament. He stood four times during the 1950s, without success, as a candidate for the Labour Party in Hitchin (North Hertfordshire). He nursed the constituency by moving his family from Bethnal Green to share a substantial farmhouse in Hertfordshire with the old Etonian Hallam Tennyson, a pacifist and campaigner for gay rights descended from the Poet Laureate.[27] Benenson's 1955 election leaflet stated that he was 'especially interested in seeing that the laws of Britain are brought up to date', while in the 1959 election he called for a foreign policy based on 'decency and prudence', criticised the decision to rearm West Germany ('an offence to the dead and a danger to the living') and called for a ban on the manufacture of 'beastly' H-bombs.[28] These latter positions placed him broadly on the left, but he was not closely associated with the bitter ideological faction-fighting within the party, and his natural political affinities lay more with social democrats such as Roy Jenkins (a close personal friend), or even liberal Tories like Ian Gilmour.

During 1954–55 Benenson, in close cooperation with his senior colleague John Foster QC, attempted unsuccessfully to create a cross-party organisation of lawyers. In July 1954 he proposed a 'British League for Human Rights', dedicated to upholding the UN Declaration of Human Rights in Britain and the colonies: this would be an all-party, non-sectarian and multi-professional body, intending to 'impress by its respectability'.[29] Benenson noted that 'there was a vacuum to be filled' as the NCCL had 'passed under the control of the Communist Party'. The initiative was eventually launched under the name of the 'British League for Civil Rights', with an emphasis now on the European Convention on Human Rights. The reason for the choice of name is unclear, but Benenson told an interviewer in 1983 that civil liberties were his passion: 'I much prefer it to "human rights"'.[30] At least one formal meeting was held, in February 1955, under the chairmanship of the Labour MP and barrister G. R. Mitchison, and in October Benenson met a member of the secretariat of the Council of Europe on behalf of the 'English Human Rights movement'.[31] But the project eventually fizzled out, and probably never went beyond the 'five or six people' that Benenson had originally approached. However, there was much to learn from this failure, not least that Benenson had concentrated on planning a structure for the organisation without offering any sense of which substantive issues might bring lawyers of different political affiliation to work together. This cross-party collaboration, after all, was his real goal, and as he later noted 'there would have been no other way of bringing Conservative and Labour lawyers together in one organisation except by diverting focus outside the UK'.[32]

This 'focus' presented itself quite suddenly in the autumn of 1956 when the Soviet repression of the Hungarian uprising coincided with the Treason Trial in South Africa. Although organisations such as Christian Action immediately saw that British lawyers had a part to play in the Treason Trial, Benenson recognised that simultaneous political trials in both communist and non-communist states offered precisely the kind of unifying cause that he sought – namely, a fair trial for the defendants irrespective of their politics. On 17 January 1957, having met with the leaders of the organisations representing Labour, Liberal and Conservative lawyers, Benenson convened a meeting in their name at Niblett Hall (part of the Inner Temple). Here, in the presence of more than 300 solicitors and barristers, he announced that they were meeting under the auspices of a new organisation, '"Justice", an imperfect acronym for the 'Joint Union of Societies to Insure Civil Liberties in England and Elsewhere'. The speakers included Gerald Gardiner, just back from South Africa, Andrew Martin of the 'Save Hungary' campaign and Norman Marsh, Secretary-General of the ICJ.[33] The meeting allowed Gardiner to report back, and also gave news of plans for legal observers to attend the Hungarian trials, but the presence of Marsh made it clear that the underlying intention was to create a permanent organisation of lawyers – in association with the ICJ – committed to defending civil liberties and the rule of law.

Barely two months later the Council of the new organisation – now formally 'the British Section of the International Commission of Jurists'[34] – met for the first time, supported by a grant of $600 and a loan of up to £1000 from the parent body.[35] (The loan was repaid in 1970 when the ICJ went through a financial crisis[36].) Tom Sargant, a former trader in metals with no legal training, whose career was in abeyance due to poor health, was hired as a part-time secretary, based in Benenson's chambers at 1 Mitre Court.[37] Sargant was a Christian socialist who had been active in Common Wealth during the war (a left-wing movement committed to radical social change). His fiery wartime polemic *These Things Shall Be* (1941) reads like a Christian version of Orwell's *The Lion and the Unicorn*. Benenson had got to know him in Labour Party circles in London after the war and, more recently, had visited him (and read some of Sargant's poems) during Sargant's convalescence in the spring of 1956.[38] The two men worked together closely in Justice, although Sargant's personal agenda often diverged from Benenson's. Benenson himself had no formal leadership position in Justice, having installed the distinguished lawyer Sir Hartley Shawcross as chairman, but he was, in Sargant's phrase, the 'kingpin'.[39] A series of significant decisions were taken at the outset. For instance, at the first meeting of the executive committee it was agreed that there should be no relations of any kind with the NCCL.[40] The parameters of Justice's work were also set. Hence, it was decided that the secretary would not take up individual legal cases except in exceptional circumstances, a ruling that Sargant (whose real interests lay in miscarriages of justice) found impossible to follow. It was also agreed that Justice would operate within the British Empire and Commonwealth, where local Bars often sought guidance from Britain, but not in Europe. Although Justice sent Gerald Gardiner to Portugal in 1957, and Benenson himself visited

Hungary in 1958, officially posing as a journalist, these kinds of investigative mission were thereafter largely discontinued until – in effect – they were revived as part of Amnesty's work.[41] The new organisation set out to recruit members from within the legal profession, and the membership had risen from 375 in June 1958 to over 1000 by the end of 1960.

During the 1960s Justice became known primarily for promoting reforms and innovations within the British legal system such as the office of the Ombudsman.[42] However, in its early years much of its work was in the Commonwealth or British dependent territories. Despite a comment in the first annual report that Justice was not a 'legal aid bureau', in the colonial sphere at least that was precisely what it was attempting to become. During 1958 Benenson held a number of meetings with Michael Scott and John Collins with a view to establishing a legal aid fund for African nationalists on trial in Northern and Southern Rhodesia. Justice obtained a £1000 grant from Christian Action, and set up a special account at Hoare's Bank for work in Africa.[43] This emphasis lasted until May 1960 when – after Shawcross complained that colonial issues took up three quarters of Justice's annual report – it was agreed that home affairs should henceforth take precedence.[44] It is not clear how far Benenson's disenchantment with Justice stemmed from this change – after all, the rapid pace of decolonisation meant that many former colonies were now becoming independent and Justice's scope for working in these countries was inevitably in decline. Moreover, Benenson was also deeply interested in domestic legal reforms and favoured doing more work in this field.[45] Even so, he did not forget the work that Justice had done in Southern Rhodesia, and it would resurface under Amnesty's banner in the mid-1960s (see Chapter 5).

There were other tensions during the early years of Justice, notably in the often-strained relationship with the ICJ. Benenson had been a great admirer of Norman Marsh, but was disappointed by the lack of leadership under his successor Jean-Flavien Lalive (Secretary-General 1958–61), who moved the headquarters from The Hague to Geneva. According to a pithy Justice internal memorandum the ICJ faced a threefold problem: 'an inept Executive Committee ... no policy ... [and] no staff'.[46] Lalive seemed to have no interest in political trials in countries such as Iraq and Romania, even though the British Foreign Office was anxious to provide the ICJ with all the relevant information. Shawcross felt that ICJ headquarters were 'infected with the characteristically neutralist Swiss attitude', and the voice of the 'free world' was not being heard.[47] Lalive also made himself unpopular by insisting – unsuccessfully – that activity within the British colonies should by undertaken by 'neutral' non-British lawyers.[48] The friction was somewhat reduced when Gerald Gardiner was invited to join the ICJ Council, giving the British Section a greater say in its overall direction. Relations were further eased when Sean MacBride (already Chairman of Amnesty International's International Executive Committee) took over as ICJ Secretary-General in 1963.

Benenson was also frustrated that other national sections of the ICJ lacked the combative instincts of Justice. This was nowhere more apparent than over the Algerian conflict, where he had taken a special interest in the allegations of torture against the French forces. In a private letter to Marsh, Benenson expressed his anger that it was a 'small but courageous group of people [within France], in the main progressive Catholics' who took a stand over repression in Algeria, while the French Section hung back. He took pride in the fact that Justice had 'automatically assumed the leadership of the Civil Liberty movement [in Britain], and in one swoop has surpassed the Communist organisations despite their twenty years of vested interest': French inaction, by comparison, would merely boost French communism. 'For the sake of the struggle against Communist totalitarianism . . . it is essential for non-Communist lawyers in Europe to lead the fight against injustice'.[49]

Although Benenson remained involved in Justice until 1967, he was increasingly unhappy with his creation and felt that it could not deliver the radical activism that he had hoped for. With hindsight Shawcross's comments as chairman in December 1957 – that their work was 'useful' but not headline-grabbing and had no 'sentimental or dramatic appeal'[50] – encapsulated much that Benenson came to feel was wrong with Justice and the ICJ. Those closest to Benenson were fully aware of his irritation. Tom Sargant recalled that Benenson felt 'confined by the legalities of Justice . . . [he] always had this wider vision of a humanitarian organisation involving not just lawyers, but all the other professions'.[51] Marsh, who later worked closely with Benenson in Amnesty, said that Benenson had wanted the ICJ to act as 'automatic protestors': when Marsh demurred, Benenson began to look for a 'body concerned simply with intervention, protest, relief'.[52] In a letter to Sargant from Sicily in March 1960 Benenson wrote that Justice would prosper not through changing the laws, but through 'altering the minds of men so that *they want* to treat their neighbours with justice. The real member of JUSTICE is he who is concerned [*sic*] with the homeless widow as with the prisoner without appeal'.[53] And once Amnesty was under way in 1961, Benenson expressed his views quite savagely in another letter to Sargant. The ICJ was a mere 'hotch-potch of individuals', backed by money raised in New York for anti-communist purposes. It could not survive because it had 'no spiritual unity. You cannot fight despotism with legal sophistry'. Tyranny could only be fought by clasping 'the Sword of the Spirit. And that is what I hope both JUSTICE and AMNESTY will do; the latter providing an instrument for all socially minded people, the former exclusively for lawyers ... '.[54] The heightened religious tone of the letter indicates how far Benenson had travelled by 1961.

The establishment of Justice reveals much about Benenson's commitment to international human rights and his readiness to work across party boundaries in pursuit of his objectives, but his attitude towards communism can appear inconsistent at times. There is no question that Benenson saw communist regimes as dictatorial and – using the language of Cold War anti-communism – 'totalitarian'. However, he never developed his political ideas at any length, and his occasional comments reveal greater nuance and pragmatism. In his book *Persecution 1961*, for instance, he espoused the idea that the ideological differences between the USA and the Soviet Union were deliberately exaggerated to mask the ever-greater similarities between their political and social systems. He also argued that both the USSR and China would treat prisoners of conscience more tolerantly if, like Yugoslavia, they could 'contract out of the Cold War'.[55] He believed that in the post-Stalin thaw some communist regimes were becoming more lawful and responsive to popular pressures, while remaining highly prone to 'acts of petty spite' by officials.[56] Benenson had some first-hand experience of the communist world, having visited Hungary in 1958. He also visited Cuba in late 1959 or early 1960, where he was encouraged 'by the stand taken by the legal profession in defence of the "Rule of Law"' a year after Fidel Castro's victory.[57] On a personal level he found individual communists to be engaging companions and colleagues. Many years later he reminisced happily about his 'extremely stimulating political discussions' while still a schoolboy with his mother's friend Joe Berger. But 'although we were both on the Left, I could not agree with him about the Communist Party'.[58] During the 1950s, for all the occasional harshness of his language, Benenson was generally willing to work amicably with communists in the IBA and the Haldane Society, while also coming to recognise the limitations on what they could achieve. Interestingly, his conversion to Catholicism during the reforming papacy of John XXIII reinforced this open-mindedness. In June 1963 he wrote a paper about the current communist campaign for political prisoners in Greece, and, citing the recent papal encyclical *Pacem in Terris*, noted that 'the fact that a policy has Communist origins does not *ipso facto* mean that it is wrong ... the *objection* to the present campaign is the methods which it employs'.[59]

3.3　　Eric Baker and Danilo Dolci

During the 1950s Benenson worked with many of those who would later collaborate closely with him in Amnesty International: Norman Marsh from the ICJ, Louis Blom-Cooper, Tom Sargant and Hilary Cartwright from Justice, Andrew Martin from the LSE and Save Hungary, and Peggy Crane from the Labour Party. However, by far the most important inter-locutor in Benenson's intellectual and spiritual progression from Justice to Amnesty was Eric Baker (1920–76). Baker, a lecturer and social activist who joined the Society of Friends while at school in Sheffield, was the perfect foil for Benenson during this period, although Benenson's char-isma has meant that Baker's role in the creation of Amnesty has been overshadowed. The two men had an intense friendship during 1958–61, developed both in correspondence and in private conversations. Baker not only responded to Benenson's ideas, but also encouraged him to expand his own ideas and reading – for instance, it was Baker who introduced Benenson to the spiritual writings of the Russian émigré Julia de Beausobre and her idea of 'Creative suffering'.[60] Above all, while Baker may have lacked Benenson's brilliance and imagination, he possessed a single-minded determination and solidity that proved invalu-able during the damaging crisis within Amnesty in 1966–67. After its resolution Neville Vincent wrote to Baker that 'in an hour of crisis I *know* that we can count on you … [you are] a great moral tonic'.[61] The difference between the two men was also evident in Baker's thinking, which evolved gradually over time, whereas Benenson could swing easily between utopian idealism and pragmatism. It would, for instance, have been unimaginable for Baker to admit – as Benenson did in 1976 – that Amnesty, in its choice of cases to be publicised, selected those (especially women) who would catch the subeditor's and the reader's eye.[62]

Baker had graduated from Cambridge in 1942, the same year that he married his wife Joyce, and the two were jointly in charge of the Quaker Centre in New Delhi from 1946 to 1948.[63] Here he had a searing experience of the inter-communal riots over partition that would later inform his work in ethnically divided Cyprus.[64] After further community and educational work in Edinburgh he was appointed in 1954 as General Secretary of the National Peace Council (NPC),[65] an umbrella organisation for peace societies estab-lished in 1908. He was involved in the early protests against testing nuclear weapons which, he recalled, 'culminated in the Campaign for Nuclear Disarmament'.[66] He also took on a role within the Society of Friends as liaison with organisations such as the UNA and the Fabian Colonial Bureau on race relations issues.[67] Baker resigned from the NPC in October 1958, partly in protest against a decision by the governing Council to join a delegation by the communist-dominated British Peace Committee to the Soviet Union,[68] but also because his time was increasingly being taken up by his involvement with two issues: the conflict in Cyprus, and his support for the Italian social campaigner Danilo Dolci.

Dolci (1924–97) was an inspirational figure amongst British activists in the late 1950s and early 1960s. Although he made little direct reference to human rights in his many publications, his work was highly influential in promoting ideas about social justice, the alleviation of poverty, and non-violent protest. He was born to a middle-class family near Trieste but became acquainted with Sicily during World War II. After training as an architect in Milan he returned to the island in 1952, determined to challenge the appalling poverty and ignorance, as well as the local elites (including the Church) and the *mafiosi* that were obstructing change. He made his home in the fishing village of Trappeto near Palermo and began to campaign for reform, employing techniques that ranged from Gandhian fasts to passive resistance and the building of local community centres. His bravery in the face of intimidation and repeated arrests soon won him an international reputation. In May 1958 he established a 'Centre for Research and Initiatives' at Partinico, and foreigners began to travel to Sicily to help his quiet revolution, while support groups sprang up across Western Europe.[69] For instance, Michael Faber, a British journalist and development economist with connections to the Anti-Slavery Society and the Africa Bureau, spent a year working with Dolci in Sicily in 1961.[70]

Dolci often frustrated his followers by naively allowing politics to inter-fere with his mission. For instance, he chose to accept the Soviet Union's Lenin Peace Prize in January 1958 because the prize money would help his work, ignoring the considerable political damage that it would cause to his standing in Italy. However, like Scott and Huddleston, for all his 'saintli-ness' Dolci was very adept at using different media to further his cause, whether through journalism, books, radio or television. His visit to Britain in September 1959 generated considerable interest and – stimulated by a review by the writer Wayland Young of his latest book in *The Observer* – raised some £3000 in donations.[71] A further visit in February/March 1960 was equally successful and more than 8000 people attended twelve meet-ings around Britain. Baker told Benenson that 'I gather nearly all of the Dolci meetings have been overflowing'. This time the success of the visit was boosted by a BBC film about Dolci's work in Sicily. Tom Sargant found the programme so 'horrifying' that he suggested that Benenson should write (in his capacity 'as a recent English convert') to the Pope to ask how such conditions were possible in a Catholic country.[72]

Baker had first met Dolci in March 1958 when he organised a press conference for him, and he played a leading role in the Danilo Dolci Society during the first two years after its foundation in 1958.[73] He also met Dolci in Palermo on his return from Cyprus in 1959. After the violence that he had witnessed in Cyprus, Baker found Dolci's willingness to accept – rather than to cause – suffering, and his 'innate sense of human dignity', deeply refreshing. Although Dolci had moved away from the Catholic Church, Baker concluded that he had 'retained the fundamental Christian belief in what is, to use a Quaker expression, "that of God in every man"'.[74] Baker must surely have transmitted his enthusiasm for the Italian's methods and beliefs to Peter Benenson, as Benenson visited Sicily in the spring of 1960, only to find that the increasingly peripatetic Dolci was abroad.

During 1960 a trust was set up alongside the Dolci committee, to raise and oversee fundraising for projects in Sicily. The trust was sponsored by the NPC and its associated United World Trust: the trustees included Ritchie Calder and Ben Whitaker, a future Labour MP and campaigner for minority rights. Dolci allotted different Sicilian villages to the various national sections, and the British were asked to work in Menfi. A young Canadian social worker, Ilys Booker, was duly recruited and sent out as a community development worker for eighteen months. Her letters home not only provide fascinating details about her work in Menfi and the problems that she faced, but also chart her progressive disillusionment with Dolci's leadership. On her departure the trust's chairman, Professor Ross Waller, left her in no doubt that Dolci was 'truly a great and good man ... a genius', while also conceding that he 'isn't and never will be' a good administrator.[75] Only a few months later Booker had concluded that Dolci was a weak dilettante with no vision for Sicily – 'he has been misled, misguided and misadvised for so long'. Henceforth she would dedicate herself to the children of Menfi and avoid any reference to Dolci in her work. Dolci was 'charming' but 'quite useless', presiding over a headquarters at Partinico torn between feuding experts: 'an amateur outfit has no business trying to run a community development project'.[76] Booker's disturbing assessment casts claims for Dolci's greatness in a starker light and helps to explain why his projects went into decline in the 1960s. Even so, he remained an inspirational figure, who attracted enthusiastic audiences in Britain into the 1970s, and the fledgling Amnesty was still eager to win his endorsement.[77]

3.4   Baker, Benenson and Cyprus

In November 1957 Eric Baker reported to the NPC that he had had a helpful meeting with Peter Benenson, a 'young Barrister with intimate knowledge of Cyprus'.[78] It was fitting that this should have been the occasion for the first recorded meeting between the two men for, although Benenson and Baker came to share many of each other's enthusiasms, their relationship was forged – in Benenson's words – 'in trying to seek a settlement of the troubles in Cyprus'.[79] However, even such a simple formulation as this conceals the substantial differences between the two men in their approach and objectives. Whereas Benenson visited Cyprus as a campaigning lawyer, determined to challenge human rights abuses by the British colonial authorities, Baker's Quaker 'concern' – which he pursued intermittently until his death – was to promote peace and reconciliation between the island's Greek and Turkish communities. Even so, the two men found that they could work together, sharing insights and contacts, and even, in January 1958 leading a delegation to brief the incoming Governor, the liberal and conciliatory diplomat Sir Hugh Foot (later Lord Caradon).[80]

Cyprus had been a British Crown Colony since 1878, when it was acquired from the Ottoman Empire. However, it gained enhanced strategic significance in the 1950s when it became Britain's major base for operations in the Eastern Mediterranean. In 1955 the Greek Cypriot EOKA (National Organisation of Cypriot Fighters) under General Grivas embarked on a campaign of violent opposition to British rule, the purpose of which was not independence but *Enosis* (union) with Greece. The prospect deeply worried members of the far smaller Turkish community, who increasingly advocated ethnic partition as the solution. A vicious struggle unfolded between the EOKA guerrillas and the British army, although compared to the contemporary events in Kenya the casualties during the Cyprus Emergency were relatively light. According to official figures 104 members of the armed forces, just over 100 EOKA fighters and 263 Greek Cypriot civilians were killed in the conflict, many of the latter killed by EOKA.[81] However, the British authorities' repressive measures, which included detention and the use of torture, plus the tendency of British troops to go in for some 'pretty rough stuff'[82] when their comrades were killed, made it difficult for Britain to win the propaganda war. EOKA secured far more international support than the Mau Mau rebels, most importantly the unofficial backing of the Greek government. The Greeks were also able to apply pressure on Britain through the new international mechanisms for the protection of human rights. The Greek government brought a case against Britain before the European Court of Human Rights in May 1956, although the British government was able to maintain the Emergency subject to some concessions, and the Nicosia Bar Association set up a Human Rights Commission in 1956 to investigate alleged cases of torture and the mistreatment of suspects.[83]

Peter Benenson first came to Cyprus in October 1956 when Ian Gilmour asked him to report on the Suez crisis for the *Spectator*. However, on arriving in Cyprus, he found that 'the entire Greek Cypriot Bar was inundated with complaints against the authorities': outside one chambers there was 'a queue of anxious parents . . . so long that it stretched outside the front door'.[84] His interest piqued, he made repeated visits to Cyprus (ten within eighteen months) and established a 'nice little [legal] practice' on the island as Advocate to the Supreme Court.[85] His first major brief was to defend Charles Foley, the owner/editor of the English-language *Times of Cyprus*, who was accused of infringing the Emergency's stringent press regulations. Thereafter, Benenson publicised numerous cases of alleged torture and mistreatment by the authorities – for instance, that of Maria Lambrou, who was punched while under interrogation and subsequently suffered a miscarriage.[86] His stance on Cyprus was broadly in line with Labour Party policy – in other words, to promote a political solution and self-determination (which might result in *Enosis*), plus guarantees for the Turkish minority. As a lawyer, he approved of the technically 'brilliant' efforts of Lord Radcliffe to devise a constitution for the island, but also believed that what was truly needed was an economic New Deal or a five-year plan.[87]

Benenson's criticism of the colonial authorities, and sympathy for the Greek Cypriots, meant that he came to be identified by the government as part of an 'Ethnarchy/Noel Baker/Peter Benenson/Foley/*Manchester Guardian* clique'.[88] This was, in fact, a very diverse group. For instance, Foley was a former Beaverbrook journalist and foreign editor of the *Daily Express* who had come to Cyprus in 1955 sensing a story. He became a thorn in the flesh for the authorities, who privately discussed ways to discredit him.[89] Philip Noel-Baker was an elder statesman of the Labour Party whose family owned large estates on the Greek island of Euboea, and who strongly supported *Enosis*.[90] His son, Francis, was also a Labour MP, on the left of the party in the 1940s and 1950s, who later supported the Greek Colonels' regime of 1967.[91] Benenson was also associated in the eyes of government with the group of anti-colonial MPs such as Fenner Brockway, Tom Driberg and Barbara Castle. Benenson hosted Castle on her visit to the island in 1958,[92] but Benenson's own politics were not sufficiently on the left to place him naturally in this company. In fact, he was, as ever, eclectic and pragmatic in the company that he chose to keep: he represented the Parliamentary Labour Party in its contacts with leaders of the Greek Cypriot community,[93] was friendly with the 'rather right wing'[94] Foley, and was well known to the left-wing LDG, membership of which was proscribed for Labour Party members. For their part, the League disliked his close links with the ICJ, of which they strongly disapproved.[95]

It is not clear exactly why Eric Baker took an interest in Cyprus, although he was firmly of the belief that it was 'the duty of Quakers to encourage international understanding' just as much as devoting themselves to 'the development of spiritual life at home'.[96] His experience of communal violence in India was surely a factor, but so too was his anxiety that there was no opportunity for a Quaker intervention on the island as there had been in Kenya.[97] He approached the question as a typical Quaker 'concern', patiently collecting information, building relationships in Cyprus and not rushing to judgement. He made two lengthy fact-finding missions to Cyprus in 1958 and 1959 (one of them paid for by *The Scotsman* newspaper), contacted the small group of Friends living there, and examined the (limited) prospects for a Quaker initiative to promote peace. Benenson's contacts were essential for the success of Baker's mission. It was, for instance, Benenson who gave him an introduction to Archbishop Makarios. (Indeed, Baker later sent Makarios some books on the history and practice of Quakerism.[98]) Baker was, moreover, eager to look at Cyprus in its wider geopolitical setting. On both trips he also visited Greece and Turkey, and in 1959 his journey started in Paris (where he met the NATO Secretary-General Paul-Henri Spaak) and Geneva.[99] Baker took a more neutral stance than Benenson on the island's politics, and he warned against seeing EOKA as a 'noble' organisation, or the Greek Cypriot Church as idealistic.[100]

The end of the Emergency came quite swiftly in February 1959 when the Zurich and London Agreements laid the basis for an independent Republic. Turkish interests would be protected by constitutional safeguards, while Britain retained sovereign military bases on the island. In August 1960 Cyprus became an independent state with Makarios, who had abandoned *Enosis* after a period of exile after 1956, as its first President. However, the fragile peace did not last and the failure of the complex political arrangements resulted in further communal violence in 1963. In 1974 a disastrous coup by extremist Greek Cypriots resulted in the temporary overthrow of Makarios, Turkish invasion and an ethnic partition that has lasted until the present day. Baker returned to Cyprus to undertake a further investigation in 1975, shortly before his death. Benenson, however, although maintaining a close interest in Greek and Turkish affairs, does not appear to have returned to Cyprus. In December 1959 he announced his intention to resign from his English legal practice and to travel in Cyprus and the Middle East,[101] but the plan did not come to fruition due to a deterioration in his health. Instead, Benenson embarked on the period of convalescence and reflection that eventually resulted in the launching of Amnesty International.

Baker and Benenson had invested much effort in Cyprus in the late 1950s, but Cyprus left strangely little imprint on Benenson's career. In 1959 when he published his book *Gangrene*, it was the case of Kenya rather than Cyprus which he chose to provide a British counterbalance to the account of torture by the French army in Algeria.[102] One tangible outcome of his involvement with Cyprus, however, was that he took a closer interest in Frank Buchman's Moral Rearmament movement (MRA).[103] The movement, which had won over some of Makarios's closest supporters, claimed that it had played a pivotal role in securing the peace settlement.[104] Cyprus could, therefore, be presented as a vindication of Buchman's strategy of targeting – and bringing about spiritual change in – leadership elites. Benenson had first encountered MRA in Bethnal Green in the mid-1950s, and they subsequently established a centre at Astonbury House in his former constituency. Writing in 1960, he joked that he only resisted an invitation to attend functions at the MRA centre because his wife took 'the strongest exception' to them.[105] He remained 'of split-mind on the subject', aware of the virulent opposition that MRA aroused, but also aware that it had 'attracted more generous-hearted men and women into the work of raising social standards and lowering race-barriers than any other recent religious movement'.[106] Baker was far more sceptical about MRA, tending to see it as a purely anti-communist organisation: indeed, for many Buchman's reputation had been deeply tarnished by comments that he made in 1936, welcoming Hitler for building a defence against the 'anti-Christ of Communism'.[107] Although Baker had received testimony that 'change in Makarios [was] due to MRA', he remained unconvinced and commented in 1959 that it was not clear 'which is the fox and which is the rabbit'.[108] However, Benenson clearly kept an open mind, and saw MRA's local activism as a useful model for what he was hoping to achieve as he moved away from Justice in pursuit of new initiatives.

3.5   The 'Amnesty' Campaigns, 1959–1968

When Peter Benenson and Eric Baker launched their 'Appeal for Amnesty' in 1961, the name 'amnesty' was hardly unknown on the British left. Indeed, from 1959 onwards there were a series of campaigns calling for an amnesty for political prisoners in Spain, Greece and Portugal. The campaigns were a response to the revival of opposition politics within these countries, but also reflected the emergence of new forms of radical activism in Britain itself. For instance, the anti-nuclear Committee of 100 (which advocated direct action) also took up the cause of Greek political prisoners in the early 1960s.[109] The Labour Party and the TUC correctly concluded that these 'amnesty' organisations were communist-inspired and communist-influenced.[110] Peter Benenson shared this view, and his adoption of the title 'Amnesty' for his own campaign should be seen not only as an attempt to universalise the question of political imprisonment, but also to wrench the concept of a political amnesty away from its left-wing moorings.[111] He succeeded to the extent that 'Amnesty' is now wholly synonymous with the organisation that he created, while the rival groups had all faded by the late-1960s. But does this mean that the other 'Amnesty' organisations were doomed to fail? A closer examination presents a more complex picture. To avoid confusion, and somewhat anachronistically, in this section I will refer to Benenson's group as Amnesty International, and the others as, respectively, Spanish, Portuguese and Greek Amnesty.

Spanish Amnesty (formally the 'Appeal for Amnesty in Spain') was launched in August 1959, timed not only to mark the twentieth anniversary of the end of the Civil War, but also to take advantage of the Franco regime's greater sensitivity to foreign opinion at a time when it was seeking international legitimacy.[112] The appeal was part of a renewed movement for solidarity with Spain across Western Europe, the first focal point of which was a major international conference held in Paris in March 1961.[113] The British campaign was organised by the Swiss-born communist Eileen Turner, whose husband – the barrister Richard Turner – had visited the 1958 trials in Barcelona on behalf of the IBA and the Haldane Society.[114] The call for a Spanish Amnesty was not only supported by the left, but also by liberals and leading artists and intellectuals. The Liberal MP Jeremy Thorpe was a prominent supporter and was due to take a petition to Spain in December 1959, until he was denied permission to enter the country.[115] Other prominent sponsors of the appeal included Isaiah Berlin, John Piper and Hugh Trevor-Roper. In addition to conferences and petitions, Turner's group also raised funds for Spanish prisoners and their families, smuggled money into Spain, and publicised high-profile cases such as the imprisonment of the poet Marcos Ana. The Spanish Amnesty campaign has left a fuller archival record than its sister campaigns for amnesties in Greece (established in May 1962) and in Portugal (November 1962).[116] The Greek Amnesty committee benefited from being closely connected to the long-standing LDG. However, the question of an amnesty was less pressing in Greece as by the early 1960s most Greek political prisoners had already been freed and Greece was enjoying a brief window of more liberal rule, prior to the Colonels' coup of April 1967.

All three organisations collected significant quantities of information about political prisoners – including their alleged crimes, their sentences and the circumstances of their families – that were not available from any other source. When Benenson launched Amnesty International, therefore, it was initially in a supplicant position with respect to existing groups such as Spanish Amnesty and the LDG, as it had no archive of its own. This meant that political qualms about working with 'communist' organisations had to be suppressed: indeed, local Amnesty International branches would often go directly to these existing organisations when they were looking for

prisoners to adopt, or wished to contact their families.[117] At one stage
Eileen Turner refused to offer any further assistance, concerned that
Benenson's enthusiastic but inexperienced supporters were making exces-
sive demands on her own organisation's resources, and fearful that they
would only endanger those that they were trying to help.[118] The balance
slowly changed as Amnesty International built up its own archive, reducing
the dependence on other organisations. Even so, in June 1963, when
Amnesty International's General Secretary Bert Lodge visited one of his
groups in Sheffield, a member told him that he preferred the 'cold unsenti-
mental professional approach' of the other Amnesty organisations to the
'naive anger' of Amnesty International's supporters.[119] At this stage he
probably had a point.

It should also be noted that the original 'Amnesty' campaigns were by
no means stuck in the past: they spoke a language of human rights, and
they deployed a visual language of imprisonment and torture that would
remain current during the 1960s and 1970s.[120] Eileen Turner saw the
propaganda value of the anniversary of the Spanish Civil War, but was
also determined to appeal to a younger generation, who were more
concerned with the present behaviour of the Franco regime than with
its origins. When Victor Gollancz complained that she had not
approached many veteran supporters of the Spanish Republic, she
replied that 'the initiative for this amnesty appeal came from comparative "youngsters", – at any rate from "under fortyfives"' who were deeply
concerned about the repression of students in Spain.[121] Accordingly,
the close focus on political imprisonment not only highlighted
a vulnerability in the Franco regime's defences, but also fitted with the
wider contemporary interest in political prisoners per se. Even so, the
historic memory of the Civil War does help to explain why the Spanish
campaign flourished more than its Portuguese counterpart. The
Portuguese Amnesty campaign could not draw on such familiar tropes
and – with its emphasis on repression in the Portuguese colonies –
increasingly had more in common with the emerging 'Third World'
liberation movements.[122] Therefore, the Spanish Amnesty campaign
linked the causes of the past and the activism of the present. The
execution of the communist leader Julian Grimau in April 1963, which
revived the campaign, neatly demonstrated this connection, as Grimau
was sentenced to death for 'armed rebellion' during the Spanish Civil
War rather than for his recent activities as an underground leader in
Madrid. His brutal treatment (he had suffered grievous injuries while
'falling' from a window in the police station) and eventual death by firing
squad aroused international disgust far beyond the communist world,
and even the Pope appealed for clemency.

All three Amnesty campaigns frequently invoked the principle of human rights. For instance, in 1959 the inveterate fellow traveller D. N. Pritt appealed for the restoration of democratic liberties in Greece, in line with the UN Charter and the 'Declaration of the Rights of Man'.[123] But such calls from the left were still too one-sided to be convincingly described as human rights activism. A speech by the Rev. Stanley Evans at the March 1963 Paris conference for a Greek Amnesty indicates some of the problems: 'because we are human beings; because the United Nations and all enlightened humanity has passed and accepted a declaration of the rights of Man; we have both a right and duty to interfere in the affairs of any country where those rights are violated'.[124] The fact that he immediately went on to cite the Nuremberg trials as a precedent, and the lack of any desire on his part to see intervention in Marxist regimes that also denied human rights, showed how instrumental his approach to the Universal Declaration was: this was still a politics of human rights that was rooted in the anti-fascist discourse of the 1940s. By contrast, as Amnesty's appeals secretary Peter Burns put it in 1967: 'Amnesty movements exist for many individual countries but Amnesty International remains the only one that transcends national boundaries and tries to protect individual human rights wherever they are abused'.[125] This divergence undoubtedly explains these organisations' differing fortunes during the 1960s, but it does not mean that the narrower conception of human rights associated with the Amnesty campaigns made them any less effective in the short term. Ultimately it was the changing situation on the ground in Spain, Greece and the Portuguese Empire, and the need for different kinds of political engagement, that would render these organisations obsolete.

Peter Benenson already knew all about campaigns for political prisoners specific to a single country as, quite apart from his other commitments in the later 1950s, he was also a leading light in the Spanish Democrats Defence Fund Committee (SDDFC). This committee was set up with the support of the Labour Party in February 1959[126] and brought together representatives of the British labour movement with exiled Spanish politicians – principally socialists, and Basque and Catalan nationalists. It never aspired to have a mass membership but rather channelled funds from trade unions to the families of prisoners, sent observers to trials and kept the Spanish cause in the public eye. As ever with Benenson's initiatives, contacts made in one tended to connect to another. For instance, the former Labour foreign minister Ernest Davies undertook missions to Spain for the SDDFC in the late 1950s and later wrote for the *Amnesty Newsletter* in the early 1960s.[127] Another important interconnection was Benenson's interest in the attempts to build a non-doctrinaire socialist opposition to Franco, and above all in the case of the imprisoned Spanish lawyer Antonio Amat. He gave the release of Amat as his principle objective for visiting Spain in 1959 and hailed him as a 'man of great devotion and personal courage'.[128] When Benenson launched Amnesty International Amat became one of the principal case studies of political imprisonment. However, his release into house arrest in June 1961 came too soon for Amnesty to claim the credit.[129]

Despite his positive experience in the SDDFC, Benenson came to believe that such country-specific campaigns did not have much to offer and might even be harmful. In the May 1961 article that launched Amnesty International Benenson wrote that: 'Campaigns in favour of freedom brought by one country, or party, against another, often achieve nothing but an intensification of persecution'.[130] Betty Ambatielos of the LDG was so affronted by this phrase that she threatened to pull out of the following day's press conference, her years of experience having taught her that 'the most effective method is concentrated campaigning in relation to particular countries and individuals'.[131] Benenson must have been aware that this choice of words would cause offence, as the League had been raising concerns about his plans for some weeks. He presumably used this damaging phrase because it emphasised two things: first, the distance between his own initiative and the country-specific campaigns which he and Baker regarded as prone to falling under communist control; and, secondly, because it represented the culmination of years of close observation and reflection on Benenson's part on the efficacy of such campaigns. For instance, in 1958 Benenson had complained to Alec Digges of the IBA that there was no value in sending observers to what he called 'trials for the record', where the authorities had clearly already agreed to release the prisoner (as had been the case with Richard Turner's recent visit). Such trials might appear to score a success, but 'the important thing is to find ways of bringing pressure on the Spanish Government to desist from arresting and arbitrarily imprisoning their political opponents'.[132] After a decade of involvement with campaigns on behalf of political prisoners in Spain, therefore, with some small victories along the way, but no sign of any weakening in the Franco regime's repressive policies, Benenson was now ready to attempt to treat the underlying wound, not to apply further bandages.

4   The Early Years of Amnesty International, 1961–1964

4.1   'Bright Idea': Benenson and Baker Launch the Appeal for Amnesty, 1961

On 13 January 1961 Peter Benenson wrote a double-sided letter to Eric Baker. The first side continued the discussion of one of their current topics of shared interest, the trial of the former Turkish Prime Minister Adnan Menderes, who would be executed later in the year. However, the second side opened with an ill-concealed invitation – 'What are you doing now?' – and went on to explain that Benenson was 'working on a scheme to make this year (anniversary of the U. S. Civil War and Emancipation of Serfs in Russia) an occasion for launching a general appeal for an Amnesty for all political prisoners everywhere. The appeal will be made on 11th November to link up with the idea of Armistice'. He was already encountering much goodwill, he added, and the *Observer* had offered space in its supplement on 12 November. Benenson asked Baker if he knew of anyone willing to undertake 'a little work', especially with helping to compile a list of all political prisoners for publication on 'Amnesty Day'.[1] The previous discussions hinted at here have left no written trace,[2] so, with this letter, Amnesty appears in the archival record – barring a few salient details such as the exact launch date – almost fully formed. Baker needed little encouragement, and over the coming year the two men worked closely together to bring this idea to fruition, initially as a year-long campaign. But where had Benenson's 'scheme' come from?

By the late 1950s Benenson had acquired a formidable and formative range of experiences, whether legal, political, as an author or as a campaigner. In other regards, however, this was an extremely difficult period in his life. First, he had fallen ill with a chronic intestinal condition, misdiagnosed at the time as tropical sprue and later identified as coeliac disease. This forced him to suspend his legal practice and take a prolonged period of leave, part of it spent in Italy at his house on Lake Orta. Secondly, after defeat in the 1959 general election he gave up on his political aspirations. Although many years later he would say that he had never wanted to be an MP, at the time this must have been a crushing setback, and in his private correspondence he would present himself as not only turning his back on a parliamentary career, but also on the Labour Party and even on socialism.[3] Thirdly, he had – as we have seen – become disillusioned not only with Justice, which seemed hopelessly limited by his fellow lawyers' 'natural caution',[4] but also with the possibility of any individual organisation taking effective action against any single repressive regime. Fourthly, in 1959 he had converted to Catholicism and during the following years was in the throes of what he would later describe as 'a very active religious period'.[5] He made regular retreats to the monastery at Cîteaux, became a lay Franciscan brother, befriended the Jesuit Fr Thomas Roberts, former Archbishop of Bombay, and actively participated in the International Catholic Lawyers Association. This intense Catholic experience, expressed in long discussions and conversations with Eric Baker, also enhanced his (already keen) European affinities. In all, his life seemed to be at something of a crossroads. The underlying issue was clearly the question of whether – as his wife Margaret wished – he should return to seek 'conventional success', either in the law or publishing. As his friend Ian Gilmour put it a few months later, could he ever settle in a 'pin stripe existence' after his lengthy break?[6] In the autumn of 1960, as his health improved and he returned from Italy, his restless energies drove him to seek a new way forward.

On 19 November 1960 Benenson had the revelatory experience that led to the formation of Amnesty. As Benenson told and retold the story – often in slightly different ways – he had read an article in the *Daily Telegraph*, while travelling on the London underground, about two Portuguese students who had been jailed for toasting liberty. After reflecting for half an hour in St Martin-in-the-Fields he realised that simply protesting to the Portuguese authorities would do no good – far better to launch a campaign for the release of 'all political prisoners everywhere'. The story has provided inspiration for many years and is still prominent on Amnesty's website.[7] The only problem is that it has proved impossible to locate the newspaper article in question, or indeed to identify the jailed students, even though there was certainly no shortage of political prisoners in Portugal, some of them jailed for actions just as innocuous as those of Benenson's students.[8] For instance, in March 1957 Kingsley Martin reported that a student had been jailed for writing 'For Peace' on a wreath on the tomb of the Unknown Soldier.[9] The iniquities of the Salazar regime were, therefore, very much in Benenson's mind at the time: in February 1961 he described the regime as a 'fossilised personal despotism', presiding over a 'listless and fatalistic population, not greatly interested in politics'.[10] It seems likely, therefore, that Benenson had indeed had a flash of inspiration, but chose to render it as a parable rather than as the logical culmination of his experiences over the previous decade. It is also worth placing more emphasis (as Benenson himself later did) on the site of this revelation. In one account Benenson recalled that 'Eyes blurred with tears, unsure what force was pulling me, I left the train at the next station and made my way up the steps of *the nearest church*, St Martin-in-the-Fields'.[11] However, St Martin's is surely far more important than this would suggest given its immense symbolic value at the forefront of charitable work and progressive causes in London. It is noteworthy that in 1963 Benenson launched a scheme to create a memorial to the victims of the concentration camps in the Crypt of St Martin's as a place where people could come to experience silent reflection 'during moments of personal crisis'.[12] Whatever had triggered his own personal crisis, the results were to prove profound.

Benenson had turned first for help to Louis Blom-Cooper who, as the *Observer*'s legal correspondent, in turn secured the backing of David Astor. This was an essential step, as it was through publication of Benenson's article in the *Observer* – syndicated worldwide – that Amnesty would become both a national and an international campaign from the moment of its inception.[13] However, it was only when Baker joined him that the project took on clearer definition. Benenson acknowledged this when he later wrote that he and Baker worked like 'box and cox' throughout the opening phase, and that from the moment that they first discussed 'the Amnesty scheme ... Eric became a partner in the launching of the project'.[14] Like Benenson, Baker was also at something of a crossroads. The Cyprus crisis was over (for the moment) and he was working again for the Friends, organising study groups.[15] He had also emerged as a trenchant critic of contemporary Quakerism, which struck him as complacent and declining in both numbers and influence. In a series of provocative articles for *The Friend* during 1960 he argued that the Quakers were in danger of becoming 'a well-meaning but average and diminishing group of citizens', no longer a 'peculiar people' who could challenge assumptions and offer a distinctive set of values. Their role in the Campaign for Nuclear Disarmament was a success – but 'after disarmament – what?' And why were they not producing great public figures to match John Collins, Donald Soper and George MacLeod in the other churches?[16] Therefore, Benenson's new project was not only attractive to Baker in its own right, but also offered the 'distinctive social testimony' that he felt the Quakers currently lacked.

Some important decisions were taken early on. For instance, the name 'Armistice' was abandoned in favour of 'Amnesty' (a choice that,

Benenson recalled, 'came out in conversation'),[17] the launch date was brought forward to Trinity Sunday, and the campaign would now culminate on 10 December, Human Rights Day. However, the point at which the phrase 'prisoners of conscience' – which came to define the human focus of the campaign – was adopted is difficult to establish. Benenson always graciously attributed the term to Baker, although less graciously also said that it was included 'to satisfy the Quakers'.[18] When Baker had asked him 'how do you define a "political" prisoner', Benenson replied that he meant anyone denied freedom of movement for 'the advocacy of any course except violence whether orally at a meeting or in writing . . .'.[19] Amidst the practicalities of organising the appeal, it was another three months until Baker offered a 'more concise' definition. Benenson cavilled at his proposal that everyone had the right to express his opinions 'except where his purpose is to stir up violence or social and religious antagonism'. For Benenson this read like a denial of freedom of speech: 'We don't go so far as that, do we? All we mean to say is that we see no reason to rub the flesh off our knuckles getting a man out of gaol, when his purpose is to put other people into gaol'.[20] The distance between the two men was never great, therefore, but the more pragmatic Benenson preferred to leave room for manoeuvre. The term 'Prisoner of Conscience' was only adopted at a late stage before the launch of the appeal in May, when the final definition was 'those physically restrained from holding an honestly-held opinion which does not advocate violence'.[21]

In addition to receiving the backing of the *Observer*, Penguin made an unsolicited offer to publish a book (indeed, a mass circulation 'Penguin Special') which would accompany the appeal and present nine case studies of political prisoners.[22] Benenson correctly judged that this emphasis on personal stories – and thereby on the fact of imprisonment rather than the causes for it – would help to 'avoid the fate of previous amnesty campaigns, which so often have become more concerned with publicising the political views of the imprisoned than with humanitarian purposes'.[23] He and Baker embarked on an – at times desperate – drive to research the book in time for publication in the autumn, fully aware that they needed not only to find enough material for each chapter, but also to strike a balance between prisoners of different ideological regimes. Inevitably, therefore, Benenson was forced to rely on some cases with which he was already familiar, such as the Spanish socialist Antonio Amat, Maurice Audin (the victim of French torture whose case had formed the basis of Benenson's book *Gangrene,* and who was already believed to be dead) and Patrick Duncan, scion of an influential South African family-cum-rebel against apartheid. Other familiar and otherwise well-qualified individuals were excluded as surplus to requirement (such as the Greek communist Tony Ambatielos), but Benenson and Baker were hard pressed to identify a convincing non-violent political prisoner in the United States. The emphasis on non-violence also precluded jailed Republicans in Northern Ireland, and it proved very difficult to obtain information on prisoners from the communist and colonial worlds. Benenson delivered his manuscript at the end of April, but Penguin editors were unhappy with the style – which they deemed overly rhetorical and emotional – and demanded rewriting of about half the text. Benenson later expressed his thanks to them for 'helping to make the style and contents, taut'.[24] Although Penguin had low expectations for the book, which they saw as merely a 'public minded gesture', it sold well on publication in late October, and by 1962 had already gone into Danish, Swedish and Italian translation.[25]

One less successful venture, but one that reveals much about the scope of Benenson's ambition, was the proposal for a global newspaper entitled *World Conscience: An International Review to Bridge the Distance between Supporters of Amnesty '61*. This existed only as a dummy run, circulated amongst prominent supporters in mid-June, but contained news about the incipient local groups, prisoners and prisoner releases and adverts by journals such as *Tribune* and the *Spectator*. There was even a letter from Benenson's old friend Roy Jenkins about the implications of Britain joining the 'European Common Market'. Would British civil servants, Jenkins mused, have to speak French, or 'some artificial international language'? Most significantly, the dummy run illustrates Benenson's internationalism: the journal would be jointly edited in London and Paris, and published simultaneously from Cyprus, Delhi and New York, to create a 'forum for the exchange of ideas which concern the "world community"'.[26] Even in October 1961, Benenson was still keenly anticipating that Amnesty's journal would be published weekly 'in several languages from distribution centres in each continent'.[27] 'World Conscience' was one of a number of ambitious projects – such as a proposed series of international contests on the theme of the appeal, aimed at artists, writers, musicians and scientists – which do not appear to have taken off.[28]

The time-pressured research for *Persecution 1961* also helped Benenson and Baker to identify sources of expertise and to weigh up potential allies. In February Benenson was complaining that 'our present task force … consists of lawyers, journalists and politicians', and that they needed to bring in colleagues from the churches and from relief organisations.[29] However, lawyers, journalists and politicians represented Benenson's oldest friends and contacts, and were also the professional groups situated most conveniently. His chambers in Mitre Court (which acted as a home for both Justice and Amnesty) lay in the middle of three interlocking worlds – the law (the office was next to the Temple and almost opposite the Royal Courts of Justice), the press (still mainly based in Fleet Street) and academia (with King's College and the LSE close by).[30] This tight nexus of experts was served by an array of pubs and restaurants, allowing regular informal meetings to be held at short notice: Benenson's comment that Amnesty was directed by 'lawyers, writers and publishers who meet weekly for lunch' was hardly inaccurate at this stage.[31] Apart from key figures such as Baker and fellow lawyers Peter Archer and Louis Blom-Cooper, their younger colleague Hilary Cartwright, praised by one insider for her intelligence and level-headedness, was also present from an early stage.[32] Benenson was highly protective towards Cartwright, privately fearful that for all her talent she might struggle in the male-dominated world of the law.[33] (She eventually went to work for the ICJ in Geneva, having spent some time promoting Amnesty in West Germany in 1962–63.) He was less considerate towards another female colleague, Peggy Crane, a politician and administrator, who had met Benenson through London Labour politics in the late 1940s. She departed Amnesty in 1962, complaining that she was fed up with being treated like a 'dog's body', to take up a prominent position in the United Nations Association.[34] In a letter of reference, Benenson explained that she had wanted to be Amnesty's General Secretary, but his committee had decided that the post must be held by a man.[35] Others who contributed during the early months included the veteran foreign correspondent James Cameron, Hugh O'Shaughnessy (journalist and expert on Latin America) and Benenson's family friend Neville Vincent (businessman and lawyer).

As the launch date loomed, Benenson and Baker sought to maximise support from a wide range of sources. They received a challenging reply from the Labour Party leader Hugh Gaitskell, who saw the Amnesty appeal as too hostile to the West and raised the practical question of how they would operate in the communist world.[36] However, Labour Party officials were swiftly convinced that Amnesty was in 'responsible' hands and would not fall under communist control: indeed, it offered party members a helpful alternative to the existing left-wing 'Amnesty' committees.[37] Their confident support helped to win over the more sceptical TUC. Benenson also received backing from the Liberals, and even the informal endorsement of Prime Minister Harold Macmillan,[38] and there were representatives of all three main political parties at the press conference to mark the appeal's launch. Like the *Observer*, the progressive newspaper *Reynolds News* also ran a series of articles on political prisoners tied into the Amnesty campaign.[39] Early funding came from an eclectic range of sources: (Lord) Tim Beaumont, an Old Etonian who had recently come into a substantial inheritance and had bought the progressive Anglican journal *Prism*; the shop workers' trade union USDAW gave £100, and the pacifist Embassies of Reconciliation gave £200 to pay for a typist.[40] More surprisingly, given Baker's involvement, the Friends Service Council gave their blessing, but offered no practical support. Baker suspected that the Friends saw Amnesty as too anti-communist and were, in any case, already supporting the Spanish Amnesty appeal.[41] Wisely, he bided his time while he built up support amongst fellow Quakers, and his 'concern' was not forwarded to the Meeting for Sufferings until April 1962, almost a year after the launch.[42]

If political and religious support was somewhat patchy, the public response to Benenson's article in the *Observer Weekend Review* and the accompanying press conference was exhilarating. The enthusiastic reply of Sean MacBride, the Irish politician and former Minister of External Affairs, was particularly gratifying and he was quickly brought into Amnesty's inner circle.[43] But even more encouraging for Benenson was that he received some 1000 letters with offers of help and funding from 30 countries – as he later recalled, his 'telephone never stopped ringing'.[44] The individuals who contacted him tended to be those – like him – who were disenchanted with traditional forms of political and religious activity, or indeed had never previously taken an interest in activism of any kind. This flood of volunteers created a problem for Benenson for, as he noted in 1962, 'other than what I wrote in the article, I'd not then formed any detailed plans for further action'.[45] In fact, it is quite clear from the launch documents that the Appeal for Amnesty was only intended to encourage *existing* voluntary or professional organisations to make a 'special effort' to support prisoners of conscience over the coming year. Hence, in June 1961 Benenson offered administrative support to the Congress for Cultural Freedom if it organised an exhibition on political prisoners in Rome.[46] The appeal's main task would merely be to set up a Central Office for the Collection of Information, which would provide details of prisoners to any organisation committed to the principle of impartiality.[47] Despite Benenson's later recollection that local 'Groups of Three' were always 'intended to be ... the basis of Amnesty's organisation',[48] there was no mention of an individual membership or local organisation at the launch. However, in the absence of any immediate wave of support from existing organisations, these local groups proved a very successful ad hoc response that allowed Benenson to make use of the 'great latent reservoir of idealism waiting to be tapped'.[49] The first of the 'Threes' groups (so-called because they adopted prisoners from the East, West and Third World) formed in Felixstowe on 9 June, 'following a spontaneous initiative by a resident writing to the local paper'.[50] By the time of the first annual report there were 70 groups, with 210 adopted prisoners.[51] However, the lack of preparation explains some of the initial chaos within the 'Threes' groups, as well as Benenson's own early ambivalence towards them.

One of the most novel features of the Appeal for Amnesty was its emphasis on publicity and advertising. Benenson was fascinated with different ways of capturing the public's imagination, such as the centenary parallels (the 1961 campaign would liberate the minds of men, just as 1861 had liberated their bodies) and, arguably, the story of the Portuguese prisoners. He was particularly good at utilising ideas already in the public domain. For instance, only a few months before the publication of 'The Forgotten Prisoners' there had been a publicity campaign by War on Want on behalf of 'The Forgotten' – in this case, refugees in Algeria.[52] As for another iconic symbol, the candle in barbed wire, Benenson claimed that it 'came to me' after Duncan Guthrie, the first Treasurer, insisted that Amnesty needed a symbol.[53] This was then turned into a graphic by the artist Diana Redhouse, but the symbol may have had a more complex parentage. At the end of July 1961 Benenson wrote to Monsignor Derek Worlock (private secretary to Cardinal Griffin) to discuss the use of candles in Amnesty's proposed Christmas vigil. He invited Worlock to think about a phrase for the accompanying posters, the current suggestion being 'Light a candle in the darkness for Peace and Goodwill'. Benenson also wanted a symbol 'to place upon the candle', and favoured Baker's proposal of the Greek 'Alpha'. Worlock immediately warned that the significance of Alpha would be 'difficult to explain to ordinary folk. Even a prison chain or bars would be easier'.[54] Worlock may not have invented the famous candle in barbed wire, but he pointed in its direction. Soon afterwards Amnesty took the bold step of hiring former Methodist minister John Pellow, now working for the Public Relations company Hereward Philips which had raised funds for St Martin-in-the-Fields, to oversee the appeal's closing events in December.[55]

When writing to Worlock, Benenson made clear that the Appeal for Amnesty would end in December, as intended, but that the annual vigils would be one of its numerous legacies.[56] At Amnesty's first international gathering in June 1961 it was already envisaged that the year would leave in place a library and a newspaper. Benenson mulled this over in August during a brief visit to Edinburgh. He told Baker that the future was a 'figment perhaps best left for imagination to pierce through the swirling Scots mist', but he had some very practical suggestions to make. Looking beyond the campaign's 'crescendo' in December he saw that Amnesty might leave three permanent organisations in place: the Prisoner of Conscience Library (which could be Baker's domain), the International Enquiry about Liberty (which could become the world's first international political party) and a newspaper to link the two. He saw his own role as purely inspirational, with Benenson as 'navigator' to Baker's 'engineer'.[57] Baker's response was far more grounded, as befitted his allotted role. While not pouring cold water on the wilder ideas, he suggested that they devote time to 'the immediate purposes of "Amnesty"'. He was particularly concerned about Benenson's current intentions. In his view organisations passed through five stages:

1) There is the Bright Idea – the Inspiration (by which you have been possessed); 2) The organisation is created; 3) The Honeymoon period – when the thing sweeps along like a gale; 4) The Initial Problems – the Crisis of Growth; 5) Their Solution[.]

He believed that he had a duty to stay until Stage 5, but feared that Benenson would leave at the end of the year ('scarcely . . . out of Stage 3'). He concluded by stating his admiration for Benenson's 'vision, energy and ability', which had 'got Amnesty off the ground in a way I never could have done'. While Baker realised that he could be a 'useful brake' on his friend's exuberance, he also understood that Benenson's brilliance needed to be nurtured and managed.[58]

While much remained uncertain, notably in terms of funding, the first Amnesty Human Rights Day Ceremony drew the year to a close with a stage-managed triumph. The amnesty candle was unveiled at St Martin-in-the-Fields and was used to burn through a white cord binding two actors, Julie Christie and the Guyanese-born Cy Grant: 'The "chains of shame" were broken by the "flame of freedom"'.[59] Then the Vicar of St Martin's gave out letters for Boy Scouts to deliver to all representatives of foreign governments, announcing the existence of Amnesty's campaign to uphold the Universal Declaration of Human Rights, and appealing to their governments to review the cases of prisoners detained for their opinions.[60] This event – and similar events in Edinburgh and elsewhere – attracted widespread coverage, and as Benenson reported to Worlock, perhaps in a nod to his inspiration, 'the symbolism of the candle surrounded by barbed wire seems to have caught the public imagination'.[61] The earlier uncertainties were passing: since 28 May Amnesty had acquired a membership, both national and international; it had also held its first international meeting (see below, Chapter 4, section 4), organised conferences and was close to sending its first mission abroad. At the start of 1962 Benenson could claim that 'the first phase' was over:

'a publicity campaign is being converted into a fully-fledged international movement with individual and affiliated membership'.[62]

Peter Benenson was fond of claiming that Amnesty could only have happened in the moment of heightened international optimism of the early 1960s, the era of Kennedy, Khrushchev and the reforming papacy of John XXIII. This was the 'exhilarating, brief springtime ... when after rebuilding the cities we set about reshaping the world'.[63] But this merely describes something of the environment of the period, and other explanations are also needed. In its report for 1961 the Haldane Society noted that – at a time of divisions on the left – 'progressive-minded young people have eschewed overtly political forms of activity', and extra-parliamentary groups ranging from CND to the Consumers' Association had 'played an exceptionally active part in the movement of protest and reform'.[64] There was no mention of Amnesty here, but it surely deserves a place. Indeed, it is striking to note how, at roughly the same time, so many people were thinking about ways in which an engagement with the cause of international justice could be used to promote social and political activity within Britain.[65] Disaffection with established forms of political and religious organisation – a mood which, in their different ways, both Benenson and Baker exemplified – was indeed defining a new activism: internationalist, idealistic, media-wise and with a powerful sense of moral purpose.

4.2   Amnesty's Emerging Practice, 1961–1964

Many of the elements of a more permanent organisation were already in place by the end of 1961, including the beginnings of a committee system, an archive of information on prisoners, and the first local groups. [66] This section will look at how these different elements developed during Amnesty's early years, but any discussion must begin with an assessment of Peter Benenson's style of leadership. There is no question that his leadership was personal and direct: he worked long hours, travelled relentlessly, and made intense demands on his colleagues. He was the first to admit that he was a poor organiser[67] and resisted formal bureaucratic constraints. In 1963 he wrote that Amnesty's supporters were not concerned with 'points of order, and all the formality of stuffy meetings'.[68] Likewise, after leaving Amnesty he would write that 'constitutions cause nothing but trouble', and (interestingly for a lawyer) that humanitarian movements should decide their actions 'from the heart, not from the book of law'.[69] According to Sean MacBride, Amnesty's first constitution, adopted on his insistence in 1968, took the place of 'bits of envelopes'.[70] A Policy Committee was only instituted towards the end of 1961, 'to centralise the work of AMNESTY ... [and] to help Eric Baker and [Peggy Crane] plan our future programmes'.[71] However, it took many months for a Chairman of some weight – the educationalist Lionel Elvin – to be appointed.[72] In difficult moments an informal group of Benenson's most respected senior colleagues, such as Norman Marsh, Tom Sargant and Neville Vincent, could be called upon for advice. During the crisis of 1966–67 the existence of this wholly non-constitutional body, referred to as 'the Godfathers', came as an uncomfortable surprise to leaders of Amnesty's European sections.[73] Matters were complicated by the failure to identify a competent, male General Secretary who could work effectively with Benenson, especially when Baker took a reduced role after the end of the initial appeal. Roger Burke, Albert Lodge (who had been expelled from Portugal for opposing the Salazar regime, and who devoted his energies to the local groups) and the South African Jack Halpern all came and went without establishing themselves in post. The first truly successful administrative appointment was that of Martin Enthoven as Executive Secretary of the International Secretariat in April 1965.[74] Some found this lightly structured way of working liberating. For instance, Clara Urquhart, who was allowed considerable autonomy while working for Amnesty in 1962–64, wrote that 'few organisations work at the same pace – and with as little red tape as Amnesty'.[75] The attractions of this approach were obvious: but so too were the inherent dangers.

Funding was one area of particular peril, especially as Amnesty was denied charitable status. It was, therefore, reliant on donations and subscriptions, subsidies from the pockets of Benenson and other leaders,[76] and grants from political, religious and voluntary groups (including Oxfam[77]). Such grants were welcome but could potentially be seen as dictating policy. One of the first Amnesty missions, to Czechoslovakia in February 1962, was, for instance, paid for by the Catholic *Universe* newspaper, and it is noteworthy that Baker had privately warned Benenson that Amnesty should not be seen as part of the 'Vatican's Cold War against Communism'.[78] One solution was to set up a special 'Prisoner of Conscience Fund', sponsored by prestigious religious and cultural figures, which would be used to fund prisoners and their families and could thereby be deemed charitable. However, it was later admitted by some leading figures that some of the fund had been 'siphoned off' to support non-charitable purposes such as research and office costs.[79] In March 1967 Benenson justified his handling of the fund in these terms: 'I have always taken the view that it was reasonable to spend a proportion of the Fund to find out where the Prisoners of Conscience are situated and what are their conditions. Without such investigation, there could be no effective relief'. But, he went on, it would have been 'unreasonable' to pass all of the money to Amnesty, as this would result in loss of charitable status and the refunding of money to the Inland Revenue.[80] In 1963 Benenson launched a further 'Fund for the Persecuted', which was intended to absorb the existing one, arguing that this was a more 'evocative' title, and that the term 'Prisoner of Conscience' did not 'immediately explain itself'. He succeeded in gaining the sponsorship of Michael Ramsey, Archbishop of Canterbury, even though the Bishop of Birmingham, a trustee of the Prisoner of Conscience Fund, warned Ramsey that Amnesty's leaders – whom he admired – were not 'cold professionals', and in matters of administration erred 'on the side of being "amateur"'. The new appeal was originally intended to create an international, tax-exempt fund, which would disburse money to all organisations working on behalf of the persecuted. It played a significant role in providing relief to the families of prisoners in southern Africa, but by 1969 Martin Ennals was noting that it did not 'exist at present'.[81]

This financial weakness made the unanticipated success of the local groups even more central to Amnesty's progress. However, there were initial differences of opinion over what their role should be. Benenson's goal had always been to mobilise public opinion in defence of human rights. Activism, therefore, was central to his vision: he was, however, not committed to any specific form of activism, and was happy to consider alternatives to the 'Groups of Three' if necessary. In June 1961, for instance, he had written that 'it matters more to harness the enthusiasm of the helpers than to bring people out of prison', and that those whom the campaign 'primarily aims to free' were not prisoners but 'the men and women imprisoned by cynicism and doubt'.[82] Later in the year, when Amnesty faced an acute shortage of funds, an internal 'office paper' (reflecting Benenson's views) acknowledged the importance of the 'Threes' groups to Amnesty's future, but also noted that they were currently unable to 'make any progress' due to a lack of central resources to support them. Accordingly, it would be better if they took on other activities such as raising money for prisoners' dependants or local educational and propaganda work. This was rejected by the Policy Committee as unacceptable to those who had joined groups to work for the release of prisoners.[83] Indeed, it is quite clear from the existing sources that volunteers were drawn to Amnesty precisely because they were excited by the opportunity to 'do something' very practical to help prisoners. Had they wished to pursue these other activities they could have done so through established organisations such as the UNA. Thereafter there was far less discussion about the purpose of the 'Threes', and more attention was paid to regularising the existing groups and creating new ones. A 'Threes' handbook acknowledged that 'The essence of Amnesty is getting on with the job of bringing men and women out of captivity'.[84] The position of the local groups was strengthened immeasurably by their rapid growth. When the 'office paper' was written there were still only 20 groups in Britain: there were 70 by July 1962, and 221 by March 1963 (when, apparently, they were being created at the rate of one per day!). Universities were particularly fertile grounds for recruitment, and at one point there were said to be ten groups in Oxford alone.[85]

The local groups took off quickly in the summer of 1961. Peter Archer's wife Margaret set up a 'Threes Centre' in Hampstead: this was intended to provide organisational support to the local groups now springing up. For instance, a group was set up in Clapham, strongly supported by the local parish church and Inter-Racial Club, while in Islington the focal point was three co-workers at a 'Family Service Unit'.[86] But the real phenomenon was the group in Eltham, south-east London, which first met in January 1962. As many as eighty-nine people attended the group's first public meeting, including John Robinson, Bishop of Woolwich, whose book *Honest to God* would shortly stimulate intense debate within the Anglican Church.[87] At Amnesty's 1963 Königswinter conference it was reported that 'the imaginations of some of the "small" [*sic*] delegates struggled to conceive the enormity of the Eltham Group . . . [with its] 70 members, 21 prisoners and busy officials'.[88] Its success was attributed to its ability to use 'the most powerful of all the media, television', after the group became the subject of a TV programme.[89] Margaret Archer was employed part-time to organise the groups, and was later replaced by Marlys Deeds, the Jewish refugee from Germany whose brother had been 'rescued' by Benenson while he was at Eton.[90] The main problem was that enthusiasm and goodwill swiftly outran the available resources, and groups often lacked direction. According to Diana Redhouse the Hampstead group wrote to Eric Baker in February 1962 because they were bored of 'waiting for something to start'.[91] In May 1962 the Eltham group appealed for help to Diana Pym at the League for Democracy in Greece as they were 'groping in the dark' to contact prisoners. Dorothy Warner, one of the group's founders, fondly recalled Pym's assistance,[92] but as we have seen, similar requests pushed Amnesty's strained relations with the Spanish Amnesty campaign over the brink.

From the beginning Benenson and Baker understood that an archive of reliable information on political prisoners would be essential for Amnesty's success. The second edition of Amnesty's journal emphasised that for any movement seeking to educate world opinion, 'Facts are its raw material, and their dissemination [to "newspaper correspondents and others"] its *raison d'être*'.[93] Indeed, in the 'Forgotten Prisoners' article the only formal action point was: 'we have set up an office in London to

collect information about the names, numbers and conditions' of prisoners of conscience.[94] Impartial facts, then, would win the trust of journalists and thereby secure wider coverage. Increasingly, however, 'facts' were
also essential to allow local groups to make reliable interventions on
behalf of prisoners. The 'live-wire' Christel Marsh, who had left
Germany in June 1939 to marry Norman Marsh, was appointed
'Librarian'. However, as she recalled, she was more like a registrar, setting
up a card-index system for the material already collected from organisations such as the writers' association PEN, and scanning the world's press
for new information on prisoners.[95] She often turned to sympathetic
experts, such as Hugh O'Shaughnessy on Latin America, or Francis
Noel-Baker on Greece, but found the 'communist-inspired' Spanish,
Portuguese and Greek Amnesty groups less cooperative: 'they disliked
our approach totally'. By July 1961 Marsh had some 400 names in the
index: by November this had risen to almost 1000, and she was appealing
for more assistance.[96] The Library turned into an Investigation
Department at the end of 1963, by which point it had amassed information on 2800 cases from 83 countries.[97] Benenson initially intended to
transfer the office to a building close to the UN Human Rights Division in
New York, while other elements would relocate to the Netherlands.[98]

While the Library expanded, Amnesty raised its profile through international conferences and overseas missions. The conferences, on topics
such as religious persecution and – separately – on the restrictions on
freedom in the East, the West and the Third World, appealed to an
academic and professional audience and helped to define Amnesty's
remit, but they declined in number after the end of 1961. Benenson and
Baker also overreached themselves when a major conference on the
'Boundaries of Freedom', scheduled for Utrecht or Leiden at the year's
end, was cancelled and transmuted into a far less ambitious event held in
London.[99] Conversely, the missions proliferated from 1962 onwards.
Benenson, as a result of his experiences during the 1950s, had already
decided that Amnesty should not be involved with sending observers to
trials – a task for the ICJ – but approved of missions that might result in
a prisoner release.[100] These missions generated information, attracted
publicity, sometimes produced beneficial results and gave a role to prominent supporters such as Gerald Gardiner who were unable to devote
time to committee work. MacBride's mission to Prague in February 1962
started a process that eventually lead to the release of Archbishop Beran
(initially, in October 1963, into house arrest). Moreover, according to
Benenson, the Beran case was a 'turning point' for Amnesty, as it 'proved
to the doubters that we were able to influence events on the other side of
the Iron Curtain'.[101] Other missions produced more heat than light –

following a visit to Portugal Neville Vincent wrote an article in *The Spectator* that was highly critical of alleged human rights abuses, only to attract a vicious counter-attack by Lord Russell of Liverpool.[102] However, in the absence of formal protocols or regulations these early initiatives always carried a risk, and had a distinct air of cloak and dagger. For instance, when Benenson went to Papa Doc's Haiti he used his love of painting to pose as a tourist; and when he was barred from entering Portugal Kathleen Rowlands went in his place, in the guise of 'a gay explorer of the country's tourist potential'.[103] Benenson produced a hard-hitting report on Haiti, but had to apologise to the British authorities for the diplomatic embarrassment caused by his subterfuge.[104] Overall, however, the success of some of the missions enhanced a positive narrative around Amnesty's early years. Benenson's early fears that there was no mechanism whereby prisoners could be released had proven unfounded. Although it was very difficult to prove Amnesty's role – it made a point of not boasting of its achievements – after five years Amnesty claimed that 2000 prisoners had been adopted and some 800 released.[105]

Amnesty's success in working towards prisoner releases – for which, at least until the Campaign for the Abolition of Torture in 1973, it remained best known – has tended to obscure the fact that from the outset one of the principal goals of the Appeal for Amnesty had been to enlarge the right of asylum. Indeed, such a right was deemed essential if repressive governments were to be convinced to release their prisoners, given that they would not want to place them at liberty in their own country. Accordingly, Benenson's *Observer* article had argued that in each host country a 'central employment office' should be set up to find work for refugees – again, regimes would be more likely to let prisoners go if they were sure that they would be gainfully employed in exile and not left idle to engage in conspiracy. In July 1961 Amnesty even set up its own travel bureau called ODYSSEY, which was intended to help those seeking asylum abroad, the first beneficiaries being a family moving from Belgium to Mexico.[106] However, the emphasis on asylum was a point of contention to the League for Democracy in Greece, which pointed out that the idea of 'release into asylum' could be 'positively harmful' given that most Greek prisoners wanted to stay and fight for democracy. In any case, thousands of Greeks were already living in exile and were denied the right to return home, sometimes because they had been deprived of their nationality. In reply Benenson somewhat backtracked, conceding that asylum was not a 'final solution', but merely a 'second best' option.[107] At the Bruges Congress in September 1962 a resolution was adopted calling for the revival of the 'ancient right of asylum', while also recognising that this was a question for a larger entity such as the Council of

Europe.[108] Over time, however, and despite the efforts of local groups to assist individual prisoners seeking refuge, the asylum question became more marginal to Amnesty's work, possibly because the anticipated flood of refugees did not materialise. Even so, as we shall see, in southern Africa Amnesty continued to remain actively involved with issues related to refugees and asylum seekers.

4.3 Amnesty and Religion

From the outset it was intended that Amnesty should campaign on behalf of those imprisoned for their religious beliefs just as much as on behalf of those imprisoned for their political beliefs. Indeed, the topic for its first conference in Paris – 'religious persecution' – was chosen precisely to show that Amnesty was not only concerned with political imprisonment.[109] However, Amnesty's religious dimension went far deeper than this, as a glance at the arrangements for Amnesty's first Human Rights Day at St Martin-in-the-Fields indicates. Although that evening's principal speech was delivered by the Labour MP James Griffiths, who also lit the Amnesty candle, the other aspects were essentially spiritual: indeed, Benenson referred to the ceremony's 'Christian purpose'. Special prayers and sermon notes were circulated in advance to the religious press; during the afternoon there was a ceremony in the Crypt of St Martin's ('to preserve an interdenominational character'); the main event was held on the steps of the church to encourage Catholic participation; and the church was to remain open all night to allow meditation and prayers for the persecuted.[110] This could be seen as Amnesty displaying a few 'post-Christian accoutrements', or, more positively, as a form of the 'religionless Christianity' that Dietrich Bonhoeffer had alluded to in his final letters from prison.[111] But a full understanding rests somewhere between Benenson's original intentions, the needs and aspirations of the emerging mass membership and the social and religious turbulence of the early 1960s, a period marked by uncertainty over how the much-vaunted 'affluence' would impact on civic and religious engagement.

Benenson never concealed his Catholicism. He was often introduced as a 'Catholic barrister', and became Treasurer of the International Secretariat of Lawyers, a branch of the Catholic cultural organisation Pax Romana.[112] The 1961 Human Rights Day sermon, with its emphasis on the damage that persecution causes to the 'personality' of the persecutor, the persecuted and the bystander, shows the imprint of a strongly Catholic approach to human rights.[113] Benenson became a close friend of Archbishop Roberts, often unburdening himself to the progressive and open-minded Jesuit, and he courted the support of the Catholic Church just as keenly as he pursued the backing of the Labour Party. He was delighted when he persuaded Cardinal Griffin to provide a special prayer for future Human Rights Days. In May 1962 he gave a talk in Swansea in which he identified Catholicism as one of five 'approaches' making up the origins of Amnesty, defining the Catholic approach as 'Holy and sincere compassion for sinners'. He even offered 'Six Catholic reasons for the Amnesty Movement'.[114] However, Catholicism shaped Benenson's personal spirituality far more than it informed the creation of Amnesty. It is striking how small a part Catholicism played in the intellectual formation of the organisation; Benenson later came to see Amnesty as essentially a product of North European, Lutheran culture.[115] Moreover, on some important issues, such as the question of political and religious persecution under ostensibly 'Catholic' dictatorships in Spain and Portugal, Benenson initially found himself at odds with his church. At the Paris conference in June 1961 Benenson welcomed – probably with some relief – the statement by Father Faidherbe, speaking on behalf of the Cardinal Archbishop of Paris, that no Catholic government could persecute Protestants in the name of the Catholic Church.[116] However, the transformative pontificate of John XXIII (1958–63) coincided with – rather than prefigured – the founding of Amnesty, which preceded both the Second Vatican Council (1962–65) and *Pacem in Terris*, John's most eloquent endorsement of human rights (1963). There appears, therefore, no reason to dispute Archbishop Roberts' assessment that, while Benenson was a devout Catholic, 'Amnesty is not a religious organisation: it's completely undenominational'.[117] Indeed, in a private letter to Clara Urquhart Benenson made clear that he did not see Amnesty 'as a means of converting others to Catholicism. There are many paths which lead to the same summit', even if, for him, Christ's path was the only 'discernible and practicable one for those of us brought up in the traditions of Western civilisation . . .'.[118]

Partly as a result of Eric Baker's involvement it was widely assumed that there was a substantial Quaker input into Amnesty, even though the Friends were slow to offer any substantive support. At the press conference to mark the launch of the Appeal for Amnesty John Foster QC commented that the campaign would 'adopt the Quaker approach'.[119] By this he presumably meant – in addition to a commitment to non-violence – traditional Quaker principles such as an obligation to follow one's conscience, to consider all sides and avoid controversy, to progress by taking small, constructive steps and to allow 'the sense of the meeting' to emerge.[120] Benenson acknowledged this in 1986 when he wrote that no specific denomination – and least of all the Church of England – could claim to have inspired Amnesty: instead, it was, 'essentially a blending of Quaker and Cistercian inspiration, that during the long silence the spirit speaks'.[121] Influenced by Baker, Benenson clearly saw Amnesty as imbued with the Quaker spirit, and this would have been reinforced by his knowledge of Archbishop Roberts' remarkable appeal in 1961 for Catholics to 'behave more like Quakers'.[122] This does not mean, however, that Benenson saw Amnesty as a vehicle for Quakerism, any more than it was for Catholicism. There is no evidence that he was ever attracted to join the Society of Friends, and as the campaign got underway Baker's unbending commitment to the highest standards of integrity caused some frictions between them. In 1963 Baker marvelled that two men so different in 'temperament, education and background' could work together at all.[123] During the interviews conducted to mark Amnesty's twentieth anniversary some of the early activists recalled Baker's dedication to principle with admiration rather than affection.[124]

In fact, both Benenson and Baker saw Amnesty as part of an ecumenical movement of spiritual renewal, challenging apathy and drawing on the best from an eclectic mixture of religious influences. Benenson's personal hero was Bonhoeffer, whose ideas were central to the religious debates of the early 1960s. But he was also devoted to St Francis, whose life and teaching were 'the epitome of religion for this day and age', and to John XXIII as the only Catholic who could reach out convincingly to non-Catholics.[125] He also admired the ability of Moral Re-Armament to organise and inspire, as well as the quiet moral determination of the Friends. Three comments from the early phase of Amnesty give a clearer guide to his thinking. First, in June 1961, responding to a leader comment in *The Times* following Michael Ramsey's appointment as Archbishop of Canterbury, Benenson wrote that 'Christianity is not on the defensive, but on the offensive'. The recent Amnesty conference in Paris, he added, was a small part of the 'Oecumenical movement ... an upsurge of the spirit which rises into the sky in a great column which over-towers even the Nuclear "mushroom"'.[126] Secondly, in summing up the first phase of Amnesty, Benenson wrote that the greatest achievement was generating 'a spirit of co-operative endeavour which has brought together men and women of so many different views, religions and nationalities ... [At the vigil around the Amnesty candle] Protestant clergymen, Catholics and Rabbis stood side by side with humanists, Conservatives next to Socialists and White, Black and Yellow races shoulder to shoulder'.[127] Finally, in his 1962 Swansea speech he returned to the theme that it was by 'struggling for the freedom of others, that we shall free ourselves. For this common struggle unites all the Christian churches, and when the unity of the church is finally and miraculously restored, then perhaps the imprisoned truth within us will be released'.[128] This suggests that his initial ideas about the 'true' purpose of Amnesty had not changed, and that he continued to believe that through the struggle for human rights lay both personal liberation and international religious harmony.

It is difficult to tell whether Amnesty's activists subscribed to Benenson's religious aspirations (in so far as they were aware of them), or simply regarded them as a religious gloss on an essentially secular endeavour. Information on Amnesty's early local groups and activists is limited, but there is no question that they were often rooted in local churches and Quaker meetings. The Eltham group, for instance, regarded itself as a 'committed Christian company'. It met in a Congregational Church vestry, was chaired by the minister, Ronald Ward, and its early meetings opened and closed with a prayer.[129] The Kensington group was said to have been founded in 1966 'from the members and friends of an ecumenical lay community in Notting Hill', and to have eventually merged with another group based in the local Unitarian Church.[130] At the Catholic Church of Our Lady of the Wayside, in Shirley in the West Midlands, a group of parishioners established an Amnesty group after reading Pope John XXIII's *Pacem in Terris*. This decision formed part of the parishioners' impressively wide humanitarian engagement with the developing world, strongly encouraged by their priest, Fr Patrick O'Mahoney.[131] Amnesty also attracted figures of religious standing, some of whom were already travelling somewhat different paths from Benenson. Eric Baker said that Amnesty developed 'under the benign encouragement of Dr Ernest Payne', a leading Baptist closely involved in the international ecumenical movement and longstanding Trustee of the Prisoners of Conscience Fund.[132] Keith Siviter, a Congregationalist minister, came to work full-time for Amnesty and eventually resigned from the Church after losing his faith. He described himself as becoming 'a revolutionary in Church ways and life' in the later 1950s, abandoning traditional ceremonies and guiding his congregation towards 'outreach' to the developing world.[133] The Rev. Paul Oestreicher, an Anglican Jew whose family had fled Germany for New Zealand in 1939, was ordained into the Church of England in 1959 and became the Chairman of Amnesty's British Section in 1974. He had a successful career in religious broadcasting for the BBC in the early 1960s and, with a long-standing interest in the relationship between Marxism and Christianity, was involved in many radical political causes.

Even so, many of those who joined Amnesty early on were motivated more by humanitarian instincts than by religious devotion. It is not surprising, therefore, that as Amnesty became better organised and more geared to the practical question of how to secure the release of prisoners, its overt religious dimension – rather like the early emphasis on asylum – declined in significance. It is likely that this, in turn, contributed to Benenson's growing disenchantment with Amnesty by the mid-1960s. His comment in 1967, following his departure from Amnesty, that he had always regarded it as 'a part of the Christian witness' could therefore be interpreted as both defiant and regretful.[134]

The high point of Amnesty's public religiosity was the service at St Paul's Cathedral to mark the 1964 Human Rights Day. Not only did the Order of Service leave little room for the prisoners of conscience, but the guest list of diplomats and civic functionaries indicated that Benenson was seeking to win over the secular establishment as well as the Established Church.[135] Perhaps sensing a misstep, the following year's event was presented as being 'of a more secular nature'.[136] The ebb and flow of Amnesty's religious engagement is not, therefore, necessarily at odds with some of the recent accounts of secularisation in Britain. Callum Brown, in particular, has emphasised the extent of religious revival that took place between the end of World War II and the late 1950s, when there was a boom in church attendances, Anglican confirmations and Sunday school enrolments. This was followed by a precipitous decline – identified by Brown and others as a full-blown religious crisis – in the mid-to-late 1960s, in which these gains were reversed and there was a collapse in the authority and associational culture of the Christian churches. Amnesty's rise, therefore, lies on the cusp of the momentous changes triggered by affluence, independent youth cultures, women's liberation and the decline of deference.[137] However, Amnesty did not become a 'secular' organisation overnight, even if Benenson's departure and the organisation's rapid internationalisation both pointed in this direction. A survey of Amnesty's British members in 1978 showed that a far higher proportion were regular church attenders than in the population as a whole.[138] Indeed, in the late 1970s the British Section forged even stronger links with the churches. The initiative may have come from Oestreicher, but – more importantly – by now change was being driven by the desire of the churches to engage more fully with human rights.[139]

4.4   Amnesty Goes International

To launch a new national movement with only a few months' planning and limited resources was very bold: to launch it simultaneously as an international movement looked foolhardy. And yet the gamble paid off, and, at a stroke, Amnesty set itself apart from all potential rivals. In principle, such a leap was necessary to fulfil Benenson's original vision, as experience had shown that a multinational approach would greatly increase the moral and political pressure on governments. Benenson had done some preparatory work, and even before the launch of the appeal knew that there would be a French Section (albeit one that did not flourish).[140] Beyond that, it was unclear what to expect: in August 1961 Benenson wondered whether Rumanians would be allowed to cooperate with Amnesty. He suspected not, but he still hoped that, when there was a thaw in the Cold War, 'individuals in Soviet Countries will be allowed to contact us, and even form National Sections'.[141] In the face of so much uncertainty, the small international meeting held in Luxembourg in June 1961 was a small but highly significant step. Nascent national sections were created in many West European countries, and in September 1962 a far more impressive gathering in Bruges gave birth to Amnesty International. The development of the new international organisation is not central to this book, but it is clearly essential to look at this opening phase, if only to understand how it impacted on Amnesty as an essentially British organisation. This is particularly important given the delineation that took place in 1963 between the British-based Amnesty International and its new 'British Section'.

On 22–23 June 1961, less than one month after the publication of 'The Forgotten Prisoners', small contingents from Britain, Ireland, West Germany, Belgium and France met at the Café Carrefour in Luxembourg, chosen for its central location. Benenson drove to Luxembourg with Peggy Crane, Neville Vincent and MacBride, and Eric Baker joined them from a tour of Germany.[142] They were joined by the Belgians Louis Kiebooms and Herman Todts, the German journalists Gerd Ruge and Carola Stern, the French lawyer Nicolas Jacob, and Gabriel Javsicas from New York. MacBride, who had only contacted Benenson in early June, took the chair.[143] Soon after the event Benenson wrote that the meeting was 'remarkable in the unanimity of its participants, and their enthusiasm to get on with the job', but what had been decided?[144] According to the official communiqué, three steps were agreed: a request to all governments to furnish information about relevant laws and the available judicial safeguards; a financial appeal in October to fund support for prisoners' families, the Library and formal representations to governments; and a fundraising week, scheduled for 24–31 December. Strangely, no mention was made of Human Rights Day at this point.[145] However, MacBride soon put a more grandiose spin on things. The 'most important aspect . . . was the birth of an international movement dedicated to the preservation of liberty'. Such a movement, he added, could have prevented the Nazi concentration camps if it had only existed in the 1930s. As for other decisions, MacBride both glossed and expanded the colourless communiqué in his article. There would be a 'world census of "Prisoners of Conscience"', and preventive action, targeting the emerging African states, to show that old colonial practices were not acceptable. This was no longer a campaign to free 'a few isolated prisoners', but a movement to secure the freedom of 'countless thousands' across twenty countries. MacBride had asserted himself, and while Benenson would have approved of his ambition, MacBride's agenda seemed rather more redolent of the ICJ.[146]

Both Benenson and Baker travelled widely to encourage and develop new national sections. These tended to be built on their existing contacts, whether lawyers (through Justice and the ICJ), international organisations in Switzerland, journalists and Quaker meetings. According to a report in May 1962, twelve national sections had been set up, but only two – in Australia and Ireland – worked 'effectively'. The failure of the French Section caused particular concern: in the report this was attributed to the political situation in France (the consolidation of de Gaulle's Fifth Republic and the violence associated with the end of French rule in Algeria), but Benenson later recalled that many extreme right-wing Catholics had been attracted to join.[147] Indeed, one of the early problems facing Amnesty was that in Europe the name was widely associated with campaigns for an amnesty for wartime collaborators, and that it was prone to infiltration by those seeking to promote that goal. The Belgian section was held back by the fact that it only attracted support in Flemish-speaking areas of the country. The US Section was also slow to develop, despite Benenson's visit to New York in September 1961, and even when it did begin to take off in the mid-1960s, its preferred modus operandi was lobbying rather than the standard adoption of prisoners of conscience.[148] By contrast, the German Section, which had registered soon after the Luxembourg meeting, based in Cologne with groups in Hamburg and Munich, developed into one of the largest national sections. It was helped by Hilary Cartwright, who lived in Germany for much of 1963 and was a member of the Cologne 'Threes' group. Just as impressive was the development of the Scandinavian sections in the mid-1960s, and the Dutch Section following its relaunch in 1968.[149]

Given these hesitant beginnings, Amnesty's 'Second International Conference', held at the Chateau de Male near Bruges, 28–30 September 1962, sumptuously hosted by the Belgian section, was a remarkable success. The conference was attended by sixty delegates, and numerous international organisations, including the Council of Europe (at which Amnesty was seeking to gain consultant status), were represented. Benenson was in his element, using the conference to call on governments to respect Articles 18 and 19 of the Universal Declaration of Human Rights, at a time when persecution on the grounds of race, colour and political intolerance 'appear to be increasing'. He summoned Amnesty's supporters to isolate and kill the 'virus' of prejudice, even if 'this meant some personal sacrifice'. The conference's most important decision – to establish an organisation called 'Amnesty International' (the name suggested by Andrew Martin[150]) with a draft Statute – was left to last, but a range of other proposals was also agreed. The UN was urged to adopt an International Code of Conduct for treatment of those suspected of being a danger to state security; concern was expressed at the erosion of the right to asylum; a World Human Rights Fund would be set up under the aegis of a group of Nobel Peace Prize winners; and initiatives would be taken to promote education in human rights and their international commemoration.[151] For Benenson, Bruges represented the 'regular establishment' of the Amnesty movement.[152] From January 1963 Amnesty International consisted of an International Secretariat, including the all-important Library, and based for the time being in London; a five-strong and genuinely international executive committee; and national sections (including for the first time Britain) which would be represented each year at international conferences. Yet new challenges were implicit in these arrangements. In particular, in January 1962 Benenson had expressed the belief that the new movement would remain 'one of ideals', and that 'unlike other international organisations it is determined not to become bogged down in constitutional wrangles and international power tussles'.[153] And yet, as the organisational structures became more complex, and the range of actors (both in Britain and internationally) became ever wider and less predictable, the question of accountability could not be easily avoided.

*

In August 1961 Benenson wrote to Eric Baker that they were both 'already engaged upon a great number of ventures, anyone of which, if so considered, might become a life's work'.[154] This was certainly true of both men, although from 1963 onwards Baker was somewhat constrained by accepting a lectureship at a college in Dagenham.[155] For Benenson, however, this continued to be a period of remarkable achievement and intense creativity. It is striking to note how, whereas Amnesty may well have appeared like a 'life's work', during the early 1960s he not only maintained his involvement with existing interests (such as Justice) but was also constantly alive to new initiatives. Some of these were potential business opportunities, such as the managing editorship of Lord Weidenfeld's 'Home University Library', or the publication of a series of 'Common Market' Law Reports.[156] Some were projects for Justice, to fulfil his promise not to let it 'grind to a standstill' while he concentrated on Amnesty. For instance, he proposed a movement called 'Scrutiny' to campaign for a court of last resort, or a 'Public Service Bureau' until the office of Ombudsman was created.[157] But others were ideas for activist-led projects that would – when they could not be accommodated within it – complement Amnesty or develop his wider vision of promoting global tolerance and an international 'community of conscience'. These ideas included an organisation 'separate from AMNESTY' dedicated to racial tolerance,[158] an organisation in support of concentration camp survivors,[159] and numerous proposals to benefit Africa developed in association with Clara Urquhart. One of these proposals that did come to fruition, and appears to have escaped notice until now, was Human Rights Policy Planning, which brought together international organisations in the human rights field on an informal basis.[160] Another, which we will return to in Chapter 5, was the Human Rights Advisory Service. These 'subsidiary ideas' (as Norman Marsh put it) were proof of Benenson's energy and intellectual fertility, but they raised questions as to his focus, and the sustainability of his style of leadership: a role that he increasingly wished to stand back from.[161]

5   'The Crisis of Growth': Amnesty International 1964–1968

5.1   Amnesty's Crisis, 1966–1967

In September 1964 the journalist Jack Halpern was appointed as Amnesty's General Secretary. The need for a new executive officer was becoming acute as Peter Benenson was currently in poor health and went on leave during the summer. In September Amnesty's conference awarded Benenson the post of President of the International Executive, a new 'advisory' position which had no defined constitutional role.[1] In many regards Halpern had strong credentials to lead an organisation promoting human rights. He was a South African Jew who had fled Nazi Germany as a boy, and – as a vocal opponent of white minority rule in southern Africa – had recently been expelled from Rhodesia.[2] During his brief tenure he had to negotiate a difficult challenge at Amnesty's conference, where it was decided that Nelson Mandela could no longer be deemed a 'prisoner of conscience' due to his support for armed struggle.[3] Even so, Halpern relished his job and in late October 1964 embarked on a tour of Amnesty's Scandinavian sections. However, he set off in the painful knowledge that Benenson had lost confidence in him and wanted to terminate his employment with immediate effect. As Halpern told Neville Vincent, 'you can imagine, I think, in what frame of mind I go'.[4] Following an intervention by Sean MacBride on his return, Halpern was allowed to serve out his six-month contract working on research projects that were never likely to come to fruition.

What had gone so swiftly and disastrously wrong? Halpern blamed his downfall on Benenson's inability to step back from Amnesty – given that he carried 'so much of the organisation in his own head'. He also believed that he had received no support from committees dominated by Benenson's friends.[5] For Benenson's part, he claimed that he had been forced to return as 'Chief Executive' due to complaints about Halpern's poor performance from the other office staff.[6] In any case, Halpern, who had been strongly recommended by Ambrose Reeves, former Bishop of Johannesburg, had not been Benenson's first choice. He would have preferred to appoint Hilary Cartwright, but her promotion was blocked by others in the office.[7] Benenson certainly felt more comfortable with Robert Swann, Halpern's successor, who was appointed in October 1965, and whose efficiency permitted Benenson to spend more time on his farm near Oxford. Swann was a Catholic Old Etonian socialist who had worked for the Foreign Office in Bangkok. What he did not initially disclose to Benenson was that he had previously been a British intelligence agent, a pertinent fact that he only revealed in March 1966.[8] Halpern's unhappy experience at Amnesty may have appeared as a mere blip had it not – by raising questions about Benenson's willingness to stand aside and his ability to work within bureaucratic structures – prefigured the much more dangerous crisis of 1966–67. The following section will give a brief overview of the crisis, while the remainder of the chapter will explore some of the implications both for Amnesty and for human rights activism more generally.[9]

The roots of the crisis lay in Amnesty's response to two separate conflicts at the end of Empire, in Rhodesia and Aden. In Rhodesia a white minority government under Ian Smith had defied Harold Wilson's Labour government by issuing a Unilateral Declaration of Independence (UDI) on 11 November 1965. Britain responded by imposing sanctions, which proved ineffective, but ruled out any settlement by force. Amnesty was already concerned about the treatment of political prisoners and detainees, and it provided local assistance through a relief worker (Hugh Vodden) for the first nine months of 1965. Following the UDI Benenson secured funding from the British government to support Amnesty's work inside Rhodesia. Crucially, at the insistence of the government, which was afraid of being seen to intervene in Rhodesia's internal affairs, it was agreed that the source of the funds should be kept secret. The money was distributed to prisoners and their families, in association with Jack Grant's Christian Council of Churches,[10] by a team of young British volunteers: these included Polly Toynbee (the future *Guardian* journalist), Aidan Foster-Carter (who became a leading expert on North Korea) and Antonia Caccia (daughter of Lord Caccia, the Provost of Eton and former permanent under-secretary at the Foreign Office). The funding for what Benenson christened 'Operation Lordship' was agreed at the highest levels in government and handled personally by the Cabinet Secretary Sir Burke Trend. The minister with the most direct personal involvement was the Attorney General (and a member of both Amnesty and Justice) Frederick Elwyn Jones.[11] Benenson was told that the money came from an anonymous donor, who – for reasons that remain unclear – he believed to be the hotelier Charles Forte. However, in the first instance at least, the funds came directly from government sources. The work started well and expanded to include legal support for opponents of the Smith regime. Benenson filed a series of optimistic situation reports, but in March 1966 the Rhodesian authorities closed the offices in Salisbury and Bulawayo and expelled the volunteers. Even so, the secret funding – despite mounting technical exchange problems – continued until later in the year.[12] Doubts about the source of the money clearly preyed on Benenson's mind, as in January 1967 he attempted, unsuccessfully, to repay it from his own pocket.[13]

In the Crown Colony of Aden meanwhile, where British forces were struggling to suppress an Arab nationalist uprising, a state of emergency had been in operation since December 1963. Between 1963 and 1966 Peter Benenson consistently lobbied the British government to allow a delegation from the International Committee of the Red Cross (ICRC) to visit the region and carry out an independent evaluation of the treatment of detainees.[14] In the summer of 1966 the Swedish Section of Amnesty sent a doctor of Kurdish origin, Selahaddin Rastgeldi, to the colony to investigate allegations of torture, and Amnesty's British Section agreed to pay half of the costs.[15] Rastgeldi returned with compelling evidence of ill treatment. However, Benenson was shocked at the way in which the British government sought to discredit him: indeed, when Rastgeldi was interviewed on BBC television, Benenson immediately received a telephone call at home from Christopher Mayhew, the recently resigned Labour defence minister and a member of Amnesty, who tried to persuade him that Rastgeldi could not be believed.[16] Benenson visited Aden himself in November, and claimed that the authorities were running a system of 'apartheid' against the Arab population 'far more cruel and humiliating than that which Smith applies in Rhodesia'.[17] On his return he filed a complaint against the British government with the European Court of Human Rights in Strasbourg for invasion of Rastgeldi's privacy.[18] When the Swedish Section published Rastgeldi's findings, the British government sought to defuse the row by commissioning an independent report by the Welsh lawyer Roderic Bowen, a former Liberal MP and another member of Justice. The significance of Bowen's report has been debated by historians, but at the time his conclusions were ambiguous enough to be presented by both the government and Amnesty as a vindication of their claims.[19]

Benenson now began to discern a disturbing pattern of events. He became convinced that Amnesty's General Secretary Robert Swann had deliberately mishandled Rastgeldi's report on Aden – either by belittling or, indeed, initially concealing it. Recalling Swann's links to British intelligence, he claimed that Swann and other members of Amnesty's staff were working to undermine Amnesty. He made a connection to another very worrying episode that had been unfolding at the same time, concerning Niels Groth, a member of the Danish Amnesty Section who had offered to carry out an investigation in Guinea into the fate of Koumanian Keita, Amnesty's 'Prisoner of the Year'. Groth, a lawyer who had been Amnesty's first representative at the UN, was arrested in Guinea on 18 July 1966 and imprisoned for more than two months as an alleged spy. Although he was released on 1 October, the episode reflected poorly on Amnesty's preparations for such missions, as Groth had proceeded to Guinea without a visa and with no formal instructions or accreditation. However, Benenson now surmised that Soviet intelligence, aware of Swann's activities, had tipped off the Guinean authorities that all those associated with Amnesty should be treated with suspicion.[20] By now, Benenson's objectives were twofold: first, a purging of the office and, secondly, for Amnesty's headquarters to move to a 'neutral' country, away from the meddling of British intelligence. In December 1966 senior figures in Amnesty, fearful of the damage which Benenson might cause both to himself and to the organisation, scrambled to contain the situation. Sean MacBride persuaded him to resign as President and to take a 'sabbatical' from his responsibilities, although Benenson later reneged on the agreement. As the crisis deepened, in January 1967 the British Section appointed a 'special chairman's committee' to provide guidance.[21] This title gave some respectability to the unelected 'Godfathers', senior figures who knew both Amnesty and Benenson well but who, on this occasion, ultimately refused to take his side. MacBride, who travelled frequently in his capacity as Chairman of the Geneva-based ICJ, left Eric Baker (Chairman of the British Section) in charge in London as his trusted deputy.

Matters came to a head in the spring of 1967 with two unforeseen and explosive developments. First, revelations were published in the *New York Times* on 19 February about the CIA's secret funding of the ICJ. MacBride immediately denied that his organisation was 'an instrument' of the CIA. However, Benenson, now seeing MacBride as another hostile agent, called on him to resign as Chairman of the Amnesty IEC and announced that he was resuming 'the active Presidency'.[22] Secondly, barely two weeks later, extracts from letters that had been taken from the Amnesty office in Salisbury by Polly Toynbee were published in two British Sunday newspapers. The published letters, written by Benenson to Swann, exposed the inner workings of 'Operation Lordship' in painful detail. The letters, which, using a comically transparent code, referred to Harold Wilson's government as 'Harry', threatened to destroy Benenson's credibility, just as MacBride's had been undermined by the ICJ revelations. Toynbee also gave an interview in which she claimed that

Amnesty's operations in Rhodesia had been chaotic: 'there was no one to check up on what I did with the money. I could have spent it on myself'.[23] Arguably, her claims of inefficiency and poor financial control caused just as much consternation amongst ordinary Amnesty members and donors as the 'Harry' letters. The Prime Minister survived the affair unscathed as, with a carefully composed – and unchallenged – statement to Parliament, Wilson was able to argue that all that the British government had done was to put Amnesty in touch with 'possible donors'.[24] Amnesty also disclaimed any knowledge of the funds' origin: Benenson was left isolated.[25]

Fortunately, a solution to the crisis was at hand. In early February 1967 David Astor asked Michael Scott to offer his services to 'minimise' the damage to Amnesty 'and other similar organisations'. On 5 February Scott, MacBride and Hilary Cartwright met Benenson in Geneva.[26] As a result, Benenson agreed that the lawyer and writer Peter Calvocoressi should prepare an independent report into his allegations.[27] Calvocoressi was a very suitable choice as he was trusted by all sides and had a formidable record as a former Nuremberg prosecutor, a member of the UN Commission for the Protection of Human Rights and Chairman of the Africa Bureau. Like Benenson, he also had experience as a wartime intelligence officer at Bletchley Park. His report, which remained secret for many years, was presented to Amnesty's International Executive Committee in Elsinore, Denmark, on 12–13 March 1967. Calvocoressi found against Benenson on the central issues raised. Benenson, he concluded, had pursued his suspicions 'the wrong way and intemperately', and his 'ill-founded suspicions' had placed Amnesty in 'some jeopardy'. Swann was, Calvocoressi determined, no longer working for British intelligence, and there was no attempt by British intelligence to 'annex or abuse Amnesty'. The IEC endorsed Calvocoressi's findings and Benenson ceased to be Amnesty President. Indeed, the IEC abolished the office and created the new post of Director General (to be held, initially, by Eric Baker). However, Swann was also criticised by Calvocoressi because, although he had served Amnesty loyally, his former employment by British intelligence 'was and is potentially dangerous to Amnesty'. The report recommended that he should remain in post for the immediate future, but by now Swann was finished. He gave a press conference after the IEC meeting that was both unconvincing and misleading and – as Calvocoressi privately predicted he would – resigned a few months later.[28] The complaint to Strasbourg against the British government was also quietly dropped. Benenson, who had refused to attend the Elsinore meeting, still had some supporters, notably in the small French Section, but accepted the outcome with dignity.

Calvocoressi's report had succeeded in resolving the immediate crisis, but it should be noted that – operating as a 'one-man commission' from his own flat – he lacked access to much significant information. He also had barely a month to pursue his investigations. Accordingly, many of his judgements were made through the application of Ockham's razor and on the 'balance of probability'.[29] Moreover, although MacBride knew about the secret British government funding when he commissioned the Calvocoressi report, he did not add it to the terms of reference. Accordingly, while Calvocoressi was clearly aware of the funding, he passed no judgement in his report.[30] The report's emphasis on Benenson's temporary mental aberration (he 'had too much on his mind, so that his judgement became fallible') suited Amnesty's immediate needs for a simple explanation, however unpalatable. As Baker wrote at the time, the problem was a 'sudden and disastrous change in Peter himself, the principal architect in whom we all trusted'.[31] However, this rationale left many questions unanswered. Indeed, one of the report's major recommendations – that there should be an urgent inquiry into the role of the intelligence services 'in relation to professional and charitable bodies and to the liberties of the citizen'[32] – does not appear to have ever been carried out.

The crisis, which, after all, struck when Amnesty was still a very young organisation, could have caused fatal damage. However, the evidence for the seriousness of its impact is mixed. Within Britain, all the senior figures within Amnesty supported MacBride and the IEC against Benenson. Moreover, letters and resolutions from branches indicate satisfaction that the crisis had been resolved and that it would be 'business as usual' for the all-important work on behalf of prisoners.[33] Regret was mixed with a new sense of purpose: in the words of one local activist 'while Peter Benenson was our guiding light it was his movement. Now he is gone, it is ours'.[34] The British Section experienced only a small fall in membership, but suffered financially as it found it difficult to attract new donors in the immediate wake of the crisis.[35] Eric Baker anticipated some criticism at the meeting of the British Section in June 1967 but thought that few critics would 'desert the ship'.[36] Even so, relations with both the Labour Party and government were badly shaken, and the 'discreet support' previously offered by government was suspended.[37] Internationally, the crisis was said to have had 'disastrous' repercussions in the Dutch Section, where the steering committee was 'decimated' by resignations.[38] However, the Irish Section, one of the largest at this point, was already preoccupied with the sudden death of its most influential member, Karin O'Donovan. The loss of this key figure (the Section's Chairman even feared that her death would cause its collapse), was compounded by mounting internal disagreements over Irish Republican politics. From the Irish standpoint, therefore, Amnesty had experienced a 'storm in a teacup blown up into a tornado' by the press.[39] More generally, the crisis left many European Amnesty sections angry and confused: angry that divisions within a wholly British leadership should have imperilled the work of the international movement and confused about the exact role of previously unknown forces such as the 'Godfathers'. This gave rise to a certain flexing of muscles, and at Elsinore the Swedish Section sought unsuccessfully to prevent MacBride from taking the chair (presumably due to the allegations against the ICJ). It was agreed at that meeting that the next Director General should be Scandinavian, although in the absence of a suitable candidate, Baker's (and Swann's) place was eventually taken in 1968 by another Briton, Martin Ennals. By this time, the two senior posts had been rolled into a single Secretary General, funded at a total cost of £5000 per year by the national sections.

Baker's willingness to step into the breach, after MacBride had appointed him as his plenipotentiary in December 1966, was crucial to the successful handling of the crisis. He was trusted by all parties and, as one of the founders of Amnesty, carried considerable weight. He was also seen as a figure of unimpeachable rectitude: Neville Vincent's tribute after Elsinore that Baker was a 'great moral tonic' echoes Benenson's of a few years previously that without Baker's 'absolute determination' he would have sailed Amnesty into 'the shelter of a more convenient port'.[40] Baker's detailed notes from the crisis illustrate just how much he was at the centre of events, defending Swann and twice persuading MacBride not to resign, while also doing his best to protect Benenson. However, even Baker knew more than he was willing to admit in public. For instance, after the newspaper revelations in March 1967 he took every opportunity to state that Amnesty knew nothing about the secret government funds, but a letter written two months earlier reveals that Benenson, as part of his 'sabbatical' handover, had briefed Baker about 'Money for Rhodesia'. Benenson made clear that there was still money available as he had 'hustled a lot through in November before putting a halt to funds from secret sources controlled by H. M. Government' when Harold Wilson engaged in talks with Smith on board HMS Tiger on 2–4 December 1966.[41] The money, which had continued to come in from Amnesty groups, and which was currently lodged in the 'Fund for the Persecuted', 'properly speaking belongs to "Amnesty"' and he would arrange for it to be paid into an Amnesty account.[42] It should also be noted that Baker was approached by a journalist from the *Sunday Telegraph* some days before it published its story, who told him that the paper had 'direct evidence' that the British government had sent money to Rhodesia via Amnesty. Baker told him that he did not 'know what to say', but agreed that it would be 'damaging if it were true'.[43] This all sits uneasily with Baker's letter to British Amnesty members of 20 March in which he endorsed Harold Wilson's evasive account of the affair to Parliament: 'whether there is any more of the matter than that I cannot say with certainty'.[44] The absence of any discussion of the Rhodesian funding revelations in the Calvocoressi report is understandable, given that it was not included in the terms of reference, but the lack of any recorded discussion at the IEC meeting on 12–13 March is perplexing. Clearly, if Amnesty were to continue, some matters were simply too sensitive to discuss openly.

5.2   'Cloak and Dagger': Amnesty, the Labour Government and the State

Should Amnesty have accepted secret British government funds for its work in Rhodesia, and had it fallen victim to improper pressures from intelligence agencies? These questions go to the heart of not only the Amnesty crisis, but, more generally, of relations between all human rights organisations and the state. Interestingly, in March 1966 the IEC had discussed whether Amnesty should accept any state funding at all, after the Swedish government offered 1 million krona, and it was agreed that this should be decided on a case-by-case basis.[45] There was, therefore, no blanket ban on such arrangements. With regard to the secret British funding, Amnesty's own position on this issue was far from clear. On 6 March 1967 Eric Baker issued a letter to Amnesty members in his capacity as Chairman of the British Section in which he wrote that while the (British) Executive Committee 'knew nothing' about the government funds, he could not 'prejudge what decision it would have come to if it had known'. In a draft version he was more open: 'Amnesty however would *probably not on that account alone* [i.e., secrecy] have declined to receive such money, on the basis that the relief of suffering in Rhodesia was of prime importance, and that gifts for such non-political purposes would not have in any way hindered or affected the work of Amnesty'.[46] In an interview during the March 1967 IEC, however, MacBride stated that the International Executive knew nothing of the secret funds and – if Polly Toynbee's allegations were true – 'these activities must have been undertaken *on the private initiative* of Mr. Benenson'.[47] For his part, in one of his few comments on the episode, Benenson stated that he had asked for £20,000 for the families of 'H. M. l[o]yal subjects detained in Rhodesia', and saw 'nothing wrong in the receipt of monies for relief purposes'.[48] This argument – that the greater good outweighed ethical or political concerns about such funding – convinced many at the time, and has continued to do so since. For instance, the musician and humanitarian Yehudi Menuhin told Baker that Amnesty should not worry about the sources of its funding because in the 'commercial capitalist world . . . money remains anonymous and non-committal'.[49] It is also noteworthy that in 1969, under the new leadership of Martin Ennals, Amnesty unsuccessfully sought further funding for Rhodesian prisoners from the British government. Ennals was fully cognisant of the earlier debacle, but 'he did not personally feel either then or now that help of this kind in any way infringed Amnesty's independence'.[50] But even if the funding was acceptable, it had been poorly handled and – when revealed – left Amnesty in considerable danger. As MacBride put it, it was 'praiseworthy' that funds had been obtained to help the families of detainees, but unfortunate that it was 'done in such a way' as to cast doubt on the 'role and efficiency of Amnesty'.[51]

Before turning to a deeper exploration of Amnesty's relationship with the state, however, a brief digression as to sources is necessary. Links between Amnesty and the intelligence community are extremely difficult to document, although its links with one particular secretive government agency – the Information Research Department (IRD) – are more fully recorded. Although more information on Amnesty's crisis has become available in recent years, one significant gap has so far been the absence of any account by Benenson himself. For instance, he said nothing about the crisis during the Amnesty oral history project of the early 1980s. However, Benenson did in fact write two lengthy accounts shortly after the crisis, and the fact that they only appear to have survived in the papers of Michael Scott is itself of interest. Scott had played a small part in Amnesty – for instance, he and Benenson had both taken part in the TV programme *Persecution 1963* – but his contribution had been restricted by the considerable time that he spent in Nagaland during the mid-1960s. Benenson, who had got to know Scott through Clara Urquhart, warmly welcomed him on his return after his expulsion from India in 1965.[52] By the time of the crisis, both men had become unhealthily prone to seeing the secret hand of the state at work. In January 1967, for instance, Benenson approvingly reported Scott's belief, following his most recent visit to the UN in New York, that the Vietnam War had been caused by the 'take-over' by the US State Department of an American relief committee in Vietnam.[53] When asked by David Astor to intervene in the Amnesty crisis Scott appears to have briefly forged a close relationship with Benenson, perhaps on the basis that both men were – in Benenson's words – 'sensitive people, neither in the first blush of youth' who had been bruised by tough political realities. In April 1967 Benenson wrote to Scott that 'recent events have brought me the great gain of your friendship, and I look forward to its long continuation'.[54] There is no evidence that the friendship did continue, but it seems likely that – in the belief that he was one of the few who could understand his recent experiences – Benenson felt able to unburden himself to Scott.[55]

Peter Benenson never displayed any inhibition in using his personal and political connections to advance Amnesty's interests. When the Appeal for Amnesty was launched in 1961 he had written to Prime Minister Harold Macmillan as a fellow Etonian and Balliol student and had received a supportive – but guarded – reply. Macmillan fully understood that overt links with government could damage Amnesty's independence, but Benenson was not deterred, noting that this should not prevent 'private understandings' or shared 'ultimate objectives'.[56] However, the situation became more propitious when Harold Wilson's Labour government secured a small majority in October 1964. Wilson, who was far more internationalist than the defeated Conservatives, understood the significance of the United Nations and of human rights. Although Benenson does not appear to have been on close terms with Wilson, he had many personal friends in the new government, such as Roy Jenkins (reforming Home Secretary 1965–67), whom he knew from Balliol and Bletchley Park.[57] Moreover, the government's law officers were all old allies from Justice and Amnesty: Gerald Gardiner (Lord Chancellor), Elwyn Jones (Attorney General) and Dingle Foot (Solicitor General). The Labour government embarked on a much-needed overhaul of the legal system, delivering many of the reforms that Justice had been campaigning for such as the introduction of the Law Commission (Amnesty's Andrew Martin and Norman Marsh were both founding commissioners) and an Ombudsman. In January 1966 Gardiner told the Society of Labour Lawyers that 'so great a programme of reform has never ... been carried through before in such a short space of time'.[58] It is hardly surprising, therefore, that Benenson should have believed that this was a time of great opportunity for Amnesty. However, this also meant that it was easy for him to become overconfident and overreach himself. For instance, during the dispute over Aden he claimed that he had visited Foreign Secretary George Brown on 29 September and mentioned to him as a 'negotiating bluff' that 'if Britain made reasonable steps to put things right in Aden, he would use his influence to see that Rastgeldi's report was not published'. If true, this was highly unwise, as Benenson did not actually have a copy of the report, and the Swedish Section – which did – could not necessarily be expected to play along.[59]

According to Anthony Marreco, Amnesty's Treasurer in the late 1960s, Benenson 'always liked to dramatize things and give him a "cloak and dagger" implication [*sic*]'.[60] Buoyed up by Amnesty's initial success, he certainly became prone to a dangerous belief that, through covert lobbying, he could discreetly influence international events. A remarkable example survives in a long letter that Benenson wrote to his friend and mentor Archbishop Roberts: the playful tone does not conceal the seriousness of the intent. In November of 1964 there was a Eucharistic Congress in Bombay, attended by Pope Paul VI and senior Catholic clerics from around the world. In the light of the recent Indian annexation of Goa (December 1961) the Congress was deemed an affront to Salazar's regime and liberal Catholics in Portugal were muzzled. Benenson saw this overreaction as little short of an opportunity to bring about regime change, and laid out a strategy to Roberts, who was attending the Congress, whereby Dr Marcelo Caetano (a former ally of Salazar who had fallen out of favour and was now Rector of Lisbon University) would be promoted as an alternative leader, acceptable to the United States and Britain. Benenson proposed a three-pronged strategy. He himself would shortly visit the Foreign Office 'at the highest political level . . . and will encourage them to indicate their attitude by announcing publicly an invitation to Caetano to lecture in, say, Oxford in the spring'. Secondly, Benenson and Roberts would engineer an invitation for Caetano to speak to the Law Faculty of the Catholic University of Paris. Thirdly, Roberts would use a press conference or a '"leak" to *Time* or some such paper' to indicate that senior cardinals admired the courage of Caetano, and thereby secure papal approval. This would attract American interest, and Roberts could then refer any questions to 'that wicked fellow, the President of Amnesty'. It is not clear how Roberts responded, and nothing seems to have come of the plot. Perhaps this was for the best, as in 1970 Caetano succeeded Salazar as Prime Minister, only to be overthrown by the Armed Forces Movement coup of April 1974.[61]

Macmillan had recommended that Benenson should keep the Foreign Office's IRD informed about Amnesty, but Benenson assured him that he was already in touch, and had been since before the launch of the Appeal.[62] Despite its innocuous title, the IRD was the government department most directly involved in fighting the Cold War, having been set up in 1948 by the Labour Foreign Office minister Christopher Mayhew, at a time when the West appeared to be losing the global propaganda war.[63] The IRD's formal task was simply to compile

information reports for British missions abroad, but its true and unac-
knowledged purpose was anti-communist propaganda, and it received
most of its funding from the Foreign Office 'secret vote'. It expanded
rapidly from a staff of 16 in 1948 to 227 in 1960 and was by far the largest
department in the Foreign Office.[64] It devised counter-propaganda,
developed links with Western opinion formers and maintained a cross-
departmental watch for communist influence. It also secretly ran
a publisher, Ampersand Books, which – amongst many texts on
Marxism and communism – published an edition of Maurice
Cranston's *Human Rights Today*.[65] The IRD had strong links to another
organisation, the Ariel Foundation, which was ostensibly independent,
but was deemed to play a valuable role in building links to politicians and
people of influence in the Middle East and Africa. The Foundation was
run by two centrist politicians, Charles Longbottom (a liberal Tory) and
Maurice Foley (a Catholic Labour candidate) on the basis of private
funding which the IRD helped to secure. In 1960 the Foundation helped
to pay for the British delegation to the ICJ conference in Lagos on African
law, and for follow-up work with Justice, and Foley provided Amnesty
with a list of speakers from the Middle East for one of its first international
seminars.[66] Despite Benenson's later suspicions about the Ariel
Foundation's funding, Foley was a co-opted member of Amnesty's
Policy Committee during 1962–63.[67]

Amidst the cultural and political turmoil of the later 1960s the IRD,
like the CIA, became cast as a cynical manipulator of Western opinion.
Prima facie, this should have made it an inappropriate partner for an
organisation such as Amnesty that was seeking to establish independent
and impartial credentials. However, the IRD was a great repository of
information on the communist world, and the attractions of a mutually
beneficial exchange of information were self-evident.[68] In addition,
Benenson was on good personal terms with the IRD's director for
1962–66, and another school acquaintance, Christopher 'Kit' Barclay.
According to Benenson the two men lunched together 'quietly every few
months to exchange a "tour d'horizon"'.[69] As early as August 1961
Benenson was sending an article that he had written for the Catholic
press to IRD to be fact-checked: he also asked for information on the pro-
regime Soviet 'Patriotic Churches'.[70] Likewise, two years later he wrote
a detailed account for Barclay of NGOs operating in the field of world
law. Benenson described with amused horror that American private
foundations were currently so awash with funds that there was an 'extra-
vaganza' of new, often overlapping, organisations that would soon end in
'farce'.[71] Such information-sharing was not in itself harmful, although,
within a few years, the revelation that these foundations were acting as

fronts for the CIA's anti-communist activities would make this correspondence appear rather naive.

However, there is evidence that the relationship with IRD went further than the mere exchange of information. In 1967 Benenson privately noted that the IRD had '"vetted" staff members of the Amnesty office in order to satisfy both the F[oreign] O[ffice] and the writer [Benenson] that they were not crypto-communists'.[72] In 1963 Benenson even suggested that an individual trusted by both IRD and Amnesty should be embedded in Amnesty as a 'liaison officer': such a person would eventually 'work in your place but have the run of ours'.[73] He also wrote that in February 1966 he had received £3000 from the IRD to fund the work of his Human Rights Advisory Service (HRAS) in financing complaints by minorities inside the Soviet Union. Although the HRAS was formally separate from Amnesty, the intention was that the investigator would also examine Soviet prison conditions for Amnesty 'without any charge'.[74] After Jack Halpern's sacking, Benenson turned to Barclay for advice as to a replacement. Shortly afterwards – Benenson implied that the two episodes were related – he was contacted by Robert Swann, who had recently lost his job at a Moroccan university for his activities on behalf of imprisoned socialists. Swann appeared to be the perfect candidate for the post and had the support of Lord Vernon, a liberal Tory peer who had served in intelligence and was Chairman of the 'Acanthus Trust' (which had funded Swann's Moroccan lectureship).[75] Six months after his appointment Swann informed Benenson of his own intelligence background, but Benenson initially paid little heed: after all, he himself – like so many of his class and generation – had served in intelligence during the war. During the crisis, however, Benenson came to regret his inaction, when he realised that Swann had kept up his contacts with his intelligence 'chums' and was even using them to support his work for Amnesty. Swann's confession to him in November 1966 that he had 'never received money [from intelligence sources] save twice to entertain people also useful to Amnesty ... '[76] came too late, as by now Benenson was convinced that Swann was working to infiltrate and undermine Amnesty.

On the basis of the available evidence, it is impossible to dispute Calvocoressi's conclusion that while Swann's past made him a poor choice of employee, his actual activity within Amnesty had been above board. His appointment – without even a formal interview[77] – was surely a symptom of the weak decision-making within Amnesty rather than evidence of a plot against it. But, just as he was mistaken in his allegations against Swann, there was also no evidence to support Benenson's supposition that British intelligence was working 'against' the Labour government rather than with it over Aden.[78] In fact, it was doing the government's bidding, and what

Amnesty had encountered was nothing more than the defensive reaction of *any* government when challenged on such a sensitive issue. Previous assumptions now counted for nothing. When Benenson accused the Foreign Office of using non-attributable briefings to smear Rastgeldi, one official privately suggested that they should 'inspire a friendly correspondent to write a condescending piece in one of the diaries educating Mr Benenson in the purpose and value of the non-attributable briefing system'.[79] More menacingly, and pertinently, when the Bowen report was about to be published it was Benenson's former allies at the IRD who were briefed about the 'strong Communist influence' in the Swedish Amnesty section, and who planned to release 'factual material about them for unattributable publication in Europe, should [the Swedes] reopen their attack'.[80]

Michael Scott's role in the crisis reinforced his growing preoccupation with the danger that the state posed to voluntary organisations, and this grew into an obsession during the 1970s. Indeed, shortly before Scott's death in 1983, David Astor reproached his old friend for seeing infiltration by intelligence officers at work in so many NGOs. After all, he went on, during the Amnesty crisis, 'Peter Calvo [*sic*] was asked to investigate. He discovered it was Benenson himself who had approached British Intelligence for help in Rhodesia ... his paranoid and confused suspicions ... nearly destroyed his own organisation'.[81] This jumbled recollection is typical of the way that Benenson's allegations were able to be dismissed due to the exaggerated terms in which they had been presented. However, Benenson did have personal insight into this secret world and was not wrong to raise these issues. The problem was that his initial confidence that he could make Amnesty an equal player with the government and its agencies had turned so swiftly into disillusionment and suspicion directed against his own colleagues. Even so, Benenson's claim that elements within the intelligence services were out of the control of elected politicians – he would even propose an organisation entitled 'Courage' to control them[82] – was a foretaste of the way that 'paranoia' would give way to disturbing reality in the 1970s. For instance, it is now known that 'Operation Condor' (run by right-wing Latin American dictatorships) targeted 'some leaders of Amnesty International' in 1977, while the South African agent Craig Williamson successfully infiltrated the anti-apartheid movement.[83] We should leave the last word on this issue to MacBride, who came to appreciate that while Benenson may have been wrong about Swann, he was correct in seeing Amnesty as under threat. In December 1971 MacBride told Amnesty's Treasurer that it needed to take more precautions in engaging staff and safeguarding documents due to the risk to those who supplied them with information from 'Southern Africa, Greece, Portugal, Brazil etc.' 'It is inevitable', he wrote, 'that in the course of our work "sensitive" or "potentially dangerous" information will pass through the Secretariat. *I know that the Secret Services of three states have been actively interested in placing agents on the staff of the ICJ and of Amnesty.* I can well imagine that several other secret services would have a like interest'.[84]

5.3   'Private Initiative'? Benenson, Amnesty and Southern Africa

The struggle for human rights in southern Africa was very important to Peter Benenson: indeed, many years later when a publicity film was being made about Amnesty he advised that showing a picture of the Sharpeville massacre would 'pitch the climate of the 60's [*sic*]' better than any other single image.[85] However, the issues were so complex and multifaceted that he found it difficult to address them through Amnesty alone. For instance, the ANC's decision to support armed struggle in 1961 made it problematic for Amnesty to provide support for its members in prison, while the plight of refugees called for more traditional humanitarian interventions. Accordingly, Benenson pursued a wide range of different initiatives, and this has somewhat concealed the full extent of his commitment to the region. These different strands came together in the ill-starred 'Operation Lordship' in 1965–66.

Benenson's own interest in southern Africa stretched back at least as far as the later 1950s, when Justice provided legal support for opponents of white minority rule in both South Africa and Rhodesia, and there are many examples of his – and Amnesty's – continuing commitment to this cause. When Amnesty was launched in 1961 one of the guest speakers at the press conference raised the plight of the Pan-Africanist leader Robert Sobukwe, jailed after Sharpeville.[86] In November 1962 Louis Blom-Cooper attended Mandela's trial on behalf of Amnesty, and the organisation received a fulsome letter of thanks from Mandela.[87] Moreover, one of the chapters in *Persecution 1961* was devoted to Patrick Duncan, the Oxford-educated son of a former Governor-General of South Africa who was jailed numerous times for his opposition to apartheid. At this point Duncan was a firm advocate of Gandhian non-violence, and he attended the 1963 Amnesty conference, but his subsequent decision to join the Pan Africanist Congress (PAC) and advocate violence made him an uncomfortable ally.[88] Duncan's story is symptomatic of how the anti-apartheid consensus of the 1950s, both in South Africa and amongst supporters in Britain, was beginning to fragment in the very different circumstances after Sharpeville. Long-standing liberal opponents of apartheid in Britain, such as David Astor and Michael Scott, were increasingly wary of the communist support for the ANC, and this coincided with their personal and political antagonism towards Canon Collins, whose Defence and Aid Fund was suspected of favouring the ANC. In 1962 the Labour Party's international secretary David Ennals launched a short-lived Southern Africa Freedom Fund, on the committee of which Benenson sat, which was intended to distribute political funds more equally – and at the same time to rein in Collins.

Amnesty's refusal to continue to treat Nelson Mandela as a 'prisoner of conscience' might appear to compromise its claim to support the anti-apartheid cause. The ANC leader's adoption by the Oxted Amnesty Group was abruptly discontinued after his conviction for sabotage on 12 June 1964,[89] a decision that was controversial at the time and has remained so due to the increasingly high esteem in which Mandela came to be held during his long captivity. However, the issue was always one of how the struggle should be conducted rather than the justice of the cause itself. In many ways, the decision was a simple one, as the Eltham group recorded at the time: Mandela and his colleagues had 'compromised themselves by their self-confessed violence'.[90] On news of Mandela's life sentence Benenson immediately announced that 'we are examining every possible means of finding a way to bring active relief to victims of South African racial policy' and appealed to the UN to establish a relief fund, but this did not address the question posed by Mandela's defence of the use of violence, which came to a head at Amnesty's Canterbury conference in September 1964.[91] As a solution, Amnesty members were asked to submit their views on two linked questions. First, should the organisation support those forced to resort to violence in defence of their racial group, and, secondly, should it prioritise the struggle against racial intolerance? The results were patchy – there were only sixty-one individual replies, half of them from Australians – and quite evenly divided. This limited consultation was the closest approximation to the 'poll [of] all its members' referred to by a number of authors, and Jack Halpern had the thankless task of advising the Amnesty conference on how to proceed. He sided with those individuals and sections who – while sympathising personally with Mandela – thought that the adoption of prisoners who advocated violence would diminish Amnesty's 'moral strength' and would put it on the 'slippery slope' to other concessions. This was the position adopted at the conference, although to soften the blow it was agreed that such prisoners – while not formally adopted – could still be provided with humanitarian support.[92] The outcome was painful, but, given that some Amnesty groups would later campaign for it to take up the case of imprisoned Baader–Meinhof group terrorists,[93] surely the correct one.

One formative influence on Benenson's thinking on these issues was Clara Urquhart, a South African who had inherited her husband's fortune at the age of nineteen and dedicated herself to supporting humanitarian causes. Indeed, in the early 1950s she had assisted Michael Scott from her base in Geneva, and she became particularly associated with the work of the French missionary Albert Schweitzer. She helped to organise the successful campaign for the award of a Nobel Peace Prize to the ANC leader Albert Luthuli in 1961.[94] She was also on good terms with the ANC leader in exile, Oliver Tambo, and fostered links between him and Benenson.[95] On meeting Benenson she immediately felt a spiritual affinity with him (she was a Jewish Quaker) and saw working for Amnesty as 'the logical sequence to my whole life'.[96] Over the next two years she made a significant contribution to Amnesty, but very much on her own terms. She made it clear that she did not wish to be involved in any committee work but preferred to work directly, and almost invisibly, through Benenson and Neville Vincent.

Urquhart contributed heavily to Amnesty's finances – including a donation of £600 per year and the proceeds from her book *A Matter of Life* (1963).[97] However, welcome as this subvention was, Urquhart's contribution was far greater than that as, for Benenson, in some respects she took the place of Eric Baker as a hard-working assistant and as a foil for religious and philosophical debate. The two often discussed South Africa, which Urquhart still visited, and in 1962 they conceived a remarkable project entitled 'Africa Calling' which was submitted to David Ennals' Freedom Fund. The proposal involved setting up a powerful radio transmitter in Tanganyika which could broadcast across southern Africa in English, Portuguese and native languages. Urquhart's contribution was to see this not only as a means to promote political change, but also to foster a dialogue between Africans and their foreign, white supporters.[98] By early 1964, however, Benenson had become convinced that no immediate political transformation was likely in South Africa and suggested long-term relief work for African women and children instead, given that women were the 'leaven of the bread'. Urquhart acknowledged that this was 'not strictly Amnesty work'.[99] Here, and at many other points in their conversations, we can see how Benenson, while deeply committed to Amnesty, also understood that its capacity to tackle the root cause of international problems was strictly limited. In that mood he told Amnesty's 1964 conference that: 'Torture and intimidation are growing in the world ... We have made no impact at all!'[100]

At the same time as these conversations, Benenson was already running a scheme to assist refugees in southern Africa. This was more clearly an Amnesty project, and one which invoked Amnesty's founding commitment to the right to asylum. In October 1963, shortly after Benenson had visited the region, Amnesty issued a report on the problems facing refugees who were fleeing South Africa and often became stranded in the neighbouring British High Commission Territories (Bechuanaland, Swaziland and Lesotho). A confidential annex to the report – circulated only to British political leaders and to Barclay at the IRD – also examined the prospect of such refugees engaging in military action, and the threats that they faced from cross-border action by the South African authorities. However, Benenson's main concern was to encourage Britain to develop a refugee policy, and – where necessary – for Amnesty to provide practical assistance.[101] Accordingly Amnesty bought a site at Francistown in Bechuanaland, close to the South African border, where it embarked on building a refugee reception centre. This was blown up two weeks before completion, and Amnesty officials believed that the explosion was the work of South African agents.[102]

In addition, Amnesty hired Commander Michael Cunningham as an 'Asylum Counsellor' for southern Africa, at a cost of some £2000. His task was to investigate ways in which refugees could be helped to travel on from Bechuanaland to asylum in emerging African states, such as neighbouring Northern Rhodesia (which formally became independent, as Zambia, from October 1964). Cunningham's appointment was tolerated by the British government, partly because Benenson had persuaded the Colonial Office that the scheme would reduce the spread of communism and the danger of refugees engaging in military action from Bechuanaland.[103] However, it was deeply resented by British officials in the Territories, who viewed Cunningham as an incompetent menace.[104] Perhaps aware of the official hostility, Benenson stressed that Cunningham would not be sent back after reporting in the summer of 1964. However, Cunningham continued to act as a representative for Amnesty in Africa, and during the Rhodesian crisis brought cash into the country as part of the funding of 'Operation Lordship'. Prior to her arrival in Rhodesia Polly Toynbee had encountered him in Nigeria with '"an enormous amount of cash" on him', and the 'Harry' letters announced Cunningham's imminent arrival in Salisbury with part of '"Harry's present"'.[105] Despite Cunningham's continuing utility, however, by July 1964 Benenson had realised that Amnesty was not the proper organisation to handle the inflow of refugees into Northern Rhodesia, and that this was a task for the UN High Commissioner for Refugees.[106]

In November 1965, following Southern Rhodesia's UDI, the plight of political prisoners and detainees held under Smith's illegal regime became pressing. Since 1959 legal aid had been handled by a voluntary 'Southern Rhodesia Legal Aid and Welfare Fund' (SRLA&WF), led by Terence and Shelagh Ranger until their expulsion, and then by the mining engineer Michael Haddon and his wife Eileen. Amnesty began to help this group soon after its own formation – in effect continuing the work that Benenson had started with Justice – and acted as an intermediary to secure funds to pay for defence lawyers from organisations such as Christian Action and Maurice Foley's Ariel Foundation. Peter Benenson maintained a correspondence with the Haddons and sent Clara Urquhart to meet them in 1964, and he himself briefly met Michael Haddon at Victoria Air Terminal, London, in February 1965 to discuss how money could be sent into Rhodesia. Amnesty's aid worker, Hugh Vodden, was highly praised by the Haddons and was said to have driven some 10,000 miles in seven months.[107] However, Guy Clutton-Brock was more doubtful of Amnesty's usefulness, arguing that it was 'good for individual cases . . . but not for general stuff'.[108] In his view, Canon Collins remained the key figure. In any case, the work of the SRLA&WF was becoming progressively more difficult, and following the UDI Michael Haddon was jailed in 1966. There was, therefore, a significant gap to be filled, but Benenson did not think that the organisation of legal defence for prisoners was necessarily a task for Amnesty. Instead, as 'none of the existing organisations could take on this work', he argued that an ad hoc committee of lawyers and representatives from other organisations was required. In November 1965 he convened an 'Association for Legal Action in Rhodesia'. He envisaged this as a 'new association . . . composed mainly of lawyers . . . to dispute . . . the legality of the new Government [of Ian Smith]', which would bring test cases against press censorship and restriction orders. He explained that Amnesty could not undertake this work for three specific reasons: that it could only adopt 'genuine prisoners of conscience'; that its groups had already adopted 102 prisoners in Rhodesia; and that Amnesty would forfeit its 'right to act as a relief agency' in Rhodesia if it became involved in court action. He had already written to the British government's law officers for support and would approach other charities and international organisations.[109]

Benenson swiftly decided to harness the committee to another of his recent initiatives, the HRAS. The HRAS had been launched in a letter to *The Times* of 21 December 1965, in response to the British government's landmark decision to allow the right of individual application to the European Court of Human Rights. As originally envisaged, it was intended to offer practical legal advice to potential complainants to

Strasbourg.[110] By the end of December, the lawyers' group described above had become the HRAS 'Rhodesia Committee'. However, the participants were essentially the same – lawyers who had worked with Amnesty plus representatives of Amnesty, Justice, the Africa Bureau and other interested parties. The barrister Patricia May acted as secretary. One significant contributor was James Lemkin, a lawyer with a strong interest in Africa who had been very active in the liberal Conservative Bow Group since the late 1950s. Legal challenges were already being investigated both in London and Salisbury, but on the advice of the Rhodesian Lord Chief Justice it was agreed that it was 'not politic' to embark on an immediate challenge to the executive power at this point.[111] Instead, a range of other activities were being looked into. For instance, it was agreed that the lawyer Bernard Sheridan should approach Shell about an 'oil action' (presumably a fuel boycott), books were sent to Salisbury for distribution in the detention camps, and a 'Register of Inhumanity' – to collate evidence against the regime for future legal action – was discussed.[112] At a late-December meeting it was reported that Amnesty would be sending a team of relief workers to Rhodesia, and the committee began to receive 'Operation Lordship' reports.[113] The overlap between Amnesty and the HRAS was therefore becoming more dangerously marked, and Benenson's reservations about the risks of confusing relief and legal interventions were being whittled away. He warned, for instance, against the danger that the Rhodesian authorities might get 'to know that the trials, or rather the [legal] defences, were being masterminded from London'.[114]

How was this work to be funded? It is clear that the campaign for legal action cannot be understood in isolation from Amnesty's intervention in Rhodesia under the umbrella of 'Operation Lordship'. Ben Whitaker (Labour MP, 1966–70, and a member of the lawyers' committee) had visited Rhodesia to investigate the case of the imprisoned British lawyer Leo Baron. On his return he and Benenson made representations for aid both for the families of detainees *and* for legal costs, which caught the attention of Gerald Gardiner and Harold Wilson. In a memorandum of 23 November, Benenson stated that the 'ad hoc' lawyers' group (which would make a separate bid for funds) had been set up precisely because Amnesty did not want to 'confuse its humanitarian role with that of taking legal action'.[115] What is not clear is how much – if any – of the secret government funding for Amnesty also went to the HRAS work. However, according to the 'Harry' letters, by early February 1966 the Chief Justice Sir Gerald Beadle had changed his mind about the desirability of legal action and the British government wanted a 'fair buzz of legal activity'. The *Sunday Times* claimed at the time that the HRAS handled the litigation mentioned in the letters.[116] This would fit with the 'Operation Lordship' situation report of 22 February 1966, which states that it was bringing two test cases within Rhodesia.[117] Later in the year, however, the HRAS became more reliant on voluntary support. Canon Collins was planning to run a fundraising appeal for it in the autumn, and the legal defence of an academic within Rhodesia was being substantially funded by money raised within British universities.[118]

The archival record of the HRAS is fragmentary and incomplete. However, two sources allow us some insight into its final phase. First, by the summer of 1966 the problem of transferring funds to Rhodesia was becoming acute and Benenson was asked to approach the Treasury, or even the Swedish Amnesty section, for assistance. These initiatives appear to have borne fruit as the final surviving minutes, for 19 October 1966, record that the Bank of England had agreed to transfer £2000 per month to Rhodesia – presumably funds from voluntary sources rather than British government funds. A tripartite panel was also set up (consisting of one barrister, one solicitor and one Rhodesian representative) to assess future cases and, effectively, took the place of the main committee.[119] Secondly, in July 1967 Stephanie Grant of Amnesty told Michael Scott that Benenson had sent Mabel Nelson to Rhodesia in the autumn of 1966 to tell lawyers that the HRAS could offer support of up to £50 per political case. However, the funding dried up when the Aden crisis broke and the HRAS 'virtually fell apart, as the person with the enthusiasm to run it had been Peter ... [no one at Amnesty] knew enough of the details to enable the Service to go on'.[120] However, some of the HRAS funds appear to have survived, as in 1970 Peter Archer suggested that they should be split with the newly founded Institute of Human Rights.[121]

Although the support for political trials dried up, it should be noted that Amnesty continued to provide significant relief in Rhodesia. For instance, in March 1967 the main Fund for the Persecuted account still had 'roughly £5000' for 'the relief of Rhodesian restrictees and their families', and there was also a standing payment of £800 per month from Amnesty's Prisoners of Conscience Fund to Christian Care in Rhodesia.[122] In 1970 Martin Ennals noted that since 1969 Amnesty had sent £700 per month to Rhodesia and that 'after the World Council of Churches we are the second largest distributor and we have a special arrangement with the Treasury allowing us to transfer funds in this way'.[123] Amnesty also distributed funds for the UN's Trust Fund for South Africa.

One of the most damaging criticisms that MacBride made during Amnesty's crisis was that Benenson had acted on his 'private initiative' over Rhodesia. It was certainly true that at the March 1966 IEC the report on Rhodesia had, for 'security' reasons, not specified the source of the funds, but MacBride had still congratulated Benenson and Swann for their work there. It is also true that the Rhodesia affair revealed significant flaws in Amnesty's governance arrangements. As Eric Baker argued at the time, Amnesty had never quite managed the transition from an informal group of Benenson's friends and colleagues – perfect for a fixed-term campaign – into a permanent international organisation. This analysis is supported by the original documentation for the Appeal for Amnesty, 1961, with its emphasis on avoiding unnecessary red tape and committee work.[124] Even so, MacBride's allegation of 'private initiative', like so much of Amnesty's formal response to the crisis, smacks of damage limitation. Nor did it calm speculation. As one perceptive journalist wrote at the time, the 'Harry' letters substantiated 'beyond doubt, that the International Secretariat was aware of what was going on, and either endorsed or condoned it'.[125] In the circumstances, it is surprising that the press lost interest in the story so quickly.[126]

A fairer interpretation would acknowledge that throughout his long career as a human rights campaigner Benenson had been seeking to create organisations that would – to cite his 1964 speech – 'make an impact'. As he became frustrated with the limitations of one organisation he was always willing to move on and try something new. In the process he accumulated a tremendous range of contacts and trusted associates across many different spheres – the law, politics, the media and religion. He was also deeply concerned about the dangers posed by white rule in southern Africa which – as Urquhart had reminded him – was 'threatening the peace of the world'. Accordingly, Benenson saw in Rhodesia the opportunity to make a new kind of intervention – both legal and humanitarian – in a region of crucial significance, and in a colony for which Britain still had sovereign responsibility. Here was an opportunity to draw on his influence with the Labour government, but also – despite his disparaging comments about the legal profession when he set up Amnesty – an opportunity to mobilise the skills and resources of lawyers. No single organisation could undertake this task, but 'Operation Lordship', by drawing on every element in his career to date, was an indication of how the next stage in his project might develop. Did the future now lie with task forces that brought together many different skills and professions, capable of making multifaceted interventions, independent of government but enjoying its quiet support? Sadly for Benenson, the edifice was too fragile to be sustained, and the Aden crisis – separate from but interrelated with the crisis over state funding – brought it crashing down.

5.4   'Towards Stability and Security': 1967–1968

It would be easy to see the Amnesty crisis as a brief moment of catharsis in which one style of leadership – charismatic, personal and gloriously unfettered – gave way to greater managerialism. [127] Eric Baker, as acting Director General, certainly understood that what was needed was for the movement to be 'more fully institutionalised' and for the staff to be more international in origin. But progress was slow, partly because the finances were in deficit. Moreover, Baker was only able to spend one afternoon a week in the office and was struggling to manage the strong-willed volunteers who did much of the work. The best solution, he noted, would be 'to staff the office completely with well chosen professionals. But then one has to face the question of costs'. [128] An alarming draft message to the sections in April 1967 warned that Amnesty was on the verge of bankruptcy and issued an urgent appeal for money. According to this analysis, the problem was partly due to poor financial management by Benenson, but it was also attributed to Amnesty's rapid growth and the lack of central funds with which to service 550 local groups. [129] A short-term transfer of funds from the British Section balanced the books and settled nerves, but the Dutch leader Cornelis van der Vlies warned that reform must not be postponed while Amnesty relied on British 'make-do and muddling through, however brilliant'. [130] MacBride promised a thorough reorganisation of Amnesty utilising the 'business-like efficiency of our Scandinavian members'. [131] In the circumstances, it is not surprising that Baker's language in the immediate aftermath of the crisis was cautious and wary. As he put it in June 1967: 'we are getting the movement to rights again, and by the Autumn all should be well again – barring unforeseen crises'. [132] However, the budget of October 1967 proved inadequate and a contentious new annual subscription of £30 for all local groups was introduced to cover the shortfall. [133]

Amnesty's revival is, therefore, more properly associated with the appointment of Martin Ennals as Secretary General in July 1968. His long and transformative period in office (1968–80) was crowned just under a decade later by the award of the Nobel Peace Prize to Amnesty. Ennals was not initially considered for the post by the small group of senior Amnesty figures (in effect, the 'Godfathers') who carried out the search. Their first choice was the former Director of the International Press Institute in Zurich, Jim Rose, who was currently conducting a landmark survey of race relations in Britain. After Rose declared his unavailability, Ennals was selected ahead of the lawyer Cedric Thornberry on account of his greater administrative experience. [134] Ennals had started his career with UNESCO in the 1950s, and already had considerable experience of working in the field of human rights as Secretary General of the NCCL, 1960–66, where he had caught Benenson's eye by steering the organisation away from its long-standing close association with the Communist Party.[135] He had then served as an officer for the ill-fated National Committee for Commonwealth Immigrants, but resigned in protest at the 1968 immigration act.[136] Ennals, along with his older brother David, attracted MI5 surveillance during the 1950s, but while it was clear that the communists admired his administrative skills there was no indication that he was ever a party member. Jonathan Power has described him as a 'dogged, persistent administrator ... a careful but wily backroom boy', who saw Amnesty's role as generating the impartial data that would convince governments to take action.[137] However, Ennals was also independent-minded: as we have seen, he was quite capable of asking for further government funds, and would repeatedly clash with MacBride in the early 1970s over his management of Amnesty.

The most important development of these years was the adoption of a new statute at Amnesty's sixth International Assembly in Stockholm, 24–25 August 1968, hailed by Ennals as introducing 'a new phase of our existence'. The statute – amended many times since – upheld the established definition of 'prisoners of conscience' and formalised the relationship between the organisation's national and international components. It also extended Amnesty's remit to include cruel, inhuman and degrading punishment (Article 5 of the UDHR).[138] Given the emphasis on clarity and accountability, there was no role now for shadowy 'Godfathers'. One important conceptual change, however, was that the former division of the world into East, West and Third World was replaced by a commitment to a 'balance' between world ideologies. As Martin Ennals pointed out, this balance must not reflect the Cold War of the 1950s, but the more complex world of the 1970s, when communism no longer had a 'sharp geographical definition'. Otherwise the statute largely codified what was already understood, but the equally important regulations 'for the conduct of field operations' – also adopted at Stockholm – marked a more definitive break with previous practices. This was a much-needed reform, as at the height of the Niels Groth affair Amnesty's IEC had already concluded that delegates must be 'properly prepared and briefed'.[139] Missions would in future be conducted openly, and with transparent, unconditional funding. Moreover, whereas before they had been staffed on the basis of 'who was available at short notice', the national sections would now be asked to recruit a panel of suitable representatives, based on appropriate professional status and 'personality'.[140]

*

As 1967 drew to a close Amnesty could feel that it had successfully negotiated a traumatic year, and members were encouraged to make the most of the opportunities presented by the UN's forthcoming Year for Human Rights. For Peter Benenson, however, the trauma was more personal, and he kept his distance from Amnesty, later explaining that '"children" must develop in their own way without parents breathing down their neck'.[141] Many in Amnesty did not see him again until he returned to attend a tenth anniversary dinner in 1971, where he recalled the 'early days and informal meetings from which Amnesty sprang'.[142] After a brief sojourn in France, he settled back in Britain and turned his energies into new campaigns, such as the Coeliac Association, while seeking new ways to shape the 'community of conscience'.[143] Yet while accepting his defeat in March 1967 he was never fully reconciled to the outcome. Indeed, allegations of torture by British forces in Northern Ireland during the new 'Troubles' reinforced his belief that Britain was not the appropriate home for Amnesty, and he never ceased to press for its headquarters to move to a more 'neutral' location. He only rejoined Amnesty in 1978 when he believed that it had finally taken a stand against the use of torture by British forces in Northern Ireland.[144] However, despite the harsh words uttered during the crisis of 1966–67, a remarkable 'bond of respect' and indeed of affection continued to connect Amnesty's senior figures. This serves to remind us what a powerful sense of mission had brought the founders of Amnesty together under Benenson's leadership, and helps to explain what Calvocoressi described as the 'unusual degree and even an unusual kind of loyalty within Amnesty'.[145] Before Benenson departed on holiday in July 1967 he wrote gracious letters to Baker and MacBride: to Baker he expressed his admiration for the manner in which he had 'soldiered on running "Amnesty"'; to MacBride he expressed surprise that their five-year association should have ended with 'a clash of arms' and assured him that 'I am just as fond of you as a person as ever before'.[146]

6   1968: the UN Year for Human Rights

6.1   The International Context

In 1963 the UN General Assembly designated 1968, the twentieth anniversary of the signing of the Universal Declaration, as the
International Year for Human Rights (IYHR). The idea was greeted
with lukewarm support by Western governments, including Britain,
which feared that the year would merely expose them to criticism from
the communist states and – more damagingly, as more difficult to rebut –
from the newly independent states of the 'Third World'. It had been these
states which, as Steven Jensen has recently shown,[1] had done much to
drive international progress on human rights during the 1960s. The
logjam of the Cold War had been broken by decolonisation, and the
UN – now composed of many more member states – had passed a series
of landmark measures, notably the Convention on the Elimination of all
forms of Racial Discrimination (December 1965). Moreover, the separate covenants on socio-economic and political rights were finally signed
in 1966, thereby giving the 1948 Declaration legal status, although the
lengthy process of ratification meant that they did not come into force
until the mid-1970s.

The Year for Human Rights has tended to be remembered – if at all – as
a failure and, even worse, as an irrelevance. For one reason, its focal point
was the somewhat grotesque international conference in Teheran,
22 April–13 May 1968, where delegates from ninety governments were
lectured by the Shah's sister about the benefits of her brother's brand of
modernising authoritarianism.[2] Sean MacBride, who attended the conference, reported to Amnesty's British Section that it had been
a 'disheartening' experience as there was much 'acrimonious debate' and
no progress on the 'burning question of implementation machinery'.[3]
Peter Burns, who was acting Secretary General of Amnesty until Martin
Ennals' arrival, put a rather more positive spin on the conference, noting
that the delegates from NGOs had demonstrated 'the demands of ordinary
people for positive international action in the field of human rights'.[4]

153

However, the high-sounding 'Proclamation of Teheran' could not disguise the sense of underachievement. At the International Conference of NGOs that met in September at UNESCO's headquarters in Paris, the General Rapporteur Germaine Cyfer-Diderich noted that Teheran's 'lacunae were many, its achievements few'. Now was the time, she added, to rely 'more on peoples than on governments' if human rights were to be pursued 'with any enthusiasm'.[5] Teheran, therefore, appeared to symbolise a world in which the Western states had lost control of, and therefore interest in, the whole human rights project, and were willing to abandon the field to emerging states which prioritised the right to social and economic development over traditional liberal freedoms. Roland Burke has described 1968's Year for Human Rights as a departure from 'the spirit of 1948', and even as marking the 'death' of the Universal Declaration.[6]

A second important factor is that the UN's 'Year' seemed increasingly marginal to the headline-making events of 1968 itself: Martin Luther King's assassination shortly before the start of the Teheran conference ushered in one of the most tumultuous and violent phases in postwar American history; opposition to the Vietnam War continued to stimulate worldwide radicalisation, notably amongst students and young people; in France, student unrest and a devastating wave of strikes brought de Gaulle's presidency close to collapse; while in Czechoslovakia Alexander Dubcek's reformist communism unleashed a heady 'Prague Spring', brutally suppressed by Warsaw Pact intervention in August. The latter case aside, the dominant discourse was not one of human rights, but of revolution, class struggle and anti-imperialism. The whole edifice of international human rights – painfully constructed through lengthy negotiations, and still difficult to monitor or implement – seemed staid and conservative compared to the contemporary mood of spontaneous radicalism and disdain for rules.

In other ways, too, world events appeared to be running contrary to the 'spirit of 1948'. In Greece thousands were imprisoned after the Colonels' coup of April 1967: a weary Betty Ambatielos, whose husband would soon be behind bars once again, wrote on resuming her work for the League for Democracy in Greece that it was like 'starting all over again'.[7] James Becket, who compiled an influential report on Greece for Amnesty, noted that Athens – where a motorcycle engine was used at the Security Police Headquarters to drown out the cries of the tortured – was 'an appropriate place to greet 1968, Human Rights Year'.[8] So long as Salazar's successor Marcelo Caetano maintained the Estado Novo (with a few liberal trimmings), and Franco lived, the tide would continue to run against democratic politics in southern Europe. In Africa, the attempt by the 'Republic of Biafra' to secede from Nigeria resulted in a bitter civil war

and a famine in which as many as 1 million perished. Some in Britain saw
the Ibo people as invoking a human right to self-determination, enshrined
in Article One of both of the new covenants, but the Labour government –
concerned about the secessionist threat to postcolonial borders – backed
the federal regime. Others, shocked by the 'spectacle of suffering' in
Biafra developed new forms of radical humanitarian interventionism.[9]
In Asia, quite apart from the continuing horrors of the war in Vietnam, as
many as 600,000 communists and other opponents had been slaughtered
by the military regime in Indonesia in 1966. One Amnesty observer
reported in April 1966 that 'the mass nature of the killings and the recent
detentions, enlarge the problem beyond "freedom of opinion and
religion" . . . it is not merely a problem of people suffering for their
religious or political beliefs but . . . of people being killed or imprisoned
for no reason at all'.[10]

The prevailing mood of the mid-1960s might, therefore, be described
as one of horror illuminated with flashes of euphoria, and one which
darkened even in the course of 1968 itself. By November one commentator was writing that: 'It may sound like a sick joke, but this is still
officially Human Rights Year'.[11] But, of course, 'moods' are of limited
help in understanding political realities, and 1968 was also a year of
conservative backlash. After all, the Paris events in May 1968 culminated
in a landslide election win for de Gaulle's supporters in the June parliamentary election, and by November the Republican Richard Nixon had
been elected US President, albeit on a pledge to bring American troops
home from Vietnam. The most severe backlash was in Czechoslovakia,
where Gustav Husak's 'normalisation' process would plunge the country
'under ice' for the next twenty years.[12] The Soviet victory appeared
complete, but the aftermath of the Prague Spring – alongside the emergence of the Soviet dissident movement – posed a long-term threat to
Soviet hegemony in Eastern Europe that tanks alone could not expunge.

6.2   The National Context

However marginal and unsuccessful the UN's Human Rights Year may
have appeared at the international level, within Britain there is
a somewhat different story to be told. Here the campaign – sponsored
by government but broadly independent – gave human rights an unprecedented and sustained prominence in national life. More importantly,
the year not only offered an umbrella for many voluntary organisations
to pursue their own agendas, but also provided the opportunity for them
to reconceive their activities as work for 'human rights'. The year 1968
did not create human rights activism in Britain, but it redefined it and

greatly extended what was already thought of as the 'field of human rights'.

The context for Human Rights Year within Britain was just as ambiguous as the international context. The authority of Harold Wilson's Labour government, which had been re-elected with a large majority in March 1966, experienced a severe blow when it was forced to devalue the pound and introduce austerity measures in November 1967. However, its record in social and legal reform was far more positive. Labour undertook an ambitious reform of the justice system, so far-reaching that Tom Sargant wondered if Justice had become a victim of its own success, and in future would merely play second fiddle to the Law Commission.[13] Moreover, principally under the liberal sway of Roy Jenkins, the Home Office introduced – or supported private members in introducing – wide-ranging reforms related to personal freedoms. These included the abolition of the death penalty in 1965 (made permanent in 1969); the legalisation of abortion on medical grounds (1967); the decriminalisation of homosexual acts, or at least those in private between men over the age of 21 (1967); the abolition of theatre censorship by the Lord Chamberlain's Office (1968) and a sweeping reform of divorce law (1969). In this so-called 'permissive society' long-standing goals were suddenly becoming achievable. For instance, the Wolfenden Report had called for homosexual law reform a decade previously, and Victor Gollancz and Gerald Gardiner had been campaigning for abolition of the death penalty since the mid-1950s.[14]

When he took office, Harold Wilson could convincingly claim to understand and support the significance of human rights, even if he also saw political advantage in making this claim. Prior to the 1964 election he had committed a Labour government to work through the UN to complete the work of the 1948 Declaration, singling out race relations and women's rights as areas where 'more progress could be made'.[15] As Prime Minister, whereas his Conservative predecessor had politely declined an invitation to attend Amnesty's Human Rights Day celebration, in December 1964 Wilson agreed to read a lesson. When suddenly called away to Washington, he began a practice of issuing an annual Human Rights Day message instead. In his message for December 1965, for instance, he noted that Rhodesia 'dominates our thoughts' and dedicated his government to securing a settlement in which the African majority's 'rights as human beings' were secured.[16] At the Labour Party's 1968 conference he declared that he led 'the party of human rights': indeed, that human rights had been 'the central theme of this Government's actions from the day we took office'. By contrast, the Conservatives were the party of Enoch Powell, white Rhodesia and Peter Griffiths (the

victorious Conservative candidate accused of fighting a racist campaign at
Smethwick in 1964).[17] By 1968, however, Wilson's claim to hold the
moral high ground was weakening, and some critics asked how Labour
could claim to be 'the party of human rights' when its government was
backing the federal forces in Biafra, and doing little to end the UDI in
Rhodesia or discrimination against the Catholic minority in Northern
Ireland.[18] Wilson's public image was rapidly changing – from the idealist
reformer of 1964 to the cynical fixer, hanging on to power, of the later
1960s. However, it was his claim to be leading a global struggle against
racialism – 'if what we assert is true for Birmingham, it is true for
Bulawayo'[19] – that rang particularly hollow, as the Year for Human
Rights in Britain was overshadowed by Labour's contradictory messages
about race and immigration.

During the economic upturn of the 1950s large-scale immigration had
been encouraged from within the Commonwealth, and many immigrants
began to make their home in Britain. In 1952 the Conservative Bow
Group claimed that there were at least 50,000 'coloured people' in
Britain but, revisiting the report in 1958 following the Notting Hill
riots, found that this had risen to 200,000, a quarter of whom lived in
London.[20] (There were an estimated 2 million immigrants in Britain by
1968.) The 1958 riots concentrated the minds of politicians on what was
increasingly being perceived as the 'problem' of race. Left-wing Labour
MPs such as Fenner Brockway and Reginald Sorenson saw this as
a problem of racial discrimination by the white majority, to be addressed
in the law through private members' bills. However, the Conservatives
were loath to legislate in this field, and instead sought to address white
concerns by introducing the first Act to restrict immigration in 1962,
greatly reducing the rights of citizens of Commonwealth countries to
come to Britain. Labour responded in 1965 with the Race Relations
Act, which was intended to outlaw racial discrimination and was patrolled
by a Race Relations Board. However, the Act – which excluded some of
the main areas affected by discrimination such as employment and rented
accommodation, and did not apply to Northern Ireland – was widely
regarded as too limited in its scope and powers to be effective. During the
mid-1960s numerous surveys were carried out into the experience of
immigrants in Britain, and in 1967 an influential report by PEP
(Political and Economic Planning) discovered shockingly high levels of
discrimination and disadvantage: in many respects these findings struck
a keynote for the Human Rights Year that followed.[21]

During 1968 race and immigration were often at the forefront of
politics. Colin Jordan's National Socialist Movement led an upsurge in
the racialist far right which continued with the rise of the National Front

in the 1970s. More significantly, the Conservative Shadow Defence Secretary Enoch Powell became the first senior politician since Oswald Mosley to adopt openly racist language and imagery. Powell was immediately sacked from the Shadow Cabinet for his infamous 'rivers of blood' speech of 20 April 1968, but he received support from groups of white workers who demonstrated outside Parliament. Wilson alluded to the 'virus of Powellism' infecting the Conservatives, but this could not conceal his own party's exposure to the charge of racism. In the spring of 1968 thousands of Asians began to flee Kenya for Britain, fearful of legislation intended to place the Kenyan economy under African control. Labour Home Secretary James Callaghan rushed a new Immigration Act into law in March 1968, privately conceding that it was intended to prevent an upsurge in 'coloured' immigration 'aggravating' racial problems in Britain.[22] Labour, Wilson told an audience in Birmingham Town Hall, had made clear where it stood in the 'world confrontation between racialism and decency', while at the same time cutting immigration to ease the strain on public services.[23] However, Tony Smythe, General Secretary of the NCCL, described the Labour government as 'committed to a racialist policy on immigration' and warned that the proposed new Race Relations Act (which was passed in October) would be 'another emasculated sop to keep us quiet'.[24] For *Peace News*, the 1968 Immigration Act was a measure worthy of the Nazis: a 'passport to fascism'.[25]

By 1968 the organisations specifically concerned with questions of immigration and race were in a state of flux as more militant voices, influenced by Black Power and Maoism, gained influence in the communities that they sought to represent. The government-sponsored National Committee for Commonwealth Immigrants (NCCI), chaired by the Archbishop of Canterbury, lost credibility when it was not consulted by government over the new immigration law. Although its chief executive, Nadine Peppard, administered a government grant of £170,000 and a multiracial staff of 16, the NCCI was branded a 'dummy committee' by the Indian Workers' Association.[26] The Campaign Against Racial Discrimination (CARD), directly inspired by Martin Luther King during his visit to Britain in 1964, was also affected by the rise of black radicalism. Some of its white supporters departed, in the case of the barrister Anthony Lester to form the Runnymede Trust with academic Dipak Nandy, with support from the Rowntree Foundation. Others, led by Professor Roy Marshall, resigned in 1968 to form the lobbying organisation Equal Rights.[27] The founder of CARD, the West Indian doctor and Labour politician David Pitt, struggled on, gamely trying to hold together the rival constituencies.[28] Similarly, the Institute for Race Relations, established in 1958 on the lines of the Royal Institute for International Relations and long regarded as a rather conservative force, was reinvented at this time as a left-wing campaigning organisation.[29]

Two other issues that were given prominence during the Human Rights Year were women's rights and the rights of travellers (generally referred to collectively at the time as 'gypsies'). As radical, 'second-wave' feminism was still in its infancy in 1968, the main issues raised during Human Rights Year were to do with fulfilling the long-standing promise of political, economic and legal equality for women, and the agenda was set by well-established organisations such as the Status of Women Committee and the National Council of Women. A briefing paper for Human Rights Year in July 1967 emphasised women's continuing lack of rights in the political, economic and legal spheres: women were still severely under-represented in Parliament (only twenty-six women were elected in 1966, and there were only eighty female candidates); equal pay was increasingly common in the public sector, but far less so in the private sector; women were still overwhelmingly employed in administrative and semi-skilled occupations, and rarely made up more than 5 per cent of the leading professions; and women were still less privileged than their husbands in areas such as child custody and assessment of income tax.[30] Although the strike by woman machinists at Ford's Dagenham plant in the summer of 1968 (which contributed to the 1970 Equal Pay Act) gave a boost to the cause of equality, the Human Rights Year was an opportunity to focus attention on 'outmoded customs, practices and prejudices' that denied women their 'basic rights as full partners in the community'.[31] However, the very longevity of the campaign for women's rights sometimes told against it. Des Wilson of Shelter, angry at the low priority given to housing issues during the Year wrote that: 'I'm sure the women of Britain could have waited another year for equality but there are families breaking up every day because of homelessness'.[32]

Both race relations and women's rights were very much in the public eye: however, the Human Rights Year also gave prominence to the less well-known problems facing travellers, although the UK Committee organising the Year quietly dropped an initial reference to tackling discrimination against 'gypsies' as one of its formal objectives.[33] The travellers' cause was strongly espoused by civil libertarians – in the words of Tony Smythe, citing a recent survey by the NCCL, no community had suffered more at the hands of the police and local authorities.[34] The West Midlands, in particular, was said to be a 'black spot so far as a human and rational approach to Travellers is concerned', and in April 1968 it was alleged that police had attacked gypsies in Walsall after 'months of persecution'.[35] The passing of the Caravan Sites Act in July 1968, which required local authorities to provide facilities (while also enhancing their powers of eviction), gave some greater security to the travellers, but reinforced the view that their lifestyle represented a 'problem' that needed to be tackled.[36] During Human Rights Year, in the absence of strong central pressure, it fell to local advocates to ensure that travellers' rights were remembered. In Nottingham, for instance, an early session of the local Human Rights Year committee came close to excluding them altogether: 'as there were no gypsies in Nottingham, we need not be concerned about their difficulties'. This was subsequently overturned when a local campaigner pointed out that there were travellers, living in very deprived conditions and facing eviction, at nearby Balloon Woods. In the event the travellers became a central theme in the local campaign, although the emphasis was on changing public perceptions rather than offering practical measures to help them.[37]

6.3   The National Committee

Although the Foreign Office remained sceptical about the virtues of the Human Rights Year, it realised that – if it had to be marked at all – it would be marked most effectively by a national committee, supported by government but otherwise independent. Such a committee could harness the energy of the voluntary organisations, and thereby enthuse and educate the public, while keeping radical influences at bay. In effect, officials wanted a series of events that would remind the world that Britain had invented human rights in 1215, while avoiding unhelpful questions about 'colonialism', and Rhodesia in particular.[38] In the event, although the Year was subject to allegations of being unduly conservative, it received such a positive response – there were eventually some 100 local committees and 160 national organisations involved[39] – that it was impossible for government to control it completely.

In May 1966 the Standing Conference on the Economic and Social Work of the UN (SCESWUN), the umbrella group for British NGOs, entrusted the UNA with organising the United Kingdom Committee for Human Rights Year.[40] The committee first met in November 1966, and the UNA seconded one of its senior officers, Gordon Evans (secretary to SCESWUN), to run it. Joost de Blank, former Archbishop of Cape Town, was appointed as Chairman, although he was in poor health and died on 1 January 1968. A memorial committee under Jack Halpern (formerly of Amnesty) set up a fund to promote race relations in his honour.[41] De Blank's place was taken by Sir Robert Birley, former Head Master of Eton and a critic of apartheid, who had recently returned from a visiting professorship at Witwatersrand University. If the national committee was in the hands of 'the establishment', both men stood firmly on the left wing of it, and had excellent credentials as opponents of racism. They were principally supported by Jocelyn Barrow, Trinidad-born teacher and educationalist (as Vice-Chair) and Humphrey Berkeley, former Tory MP and advocate of homosexual rights who had lost his seat in 1966 (Treasurer). All three of the main party leaders, Wilson, Edward Heath and Jeremy Thorpe, were appointed Honorary Presidents to demonstrate cross-party support. One particularly prominent supporter was Ritchie Calder (by now, Lord Ritchie-Calder) who offered a personal link to the Sankey/Wells initiative of 1940. During 1968 Calder frequently lectured about his memories of 1940, and his hopes for human rights in the modern world, and was considered as a possible chair of the UK Committee following the death of Archbishop de Blank.[42]

In July 1967 de Blank set out the committee's four main objectives as follows: to publicise and elucidate the Universal Declaration of Human Rights; to work towards the elimination of racial discrimination; to work towards the elimination of discrimination against women; and to assist those living in the UK's dependent territories to achieve human rights.[43] These aims remained unchanged, although at the launch ceremony on 11 December Humphrey Berkeley emphasised the underlying target of encouraging the government to ratify three key international conventions (which the UN had set as one of the goals for the year).[44] In April 1968, however, as race and immigration surged up the political agenda, Gordon Evans gave priority to a single aim: *'The thing of paramount importance we have to do in Human Rights Year is to ensure by all means in our power that the Race Relations Act, which will be passed by Parliament in a few months' time, shall be as fully effective as possible as an instrument for checking racial discrimination'.*[45]

How were these ambitious goals to be achieved? The government made available a miserly £5000, with a possible further £5000 to follow: this was supplemented by a £3000 grant from the UNA and subscriptions from affiliated organisations.[46] The committee's work was organised through a number of working groups, assembled around specific tasks or by common areas of interest: Education; Information and Publicity; Religious Organisations; Youth Organisations; Student Organisations; and Legislation and Conventions. These were later joined by groups on the Advancement of Women's Rights and on Housing. The reason for the delay in the former case was that the field was already congested, while, in the latter case, the key organisation – Shelter – had only recently been set up. However, the Executive Committee decided not to pursue the suggestion of establishing a working group for 'coloured immigrants' for fear that it would intensify prejudice: only a few months later, however, concern was expressed that immigrants were not taking a sufficient part in the Year.[47] These working groups varied in their level of activity. The Youth Organisations group was largely moribund, and the British Youth Council stated that it was 'unable to interest its member groups in Human Rights';[48] conversely, the student group campaigned hard over issues such as apartheid and Rhodesia. The multifaith Religious Organisations group commissioned notes for sermons and other religious services around the theme of human rights.[49] The women's group, which identified unequal pay for equal work as the 'chief' form of discrimination against women, sponsored some important local and national surveys. It held a highly successful closing conference (or 'talk-in') which issued a 'Declaration on the Advancement of Women's Rights'.[50]

The committee made good use of three prestigious, widely reported public events to project its message. At a special service at Westminster Abbey on 10 December 1967, attended by 'virtually all' churches and denominations, Archbishop Ramsey called for 'a year of spiritual warfare for human rights'. In more practical terms, he stated that 'the building up of community relations is the best answer to actions which are contrary to human rights'. The following day, there was an official launch at Central Hall, Westminster. In a message read out by Lord Chancellor Gerald Gardiner, Harold Wilson welcomed the Year as an 'opportunity to recapture the far-sighted idealism' of the Universal Declaration and pledged the government's support for its complete realisation.[51] The third major event was a conference for 2500 sixth-form students, organised early in the New Year by the Council for Education in World Citizenship (a UNA affiliate). The students listened to an address by Britain's Ambassador to the UN, Lord Caradon (who, as Hugh Foot, had been Governor at the height of the Cyprus Emergency), and were then left to debate a suitably provocative motion: 'This House holds that the Universal Declaration of Human Rights is based on a fallacy, lays down an impossible standard of achievement, and is entirely unrealistic in the world of the twentieth century'. After a 'flat and uninspiring' discussion the motion was heavily defeated.[52] Plans to mark the end of the Year with a major event at the Royal Albert Hall were abandoned, partly due to lack of funds, but also because 'Red Robert' Birley, alarmed at the anti-Americanism that he had witnessed at a similar event, thought that it would be unwise. Instead, the Foreign Office paid for a cocktail reception at Lancaster House.[53]

Throughout the Year, the committee was willing to make pointed interventions in public life. For instance, in February 1968 it expressed its 'complete opposition' to the Immigration Bill, which it saw as both discriminatory and a breach of faith towards East African Asians. It also recalled the pledges made by party leaders only a few months before to uphold the Year's objectives, but resisted calls for the removal of Wilson and his Conservative counterpart Edward Heath as Honorary Presidents.[54] Likewise, Robert Birley wrote an open letter to Enoch Powell, at the committee's request, immediately after his 'rivers of blood' speech. The tone and character of Powell's speech, he argued, was an affront to the dignity of Commonwealth immigrants, and thereby offended against Article 29 of the Universal Declaration ('dignity and free development of the personality') – a right with which the committee was 'particularly concerned'. To prevent the entry of immigrants' family members, as Powell proposed, was contrary to the Declaration's emphasis on the protection of family life and was not acceptable in a 'Christian country'.[55] While, the religious emphasis aside, Birley's comments may seem unexceptional today, it should be borne in mind that this was far from apparent at the time. The committee was hearing from its Field Officer, Keith Dowding, that 'people of good will were keeping silent on the subject of race relations', and during his tour of the local committees he noted that none were willing to take a public stand against Powell.[56] The final public statement by the committee in January 1969, a 'National Declaration on Race Relations', returned to the theme: it castigated racism as a 'false belief' and called for action against it in every sphere of life.[57]

The question of Rhodesia proved the most difficult to handle. At the outset the Foreign Office had discouraged the committee from taking up external issues such as Vietnam but accepted that 'some attention to United Kingdom colonial territories and Rhodesia would be reasonable'.[58] Indeed, as officials realised, not to take a position on Rhodesia would have fatally undermined the committee's credibility. However, doing so exposed it to political tensions, as left-wing politicians, such as Idris Cox of the Communist Party International Department and Abdul Minty of Anti-Apartheid, swiftly gravitated to the working group on dependent territories, much to the horror of the Foreign Office.[59] The chair, Labour MP Joan Lestor, was able to keep the working group under control. However, the committee would not allow her to present her group's findings at the Year's closing event, or to express her concerns about the government's commitment to the principle of no independence before majority rule in Rhodesia (or 'NIBMAR'). 'A controversial issue such as this', the committee decided, 'could not be raised in the presence of [the committee's patron] Prince Philip': instead, Birley promised merely to refer to the committee's work in his closing speech.[60] However, one more daring scheme did come to fruition in October 1968 when some 2500 envelopes were sent to people whose names were 'taken at random from the Rhodesian telephone directory'.

The packages contained copies of the Universal Declaration translated into English, Ndebele and Shona, as well as a list of political detainees and a letter from the committee expressing its concern.[61]

As the Rhodesia case demonstrates, the organisers of Human Rights Year in Britain had to strike a very difficult balance. It was almost impossible to pursue the patronage of royalty, the Foreign Office and the political parties while, at the same time, treating the Universal Declaration as – as Gordon Evans had told activists – an 'incredibly explosive document'.[62] Idris Cox accepted this compromise when he encouraged fellow communists to help to set up local committees: 'We cannot expect that such a committee will do everything we would like, but at least it would be a means of bringing together different progressive trends around this campaign … '.[63] This was part of a more thorough-going identification of the Communist Party with human rights, most visibly in a series of articles in the *Morning Star* to mark the start of Human Rights Year.[64] Others felt a keener sense of dissatisfaction. Tony Smythe of the NCCL derided the launch event in London's Central Hall as a takeover by the 'Establishment' – this was the signal for 'those who really want social change to walk out'.[65] (Interestingly, Gordon Evans had made a similar point a few weeks earlier when he briefed activists not to be too 'establishment-minded' and lose their 'moral fervour'.[66]) In part, however, Smythe's hostility was a way of asserting his own organisa-tion's claim to have made a distinctive, long-standing contribution: the NCCL had been protecting human rights 'since 1934', he noted, and could see beyond mere 'platform rhetoric' to the real 'victims of prejudice and neglect'. Smythe had relaunched the NCCL in the mid-1960s with some hyperbolic claims about the diminution of civil liberties (or 'creep-ing Fascism'[67]) under Labour and was not ready to take any lessons from Gerald Gardiner. At the end of the year, Des Wilson of Shelter, annoyed by the low priority given to the housing crisis by the national committee, launched a strong attack on the Year's 'contemptible' record. He and Shelter's Secretary Eileen Ware refused an invitation to attend the closing reception at Lancaster House, presided over by Prince Philip, stating that they would like a homeless couple to attend in their place.[68]

The record of the national committee was undoubtedly mixed. At least one flagship initiative – a proposed survey of human rights in the UK which was intended to serve as a 'baseline' for judging the success of the Year – generated much discussion but never materialised.[69] However, while never straying far from its 'establishment' connections, the com-mittee had offered an independent voice in national politics and facili-tated the work of the local groups. Looking back, the NCCL's annual report captured this ambivalence nicely. The Year had been a disappointment to those who had hoped for a 'positive improvement in the state of Human Rights in Britain'. Even so, there were some gains: the public had gained a clearer understanding of the Declaration of Human Rights, and local organisations worked together 'on human rights issues as never before'. Some even discovered 'serious problems that they never knew existed'.[70]

6.4   Participants: Organisations and Localities

The Year for Human Rights in Britain rested on two pillars, the 160 national organisations which affiliated to the central committee, and the roughly 100 local and regional committees. (Joost de Blank had originally hoped for 'several hundreds' of them.[71]) Given that many of these national organisations simply encouraged their members to participate in local events, it is the local committees – typically started from scratch with minimal resources – that provide the greatest insight into the public's response.

The participating national organisations (listed in Appendix 6.1) fall broadly into three categories. First, there were those which took the decision not to affiliate, in some cases because they were already too busy (such as the Howard League for Penal Reform). The response of the TUC was particularly disappointing. It saw the Human Rights Year committee as just the kind of amorphous, 'miscellaneous' body of which it was traditionally wary, especially as it already felt under pressure over certain human rights issues (such as equal pay and the closed shop). It settled for making a small donation instead.[72] Other groups, however, such as the Anti-Slavery Society, were initially non-committal but joined in enthusiastically once they realised the possibilities that participation offered for promoting their campaigns.[73] Secondly, the mass of organisations – such as political parties, trade unions, religious bodies and interest or vocational groups – had not previously taken a strong interest in human rights, but chose to affiliate because they broadly identified with the Year's goals.[74] In some cases these groups began through participation to redefine their activities *as* work for human rights. For instance, the Soroptimists, a non-political organisation dedicated to advancing the status of women, and promoting international friendship and understanding, became closely involved in Human Rights Year. They circulated journals and circulars around their clubs, eighty-five of which affiliated to local committees. Although the Soroptimists had always worked closely with the UN and its institutions, and had occasionally taken a position on broader issues such as the 1949 Genocide Convention,[75] after 1968 there was a marked increase in their willingness to take up human rights issues, In 1969 they enthusiastically adopted a UN campaign on the impact of science and technology on human personality, and they also joined the UNA's Human Rights Committee, established in the wake of Human Rights Year.[76]

Finally, there were the groups which already had a commitment to human rights: such groups were always likely to affiliate but may still have had to make certain accommodations in doing so. For Amnesty International the Year offered the British Section a way forwards after the crisis of 1966–67: as Eric Baker put it, it was a great opportunity 'to expand our active membership and to strengthen our finances'.[77] Amnesty described its Prisoner of Conscience week in November 1968 as its 'special contribution' to the Year.[78] The week certainly gained global publicity, but Amnesty – with its resolutely international focus – had to reorient itself in order to make the most of the Year's predominantly domestic focus. For instance, a conference at the LSE organised by the British Section took the theme of 'The Political Offender in Britain'.[79] The NCCL pledged its support to the Year while acknowledging that civil liberties issues did not always 'fall easily within the terms of the [Universal] Declaration'. It intended to use the Year to place questions such as police powers 'firmly before the public as a human rights issue'.[80] Discussions within the NCCL emphasised the many benefits of participation, such as the dissemination of its existing publications to a new audience, grants, access to younger age groups and publicity through the media.[81] Finally, Shelter, which had been founded in December 1966, saw the opportunity to raise public interest in homelessness at a time when most people in Britain 'would not . . . regard housing as a human right'. The national Human Rights Year committee's Housing Working Group – which Shelter dominated – was disappointed that housing was not given a more central role during the launch event. The persistence of this complaint helps to explain Des Wilson's outspoken comments at the Year's close.[82]

Turning to the localities, the fact that only about 100 out of the 1700 local and regional authorities approached set up a committee might, at first sight, be taken as an indication of failure. However, this figure is somewhat misleading as to some extent regional and national organisations compensated for a lack of committees in specific localities: in Wales, for instance, Human Rights Year was taken up very widely by a Welsh national committee, especially as an educational activity.[83] A Yorkshire committee was formed, under the chairmanship of the Liberal politician Lord Wade, which sought to address regional issues and to encourage participation by the large immigrant community.[84] Moreover, branches of organisations such as the UNA undertook much local activity without necessarily creating the formal structure of a town or city committee.[85] The sheer effort and element of risk in setting up a committee should also be taken into account. After all, no central funding was available, and, in the absence of precedent, any local initiative was inevitably a leap in the dark. When activists called an initial meeting to test the local interest in Nottingham they invited 400 organisations to attend, but the assumption was that they would be 'lucky' to attract 60 people. In the event, double that number attended. Even so, local activists still feared for a fiasco until the campaign was safely underway.[86] For any local committee, therefore, the initiative had to come from supportive councillors and/or activists and was most likely to succeed when other factors were also present: these included a strong civic culture, existing local networks of voluntary organisations (above all, an active UNA), religious ecumenism and a local awareness of social and racial tensions. However, the list of participant committees (see Appendix 6.2) does not reveal any obvious pattern as it represents a cross-section of British society: urban industrial areas, prosperous suburbs and market towns in roughly equal measure. Nor could success be taken for granted, as even in traditionally liberal Oxford the initial response to the Year was so poor that the Lord Mayor said that local people should 'be ashamed' of it. It may be that a city that was the home to Oxfam and some pioneering local initiatives to promote racial integration, and was represented in Parliament by a leading authority on human rights and internationalism (Labour MP Evan Luard), felt less urgency in marking Human Rights Year.[87] Overall, however, while Human Rights Year was hardly an unalloyed triumph in the localities, the level of achievement was still striking, and deserves further exploration.

Although some regional planning conferences were held as early as the spring of 1967, the national campaign deemed local committees to be autonomous and devoted little attention to them. Indeed, a half of them were only beginning to function once the Year had begun.[88] Unfortunately, the lack of a central archive for Human Rights Year limits any comprehensive nationwide analysis of the campaign, compounded by the fact that only one of these local committees (Nottingham, which also claimed to be the first) appears to have left substantial documentation. Moreover, the national committee only appointed a Field Officer to assist the local groups (Keith Dowding) in January 1968, and his reports have not survived in any detail, apart from a few tantalising comments. As we have seen, he was evidently critical of what he found, and according to Tony Smythe his reports showed that prejudice was 'rife' in the local committees and UNA branches.[89] In the absence of fuller national reporting, the following account draws heavily on the Nottingham archives and the reasonably good local press coverage of some other localities.

In April 1967 the national committee issued formal guidance to the local groups. The aim was to carry out a programme of education and study of human rights, to be delivered by a 'widely representative Human Rights committee ... under civic leadership'.[90] Two important points emerged from this advice: the first was that the leadership and help of the civic authorities was deemed to be crucial; secondly, a comprehensive list of the kinds of organisations which should be invited to take part ranged from adult education providers, churches and political parties, to organisations representing women, employers and the Jewish community. However, although they were not excluded, there was no mention of those organisations specifically interested in human rights, such as Amnesty and the NCCL. One document prepared for the Nottingham committee sheds light on this: it makes clear that promoting an awareness of international human rights was the distant goal, but that many organisations would be primarily interested in the local and national situation and their efforts should not be 'decried'. The focus must be on the '"pay off" which will benefit the whole community rather than the very high moral standards which very few of us are capable of maintaining'.[91] By implication, groups with 'high moral standards' such as Amnesty might even deter participation by less committed groups. The primary intention was to make 'the whole community ... human rights conscious', and this would – for most – begin close to their home.[92] As a Nottingham circular put it: 'Problems of Human Rights seem far off when compared to the life in our City but we have problems too and find extreme poverty, loneliness, racial discrimination and deliberate ignorance of human feelings on our own doorsteps'.[93] The Yorkshire committee highlighted the '"social services" aspects of human rights ... lively concern for the elderly, the lonely, the handicapped, the isolated'.[94]

In the absence of central funding, the local groups were reliant on whatever money they could raise, alongside very variable levels of local authority support. In Camden, a London borough with a large immigrant population stretching from the City of London to Hampstead, the council provided a £450 grant to cover the administrative costs of the local campaign. The campaign had its own office to coordinate local activity and set up local working groups that corresponded to those at the national level.[95] However, in Nottingham, despite personal support from council officials, the committee faced financial difficulties even when still in the preparatory stage. A circular noted that the committee was being 'carried' by the Nottingham Council for Social Service: however, with the city council in deficit and no more 'hidden subsidy' available, fundraising was now essential. Proposed activities included a 'pub-crawl' by students who would collect money from customers 'instead of accepting drinks from them'.[96] The committee flirted with bankruptcy, and by May 1968 it was told that it must raise funds quickly or 'fold up'. It was kept afloat with a small unpublicised grant from the national committee.[97] With funding at such a premium, the main resource was the unpaid support – and skills – of the local voluntary sector. In Nottingham, for instance, some 120 local organisations were affiliated, with interests ranging, it was said, 'from underdeveloped countries to Boy Soldiers, the United Nations to Gypsies, Child Poverty to International Voluntary Service'.[98] Another resource was to borrow ideas from other localities. Some councils thought about copying Camden's proposal for a 'non-discrimination clause' for all the employment agencies in the borough.[99] Others took inspiration from Tunbridge Wells' decision to display a sumptuous copy of the Universal Declaration – leather-bound, with the Human Rights Year symbol in gold leaf, hand-printed on parchment and mounted on a carved wooden stand – in the Town Hall. This 'beautiful book ... a labour of love' by a sympathetic local calligrapher, was paid for by coffee mornings organised by the local Human Rights Committee.[100]

Tunbridge Wells was simply carrying out – albeit lavishly – one of the original recommendations of the national committee, as Evans had suggested that copies of the Declaration 'inscribed on worthy material' should be 'ceremonially unveiled like a war memorial'.[101] However, this case serves to underline the absolute centrality of the Universal Declaration, both as a text and as an artefact, to the celebration of Human Rights Year. Indeed, there are many other local examples of plaques or framed copies being unveiled – Poole, for instance, was described as 'one of the first places in England to have the declaration inscribed for all to see'.[102] Other forms of promoting the Declaration might include asking local newspapers to write a series of reports dealing with each Article in turn.[103] In May 1968 the Declaration was read out in full in an Oxford Methodist Church, whereupon the Rev. J. A. Gibbon made a vigorous defence of immigration.[104] What is not known is the extent to which, as a result of this local activism, the 'universal Magna Carta'[105] was actually read, understood and internalised by the public. In a briefing session for local groups Gordon Evans made a somewhat unfortunate point when he said that 'in the Western world [the Universal Declaration] may be compared with Mao Tse Dung's [sic] little red book in the East'.[106] The leader of the UNA in Nottingham made a more practical suggestion when she told the first meeting of the local committee that they should all study the Declaration in detail and then look at how it was applied in 'our own city ... in practice'.[107] The Year ended with the committee's Chairman presenting a bound copy of the Universal Declaration to the Lord Mayor of Nottingham, before the full city council. He handed it over in the firm belief that the city council acknowledged 'the various articles embodied within', but also noted that there were 'still too many areas of our Community life which are a denial' of its principles.[108]

Alongside the emphasis on the Declaration, another striking feature of local campaigning was the importance of religion. It was implicitly understood, from the national launch in Westminster Abbey onwards, that Human Rights Year was underpinned by religious values (primarily, but by no means exclusively, Christian) and that religious organisations would be a principal source of support and guidance. In its advice to local groups about their launch events, the national committee specified that – mindful that Human Rights Day fell on a Sunday – 'in addition to a civic launching ceremony, special efforts should be made to enlist the help of all clergy and ministers and leaders of all religious organisations, including those of non-Christian religions ... .'[109] In Nottingham, for instance, the initial proposal was to hold an interfaith service, although this was abandoned for the intriguing reason that 'the scriptures and sacred books of some of the religious denominations ... did not provide any material to support the Human Rights theme'.[110] Instead an inter-denominational service was held in the Castle Gate Congregational Church. The sermon was delivered by the Barbados-born Rev. Wilfred Wood, who took as his text Amos 5: 22–4: 'let justice roll down like waters, and righteousness like an ever-flowing stream'.[111] Both at the national and local levels, formal religious involvement was less in evidence after the launch events, and closing ceremonies were typically secular (although in Wales the Year ended with a multifaith ceremony in the Temple of Peace, Cardiff[112]). There is no record of the amount of use made of the generic materials for religious services produced for Human Rights Year. However, religion returned sharply and unexpectedly to the fore after Martin Luther King's assassination in April 1968, when many local committees organised commemorative religious services.

The record of Human Rights Year in the localities remains open to widely differing interpretations. One can choose to emphasise those areas which saw a high level of activity, or, alternatively, the swathes of the country where there appears to have been little or no formal commemoration. Gordon Evans saw the Year in Britain as 'a sowing of seeds and putting down of roots ... a year of fertiliser and ferment'. The Chairman of the Leeds committee emphasised how people from very diverse backgrounds worked together in study groups – 'concern for Human Rights can overcome barriers which have existed for years'.[113] The Chairman of the campaign in Nottingham put it very well: they did not 'attempt the spectacular' but 'in a quiet way a steady educational process went on ...'.[114]

6.5   Northern Ireland's Year of Human Rights

While copies of the Universal Declaration were being exhibited in town halls across mainland Britain, in Northern Ireland civil rights campaigners were reading out the Declaration in front of the Guildhall in Derry (Londonderry).[115] The contrast could not have been sharper – in Northern Ireland, the Declaration truly was Gordon Evans' 'explosive document'. Indeed, nothing posed a greater challenge to the entire conception of the Human Rights Year in Britain than the surge of protests and increasing political polarisation in the province that took place during 1968. How could Britain proclaim its commitment to – indeed, assert a claim to leadership in – human rights when a Catholic minority in one part of the United Kingdom felt deprived of basic democratic and civil rights? The Labour politician Paul Rose, who took a keen interest in Northern Ireland in the mid-1960s, wrote that, within Britain, he encountered a 'black wall of incomprehension and ignorance about Ulster'. Saigon and Salisbury loomed far larger, it seemed to him, than Belfast and Londonderry.[116] The events of 1968 punctured this complacency and ensured that Northern Ireland could no longer be ignored. By June 1969 the ICJ would add Northern Ireland to a list of places in Europe where human rights and the rule of law were regressing – a list that included Spain, Portugal, Greece and Czechoslovakia. The good reputation of Britain was, the ICJ noted, thereby 'vicariously damaged'.[117]

The tensions in Northern Ireland had largely been contained since partition and the first round of sectarian 'Troubles' in 1920–22. The Unionist domination of the devolved state, government and Parliament rested not only on a simple Protestant majority, but also on continued resort to the repressive Special Powers Act, Protestant domination of the ill-disciplined Special Constabulary (or 'B-Specials'), widespread discrimination in terms of access to local authority housing and employment opportunities, and electoral gerrymandering. At its simplest the demand of the civil rights movement was for 'One Man – One Vote'. The Catholic minority, meanwhile, was politically weak and divided. The long-established Nationalist Party was fragmented and for many years conflicted over whether to even contest elections for Northern Ireland

Parliament at Stormont, where it had only recently formed an official opposition. The Northern Ireland Labour Party had lost Catholic support when it adopted a Unionist platform in 1949, although some working-class Catholics turned to Gerry Fitt's Republican Labour Party in the mid-1960s. There was also some limited support for militant Republicanism, but the IRA's 'border campaign' of 1956–61 had been defeated amidst the widespread jailing and internment of Republican sympathisers.

By the mid-1960s, however, there were indications of a fresh approach to politics, as the Catholic middle class came to the fore. Sheelagh Murnaghan, who had helped to revive the Liberal Party in the province in 1959 and represented Queen's University Belfast at Stormont, introduced four human rights bills in the Northern Ireland Parliament between 1964 and 1968. According to the local press she epitomised 'the Human Rights movement in Ulster' – but her efforts were consistently blocked by the Unionist majority.[118] Another prominent figure was the Catholic activist Patricia McCluskey, who established the Campaign for Social Justice (CSJ) with her husband Conn following a campaign for fairer access to housing in Dungannon. Like Murnaghan, McCluskey was not concerned with Irish unification, but rather wanted the rights enjoyed by British citizens on the mainland to be extended to the North. Harold Wilson corresponded with the CSJ shortly before his election victory in 1964 and – in an often-cited letter – pledged a future Labour government to 'do everything in its power' to deal with the 'infringements of justice'.[119] Once in office, however – despite Wilson's later claim that Labour MPs had been 'united in their determination to establish human rights in Northern Ireland' – the cross-party convention of non-interference in Northern Irish affairs, the demands of other political priorities and a lack of resolve meant that his 'good intentions ... came to nothing'.[120] However, the CSJ had at least galvanised interest at Westminster, where Paul Rose, a Labour MP, barrister and member of Amnesty, was inspired to set up the Campaign for Democracy in Ulster in 1964.

The principal hope for political change lay briefly with the rise of the reformist Unionist Captain Terence O'Neill, who became Prime Minister of Northern Ireland in 1963. O'Neill understood the benefits of cross-border economic cooperation with the Republic and established good relations with his counterpart Sean Lemass in the South.[121] However, O'Neill aroused hostility amongst many working-class Protestants, who feared that his modernising reforms would be at the expense of their own interests. O'Neill encountered mounting opposition both within his own party, from hardliners such as William Craig, and without, from the evangelical minister and grass-roots Belfast politician Rev. Ian Paisley. To the frustration of Harold Wilson, who had hoped that a successful programme of reforms could save his government from having to intervene, an embattled O'Neill found himself trapped on a vanishing middle ground, caught between Catholic demands for civil rights and Unionist reaction. The Northern Ireland Civil Rights Association (NICRA), established in January 1967 and inspired by civil rights campaigns in the United States, was the principal vehicle for Catholic campaigning.[122] However, other political forces were also in motion – left-wing university students (who would become the People's Democracy movement), local mobilisations around housing and other grievances in Belfast and Derry, and representatives of older Nationalist, Republican and left-wing traditions that were adapting to the more activist politics of the mid-1960s. The young Nationalist politician Austin Currie worked with local campaigns for improved housing, and Gerry Fitt, elected to Westminster in 1966, was determined to break down the conventions that restricted serious discussion of Northern Ireland on the floor of the House.[123] This was an uneasy combination, but in 1967–68 it was still characterised by a belief that rights for the minority could be secured by peaceful protest.

Human rights campaigners in mainland Britain had not completely neglected Northern Ireland. The NCCL laid claim to an honourable heritage dating back to its pioneering inquiry of 1936, and in 1962 Martin Ennals reported on the persistence of 'grave violations of civil liberties' in the province.[124] A short-lived Northern Ireland Council for Civil Liberties was established in 1960, mainly concerned with supporting Republican prisoners jailed during the recent border campaign. In 1967–68 the NCCL actively supported NICRA, but found it to be a difficult partner and pupil, given that NICRA favoured political activism over the NCCL's more discreet application of legal and political pressure.[125] Amnesty had also expressed an initial interest in Northern Ireland. Peter Benenson and Eric Baker had looked for political prisoners there while planning the launch of their Appeal in 1961, but they discovered that there were no 'deserving cases' as all the jailed Republicans had advocated violence.[126] On Human Rights Day 1961 Benenson and Baker wrote to the Ulster Agent in London to inform him of Amnesty's work. They received a rather tart response from Stormont's Minister for Home Affairs, Brian Faulkner, who felt that they were 'under a serious misapprehension': terrorists might be jailed or detained in Northern Ireland, but nobody was deprived of their liberty for their opinions or religion.[127] Benenson spoke at Queen's Belfast in November 1962 and an Amnesty branch was established in the city in 1963. It had a membership of fifty by 1968, and was hoping to expand further, especially amongst students. However, like all Amnesty groups, its work was limited to foreign prisoners (it claimed to have secured the release of an 'influential Moroccan newspaper editor'), and any intervention in the new 'Troubles' would have to come from Amnesty sections in other countries.[128] In July 1968 representatives of the Irish and Northern Irish sections met on the border and agreed, in principle, to form 'one national section', but nothing appears to have come of the initiative.[129]

Northern Ireland claimed to have established one of the first Human Rights Year committees, which was formed as early as the autumn of 1966.[130] In May 1967 thirty representatives out of some eighty invited organisations took part in a meeting in Belfast City Hall, addressed by the UNA's Director General John Ennals. However, the campaign was not formally launched until the spring of 1968.[131] One reason for the delay may have been the difficulty in identifying a Chairman – at least one turned the post down, fearing correctly that it was 'likely to be quite a serious task for Northern Ireland'.[132] The committee broadly resembled those on the mainland, in that it was sponsored by civic authorities and local politicians (Terence O'Neill and the Nationalist leader Eddie McAteer, alongside church leaders, were amongst the honorary Presidents). It drew its support from liberal-minded, middle-class Catholics and Protestants, above all the UNA and the Society of Friends. One influential participant was the prominent Quaker and peace campaigner Denis Barritt, the author of respected studies of community relations in the province.[133] In the course of 1968 the committee organised school conferences on human rights, and a subcommittee reviewed Northern Ireland legislation, including the Special Powers Act. The campaign also agreed to raise funds for a research project in association with Queen's University Belfast to examine the origins and impact of sectarian prejudice. By the end of the year some £1500 of the £5000 required to fund a fellowship had been raised, at which point the fundraising was taken over by the local UNA.[134]

Such otherwise worthy activities were wholly inadequate for addressing the surge of radical protest, under the banner of civil rights, that swept Northern Ireland in the autumn of 1968. On 5 October 1968 the Derry Housing Action Committee, backed by NICRA, decided to go ahead with a banned march in the city centre. The marchers, who included moderate Catholic activists such as John Hume, were savagely beaten by the police, in full view of the TV cameras and three Labour MPs. On 9 October the Northern Ireland Human Rights Year committee's officers issued a statement in which they listed the articles of the Universal Declaration not observed in the province and called on the government to tackle 'long-standing grievances with energy and determination'.[135] When Tony

Smythe of the NCCL expressed disappointment that the statement did not go far enough, he was told by the Secretary of the Northern Ireland committee that it was the best that such a broadly based body could achieve, and 'it was felt that they could make a useful contribution by giving expression to moderate opinion'.[136] Others were more forceful. At the UNA Executive in mid-November Brian Walker, representing Northern Ireland, warned about the dangers: 'if civil war broke out this weekend, as it might well do, it could easily spread to London and other cities in England'.[137] Speaking in Oxford in December Gerry Fitt also warned that if civil rights were not granted 'the only other solution will be civil war'.[138]

Civil rights campaigners and Catholic politicians such as McAteer and Fitt repeatedly referred to the crisis in Northern Ireland as being due to the denial of 'basic human rights'.[139] On Human Rights Day (10 December) the Derry Citizens' Action Committee, which had been created in response to the police actions of 5 October, organised a petition calling on the British government to implement the Universal Declaration throughout the whole of the UK.[140] By the autumn, therefore, there were in effect two human rights campaigns in Northern Ireland: one of them moderate, educational and closely analogous to the national campaign; the other radical, activist and seeking to use the Declaration as a lever for promoting immediate reforms. The distance between them was broad, but not wholly unbridgeable. Interestingly, Sir Robert Birley chose to come to Derry in the closing days of Human Rights Year to speak to the local UNA on 'The History of a Great Ideal'. He observed that the civil rights movement in Northern Ireland 'was asking for many of the things which the Human Rights movement was asking for all over the world'. His recollections of apartheid in South Africa helped branch members – as one wrote –'to put our own difficult local problems in wider perspective and to strengthen our determination to do our best to help overcome them'.[141] Only a few weeks later, however, in early January 1969, a People's Democracy march from Belfast to Derry was brutally attacked by Unionists at Burntollet Bridge, as police stood by. In response, the first barricades went up in Derry's Catholic Bogside area. In February O'Neill called fresh elections and – having failed to receive the mandate he had hoped for – resigned on 28 April. By August, amidst outbreaks of severe sectarian violence, premonitions of civil war did not seem misplaced and the British army was dispatched to keep the peace.

6.6   Legacies: the British Institute of Human Rights

During 1968 a debate began as to how the 'spirit of the Human Rights Year' could be kept alive.[142] One imaginative proposal – the brainchild of Amnesty's Anthony Marreco – was for a 'Human Rights Television Trust', which would utilise the power of film to avert future human rights catastrophe. Marreco's interest in the potential for televised drama and documentary was sparked by the success of *Cathy Come Home* – Ken Loach's 1966 film which did much to alert public opinion to Britain's housing crisis – although his idea that television reporting could have averted the drift to dictatorship in the 1930s was surely over-optimistic.[143] The project failed to take off, although Marreco had judged correctly that the media would come to play an increasingly influential role in publicising human rights violations, through the pioneering work of film-makers such as Vanya Kewley.[144] The most enduring proposal was for a permanent Human Rights Institute, which would carry out research into human rights and lobby government. This enjoyed consid-erable support within the Human Rights Year national committee, but also encountered a surprising amount of opposition – both on institu-tional and conceptual grounds – which sheds interesting light on the current state of human rights activism.

The Institute was mainly the work of John Alexander-Sinclair,[145] a retired international civil servant who was appointed as Campaign Director for the national Human Rights Year committee in late 1967. Alexander-Sinclair aroused some hostility due to his alleged 'establish-ment' connections, but there is no question that without his persistence the project would have been abandoned at an early stage. A brief survey of his career shows how, in his case, human rights offered a new focus for a wide-ranging set of skills and experiences, acquired over many years.[146] Alexander-Sinclair (1906–88) had started his career as a British Consul and embassy official in China during the 1930s, where he had helped found the famous Chinese Industrial Cooperatives movement and was briefly interned in 1941–42. At the end of the war he joined the British delegation to the UN (Social and Economic Affairs section), where he was Chairman of the Non-Governmental Organisations Committee 1946–47. It was said that he found his 'cause' in working for the resettle-ment of refugees and served with the United Nations Relief and Rehabilitation Administration (UNRRA) and various UN agencies before, as European Director of the International Rescue Committee (IRC), working with Hungarian exiles. In 1959 he won an IRC Distinguished Service Award for 'devotion to the cause of freedom' in helping 'refugees from totalitarianism'. Despite a career spent in organi-sations, Alexander-Sinclair was independent-minded: he left the UN High Commission for Refugees in 1955 when, by his own admission, he 'became too difficult to handle', and the IRC was unenthusiastic about his master plan to resettle refugees on Sardinia. On leaving the UN he went to work for the Liberal International, 1962–64, before joining an early incarnation of the Minority Rights Group, and, eventually, the Anti-Slavery Society. As a libertarian and an opponent of official secrecy, the attraction of working for Human Rights Year was obvious: but after an itinerant career, so too was the attraction of personally shaping what came after it. In effect, the legacy of the Human Rights' Year in Britain would also be that of John Alexander-Sinclair.

In the spring of 1968 Alexander-Sinclair floated the idea of 'some sort of organisation which could carry on the work of the UK Committee' to an informal group that included the lawyers Hilary Cartwright, Anthony Lester and Sam Silkin. The UK Committee commissioned him to set up a new working group to explore the idea further.[147] Silkin, a Labour MP and future Attorney General (1974–79), acted as rapporteur and produced a highly ambitious threefold plan. In addition to a Human Rights Institute, he also called for the creation of a new post of UK Human Rights Commissioner (akin to the recently created Ombudsman), and a 'specifically British' Bill of Rights. The problem was that only the first of these was within the scope of voluntary agency to achieve: the other two were political projects requiring high-level support within government. The national committee accepted this point when in January 1969 it agreed to back (albeit not wholeheartedly) the Institute, but reserved judgement on the other two proposals.[148] The working group then turned into a smaller preparatory committee, which in turn established a charitable Human Rights Trust in early 1970.

The project aroused an angry response from Tony Smythe of the NCCL, who – despite Alexander-Sinclair's attempts to reassure him – saw it as an unnecessary distraction, a possible rival for grants and an attempt by the establishment to exercise 'benevolent supervision' over human rights organisations in the field. What the NCCL needed from the Human Rights Year committee, Smythe argued, was help securing more members and funds, not competition.[149] His response was to boycott the discussions, and as a result he wrongly believed that the UK Committee had refused to back the proposed institute: accordingly, and rather unfairly, when it finally became operational in 1971 he felt that he had been deliberately kept in the dark.[150] Given that the field was far from overcrowded (as one colleague told Smythe, there was enough work for six organisations like the NCCL) Smythe's opposition was instinctively political. After all, his first response had been to claim that Alexander-Sinclair was seeking support from the Confederation of British Industry and to question his motives.[151] More significantly, perhaps, he understood that as the human rights movement grew and became more mainstream it would be increasingly torn between radical activism and working for change from within. As he put it in 1972, one reason for concern about the new institute was that it was 'forcing us away from the middle ground': it was time for the NCCL to decide where it stood.[152]

The Institute also stirred some hostility on the part of the UNA. One thinly veiled source of tension during Human Rights Year had been the assumption that the UNA was '"first among equals"' in the campaign, and, at the year's end, Birley was careful to thank it for its 'major and indispensable' support.[153] Indeed, Gordon Evans had briefly resigned as General Secretary of the national committee over the issue of whether it was a truly independent organisation, or one directed by the UNA.[154] This friction became more significant now for two reasons. First, the UNA was itself eager to lay claim to be the 'residual legatee' of Human Rights Year. It was in the process of setting up its own Human Rights Committee and this gave it a strong case, as many members of the national committee simply transferred onto the new one. Moreover, the new committee was chaired by Jocelyn Barrow, and was joined by the entire Human Rights Year working groups on dependent territories, women's rights and legislation. The UNA was therefore hostile to any claim by Alexander-Sinclair's project to be the legatee of Human Rights Year, especially – the second key point – as there was still some money in the Human Rights Year committee's coffers. Indeed, the UNA Trust received some £4500 to support the continuing activities of the working groups.[155] Counterproductive as some of these arguments may have been, they did at least prove that – with Human Rights Year at an end – there was a legacy worth fighting over.

In the event, the Institute did not start work in earnest until 1972, when it ran a conference on the rights of detainees. It was only able to employ its first salaried Director – Tony McNulty, formerly Secretary to the European Commission of Human Rights – in 1977.[156] For all his assumed links to the establishment, the project was always a labour of love for Alexander-Sinclair. At one point he revealed that he was paying for all its administrative costs himself, 'out of my FO pension . . . and you can imagine what THAT is'.[157]

*

During the final months of 1968 the Society of Portrait Sculptors staged an exhibition of its members' work in the Crypt of St Paul's Cathedral 'in honour of men and women of all nationalities who have fought in the furtherance of human rights'. It was a marvellously eclectic selection of six women and forty-one men (listed in Appendix 6.3): popes, presidents and humanitarians alongside less familiar names such as Hiroshima survivor Mashashi Nii, who was currently touring Britain.[158] These were, for the most part, people who had lived exemplary lives and contributed to the general good, now grouped together as fighters for human rights. This makes a good metaphor for understanding the impact of Human Rights Year in Britain. For, where it had been customary to refer to diverse organisations working together loosely in 'the field of human rights', by 1968 the 'field' was becoming a club. Being identified with human rights was now desirable – even fashionable. It offered a new sense of purpose, valuable connections, an enhanced public profile, and access to funds from the state and wealthy foundations.

Appendix 6.1 The Affiliated National Organisations

(As of 1 June 1967: TNA FCO 61/179) Amnesty International, Anglo-Jewish Association, Anti-Apartheid, Anti-Slavery Society, Association for Jewish Youth, Board of Deputies, British Council of Churches, British Federation of University Women, Brotherhood Movement, Catholic Institute of International Relations, Civil Service Clerical Association, Council of Christians and Jews, Council for Education in World Citizenship, Education Advisory Committee of the Parliamentary Group for World Government, Fawcett Society, Federation of Conservative Students, Fédération internationale des femmes des carrières juridique (UK Section), Federation of Soroptimist Clubs, Federation of Women Zionists, General Assembly of Unitarian and Free Christian Churches, Health Visitors Association, International Friendship League, International Planned Parenthood Federation, Josephine Butler Society, Labour Party, League of Jewish Women, Liberal Party, National Association for Mental Health, National Association of Schoolmasters, National British Women's Total Abstinence Union, National Committee for Commonwealth Immigrants, National Council for the Unmarried Mother and Her Child, National Council of Women, National Federation of Community Associations, National Federation of Young Farmers' Clubs, National Joint Committee of Working Women's Organisations, National Peace Council, National Secular Society, National Union of Agricultural Workers, National Union of Boot and Shoe Operatives, National Union of Municipal Workers, National Union of Teachers, National Women Citizens Association, Racial Unity, St Joan's Alliance, Salvation Army, Save the Children Fund, Shelter, Society of Technical Civil Servants, Student Christian Movement, Tobacco Workers' Union, Trades Advisory Council, Union of Catholic Mothers, Union of Jewish Women, Union of Liberal and Progressive Synagogues, Union of Post Office Workers, UNA, United Nations Students' Association, United

World Education and Research Trust, War on Want, Women's International League for Peace and Freedom, Women's Liberal Federation, World Goodwill, World Jewish Congress (British Section), World University Service, Young Women's Christian Association of Great Britain, National Spiritual Assembly of the Ba'hai of the British Isles.

Appendix 6.2 The Local Committees

There is no definitive list: the most authoritative is Bodleian Library, Anti-Slavery Society, S.22 G881 4 R, File B, for 27 March 1968. This identifies ninety-seven committees, including 'national committees' for Scotland, Northern Ireland and Wales, and 'regional committees' for the Isle of Wight and Yorkshire. It lists the following local committees in England and Wales: Abingdon, Barnsley, Bath, Bideford, Birmingham, Bolton, Bournemouth, Bradford, Brent, Bridgend, Bristol, Burnley, Bury St Edmunds, Cambridge, Camden, Cardiff, Carlisle, Chard, Chelmsford, City of London, Coventry, Crosby, Deal, Doncaster, Durham, Ealing, Eastbourne, Exeter, Folkestone, Hackney, Haringey, Harlow, Harrogate, Hastings, Havant, Havering, High Wycombe, Hounslow, Huddersfield, Hull, Ilkeston, Keynsham, Leeds, Leicester, Lewisham, Lincoln and County, Liverpool, Manchester, Marlborough, Marple, Middlesbrough, Newbury, Newcastle upon Tyne, Norwich, Nottingham, Oxford, Oxted, Peterborough, Plymouth, Pontypridd, Poole, Port Talbot, Princes Risborough, Reading, Reigate, Richmond, Risca, St Albans, Salisbury, Sheffield, Skipton, Southampton, Southport, Stockton-on-Tees, Sutton Coldfield, Swansea, Tunbridge Wells, Wandsworth, Warrington, Watford, Westminster, Weymouth, Whitstable, Wimbledon, Winchester, Wolverhampton, Worthing, Wortley, Wrexham.

However, in June 1968 Gardiner told a UN seminar that there were 'more than a hundred' local committees (Churchill College, GARD 2/4, text of speech, 18 June 1968, p. 2), and Birley also referred to committees in 'over a hundred towns and cities' in his closing report (*New World*, September 1969, p. 7.) This indicates that there were a few unrecorded latecomers, amongst which I have been able to identify examples in Barnet, Colchester and Croydon (*New World*, September 1968, p. 10 and November 1968, p. 10).

Appendix 6.3 The Society of Portrait Sculptors Human Rights Exhibition, St Paul's, 27 September–20 December 1968 (Source: Bodleian Library, Anti-Slavery Society, S.22 G881, File J).

Subjects represented three times in the exhibition: Pope John [XXIII]; Dr Albert Schweitzer.

Represented twice: Mahatma Gandhi; Tom Paine; Hugh McDiarmid; Mrs Eleanor Roosevelt; President John F. Kennedy.

Represented once: Colonel Mary Booth; David Lloyd George; Cardinal Bea; Sir Leary Constantine; Dr Du Bois; Canon Collins; Keir Hardie; Elizabeth Fry; Emmeline Pankhurst; Dr Billy Graham; Dr Harold Moody; William Morris; Prof. Gilbert Murray; Mrs Luther King; Lord Denning; James Cameron; Masashi Nii; Bishop Colenso; Lord Balfour; Col. Van der Post; Lord Beveridge; Earl Attlee; Lord Robert Cecil; Josephine Butler; Lord Boyd Orr; Paul Robeson; Dr Martin Luther King; Aneurin Bevan; Sir Alan Herbert; Robert Kennedy; Abraham Lincoln; Rev. P. B. Clayton; Pope Paul; Florence Nightingale; Sir Winston Churchill; Melina Mercouri; Father Borelli; Sir Thomas More.

7 Torture States: 1967–1975

7.1 'The Recrudescence of Torture'

Amidst the many conflicts of the late 1960s and early 1970s, arguably the greatest shock for human rights activists was the installation of ruthless military dictatorships in Greece and Chile. The Greek Colonels' *coup d'état* of April 1967 was particularly alarming as it took place in a state that was a member of NATO and the Council of Europe, and was often referred to as the cradle of democracy.[1] Chile, where General Augusto Pinochet's junta seized power on 11 September 1973, was less well known in Britain, but it had a long democratic tradition, and the progressive Allende government of 1970–73 was popular on the British left. Both of the new regimes were characterised by the systematic use of torture against their opponents, as well as, in Chile, by extrajudicial killings. The reports by Amnesty's investigators marked a shift towards a new, unflinching intensity in the description of torture, often accompanied by disturbing visual representations.[2] Whereas Amnesty had previously focused on the psychological isolation of the 'forgotten' prisoner, it increasingly placed a spotlight on prisoners whose physical well-being – even their lives – were also in immediate jeopardy. (Hence Amnesty's introduction of 'Urgent Action' campaigns for the most vulnerable cases.) Such a retreat from democratic rule into 'barbarism' had not been seen since the 1930s, but it was concerns over an 'epidemic' of torture that above all galvanised action. As Joseph Needham, the Cambridge Sinologist and prominent supporter of Amnesty, wrote privately in 1974: 'I feel very disturbed at the recrudescence of torture of political prisoners in so many countries, and fear the growth of a new "scientific" and "hygienic" sadism, designed to terrorise opponents of establishments ... [Torture had been considered barbarous between *c.*1830 and 1930 but] are we in for another couple of centuries of horrors while a new stabilisation occurs'?[3]

Activists also had to contend with the fact that Britain itself had become the site for alleged serious abuses of human rights, arguably amounting to torture. Following the decision to deploy soldiers in Northern Ireland in August 1969, initially to impose order between the province's bitterly divided communities but increasingly to confront the Republican Provisional IRA, the army's conduct came under unprecedented scrutiny. The scale of the crisis facing successive governments should not be underestimated, as more than 3000 people died in the 'Troubles' of 1969–98, more than half of them during the period 1971–76. However, the risk to Britain's reputation as a tolerant, liberal society was also severe. There were three pivotal moments. First, in August 1971 – with British approval – the Northern Ireland government introduced internment without trial, overwhelmingly of Catholics. This in turn led directly to 'Bloody Sunday' in January 1972, when the army shot dead thirteen unarmed anti-internment protestors in Derry, and to the introduction of direct rule from Westminster in March. Secondly, the army used 'interrogation in depth' to gather intelligence from detainees. (These were the so-called 'five techniques', including sleep deprivation and hooding, that had been developed in Aden.) In 1976 the European Commission of Human Rights determined that the methods used amounted to torture, although the European Court subsequently decided that the British authorities had been guilty of no more than inhuman and degrading treatment.[4] Thirdly, the Prevention of Terrorism Act (PTA) was passed through Parliament in a few days following the IRA Birmingham pub bombings in November 1974 and was described even by Home Secretary Roy Jenkins as 'Draconian'.[5] Northern Ireland, therefore, posed severe challenges for British human rights organisations. They were divided over whether to criticise the actions of the British government,[6] their assumptions about Britain's claims to moral leadership were questioned, and they realised that they could not always take public sympathy for granted. Eric Baker noted that 'I do not believe that we have yet grasped the degree of public support' for 'interrogation in depth' during a period of emergency, and he had even encountered support for it at Friends' meetings.[7]

The revival of torture, therefore, cast a dark cloud over this period: even in an age of violence, it was noted, torture held a 'special horror'.[8] In a booklet published in 1973 Victor Jokel, Director of Amnesty's British Section, wrote that 'we can speak of the existence of "Torture States" as a political reality of our times. The malignancy has become epidemic, and knows no ideological, racial or economic boundaries'.[9] Likewise, Eric Baker frequently referred to torture as a 'cancer in the body politic'.[10] These dark times, globally as well as within Britain, produced vivid, even apocalyptic, language. The NCCL concluded in 1974 that civil liberties were 'in retreat', and in 1975, following the 'near-hysterical debate' over the PTA, it noted that it was becoming 'commonplace ... to talk of the collapse, amidst inflation and world recession, of Parliamentary democracy ... .'[11] In 1973 Sean MacBride described the worldwide spread of torture – and brutality against civilians more generally – as a 'massive breakdown of public morality and of civilisation itself'.[12]

7.2   Greece, Chile and Spain

The opposition to the Greek coup in Britain was led by the long-standing League for Democracy in Greece, which had strong links with the Communist Party and the left wing of the labour movement. It was accompanied by new organisations such as the Greek Committee against Dictatorship, which derived support from academics, political refugees and Greeks living in Britain. The propaganda war was relatively easily won, as the Colonels failed to understand the power of public opinion in the West and lacked convincing advocates.[13] The Junta was swiftly branded as a 'barbarous', 'Fascist' regime, not only redolent of the Nazi occupation of 1940–44, but even tormenting its victims in the very same buildings that the Nazis had used. In June 1968 Harold Wilson referred in Parliament to the 'bestialities' perpetrated by the Greek dictatorship.[14] However, as the Colonels consolidated their hold on power it became clear that mere condemnation was not enough. Western governments, including Britain's Labour government, might regard the new regime with distaste, but they were unwilling to destabilise a NATO ally in a region of such high strategic significance.[15] Accordingly, enemies of the Junta soon realised the significance of torture: Greece, as a member of the Council of Europe and signatory of the European Convention on Human Rights, might claim exemption for the temporary detention of thousands of opponents, but there could be no derogation for torture.[16]

The first allegations of torture came to light in October 1967 when the legal scholar Cedric Thornberry, who was working for the *Guardian*, published two anonymous letters sent to him by political prisoners.[17] One, from the concentration camp on the island of Yaros, referred only to emotional blackmail, poor food and other forms of 'inhuman' treatment. The second letter, however, smuggled from the security jail on Bouboulinas Street in Athens, described an 'abominable mechanism of arrests, pressures and tortures' that was 'at work ... day and night ...'. Some of the techniques described, such as the *falanga* (beating of the soles of the feet), would soon become well known in the fast-growing literature on torture. In November Thornberry collected evidence in Greece which formed the basis of a further article,[18] but he became *persona non grata* and was refused further entry to Greece in April 1968. In the interim, however, Amnesty International had sent a mission (or 'Delegation') to Greece, charged with investigating the effectiveness of a recent official amnesty and examining the conditions of prisoners' families.[19] The undeclared purpose of the mission was to establish a permanent office on Athens, which could relay reliable information to London, and to investigate conditions on the prison islands.[20] The mission, which arrived in late December and stayed for almost a month, was comprised of Anthony Marreco (whose task was to meet with government officials) and James Becket, an American lawyer who would interview prisoners and their families. Becket knew Greece well through his Greek wife Maria, who was also a prominent opponent of the dictatorship. Marreco was a former Junior Counsel for the British prosecution team at the Nuremberg trials who had made his career in banking and publishing. He had been involved with Amnesty since its early days, having been put in touch with Peter Benenson by Lord Weidenfeld and Benenson's mother Flora,[21] and had already carried out investigative work for Amnesty in Latin America. Like Benenson, Marreco thrived on being a somewhat dissident member of the establishment and had no qualms about confronting Greek government ministers with damaging allegations.

Marreco would later describe the mission as a 'routine Amnesty job'.[22] Given the report's impact this was false modesty, but the mission was also far from routine in another way: its most important finding – the evidence of torture – was not even part of the original brief. Amnesty only added torture to its statute in mid-1968, although in 1966 the International Assembly had enjoined national sections to give it their 'special attention'.[23] Becket later wrote that 'we had gone to Greece with no intention of investigating torture'. Instead, the delegation heard reports of police brutality while interviewing prisoners and were instructed by the International Secretariat to look into them.[24] Becket's account emphasises the shock that he felt on hearing the allegations of torture, as well as his naivety in expecting that victims would simply sign an affidavit, whereas, in fact, most would only speak to him on the grounds of anonymity. His comment that 'my stomach was to stay in a knot that whole month in Greece' contrasts with Marreco's insouciance (perhaps reflecting the latter's greater experience). Their report, published on 27 January 1968, found that there were still 2777 prisoners in detention, and that the government had persecuted some of their relatives. However, the final paragraph was the most significant, as the authors claimed to have received testimony from sixteen victims of torture, as well as hearing of thirty-two other alleged cases concerning those still in prison. The report concluded that: '*the Delegation can objectively state that torture is deliberately and officially used and was convinced that the use of torture is a widespread practice against Greek citizens suspected of active opposition to the Government*.[25] In late March, following an intervention by the Labour MP Francis Noel-Baker (who supported the Junta), Marreco was allowed to return to Greece, where he met senior ministers and gathered further evidence of the use of torture. This second report was published – crucially, this time, offering prima facie evidence of the torture of *named* prisoners – in early April 1968.[26]

The report of January 1968 was remarkably brief – less than two sides, plus an appendix – and in the absence of any signed statements offered no concrete evidence. Inevitably it attracted critics: Francis Noel-Baker described it in Parliament as 'wildly inaccurate', while the writer Kenneth Young stated that Marreco's methods 'did not satisfy the criteria of objectivity and the checking of facts'. (He was successfully sued for libel by Marreco in 1974.)[27] However, the damage to the Greek Junta's reputation had been done, and the idea became widely accepted that – as Marreco told the British Section's annual meeting in June 1968 – 'torture *was* practiced on a deplorably large scale in Greece'.[28] Impressed by the report, Scandinavian governments added torture to the case that they were already bringing against Greece at the European Court of Human Rights. Marreco and the Beckets remained closely involved in briefing the Strasbourg court and providing reliable witnesses. A four-volume report was published by a subcommittee of the European Human Rights Commission in mid-1969 and, facing certain defeat, the Greek government chose to withdraw from the Council of Europe in December.[29] Despite its flaws the Amnesty report had been 'accurate in essentials', and, although the Junta remained in power until 1974, this victory for the utility of simple but courageous investigation had a powerful impact on the human rights activism of the 1970s.[30] The evidence of torture which the team had stumbled upon had proved remarkably compelling, but it remained incidental to the mission's principal tasks. Tellingly, in February 1968 Amnesty briefed one of the young men sent out to replace Marreco that 'enough evidence has probably been assembled on torture for the time being' and that he should concentrate on investigating the prison islands.[31]

*

The Chilean coup of September 1973 triggered a frenzy of violence. Thousands of supporters of Salvador Allende's Popular Unity government were rounded up and kept in temporary camps such as the National Stadium. Many were tortured and – although initial estimates were inflated – it seems likely that some 3500 were killed in the first years of the Pinochet regime;[32] others simply 'disappeared'. Prominent victims included President Allende, who died during the storming of his palace, and one of his best-known supporters, the popular singer Victor Jara, who was tortured and murdered in the stadium. More so than in the Greek case, the Chilean coup created a humanitarian emergency. Thousands of Latin Americans who had sought asylum in Chile under Allende were placed at risk and joined many Chileans in seeking to flee the country.[33] In Britain, the crisis generated an intense desire to help that encompassed human rights activists and religious groups as well as trade unions and the political parties of the left. However, the unprecedented set of challenges was more than any single organisation had the skills or resources to cope with: indeed, Amnesty's annual report referred to the immense strain that the coup placed upon it.[34] Accordingly, what emerged during the winter of 1973–74 was a novel combination of the organisational base and internationalism of the left with the techniques and emphases of human rights activism.

Despite the left's enthusiasm for the government of Salvador Allende, a Chile Solidarity Campaign (CSC) had to be improvised at short notice after the coup.[35] One of its leading figures was Mike Gatehouse, who had been working for the Forestry Institute in Santiago prior to the coup. Appalled by the 'precision and totality' of the military takeover, Gatehouse witnessed the collapse of resistance and was briefly incarcerated in the notorious National Stadium.[36] On his return to Britain he wrote a lengthy account of these events, including an early description of the torture of detainees, which was published (unattributed) within a month of the coup by Amnesty.[37] The CSC was an umbrella for a wide range of organisations, but it was located firmly on the left, with strong links to the Communist Party, the trade unions and the Labour left (notably through Judith Hart, minister for Overseas Development 1974–75 and 1977–79). Once Labour had returned to power in March 1974 the CSC had the ear of government and pressed for ever stronger measures to isolate the Pinochet regime both diplomatically and economically.

Given the sheer scale and urgency of the crisis the CSC decided to extend the reach – and fundraising capacity – of the campaign. In December 1973 it convened a meeting at the House of Commons with a view to co-ordinating work on behalf of refugees. The outcome was disappointing, as none of the other organisations present were able to dedicate themselves full-time to the Chilean crisis, and the CSC warned that they all faced a 'very uphill task' in offering 'any real help in Britain'.[38] Accordingly, early in the New Year the CSC set up a separate Chile Committee for Human Rights (CCHR) with its own Chile Relief Fund.

Joan Jara, the British-born widow of Victor Jara, was appointed President. In addition to raising funds, the new committee's remit was to promote awareness in Britain of the Pinochet regime's 'barbarous crimes', to facilitate the arrival of Chilean refugees in Britain and to protest to the Junta about 'political prisoners, torture and economic repression'.[39] Over time the CCHR developed an active network of local committees and became a successful fundraiser – a concert by the exiled group Inti-Illimani in December 1974 alone raised more than £2000. Its principal task was to assist refugees, 3000 of whom arrived under the more welcoming Labour government which took office in March 1974. Such was the pressure of helping and integrating these new arrivals that the CCHR set up a separate Joint Working Group with other refugee organisations in June 1974.[40] Meanwhile, the Chile Relief Fund – a registered charity – sent funds direct to Chile, where they were used to help victims of repression by the ecumenical Committee for Co-Operation for Peace.[41] The CCHR also developed activities modelled on the work of Amnesty: for instance, with Amnesty's advice, trade union branches and student unions began to adopt political prisoners, and the organisation's secretary Wendy Tyndale made her own fact-finding mission to Chile to mark the first anniversary of the coup.[42]

There was nothing inherently new in the left setting up parallel organisations to fundraise and campaign on behalf of political prisoners – this was, after all, a pattern that had been well established in the 1930s. What was new was the way in which this now took place under the banner of human rights, as well as the CCHR's determination to define its own sphere of activity. At the outset the CCHR had been described as a subcommittee of the CSC with 'an independent fund and, to a certain extent, independent action'. It was intended to work on a 'purely humanitarian basis ... because there are many people in Britain who feel sympathetic to humanitarian causes but who would not necessarily want to support any resistance in Chile'.[43] However, in order to embrace this wider constituency, the CCHR's distinctive character – separate from the politics of the left as well as the often-fractious world of the Chilean exiles – had to be stated emphatically. In 1976, for instance, the CCHR strongly recommended that its local committees should be separate from local CSCs, and that, to avoid 'sectarianism' Chilean exiles should not play a leadership role in them or have voting rights. 'Political representation' it was noted 'was alien to the nature of the CCHR'.[44]

Although a series of investigations by Amnesty and other organisations soon established that sustained and systematic abuse of human rights was taking place under the Chilean Junta,[45] they lacked the impact of the Becket/Marreco report on Greece until the shocking case of the British doctor Sheila Cassidy. Cassidy, who had tended to a wounded opponent of the regime, was arrested by the DINA (the Chilean secret police) on 1 November 1975 and severely tortured. The terrible abuse that she had suffered caused outrage and after her return to Britain Foreign Secretary James Callaghan withdrew the British Ambassador from Chile in protest. Courageously, Cassidy gave detailed evidence of her experiences to a UN Working Group in January 1976, as well as giving interviews to the British press.[46] Mike Gatehouse's acknowledgement of the importance of this case was tinged with an awareness that it had greater impact than the everyday suffering of many Chileans: 'it grieves us that *until* the case of a British citizen, Dr Cassidy, was publicised, Chile had almost dropped out of the news altogether ... '.[47] Others were less inhibited. The CSC told its local committees that Cassidy's suffering had, brought 'more favourable publicity to our cause' than any event since the coup, and 'every opportunity' should be taken to press home the point. Her case gave 'tremendous credibility to everything we have been saying about Chile, precisely because she is British, a woman, non-political, a professional, and a deeply religious person who intends to become a nun'.[48] Local committees were encouraged to place collages of press cuttings in public spaces – 'perhaps a local catholic church' – and to encourage Chilean refugees who had been tortured to give interviews in the local media. As Shirin Hirsch has commented, Cassidy quickly became 'the human face of solidarity'.[49]

This does not mean, however, that the growing focus on human rights within the CSC – of which this was merely the most prominent example – should be interpreted as a retreat from politics, whereby the passive victim of oppression took the place of the heroic resistance fighter. After all, as with the Greek case, human rights made for good politics, and the unique features of Cassidy's story made her case highly politically damaging to the Chilean regime. In some respects, therefore, little had changed since the campaigns for an 'Amnesty' in Spain, Portugal and Greece, when human rights abuses were also utilised for political ends. What had changed in the intervening years was the advance of human rights organisations which had a credibility that the more politicised solidarity campaigns lacked. Mike Gatehouse was able to defend the CSC from claims of partiality by citing Amnesty's reports on Chile and pointing out that Amnesty was 'not prone to the same charges of "partisan" pleading that we are ... '.[50] The Chile campaign was, therefore, simply a more advanced stage in a continually evolving relationship between traditional solidarity movements and human rights activists. While the left hoped to reach new audiences, who were more likely to be interested in human rights abuses than the internal politics of the Chilean opposition, the concerns of human rights activists could hardly fail, in turn, to exert an influence over the campaigns of the left.

*

A similar two-way dynamic was at work amongst activists campaigning against the Franco regime in Spain during the early 1970s. Franco had presided over rapid economic growth during the 1960s and had even introduced a modest relaxation of political controls. This changed during the 1970s, not only because Franco's increasing physical frailty created instability and hope in equal measure, but also because of an economic downturn, the rise of assertive new opposition movements and the beginning of the Basque nationalist ETA movement's terrorist struggle. Amidst soaring repression, Amnesty conceded in 1975 that Spain remained one of its 'deep concerns'.[51] There were well over 400 prisoners of conscience in Spain, a remarkably high proportion of Amnesty's worldwide total, and the unwelcome revival of the death penalty restored the regime's reputation for callous violence. Allegations of the torture of prisoners in Spain – first brought to Amnesty's attention in 1964 – were now levelled against the Franco regime with increasing frequency in the turbulent period leading up to Franco's death on 20 November 1975.[52] Two examples from this period show how human rights activists and left-wing campaigners were learning from each other.

In April 1970 local Amnesty groups erected giant billboards outside five British airports. The posters, which juxtaposed the mask-like faces of political prisoners against a stylised beach resort, carried the slogan: 'Have a good time – but remember, Amnesty for Spain's political prisoners'. The boards, which were paid for by the local activists and designed by the talented graphic artist Robin Fior, were clearly aimed at the British tourists who were now flocking to the beaches of southern European dictatorships in unprecedented numbers. The campaign had germinated a year previously, when Amnesty's British Section published an appeal for British holidaymakers travelling to countries where there were prisoners of conscience to 'tax' themselves 2.5 per cent of the cost of their holiday and send the proceeds to Amnesty. Some consciences were clearly pricked as the appeal raised almost £50 and, as the British Section sought to plan out the coming year's activities, a 'Holiday scheme – taking a wider basis than in 1969' was pencilled in. The poster campaign, initiated by activists from the St John's Wood group, attracted considerable press attention, but it is impossible to judge the impact on holidaymakers.[53] Amnesty International was, itself, somewhat ambivalent about the scheme as it potentially interfered with – ultimately successful – negotiations between the International Secretariat and the

Spanish government for the release of jailed conscientious objectors.[54] The action of these Amnesty groups formed part of a wider attempt to target tourism, as a way of eroding the revenues and legitimacy of undemocratic regimes. For instance, opponents of the Greek Colonels had embarked with enthusiasm on such a scheme in 1968: on one occasion they picketed the Greek tourist office, while hiring military vehicles to create a sense of menace in London's West End. However, the 'Anti-Tourist campaign' failed to be the magic bullet that many campaigners had hoped for. By July 1970 the Greek Committee against Dictatorship had conceded that such a boycott 'was bound to be unrewarding because tourists in general are not an identifiable group towards which one can direct a campaign'.[55] Even so, in the Spanish case the idea persisted, as in 1971 one local group even called for the picketing of airports.[56]

Influences also passed the other way. For instance, in 1973–74 plans were drawn up to hold an unofficial international tribunal to put the Franco regime 'on trial' for violations of the Universal Declaration of Human Rights (which Spain, as an international pariah, had not signed in 1948).[57] The project, inspired by Bertrand Russell's 1966–67 tribunal on Vietnam, was the work of the Labour Party's Spanish Democrats Defence Fund Committee (SDDF). The committee had been set up by Peter Benenson and others in 1957 but was now controlled by senior figures in the labour movement who had fought in the Spanish Civil War, such as Jack Jones of the Transport and General Workers' Union, the former miners' leader Will Paynter and Labour MP Bob Edwards. Amnesty, which began to work closely with the SDDF in the mid-1960s, conceded that the committee's 'wider sphere of influence and bigger resources have helped our efforts immeasurably'.[58] In 1973 Paynter drafted an outline of how a tribunal could be conducted. The indictment would list 'crimes against the Charter of Human [R]ights, giving dates of repressive legislation, trials, detentions, gaol and torture and wherever possible naming the perpetrators'.[59] The project was supported by the TUC in Britain, by opposition groups in Spain and by Victor Jokel, the Director of the British Amnesty Section, although he pointed out that such a tribunal could be deployed against many other states 'in breach of fundamental human rights'.[60] However, the scheme was overtaken by events. Labour's return to government made some key legal figures unavailable as they were appointed to high office, and the demands of more pressing events in Spain (such as the trial of the trade union leaders known as the 'Carabanchel Ten') took precedence. Ultimately, Franco's prolonged final illness focused attention on the imminent changes that would follow his death. The tribunal was postponed indefinitely in July 1975.[61]

7.3   'You Really Started Something': Eric Baker and the Campaign for the Abolition of Torture

In December 1972 Amnesty International launched its Campaign for the Abolition of Torture (CAT), the first phase of which culminated in a major conference in Paris one year later. The objective was not only to raise awareness but also to galvanise international action, and in this the CAT was remarkably successful. It contributed to a succession of UN resolutions, and, twelve years later, to the signing of the UN 'Convention against Torture and Other Cruel, Inhuman or Degrading Treatment or Punishment'. The campaign has been presented as a textbook case of how an NGO can generate – and then persuade states to agree to – new norms of conduct.[62] But where did this particular norm come from? After all, torture was hardly new in the early 1970s, even if it was taking ominous new forms and states appeared to be more inclined to make use of it. Indeed, when the CAT was launched the first task was thought to be one of tackling 'popular indifference'.[63] The success of the campaign clearly had many different roots, not least the increasingly flagrant behaviour of the 'torture states' themselves. However, one significant and previously neglected source was activism, and more specifically the energy and commitment of Amnesty's Eric Baker. Baker was uniquely qualified to drive forward a campaign against torture as he was not only a highly respected member of Amnesty and the Society of Friends, but he also held leadership roles (such as Chairman of Amnesty's British Section and Vice-Chair of Amnesty's IEC) that allowed him to interact at a senior level with the UN and its agencies. By comparison, Sean MacBride, who also played an important role, was more prominent internationally but lacked Baker's connection to the grass roots.[64]

In the late 1950s Peter Benenson had taken a keen interest in France's use of torture in Algeria, and his introduction to the book *Gangrene* (1959) contains many powerful insights – not least into the psychology of the torturers. There is no question that Benenson was passionately opposed to torture and was deeply shaken by the allegations in 1966 against the British authorities in Aden. However, in setting up Amnesty International he chose to focus on political imprisonment rather than the ill-treatment of prisoners, and his later remarks indicate that he tended to see torture as merely a symptom of a wider malaise. In a self-critical speech in 1976 he regretted some of Amnesty's early publicity, which pandered to the prurience of the public:

It was and is a cheap way of obtaining publicity to suggest that there is some special category of prisoner, the tortured Prisoner of Conscience. The truth is that all prisoners everywhere are subjected to inadmissible indignities, many are incarcerated in conditions of extreme heat or cold, few are adequately fed – and a very few are subjected to deliberate torture.[65]

He may have been thinking of the annual meeting of Amnesty's British Section in 1965, where a 'life-size painting of a suspect, tied to an iron bar and being given electric shocks to make him talk, dramatically illustrated a resolution condemning the use of torture on political detainees. A replica of one such torture machine was on view'.[66] In fact, Benenson only adopted torture as a cause per se much later, in the 1990s, within the organisation Christians Against Torture.

During Amnesty's formative years there were only occasional hints that Eric Baker took a different view of the significance of torture, such as his note in 1965 that, even if it was diminishing, there was still too much of this 'ancient evil of wh[ich] man has always been capable'.[67] The Greek coup sharpened his thinking, however, and in April 1968 he wrote an 'exploratory' paper on the ill-treatment of prisoners, which prefigured much that was to follow. Amnesty, he wrote, could no longer ignore the abuse and poor conditions which many prisoners of conscience faced and should campaign for new, enforceable international standards for *all* prisoners (while recognising that its own focus remained on helping prisoners of conscience). Turning specifically to torture, he noted that the Greek case proved that Article Five of the Universal Declaration and Article Three of the European Convention – which both prohibited it – were insufficient. Part of the problem was a lack of clarity as to what currently constituted torture, at a time when torturers were developing ever more sophisticated methods. These ranged from the infliction of pain without leaving a visible trace to forms of 'mental torture' (such as being subjected to the sound of the abuse of others). The exact definition of torture remained surprisingly difficult to agree on and the question continued to bedevil the planning of the CAT: in 1976 Baker ruefully commented that 'what anyone feels is torture is torture for them'.[68] His 1968 paper concluded with an appeal for an effective Convention and enforcement mechanism to protect civilian detainees and prisoners. 'To begin by trying to eliminate torture', he added, 'may not be the best starting point, but it is[,] at least, one starting point'. Referring again to Greece, he noted that this applied not only to men but 'a fortiori' to women.[69] Baker presented his paper to Amnesty's special conference on torture in Stockholm on 23 August 1968, and, at the AI International Assembly which immediately followed it, a commitment to upholding Article Five was added to the organisation's statute.[70]

Although the revision of the statute was an important step it did not produce any immediate results. As late as September 1970 torture ranked as low as item 16 on the agenda of Amnesty's International Council meeting.[71] Baker realised that change would not come simply through making representations to international bodies such as the UN: they must be matched by an 'awakening' and mobilisation of public opinion, and this in turn would require Amnesty to work with churches, professional groups, women's groups and trade unions. Amnesty must, he wrote, foster an 'international conscience' on torture.[72] In July 1970, in an article entitled 'What Can Be Done about Torture?', he noted that two years after drafting his paper, torture had become 'accepted policy in far more countries than one cares to think of'. Isolated atrocities might periodically cause a stir, as had been the case over Algeria, but there was no sustained campaign against torture.[73] He had in mind the revelations about the abuse of prisoners in the 'Tiger Cages' of South Vietnam's Con Son Island, photographs of which had been published in *Life* magazine earlier that month. It is significant that his article was published in *The Friend*, an indication that Baker was seeking to stimulate action amongst his fellow Quakers, many of whom were also members of Amnesty. In April 1971 he presented his 'concern' about torture to the monthly 'Meeting for Sufferings'. He did not want to delegate the matter to a committee, he said, but rather for 'a few Friends to join him in this concern with the same faith and courage as inspired our forebears who joined in the fight against slavery'.[74] Baker found a receptive audience, but the impact of his appeal was greatly magnified by the subsequent events in Northern Ireland: internment, the alleged mistreatment of detainees and the failure of the government-appointed Compton and Parker commissions to condemn these as torture. As Baker put it, torture – which until recently he had described as quite unknown to modern Britain – was now 'on our own doorstep'.[75] Northern Ireland was Britain's 'Algeria ... the graveyard of many ideals of conduct'.[76] It was left to the former Lord Chancellor Gerald Gardiner, one of the three-man Parker Commission, to enter a minority report and shame the government into banning the infamous 'five techniques'.

As Baker's 'concern' gained momentum amongst Quaker activists, steps were also being taken to promote action through the UN. In November 1971 Baker and other representatives of Amnesty called a meeting with other interested bodies such as the Red Cross, the World Federation of United Nations Associations and the World Veterans Federation, and passed a resolution in favour of a UN convention against torture. This was adopted by the UN's three-yearly International NGOs' Special Committee on Human Rights (chaired by MacBride).[77] Baker told Friends that they could now contemplate 'a much more emphatic campaign this coming autumn', aimed not only at the public, but specifically at groups with a professional interest such as doctors and lawyers.[78] In September 1972 Amnesty's International Council agreed to launch a worldwide campaign for the abolition of torture, which would co-ordinate the individual campaigns of national sections while the secretariat prepared a global survey of torture for publication.[79] During the initial year-long campaign there was, therefore, a combination of international and national initiatives. National sections ran their own campaigns, collecting thousands of names for a petition in countries such as Sweden and the Netherlands.[80] The British Section organised its own conference in October 1973 and agreed to form a Standing Committee to oversee the campaign in Britain.[81] One of the most important features of the build-up to the Paris conference was the successful mobilisation of professional groups such as lawyers and, in particular, doctors – the latter a recognition of the need both to document allegations of torture and to address the trauma of the victims – through a series of international seminars.[82]

The international conference in Paris in December was deemed a success even though a new venue had to be found at very short notice when UNESCO became alarmed that Amnesty's report criticised some of its member states.[83] Baker was so enthused by the outcome that he declared that the battle against torture 'can probably be won within the generation', although he also appreciated that Paris was 'only the opening of a campaign'. He was delighted that Danilo Dolci – 'immense as ever' – attended and dedicated a poem to the occasion.[84] Despite the success of the conference, however, and the agreement that this was indeed a 'continuing campaign',[85] what was less clear was whether it would continue indefinitely as an *Amnesty* campaign. In a paper drawn up prior to the Paris conference, Baker reviewed the options, which included the creation of a parallel organisation that would have a more 'humanitarian' basis than Amnesty. After all, Amnesty itself had started as a year-long campaign, and there was no reason why the CAT should not evolve into a separate organisation akin to the campaign for the abolition of the death penalty. In fact, Baker had no stomach for such a move: he was well aware of the damage that it would cause to Amnesty, and the inevitable dislocation would also hurt the interests of the victims of torture, to whom he felt a strong moral commitment. Even so, there were costs to the course that was eventually adopted – whereby the CAT became a department within Amnesty International – and these were not simply financial costs. In 1976, for instance, Amnesty's CAT co-ordinating committee noted that 'to many outsiders, torture seems to be AI's main preoccupation – at least it is the face that is most easily presented with the most emphasis'.[86]

When Baker died in 1976 British Amnesty's tribute noted that 'he organised [the CAT] within the Quaker movement as well as within Amnesty'.[87] However, this fails to do justice to the extent of his contribution, given that these were not two parallel campaigns, but in many respects facets of the same campaign. These interconnections were apparent when Baker briefed the British Council of Churches (BCC) in February 1973 and invited its participation in the forthcoming autumn's seminar on the moral implications of torture. He told the BCC that the Society of Friends 'would be taking full administrative responsibility for the whole campaign [for the seminar] as far as Britain was concerned'.[88] Moreover, local Quaker activists, inspired directly or indirectly by Baker, and often also involved with Amnesty groups, were amongst the first to support the CAT and to organise regional conferences on torture. Baker's papers are full of instances of local Quaker groups organising meetings on torture, as a result of which money was raised for Amnesty or, indeed, new Amnesty branches were formed.[89] Dorothy Birtles of the Oxford Society of Friends, who was encouraged by Baker to organise a regional conference in the spring of 1974, was 'heartened by the ready response of local Councils of Churches, United Nations Associations, Amnesty Groups, Quaker Meetings and similar bodies' in joining a 'corporate witness' against torture.[90] Given the degree of support from the Friends it was small wonder that when Amnesty opened its new headquarters in January 1973 Sean MacBride made sure to invite 'quite a few Quakers as we will need their support'.[91]

Baker's campaigning over torture faced many obstacles. The subject matter was inevitably traumatic, and activists struggled to persuade their colleagues that meetings would not dwell on 'harrowing' or 'horrifying' details.[92] Many Friends were unconvinced by Baker's case and the most persistent request from his supporters was for more 'facts' so that they could convince the sceptics. At the Yearly Meeting in 1974 Baker's session on 'The Contagion of Torture' failed to fill the hall, and only a handful of volunteers came to a follow-up meeting with him. Baker wryly observed that 'we had an enthusiastic response to the idea of setting up regional conferences, particularly with the churches, and an unenthusiastic response to the idea of speaking at them'.[93] When the Yearly Meeting adopted Baker's concern and wrote to all other churches for support, Baker noted that there was much sympathy but 'very little came of it'.[94] He remained sceptical of the value of such institutional contacts and always preferred to engage with small numbers of individuals: 'laborious, perhaps, but worthwhile'.[95] The high moral stakes called for nothing less than immense patience and dedication. For Baker this was, above all, a spiritual struggle against evil, to be conducted not only by organisation but also by prayer (for both the victims and the perpetrators of torture). Accordingly, Friends should support the campaign 'whether any other organisation does so or not'.[96]

Such setbacks, however, should not diminish Baker's achievement. He had enthused Friends with a moral cause that many compared to the 'fire' of the struggle against slavery:[97] in the process he had offered them a way forward out of the dilemmas of the 1960s (see Chapter 4) while also helping to give a new direction to human rights campaigning. Moreover, he had shown how the individual could combine an activist's zeal with the diplomatic skills needed to bring together diverse coalitions – nationally as well as internationally – and wage effective campaigns. Although he was honoured by being made President of Amnesty International less than a year before his death, his role in the CAT, just as does his role in the formation of Amnesty itself, deserves greater attention. But close observers were fully aware of his contribution. In 1974 the editor of *British Amnesty* noted that 'we should not forget that three years ago the support of the British AGM given to Eric Baker's concern over torture started Amnesty on new work which has become a world-wide campaign'.[98] Peter Benenson wrote to Baker in December 1972 to say how delighted he was that Amnesty had launched its campaign against torture, 'which I am sure is very much your doing'.[99] And, in 1974 the clerk of one of the Friends' Monthly Meetings wrote to tell Baker that 'you really started something in our [meeting] when you came to talk with us about Torture in 1971'.[100]

7.4   'Dissent as Disease': Human Rights in the Soviet Union and the Abuse of Psychiatry

When Eric Baker wrote his pioneering paper in April 1968 for Amnesty's Stockholm conference he was well aware that there were other forms of punishment 'amounting to torture', of which the most egregious was the confinement of political and religious dissenters in 'lunatic asylums' in the Soviet Union. [101] At this stage, he acknowledged that it would be an achievement merely to address torture in conventional places of detention, and that these other forms would have to wait.[102] However, amidst mounting evidence of abuse in Soviet psychiatric institutions, the issue rose rapidly up the agenda to become, by 1972, a 'dominant feature' of Amnesty's work on the USSR.[103] So much so, indeed, that the *Human Rights Handbook* noted that Soviet psychiatric abuse had come 'to occupy something of a privileged position amongst human rights activities in Britain'.[104] The decisive moment was the success of the Soviet dissident Vladimir Bukovsky in smuggling a collection of Soviet psychiatric diagnoses to the West in 1971: their publication had a tremendous impact, not least within the psychiatric profession, but Bukovsky paid for his defiance with a further prison sentence.[105] Amnesty's *Report on Torture* (1973) accepted the evidence presented by the International Committee for the Defence of Human Rights in the USSR that the psychological and physical treatment of dissidents detained in prison psychiatric hospitals appeared 'to constitute torture as an administrative practice'. These abuses formed a major chapter in Amnesty's first substantive report into the treatment of political prisoners in the USSR in 1975, which concluded that Soviet psychiatrists, especially members of the notorious Serbsky Institute, were highly politicised and did not 'meet a reasonable standard of objectivity and scientific authority'.[106] The issue was also being taken up by other organisations at this time. For instance, in April 1974 the UNA's General Council passed a resolution condemning the 'inhuman practice of misusing psychiatry to incarcerate dissenters', contrary to medical ethics and Article 5 of the Universal Declaration.[107] The Parliamentary Human Rights Group devoted two out of its first eight meetings to this topic.[108] Although the numbers detained in this way only represented a small fraction of the 350 or so prisoners of conscience in the Soviet Union (Amnesty estimated a mere 15 per cent of its adoptees were held in prisons or psychiatric hospitals in 1975), their significance for human rights activists in Britain and Western Europe was disproportionately large.[109]

There are numerous reasons for this special focus on the abuse of psychiatry. Above all, this was a grotesque, nightmarish abuse of human rights, which dramatised the suppression of free intellects by a totalitarian regime and thereby undermined the idea that the leadership of the Soviet Union had broken with Stalin's methods. Secondly, at a time when the Soviet state was suspected of perfecting methods of torture that left no physical mark or scar, the evidence of the abuse of psychiatry offered critics a powerful weapon for challenging the repressive apparatus. Accordingly, the concerns expressed by psychiatrists in Britain and elsewhere matched the more general mobilisation of concerned medical professionals behind the Campaign for the Abolition of Torture. Finally, the allegations against Soviet psychiatry coincided with a wider contemporary suspicion of the function of psychiatry, in the West as well as in the Eastern bloc. In responding to the Soviet abuse of psychiatry, human rights activists were also responding to influences within Western culture such as the writings of R. D. Laing, Ken Kesey's novel *One Flew over the Cuckoo's Nest* (1962; the movie was released in 1975) and the Italian Psichiatria Democratica movement.[110] Professor Alec Jenner, one of the leading British psychiatrists to campaign against Soviet abuses, and also a prominent advocate of 'democratic psychiatry', later recalled that 'that whole issue made me more aware of the thought-police function of psychiatry. One could easily see how deviance from the party line could get close to being called madness'.[111] This line of thought enabled him to understand, while not condoning, the attitude of his Soviet counterparts. As he told the *Guardian* in 1971, the term 'madness' was often used to describe people who did not fit into 'acceptable patterns of behaviour' such as, in Britain, 'if a kid is taking cannabis'.[112] The title of the 'Working Group on the Internment of Dissenters in Mental Hospitals' (WGIDMH), of which Jenner was a leading member, was deliberately chosen so as not to limit the group to a critique of Soviet psychiatry alone, even if the weight of evidence pointed in that direction.[113]

Soviet psychiatric abuse had first come to public notice in the West in the early 1960s, with the publication of *Ward 7*, a broadly autobiographical novel by the Soviet writer Valery Tarsis, who had been detained in a mental hospital and was eventually exiled in 1966. Extracts were published in *The Observer* in May 1965. Peter Benenson had a more than casual acquaintance with *Ward 7* as it had been published by his aunt, Manya Harari. Indeed, at the height of his war of words with Sean MacBride during the Amnesty crisis Benenson had pointedly suggested that the Irishman should read it: 'it's a regular Communist technique to work on an awkward Party member suggesting that he needs a rest . . .'.[114] Tarsis was already an established Soviet writer, in the tradition of Chekov and Gogol,[115] but the plight of a younger critic of the regime, Evgeny Belov, also had a powerful impact in Britain. Belov had been befriended by four British students on a visit to the USSR and, on learning of his incarceration in a mental hospital, they campaigned actively with Amnesty for his release. Amnesty reported that it was overwhelmed by the public response and appealed for volunteers to come forward to deal with the mass of letters that was arriving.[116] Victor Zorza, a seasoned *Guardian* correspondent on Eastern Europe, had been initially sceptical about the claims made by Tarsis, stating that he did not see the use of lunatic asylums as the 'settled policy' of the Soviet government: reporting on the Belov case a few months later he concluded that he would have to 'eat [his] words'.[117]

These episodes aside, however, human rights abuses in the Soviet Union had been somewhat neglected during Amnesty's early years, not because of any tenderness towards the regime, but because the lack of resources to conduct research compounded the difficulty of obtaining the reliable information needed to create cases for adoption.[118] This began to change in the mid-1960s with the emergence of the dissident movement within the USSR and, in particular, the circulation of information through *samizdat* ('self-published') writings such as the *Chronicle of Current Events*.[119] Indeed, from the early 1970s Amnesty sponsored the translation and circulation of the *Chronicle* in Britain. The trial and sentencing in February 1966 of the writers Andrei Sinyavsky and Yuli Daniel, who were charged with anti-Soviet agitation and propaganda, did much to galvanise the emerging dissident movement and attracted considerable interest abroad. In 1968, for instance, Violet Bonham Carter sought to raise the matter within the Great Britain–USSR Association, an elite body that brought together writers and politicians from both countries and was presided over by Fitzroy Maclean. Bonham Carter pleaded that the Association could not remain silent about the treatment of Soviet writers during the UN's Human Rights Year, and eventually resigned in exasperation.[120]

Initially, therefore, attention focused on networks of dissenting writers and intellectuals, mainly based in the larger cities, rather than on psychiatric abuse. At the same time two other groups within Soviet society were beginning to attract their own support networks within Britain. The cause of religious dissenters was taken up by the Anglican priest Michael Bourdeaux, who established the influential Centre for the Study of Religion and Communism (later known as Keston College) in 1969, and subsequently the journal *Religion in Communist Lands*.[121] Dissident Baptists alone accounted for almost 50 per cent of the 350 Soviet prisoners that had been adopted by Amnesty by 1973–74, although these numbers declined sharply thereafter. The second group was Soviet Jews, especially the so-called '*refuseniks*' who faced harassment and persecution for seeking to leave the Soviet Union, in many cases for Israel. Amnesty made few adoptions of Jews because they often did not meet its criteria as prisoners of conscience. In 1967 Amnesty reported that most imprisoned Jews were guilty of 'economic offences' against the stringent anti-capitalist laws, even though it was recognised from an early stage within Amnesty that allegations of black-marketeering often cloaked anti-Semitism.[122] In 1970 it noted that the Jews' problems were 'mostly religious, cultural and linguistic and do not involve imprisonment'.[123] When a group of Jews attempted to hijack an aircraft and fly it to the West in June 1970, Amnesty appealed against the death penalty but did not adopt them as prisoners of conscience. Other activist groups did not feel so constrained: in particular, the Women's Campaign for Soviet Jewry (also known as 'the 35s') initially relied on direct action, such as stage invasions of visiting Soviet cultural productions, to publicise their cause. When Amnesty activists were planning the CAT, one participant presumably had these attention-grabbing tactics in mind when warning against 'over-exposure of the kind which had weakened the campaign on behalf of Soviet Jewry'.[124]

In the early 1970s Bukovsky's release of powerful evidence of psychiatric abuse, combined with some victories for Amnesty's established methods of protest, served to intensify interest in the question. Victor Feinberg, an art critic incarcerated on psychiatric grounds for protesting against the Warsaw Pact invasion of Czechoslovakia, was adopted by Amnesty and eventually released. He toured Britain in 1974 and appealed to Amnesty's British members not to be despondent about the impact of their letter-writing campaigns, or fooled by the current relaxation in superpower relations: 'only when you stop sending [the letters] do the thousands of political prisoners know the bad side of détente'.[125] Likewise, the Ukrainian activist Leonid Plyushch was released after an international campaign by fellow mathematicians, supported by Amnesty's French Section and even the French Communist Party. An unidentified Amnesty representative is also reported to have visited the Director of the Serbsky Institute and secured the release of a prisoner.[126] When Amnesty held a meeting in Westminster Hall in November 1975 to publicise the plight of Soviet dissidents and appeal for Bukovsky's release, prisoners freed from psychiatric detention such as Plyushch and the poet Natalia Gorbanevskaya had pride of place on the platform. However, the presence of a jeering picket outside, whose members claimed that Amnesty was a CIA front, served as a reminder that the dissidents were by no means heroes to some on the British left, no matter how harsh their treatment.[127] These divisions became more marked in the late 1970s when Margaret Thatcher, newly elected as Conservative leader, enthusiastically took up the dissidents' cause. In January 1977 she attended a meeting of the right-wing National Association for Freedom that was dominated by speeches attacking détente and the Soviet Union: the other guest of honour was Vladimir Bukovsky, who had just been expelled from the USSR in an exchange for the imprisoned Chilean communist leader Luis Corvalán.[128]

Increasingly, the struggle was conducted within the national and international psychiatric organisations which had initially been reluctant to confront the Soviet Union over its practices. The failure of the World Association of Psychiatrists (WAP) to take a critical stance at its 1971 congress in Mexico, compounded by the attendance of a number of British psychiatrists at a conference on schizophrenia in Moscow two years later, stimulated activism within the profession. The Working Group (WGIDMH) was set up in February 1971 following the publication of Bukovsky's papers. Its organiser was the actor David Markham, a member of the NCCL who had briefly been detained at Moscow airport and was often seen leading vigils outside the Soviet embassy.[129] However, the key figure was Peter Reddaway, a political scientist specialising in the Soviet Union at the LSE, who led the way in translating and circulating the *Chronicle of Current Events*.[130] They were joined by some prominent practising psychiatrists, including Alec Jenner, the Czech-born Gerhard Low-Beer and Harold Merskey. All drew strength from the almost pre-ternatural courage of Bukovsky: as Jenner put it, if Bukovsky was 'abnormal ... he is ill in a way which makes me not very proud to be well'.[131] The Working Group, which focused on the psychiatric profession, was joined from 1975 by a broader and more public Campaign Against Psychiatric Abuse (CAPA). The combination of this small but vocal group inside the profession, aided by picketing and leafleting by activists on the outside, helped to change opinions, initially within the Royal College of Psychiatrists and, in 1977, within the WAP itself. The battle was by no means won,[132] and in many respects the situation for all Soviet dissidents deteriorated in the later 1970s. For instance, the members of the fledgling Amnesty group in Moscow, recognised – amidst some internal controversy – by the IEC in September 1974, all faced persecution and arrest.[133] Nevertheless, with the signing of the Helsinki Final Act of 1 August 1975 the nature of the game was to be fundamentally and permanently altered, both for Soviet critics of the regime and for their supporters in the West.[134]

*

The Campaign for the Abolition of Torture was tantamount to a relaunching of Amnesty International, and of human rights campaigning more generally. Stella Joyce's comment, during the row over Amnesty's criticism of alleged Israeli use of torture in 1970, that 'this kind of thing is only a small part of our work. Most of it is concerned with the release of Prisoners of Conscience', appeared less and less apt during the following decade.[135] Whereas, during the 1940s and 1950s, activists' focus had been on the unknown political prisoners, and, in the 1960s, the known political prisoners, the new emphasis was on the personal, bodily suffering of the torturer's victims. Images of barbed wire or the prison cage did not lose their potency, but by the 1970s they were being matched in activist literature by images of the practice and instruments of torture. The very weakness and suffering of the victims empowered those who supported them, as they discovered that states were uniquely sensitive to allegations of torture. No other abuse of human rights was so abhorrent, or so corrupting to those who practised it.[136] It was opposition to torture that allowed Amnesty to become more than David Astor's organisation whose aim was simply to 'rescue people'. As the understanding grew that torture was being facilitated by medical professionals, and that the trauma did not end with release, the CAT opened doors within the professional world, allowing activists to work more closely with concerned doctors, psychiatrists, ethicists and lawyers. In 1974 Helen Bamber, the chair of Amnesty's Hampstead branch who had, as a young woman, worked with a Jewish relief unit at Belsen, established Amnesty's medical group. In 1985 this became the separate Medical Foundation for Care of Victims of Torture.[137]

The very success of the campaign against torture, however, raised some challenging questions for human rights activists. In particular, if one gave centrality to the act of torture itself, did it matter what crime – if any – the victim had committed? How did one draw the line between different kinds of prisoner when the fundamental issue was now their mistreatment? Peter Benenson made a fascinating digression on this theme in his speech to mark Amnesty's fifteenth anniversary: 'The 'Amnesty' Movement is very properly concerned with torture, but has not the time come now to extend the area of concern to the whole of brutality? . . . It is impossible to eradicate brutality, which embraces torture, without closing down prisons [. . . which] brutalise those who are imprisoned as well as their jailers, and they brutalise those who read about them in books and papers'.[138] The aim of abolishing torture still seemed attainable, although harder to achieve than Eric Baker had imagined. But Benenson may have been subtly indicating that the CAT had opened a Pandora's box to ever less attainable claims in the future.

8 'All Things Come to Those Who Wait': the Later 1970s

8.1 Amnesty's Prize

On 10 October 1977 the Nobel Peace Prize Committee of the Norwegian Parliament announced that the prize for 1977 (worth £80,000) had been awarded to Amnesty International, the 'world-embracing movement working for the protection of human rights'. In Britain the news was somewhat overshadowed by the simultaneous award of the 1976 prize to Betty Williams and Mairead Corrigan, founders of the Northern Ireland Peace People, a grass-roots initiative that had enjoyed brief success but was already being described as a 'spent force'.[1] However, if for the Peace People the Nobel Prize was a high-water mark, and even a factor in precipitating the movement's decline,[2] for Amnesty the award set the seal on its emergence as a serious international actor. Amnesty's remarkably downbeat public response – as if the prize merely saddled it with unrealistic expectations for the future and clouded its real purpose – could not quite conceal the organisation's own sense of wonderment at the vertiginous growth of its membership and influence since the crisis of 1966–67.[3] Just as importantly, the prize offered recognition for human rights activism in general. Clearly Amnesty was now the pre-eminent international human rights organisation, with 1874 groups in 33 countries and a global membership of some 168,000, but it no longer stood alone. Instead, by the late 1970s a dense thicket of campaigning organisations had grown up – many also British-based, and many of them inspired by Amnesty's success. *The Human Rights Handbook* (1979), a publication whose very existence was a sign of the changing times, listed some seventy British voluntary groups concerned specifically with human rights.[4]

Amnesty's success fits with an influential interpretation that views the 1970s as the period in which human rights experienced a 'breakthrough', emerging 'seemingly from nowhere' as a significant force in international politics.[5] If the decade had opened on a pessimistic note, with the spread of military rule and state-sanctioned torture in many parts of the world, events took a far more hopeful turn with the Helsinki Final Accords of

1975, the coming into force of the UN's two human rights covenants in March 1976 and the election of Jimmy Carter, a US President who in 1978 would describe human rights as 'the soul of our foreign policy'.[6] During the 1970s Western governments discovered that embracing human rights not only made them look virtuous but also offered them diplomatic leverage over their undemocratic rivals – indeed, when accepting the Nobel Prize for Amnesty, the Turkish activist Mümtaz Soysal pointedly remarked that human rights were an end and not a means, and certainly should not be used as a weapon.[7] Clearly, therefore, much had changed during the 1970s, but how is this 'human rights revolution', as it has been described, to be explained? Jan Eckel has offered a helpful frame for analysis which combines changes in the international environment (such as the end of European colonial rule, the decline of Cold War tensions, advances in mass media and changes in the spheres of religion and politics) with the growing intrinsic appeal of human rights. Above all, both Eckel and Samuel Moyn have argued that the new attraction of human rights was a response to the apparent failure of all previous over-arching, utopian political projects. In the United States, for instance, Amnesty offered a home to disillusioned radicals of the late 1960s who were drawn to the more limited, pragmatic scale of its ambitions. Hence, Amnesty's 'groups did not set out to free the world from evil but wanted to assuage suffering in cases they had learned about and that promised a measure of success'.[8]

With regard to activism in Britain, the concept of a 'breakthrough' for human rights corresponds closely to what activists and other commentators believed that they were witnessing at the time. For instance, there were frequent references to a 'boom' in human rights, and to the idea that human rights had become 'fashionable'.[9] In 1978 the Deputy Chairman of Amnesty's British Section alluded to 'these days when the term 'human rights' has become topical and makes daily headlines in the media'.[10] Third World First referred to human rights as the new 'catchword of international politics'.[11] By the later 1970s, therefore, human rights activists felt that they were riding a wave of public and media interest. The question now was how non-governmental organisations could best exploit the 'boom' to influence governments and 'feed human rights material into the Government machine'?[12] At the same time, however, activists were hardly complacent. After all, a boom could easily end in bust: the fashionable could soon become passé. Foreign Secretary David Owen, when invited to speak at the 1978 Human Rights Day event, warned against 'over-repetition' of the human rights message, as if the public could easily tire of it.[13] Positive comments were frequently qualified. The *Human Rights Handbook* noted that human rights was a 'common currency ... constantly on the lips of newscasters, pundits and presidents', but added that some would surely see this as 'the kiss of death for the authenticity of the human rights movement'.[14] Journalist David Watts, who had himself launched a regular column on 'Prisoners of Conscience' in *The Times*, commented apropos Amnesty's prize that 'most people have heard of [human rights] but few understand its subtleties'.[15] If there was a 'breakthrough' for British human rights activists in the later 1970s, therefore, it was by no means taken for granted.

8.2   Contexts

Few British human rights activists in the early 1970s would have predicted this positive turn, given that there was a widespread perception that, both globally and within Britain itself, progress was faltering – or even moving into reverse. There was certainly much to trouble British activists in the late 1960s and early 1970s, ranging from the seemingly boundless conflicts in South East Asia and the atrocities accompanying the birth of Bangladesh in 1971, to the Warsaw Pact's crushing of the Prague Spring in August 1968, and the Soviet Union's decision to detain dissidents in psychiatric hospitals. The twenty-fifth anniversary of the Universal Declaration fell in December 1973, but the mood amongst activists was far from positive. The prominent Quaker Cecil Evans wrote that many of the rights listed in 1948 could be even more grossly violated in 1973,[16] while the journal of the UNA saw little to celebrate so long as the likes of Mandela and Bukovsky still languished in jail.[17] In a speech to Parliament to mark the anniversary, Peter Archer, Chair of Amnesty's British Section and a lay preacher, noted the disparity between the actions of NGOs to promote human rights over the last twenty-five years and the inaction of governments: 'while the Samaritans were being effectively busy, the priests and the Levites have learnt nothing in 2,000 years'.[18] A year later he alluded to a 'sense of ineffectiveness' amongst British Amnesty members, and calculated that, at the current rate of progress, it would take some 2000 years for all the prisoners of conscience to be freed.[19] Two separate NGOs, the Minority Rights Group and Oxfam, ran publicity campaigns claiming that the Universal Declaration had been forgotten, or that something had 'gone wrong' with it.[20]

During the mid-1970s the world did not become a better place overnight. But there were significant improvements in the environment for human rights campaigning. For instance – allowing for terrible exceptions such as Argentina, where thousands 'disappeared' in the army's 'Dirty War' after the March 1976 coup – the tide of military dictatorship slowly began to turn. Whereas the Chilean coup had overthrown an elected government, in April 1974 the coup by the Portuguese Armed Forces Movement destroyed the authoritarian Estado Novo and set Portugal on a circuitous route to democratic rule. Moreover, the new government's decision to withdraw from Portugal's African colonies not only brought independence for Angola, Mozambique and Guinea, but posed a significant challenge to the continuation of white minority rule across southern Africa. In Greece, meanwhile, the Junta collapsed in July 1974, having overreached itself with its disastrous intervention in Cyprus. The collapse of dictatorship in Portugal and Greece made possible the trials of Junta members and torturers and shed light on the inner workings of the 'Torture States'.[21] Franco's death in November 1975, and Spain's transition to democracy over the next few years, completed the process whereby southern Europe eventually ceased to be a principal focus for the concerns of British human rights campaigners.

A second important change was the reduction in East–West tensions during the mid-1970s. The Helsinki Final Act of 1 August 1975 wrote human rights for the first time into an international agreement signed jointly by the European states, the USSR and the United States. Although the Cold War revived towards the end of the decade, the Helsinki Accords gave internal 'dissidents' an agreed standard against which to judge their own governments, and began a process of review and evaluation that greatly encouraged the formation of international activist networks straddling the Iron Curtain.[22] As the decade progressed the full extent of human rights abuse, as reported in Amnesty's ever-expanding annual reports, tended to obscure the fact that far more was now known about the communist world. Whereas in the mid-1960s, communist states – including the People's Republic of China (PRC) – were largely impervious to outside scrutiny, during the 1970s reporting became possible in previously uncharted areas. For instance, Amnesty's first report on the PRC was published in 1978. By the late 1970s only isolated states, such as North Korea, and Cambodia under the Khmer Rouge, were completely beyond the reach of human rights investigators. In this sense, knowledge of the scale of international violation of human rights – humbling and demotivating as it might be – was also the precursor to action.

Another significant development, Britain's decision to join the European Economic Community (EEC, often referred to as 'the Common Market') on 1 January 1973, was broadly welcomed by human rights activists, although the implications were initially far from clear. British Amnesty briefed its members that the Common Market and other European organisations 'might seem unrelated to Amnesty's work ... but in fact they do present us with opportunities'. It alluded to the EEC's close relations with Turkey and the undemocratic regimes of southern Europe as a case in point.[23] Likewise, when the NCCL launched a series of annual Human Rights Day lectures in 1973 the General Secretary, Martin Loney, hoped that a suitably European theme would assist their drive to fund a 'European Officer', and even to create a European Council for Civil Liberties 'to keep an eye on the supra-national activities of the EEC'. In the event John Berger's lecture on the migrant worker in Europe was poorly attended, something which Loney blamed on 'the energy crisis and British apathy about Europe'.[24] Britain's membership of the EEC also sparked renewed interest in the European Convention on Human Rights, coinciding with the Strasbourg court's increasing levels of activity. During the mid-1970s there was a serious discussion within the Labour Party about the incorporation of the European Convention into British law, partly as a riposte to a Conservative proposal for a Bill of Rights, which was perceived as an attempt to shackle the Labour government. However, at this point there was still significant resistance to incorporation from within the Labour movement: some feared that they would weaken Parliament by handing powers to an inherently conservative judiciary, while the trade unions were concerned for the future of the 'closed shop' and the right to strike. The TUC's leaders remained firmly opposed to incorporation but – with an election likely – had no intention of giving 'the individualist lobby a field day' by publicising their position.[25]

After the Labour Party's unexpected return to power in March 1974, campaigners found government rather more favourably disposed towards human rights issues. Parliament finally ratified the UN human rights covenants in May 1976, eliciting a rather weary comment from Peter Archer: 'All things come to those who wait'.[26] David Owen (Foreign Secretary, 1977–79) published a book about human rights in 1978 and had once been suggested as a potential Amnesty Secretary-General.[27] Owen and his junior minister at the Foreign and Commonwealth Office, Evan Luard, were happy to meet with human rights organisations, in order to share expertise and current thinking. A high-profile seminar at Oxford in June 1978 brought together officials, opinion formers and activists from both sides of the Atlantic. After 1976 the formation of a Parliamentary Human Rights Group, chaired by Lord Avebury (formerly the Liberal MP Eric Lubbock), meant that government could be held to account more easily. Avebury was a forthright defender of individual liberties who took part in one of Amnesty's most significant – and dangerous – missions of the period, to Argentina in 1976.[28]

Human rights campaigning was also influenced by wider changes within the voluntary sector. Most organisations could not rely on a large membership for funding, and charitable trusts both in Britain and the United States became increasingly important as sources of finance. For instance, Amnesty received a 'considerable annual grant from the Quaker Rowntree Social Service Trust',[29] Index on Censorship was supported by the Wolfson Foundation, and the Minority Rights Group received several tranches of funding from the US Ford Foundation from 1968 onwards. In June 1976 a senior executive told the Group's co-founder David Astor that the Ford Foundation viewed human rights 'as a field of activity of increasing importance ... almost replacing economic development in priority'.[30] Such support helped to shape the sector, as funders favoured higher levels of professionalism and encouraged cooperation with other organisations. This pressure, alongside the overall proliferation of NGOs in the 1970s, promoted managerial abilities, lobbying skills and a career structure. David Simpson, the Director of the British Section of Amnesty (1974–79) joined Amnesty from Shelter and later moved on to run Action on Smoking and Health (ASH), neither of which was explicitly a 'human rights' organisation. Likewise, Tony Smythe of the NCCL went on to lead the mental health charity MIND, and Peter Burns, who fulfilled a variety of roles at Amnesty during the period 1967–68, came originally from Oxfam and later worked for the NCCL and Anti-Apartheid before becoming the General Secretary of War on Want (1972–76).[31]

During this period new movements were emerging to press claims to rights related to gender, sexuality and personal choice – claims which had not previously been couched in terms of human rights. The Campaign for Homosexual Equality (CHE) had been pressing ever since the 1957 Wolfenden Report for reform of Britain's discriminatory and oppressive laws on same-sex relationships, although it was briefly eclipsed by the more radical Gay Liberation Front (1970–73), which was heavily influenced by US countercultural politics.[32] Likewise, the late 1960s and early 1970s witnessed the emergence of 'second-wave' feminism in Britain, which shifted the focus away from political representation and legal equality towards a more radical questioning of women's place in society, while adopting more militant tactics. These new movements greatly expanded the range of those interested in human rights questions, so that, for instance, the feminist magazine *Spare Rib* often ran items about torture in Spain and Chile.[33] At the same time, these movements created a challenge for existing organisations as they quite properly wanted to see their own concerns taken up. However, human rights activists were anti-authoritarian but not necessarily libertarian, and in some cases were quite socially conservative. This was not the case with the NCCL, which was quick to establish separate Gay Rights and Women's Rights committees and was later criticised for its close association with the Paedophile Information Exchange.[34] In June 1978, however, the AGM of Amnesty's British Section rejected a decision by the International

Council to recognise those imprisoned for their sexual behaviour and orientation as prisoners of conscience. One member of the British Amnesty Council pointed out that there was no explicit mention of sexual orientation in the Universal Declaration: Amnesty had a clear 'moral obligation' to act, but should it do so at the expense of diverting resources from its 'already massive task … whatever the cost'? In 1979 the new chair, Jacques Berthoud, stated that he considered 'the 'trade and aid' problem to be much more significant than the 'homosexuality' question'.[35] Senior figures also appeared uncomfortable with the implication that there may be gendered differences within the organisation, struggling, for instance, to answer the question of why so many prisoners of conscience were male. The findings of a membership survey which revealed that far more women than men had joined Amnesty due to their concerns over torture passed without comment.[36] Absurdly, when *British Amnesty* ran a profile of the peace campaigner and former prisoner of conscience (and Amnesty worker) Pat Arrowsmith, some readers protested that – in addition to her views on Northern Ireland – they did not approve of her being photographed holding a 'homosexual sex aid'. It was, in fact, a rubber bullet that had been fired at her![37]

By the later 1970s concepts of rights were increasingly subject to political contestation. In 1978 right-wing commentators queued up to criticise Amnesty International's apparent abandonment of impartiality when it appointed Derek Roebuck, a long-standing member of the Australian Communist Party, as its head of research.[38] In this instance the criticism was unfounded, as Roebuck was a distinguished legal scholar, committed to Amnesty's principles, but the episode was indicative of a broad association of human rights with the political left by the later 1970s. Even so, the distinction was not a sharp one, and Sir Keith Joseph, a senior Conservative who had the ear of Margaret Thatcher, was happy to remain a member of Amnesty so long as it was not 'blind to the evils in communist countries'.[39] It was during precisely this period that the resurgent right was embarking on a successful attempt to reclaim the language of individual freedoms. The left was slow to appreciate that the idea of the right to work, the right to home ownership and the right not to join a trade union had a powerful resonance, not only in the middle class, but also amongst sections of the working class. Margaret Thatcher successfully turned many of these themes into policy as Prime Minister (1979–90). During the 1970s they had been articulated by forerunners such as the National Association for Freedom (NAFF). The NAFF organisation, which claimed that Labour – with a vanishingly small parliamentary majority – was governing dictatorially, spoke above all to middle-class insecurities about trade union power, crime and Soviet expansionism. It took its cue from 1215 rather than 1948:

the first item in its Charter of Rights and Liberties was the right to be defended against the country's enemies: the second, to live under the Queen's Peace. It attracted some champions of human rights to its cause, and Peter Benenson's old mentor, Sir John Foster QC, was a patron.[40] Human rights played no specific part in its discourse, but, following the lead of the new Pope John Paul II (1978–2005), they were easily woven into it when needed.[41]

8.3   Does Size Matter? Amnesty International

Amnesty International's success in the 1970s was the result of careful planning and strategic decision-making at the start of the decade, with the goal of increasing and diversifying membership around the world, while retaining the organisation's hard-won reputation for integrity, accuracy and impartiality.[42] Accordingly, between 1970 and 1973 resources were devoted to building up the Research Department in London under the Czech-born academic Zbynek Zeman. Whereas in 1968 Amnesty had envisaged a full-time research staff of four, by 1976 ten times that number were employed in the department.[43] The growth of Amnesty's research capacity enabled a far wider range of countries to be monitored and generated the all-important case histories of prisoners of conscience for adoption by the local groups. Meanwhile, ambitious, innovative new campaigns such as the CAT or the international campaign over repression in Uruguay (spring 1976) energised existing members and boosted recruitment. The result was a prodigious growth in Amnesty's international membership, notably in the United States. However, Amnesty's transformation was by no means painless. This section will discuss some of the difficult issues that accompanied its growth, and, with special regard to the British Section, question some of the conclusions that have been drawn about the nature and characteristics of the expanding membership.

Amnesty International benefited immensely from the stability provided by Martin Ennals' leadership as Secretary General between 1968 and 1980, but it continued to be troubled by internal controversies and resignations. This fractiousness exasperated leaders, and in the case of Eric Baker drove him to a remarkable reflection on the organisation which he served: 'One of the unfortunate things about Amnesty over the years is the fatal consequence which it seems to have had for so many. Well-intentioned, capable and hard-working, they have all given a great deal to Amnesty – and in the end have destroyed themselves or been destroyed'.[44]

The most high-profile split came in November 1971 when the Treasurer Anthony Marreco resigned over Amnesty's readiness to criticise British conduct in Northern Ireland after the introduction of internment. Marreco, who owned a farm in County Donegal and was a member of the Irish Section, claimed that Amnesty had violated its own codes of neutrality and evidence gathering, and was guilty of 'crying "torture" where it knew that no torture within the meaning of the ECHR had taken place'.[45] Marreco took a benign view of the British army's role in Northern Ireland and argued that – unlike the Greek army – British troops were acting 'to protect Human Rights'.[46] The dispute was compounded by Marreco's belief that IEC Chairman Sean MacBride (a former Chief of Staff of the IRA in the mid-1930s, whose father had been executed by the British authorities in 1916) was prejudiced against Britain, and was not recusing himself on this issue as he had claimed. To a certain extent Marreco's criticism was justified as there is no question that MacBride could not resist quietly attempting to nudge the Secretariat into action over internment without trial.[47] Marreco was something of a maverick who also caused dissension with his scheme to create a tax-exempt fundraising arm for Amnesty in the United States,[48] but MacBride's personal correspondence reveals that he too could be a destabilising force. MacBride's fierce desire to impose his own authority on the Secretariat, and especially its finances, made him highly critical of Ennals, whom he accused of being incompetent and of concealing vital information from him. At one point he toyed with firing both Ennals and the Research Director Zeman, whom he viewed as a 'cold warrior'. When appointing a new Treasurer, he stated that it would not worry him at all if – as reported – there was 'no love lost' between his candidate and Ennals. It was perhaps fortunate for Amnesty that MacBride stood down in 1973 when appointed UN Commissioner for Namibia. He was awarded the Nobel Peace Prize the following year for his many 'efforts on behalf of human rights'.[49]

One of the issues over which Ennals and MacBride clashed was the Prisoner of Conscience Fund, which also bedevilled relations between Amnesty and its British Section. There were a number of issues at stake, quite apart from the central question of what the proceeds could be spent on – a bone of contention with the Inland Revenue and Charity Commissioners, still unresolved in the mid-1970s. The British Section's major grievance was that one of the Fund's main sources of income was British members, who paid their subscriptions into it with a tax covenant. As the Treasurer of the British Section put it in 1969, this represented a 'hidden contribution' of as much as £5000 to Amnesty International, as the international movement reaped the financial benefits while the British Section still had to provide services to its members.[50] Over the years this question was addressed by a series of elaborate 'offset' arrangements, although these too had to be cleared with the authorities. Secondly, the question of control over the fund proved contentious. Formally, it was controlled by independent managers and trustees (such as Archbishop Roberts and Ritchie Calder), rather than the IEC. After the crisis of 1966–67 Norman Marsh and Tom Sargant took over as managers, without realising what a complex administrative task they had taken on.[51] In the early 1970s MacBride became convinced that Ennals was using the fund without due accountability and was determined to bring it under IEC control.[52] Amidst the acrimony and resignations generated by what Baker once termed 'the mysteries of the Prisoner of Conscience Fund',[53] however, it should not be forgotten that the fund paid for a great deal of good work to be carried out, especially on behalf of the families of political prisoners.

The fund was one example of how unresolved problems from the past could create problems in the present: another was the strange case of George Lennox, a former British soldier who had offered first-hand evidence in support of Amnesty's allegations of torture in Aden, and then spoke out against British abuses in Northern Ireland in 1971. Lennox was subsequently jailed for robbery – he claimed that he had been framed – and served three years in jail. However, Amnesty refused to accept him as a prisoner of conscience after his case was reviewed by its 'Borderline Committee', the body set up in 1968 to determine precisely such difficult cases.[54] Lennox's case was taken up by a Dutch anarchist organisation called HAPOTOC that succeeded – to Amnesty's embarrassment – in interesting a new generation of Amnesty activists in the murky events of 1966–67.[55] The debate over Lennox was particularly unwelcome as some of the radicals, both in Britain and Europe, who supported Lennox also favoured a revision of its statute so as to allow Amnesty to assist imprisoned Baader–Meinhof group terrorists. This, again, was an issue from the past as the IEC had decided in 1969 not to revise the statute, a position overwhelmingly backed by the British Section (by forty-four votes to five).[56] In November 1974 Rev. Paul Oestreicher, Chairman of the British Section, made a private visit to West Germany to investigate the conditions of the prisoners, who were on hunger strike. He concluded that their conditions should be improved, but that their allegations of torture could not be upheld.[57] However, some British Amnesty groups continued to press for change: one proposal was to introduce a new category of 'prisoners without rights'.[58]

The continuing debate over prisoners who advocated the use of violence was an extreme example of the lingering uncertainty over exactly what kind of organisation Amnesty was. How could Amnesty earn the respect of governments and international agencies while also retaining its critical edge and the unpolished, somewhat ramshackle image it presented to the outside world? Tricia Feeney, who came to work for Amnesty International in the mid-1970s, wrote that it was housed in a 'narrow, crooked building and visitors had to squeeze their way past rows of bikes to enter what looked like a shabby workshop rather than the headquarters of an international organization'.[59] These dilemmas were frequently aired at the time. In 1972 MacBride spoke of Amnesty needing efficiency, but not 'without a soul', while Ennals warned the annual meeting of the British Section that Amnesty's planned growth carried inherent risks of 'professionalisation, bureocracy [sic], over-administration and the putting off of voluntary aid'.[60] At the same occasion a few years later the question arose as to whether Amnesty was an '"Establishment Organisation" or a pressure group'. Ennals' cannily evasive response was that it should be '"as established as the Red Cross and as militant as the anti-apartheid movement"'.[61]

There were also doubts related to the rapid growth of Amnesty's world-wide membership, which had been regarded as an unalloyed good ever since the 'Long-Range Planning Committee' of the early 1970s had targeted growth outside of Europe, especially in the developing world. Amnesty had appointed Richard Reoch as its first field officer in South Asia in order to facilitate this process.[62] However, although growth was achieved, much of it took place in Europe and, more surprisingly, in the United States, where Amnesty had struggled to take off in the 1960s.[63] Barbara Keys has argued that AI USA's claim that its membership rose from 3000 to 50,000 in a year and a half (1975–76) should be treated with caution, although she goes on to say that the overall numbers do indicate a 'stunning turnaround' in its fortunes. She adds that Amnesty was developing rather differently in the United States, and members tended to be 'one-time donors or subscribers to the newsletter' rather than European-style adoption groups.[64] By the later 1970s one finds frequent, thinly veiled notes of concern about the new mass membership: concern that it might be motivated by a 'generalised human rights orientation' rather than by Amnesty's specific mandate, and that Amnesty might be mistaken for a 'movement embracing all good causes'.[65] Moreover, membership growth created something of a vicious circle as the larger the membership the more prisoners were needed for adoption: yet the difficulty of obtaining information from the communist world made it impossible to obtain the balance between different political systems that the original 'threes' system had required. Indeed, this 'shortage' of prisoners meant that in the mid-1970s the main source of discontent amongst British groups was the practice of 'double adoption', whereby the same prisoners were allocated to more than one group. Some members responded creatively, by co-ordinating their activities around specific themes or forming specialist interest groups. However, alternative forms of campaigning carried the risk of undermining Amnesty's distinctive modus operandi.[66]

The British Section had been established in 1963 but was consistently overshadowed by the international organisation. As Baker put it in 1970, the London-based International Secretariat tended to treat the UK as 'part of their own backyard', and often forgot to consult with the British Section.[67] The AI annual report for 1968–69 explained that, in the attempt to distinguish between the two, efforts had been made to 'separate the two secretariats while retaining the closest practical communication between them'.[68] However, the British Section continued to suffer from something of an identity problem despite moving into separate premises and developing its own leadership structure. It only had a handful of staff but was a major contributor to the rapidly expanding central budget, which it struggled to contain.[69] The British Section experienced substantial growth in the mid-1970s, but nowhere near the levels claimed by AI USA. In the autumn of 1975 the section launched a 'Huge Membership Drive', calling for 'thousands more members . . . to give us a really firm base'. At this point the membership stood at almost 3000: this had risen to 5000 one year later, 7500 in June 1978, and finally passed 10,000 in the spring of 1979 with little fanfare.[70] This was a significant achievement, although almost as many groups were listed as closing (especially in universities) as opening, and the growth in members was not reflected in an equal expansion in the overall number of groups. Moreover, to put it in perspective, the Labour Party had more than 500,000 members during the mid-1970s, and the Conservative Party 1.5 million: in the voluntary sector, the National Trust grew from under 300,000 to over 1 million during the decade, and Amnesty was considerably smaller than Greenpeace and Friends of the Earth.[71] When Oestreicher stood down as Chairman at the end of 1979 he noted very sensibly that it was not the size of the membership that counted but the creation of structures through which individuals could commit to others.[72] The relatively modest growth meant that the members remained activists: Stefan-Ludwig Hoffman's comment that Amnesty members were 'content for the most part with paying membership fees' may apply to the AI USA, but not in Britain.[73]

As to the characteristics of the British Amnesty membership, Director David Simpson told an interviewer in 1977 that his members were no longer 'Hampstead liberals and middle-aged, middle-class people. They're much broader-based than they were'.[74] Certainly the limited available evidence suggests that while the British Section's strongholds remained in London and the universities, growth during the 1970s often took place in suburbs and middle-sized towns such as Hemel Hempstead. There were, for instance, targeted campaigns in East Anglia and the North West of England in 1973.[75] The most illuminating guide is a survey carried out with help from National Opinion Polls in June 1978, which was sent to 10 per cent of members, with a 70 per cent reply rate. The headline results were published in the section's newsletter although, unfortunately, none of the information collected about occupation, income, trade union membership or political affiliation was made public. Most members, it transpired, had found their way to Amnesty either in response to an item in the media or through the efforts of existing members to recruit them. When asked why they had joined Amnesty, the main reason given was concern over injustice, followed by a sense that it was a 'worthwhile' organisation and a concern about oppression and tyranny: only one in five identified 'human rights' as the reason. Ninety-two per cent expressed some degree of satisfaction with their decision to join, and levels of satisfaction were far higher amongst active members. The most interesting findings concerned religion: 46 per cent stated that they attended church regularly, a far higher proportion than in the overall population. The single largest group was members of the Church of England (27 per cent), followed – in order of size – by agnostic/don't know (18 per cent), atheist (16 per cent), Roman Catholics, Quakers, Non-Conformists, Methodists, Jews (2 per cent) and Unitarians. The editor's attempt to gloss this result with the comment that Amnesty was a 'religious' movement – in so far as concern for others was a 'religious' impulse – went down badly with some of the substantial non-religious membership.[76] Activists in the London region noted that, while the figures indicated 'some kind of Christian quasi-identification … Amnesty is not co-terminus with a Christian witness'.[77]

The available evidence, therefore, suggests that Amnesty's membership growth in Britain was significant without being spectacular. The new members were largely recruited by – and absorbed into – the existing groups, and do not appear to have changed the overall social, religious or political composition of the section. The groups' core activities remained the same, although they evolved in response to the shortage of sufficient numbers of appropriate prisoners for adoption. There is no evidence that membership was swollen by an influx of post-revolutionary idealists, disenchanted with politics and happy to focus instead on alleviating the suffering of specific individuals. Admittedly, the Director of the British Section (1972–74), Victor Jokel, was an American Unitarian Minister who had campaigned against the Vietnam War, but even he was careful to label himself as a 'humanitarian' rather than a left-winger.[78] Such an interpretation applies far more to an organisation such as War on Want which, under Peter Burns, moved self-consciously to the left and sought to 'harness the energy of the Sixties protest generation'.[79] There is clearly a danger, therefore, in taking the changes in the size and composition of the highly volatile American Section as characteristic of Amnesty as a whole.

8.4   Echoes of Amnesty

Of all the new human rights groups established at this time, perhaps the closest to Amnesty was the Writers and Scholars International (WSI), better known through the title of its publication *Index on Censorship*. The two organisations enjoyed a close, complementary relationship in the 1970s, whereby the WSI published the translation of the Soviet dissidents' *Chronicle of Current Events* on behalf of Amnesty, while Amnesty described *Index* as its 'literary counterpart' and encouraged its members to subscribe.[80] Although the WSI never sought to acquire a large membership, its global remit and non-ideological stance were both modelled on those of Amnesty: in the words of Michael Scammell, who edited *Index* from 1972 to 1980, it was a 'deliberate echo of Amnesty International'.[81]

The WSI was formed by a group of British liberal intellectuals, led by the poet Stephen Spender and the philosopher Stuart Hampshire, in response to an open letter from Pavel Litvinov and other Soviet intellectuals protesting at the trial of Sinyavsky and Daniel in 1966. In a letter to Spender, Litvinov invited him to form an international committee in support of the 'democratic movement' in the USSR, but wisely recommended that the new committee should not have an 'anti-communist or anti-Soviet character' and that its remit might even include those jailed for espousing communism in countries such as Greece.[82] The contact was timely for Spender and Hampshire as they were looking for a new venture after the collapse of *Encounter* magazine, following revelations that it had received secret CIA funding. Arguably, however, the true 'founding father' of WSI was Edward Crankshaw, the well-connected *Observer* journalist and Russian historian who, with his background in British intelligence and status as *persona non grata* in the Soviet Union, preferred to keep a low profile.[83] It was Crankshaw who began to flesh out the project, although his original conception of a committee of 'respected academics', publishing banned books from dissident Soviet authors alongside a 'little magazine', did not fully correspond to the organisation that eventually emerged.[84] Crankshaw also provided a key point of contact to Lord Wolfson who, along with David Astor, was one of the WSI's most significant backers. In 1974 Edward Crankshaw noted that Leonard Wolfson was 'above all concerned with the Jews', and that he had told him that 'many of the people that we are trying to help are in fact Jews'.[85]

The WSI was formally launched on 15 October 1971, under the auspices of a Council chaired by Lord Gardiner and containing experienced campaigners, often with strong associations with Amnesty, such as Peter Calvocoressi, Louis Blom-Cooper and Zbynek Zeman. The organisation, 'formed by a group of individuals who have no political, or ideological axe to grind' was intended to make the public aware of 'the suppression of freedom of expression, wherever it occurs'.[86] The first edition of *Index* was appropriately wide-ranging – poems by Natalya Gorbanevskaya, the poet confined to a psychiatric hospital, a short story by the dissident Yugoslav communist Milovan Djilas, a piece by Spender and articles on Bangladesh, Brazil and Portugal. In the absence of a mass membership the new organisation struggled to shake off the image of being a group of 'splendid liberals' (as Crankshaw put it) or participants in 'one of David Astor's pet schemes' (in the words of David Kessler, Chairman of the *Jewish Chronicle*).[87] Even so, during the 1970s it achieved considerable success – perhaps most importantly, WSI avoided the dangers of becoming a purely Cold War, anti-Soviet movement by taking its stand on the global defence of intellectual freedom. Summing up in 1979, Scammell noted that in addition to publishing *Index* and a series of research studies, WSI was acknowledged as the centre of expertise on political censorship and had 'substantial links' with the dissidents of Eastern Europe. It had an annual turnover of some £100,000 – a third from private donations and the rest from foundations – and a staff of twelve.[88] *Index* was also beginning to gain a reputation in the USA where, by August 1975, a quarter of the 4000 copies were being sold. During a visit in 1977 Scammell received a sympathetic hearing from American foundations and found Marilyn Haft, one of Carter's special advisers on human rights, gratifyingly 'full of praise for *Index*'.[89] One unforeseen obstacle to gaining support in the United States was the journal's name, however, as Scammell reported that censorship was not widely regarded as a human rights issue, and was more likely to be identified with attempts to restrict pornography. In 1976 the WSI agreed in principle to abandon the term 'censorship' for a title that more explicitly defined it as a 'human rights journal' but failed to agree on an alternative.[90]

*

Like the WSI, the Minority Rights Group (MRG) also measured itself against Amnesty, while developing as a small community of experts rather than as a mass-membership organisation. The MRG had had a troubled beginning in the 1960s,[91] having been established by David Astor as a vehicle for addressing Michael Scott's concerns over the fate of ethnic and religious minorities in newly independent states. Scott saw the lack of provision for minorities as the 'fatal flaw' in the UN Charter and Declaration of Human Rights.[92] Astor envisaged assembling a group of regional specialists who would prompt newspapers and other media to report on emerging crises and thereby trigger international public concern. Accordingly, his initial choices as Chief Executive were prominent journalists such as the Sri Lankan Tarzie Vittachi, who was currently working for the International Press Institute, and Laurence Gandar, editor of the *Rand Daily Mail,* who had recently stood trial in South Africa for his reporting of jail conditions. Neither appointment was deemed particularly successful: to Astor's disappointment Gandar, 'the famous campaigning editor', showed no taste for campaigning, and only stayed for a short period.[93] The MRG also experienced a frisson of competition in 1969 following the formation of the Primitive People's Fund (later Survival International), although the newcomer's focus on indigenous people's rights, and its roots in anthropology and Amazonian exploration, kept friction to a minimum.[94] The MRG truly began to take shape in the 1970s under the direction of Ben Whitaker, an Old Etonian and former Labour MP who – partly because of his support for the Vietnam War – had lost his Hampstead seat in the May 1970 general election. Whitaker turned the MRG into a respected source of information about the problems facing minorities around the world,[95] albeit at the expense of alienating its founders.

Astor's original vision, as he later explained it, had been for an organisation that would provide information about the worst-treated minorities, 'rather as Amnesty goes for the worst-treated political prisoners'. Yet he wanted to square a circle. How would such an organisation gain a reputation for 'truthfulness, accuracy, independence' in its reporting and also act as the minorities' friend and adviser – 'without becoming their propagandists'?[96] Scott had certainly failed to convince the Indian government of the impartiality of his work with the Nagas and had been expelled in 1965. When Whitaker took over as Director in 1971 he realised that his predecessors had, in fact, made invaluable progress in certain essential areas: first, they had obtained funding from the Ford Foundation in 1968, and this was regularly renewed; secondly, they had obtained charitable status, something that Amnesty had failed to achieve and which WSI faced considerable difficulty in securing. The MRG's lawyer offered the opinion that 'it was a miracle that MRG ever became a charity',[97] and to preserve that status the organisation must refrain from acting as a lobby or pressure group. Whitaker's strategy for leading the MRG was therefore determined by the harsh reality that it must maintain charitable status or lose most of its funding. Accordingly, he saw its primary task as 'describing and publicising the facts' through a series of reports by experts, acknowledging that – like Amnesty – it would take some years to gain a reputation and begin to influence governments. Although the reports were well regarded, Astor and Scott became increasingly disenchanted with the dry 'academic' route that the MRG had taken, and the apparent abandonment of advocacy and activism, especially with regard to minorities in the developing world.[98] The final straw for Scott was the decision to carry out a major research project into the status of Gypsies in Britain, which he believed was chosen to 'cause least embarrassment in government circles'.[99] Scott and Astor finally resigned in 1977, claiming that the MRG was doing little more than 'informing the general reader of all the different minorities in the world'.[100] In the early 1980s Scott set up an organisation called 'Rights and Justice' (itself an echo of his very first campaign in South Africa in the 1940s) which was intended to fulfil the MRG's original vision, before it had been taken over by those who wanted to keep it as a 'strictly academic study group'.[101]

In some respects, the decision by MRG's founders to walk away from the organisation merely reflects the decline of Scott's brand of awkward, one-man crusading. At the same time, however, Whitaker's ambition of doing 'for minority groups what Amnesty does for individuals' and developing a staff and budget commensurate with Amnesty's remained a remote prospect during the 1970s: in 1977 MRG still only had an annual budget of £25,000, while Amnesty's had risen to £492,000.[102] A major factor shaping MRG's development was surely the decision not to attempt to build a membership base, on the understanding that its task was to inform the press and public rather than to form opinion. Even so, there is evidence that Whitaker's long game was beginning to pay off. In addition to an expanding portfolio of publications on problems facing minorities ranging from the Japanese Burakumin to the Crimean Tartars and the Asians of East Africa, the organisation was becoming more international – for instance, a Swiss group was set up in 1973.[103] It was also becoming more like the advocacy organisation that Astor had envisaged. Its energies were increasingly focused on the UN, where it gained consultative status in 1974, and where Whitaker served for many years on the Human Rights Commission.

*

Attractive as the Amnesty model was in the 1970s, some human rights organisations trod a rather different path. Perhaps the most interesting was the Centre for Human Rights and Responsibilities (CHRR), which was the creation of the Austrian-born sociologist Richard Hauser and his wife, the musician Hepzibah Menuhin. Hauser was intermittently involved with Amnesty in its early years, and Hepzibah memorably performed with her brother Yehudi at Amnesty's 1964 Human Rights Day commemoration.[104] Hauser and his wife had set up an Institute for Group Studies in 1958, with the goal of encouraging 'problem groups within society to face and solve their own problems': they listed five target groups, 'unintelligent young people', coloured people, isolated housewives, sufferers from mental illness and homosexuals.[105] The couple collaborated on a book, *The Fraternal Society* (1962) which set out the theory underpinning their activities. They argued that the 'paternal society', characterised by greed, exploitation and war, was coming to an end, and that a new 'fraternal' society, which would be more democratic and based on a greater sense of social responsibility, was struggling to be born. Their own contribution would be to facilitate the arrival of this new era by making a series of practical interventions, thereby 'working out their ideas in society'.[106] Accordingly, they moved to Bethnal Green in 1967, where they opened a youth club in a 'rough area' and mobilised local volunteers to tackle the pressing social problems there. As the project came to an end three years later one of their team commented rather sceptically that 'our skinheads are now growing their hair and leaving off the tuf boots and discarding the braces. Their morals remain unchanged'.[107] Like Peter Benenson, therefore, Hauser believed that activism – whether through local 'community activation' projects or internationally – was the key to individual self-transformation. Indeed, the similarities were even greater than this: when Hauser identified four aspects of the struggle for peace in 1960, the fourth was 'identification with all those suffering possibly "in countries far away" of which we know but little – such as Algeria, South Africa, Hungary and the Portuguese Colonies, Spain and Tibet ...'.[108]

During the 1970s Hauser secured some very prestigious collaborators for the now renamed CHRR, such as Philip Noel-Baker (the 1959 Nobel Peace Prize laureate), Quaker peace campaigner Kenneth Lee, Brigadier Michael Harbottle and his wife Eirwen, Archbishop Roberts and the American Jesuit Ray Helmick. Reflecting these associations, the Centre became more focused on international issues, and offered its services in promoting conflict resolution and conciliation in areas such as Northern Ireland and Cyprus (where Harbottle had been head of UN peacekeeping in the late 1960s). It also opened an India Bureau to bring together those concerned with human rights violations during the Indian Emergency of 1975–77, and founded the British Kurdish

Friendship Society.[109] However, the Centre also continued to pursue local initiatives, and in February 1975 claimed to be running thirty-one 'pilots and projects', although it is impossible to establish how substantial they were.[110] In 1975 an Anglican nun, Sister Florence, undertook a project for the CHRR on society's neglect of the elderly. The intention was to give the young a greater understanding of the 'Third Age', while the elderly would be encouraged to show that they could still make a valuable contribution to society: 'we need more provocation, indignation and protest, not least among the elderly themselves'. The CHRR, therefore, rejected both the current 'clamour for rights' (while responsibilities were being forgotten) and what it saw as a disempowering welfare state.[111]

The CHRR was undeniably quirky – its 1979 annual report concluded with a bizarre encomium for the Romanian President Nicolae Ceauşescu, who was hailed as a catalyst for change within the Soviet bloc who, as yet, had no equivalent in the West. The Centre even proposed its own five-year plan for change, stimulated in part by discussions held by unnamed members of the group with Ceauşescu and his wife![112] Even so, the organisation remains worthy of serious attention for several reasons. First, the charge often levelled against the human rights campaigners of the 1970s – that they lacked a theoretical basis and were simply seeking to do good – clearly does not apply here. The CHRR had a carefully thought-out view of the world, and in all their surviving documentation sought to relate their very diverse activities to it. Secondly, it did not see human rights abuses as something that only happened 'abroad', but also as a cause to be fought and won in Britain. As Hauser put it, 'we see the task as being local, national and international, with local groups looking at international issues, and vice versa'.[113] The Centre's concern with the human rights of old people contrasts with the UNA Human Rights Committee's decision – when urged by one of the branches – not to prioritise the right to security in old age (as specified under Article 25 of the Universal Declaration).[114] Finally, the CHRR embodied an important, but often overlooked, strand within the history of human rights: Gandhi's emphasis on duties (or responsibilities) rather than rights.[115]

8.5   Fields and Networks

In 1979 *The Human Rights Handbook* commented that the human rights lobby in Britain had 'never had a strong centre. It is only in the last few years that the label "human rights" has come to be applied, with varying degrees of reluctance, to a disparate collection of humanitarian organisations. Most of them small, all of them independent' and some predating the Universal Declaration.[116] This captured perfectly how – for all the individual success of organisations such as Amnesty – the 'field of human rights' remained the loose, decentralised collection of campaigning NGOs that had come together a decade earlier, in response to the UN's Year of Human Rights. Latterly, however, as the handbook pointed out, an attempt had been made to bring some order to this disparate world: a 'Human Rights Network' which would provide mutual benefits without endangering the cherished freedom and flexibility that constituent organisations enjoyed.

The UNA's Human Rights Committee had been charged with taking forward the work of Human Rights Year and was supported by a modest, time-limited grant from the UNA Trust. In the early 1970s the committee sought to offer a degree of leadership across the field, and persuaded Amnesty's Martin Ennals to act as chair. However, the lack of progress in the period since 1968 prompted a new approach. In particular, the UNA was disappointed that the Conservative government was planning no formal commemoration of the twenty-fifth anniversary of the Universal Declaration in 1973 and had made little effort to ratify the human rights covenants. Moreover, a report by the young Australian activist Keith Suter, who acted as rapporteur for the Human Rights Committee, indicated that the UNA's grass roots found human rights 'boring', and were far more enthusiastic about protecting the environment. According to Suter, the committee was in danger of being a 'cosy coterie' of London-based professionals, cut off from the UNA's branches.[117] Accordingly, at a series of meetings in 1975, the UNA embarked on discussions with other human rights organisations which resulted in the formation of the network. This proposal clearly struck a chord, as a meeting in September 1975 was described as 'packed like sardines'.[118] In 1975 Gordon Evans congratulated the network's convenor Leah Levin (who would later succeed Tom Sargant as Director of Justice) on 'what a wonderful job you have done and are doing for the Human Rights cause. Even just keeping the H. R. [sic] community together and in focus is invaluable'.[119]

The network was run by the UNA until March 1976, when it was handed over to the National Council for Social Service to administer. Within eighteen months some forty organisations were sending representatives to meetings, while a further ninety received papers.[120] A richly diverse group attended the meetings. Alongside the national organisations such as Amnesty, Justice and the NCCL, many members represented oppressed groups around the world, such as TAPOL, which campaigned on behalf of prisoners in Indonesia, or the British

Committee for Portuguese War Resisters. The voices of the Eritreans, struggling against Ethiopian 'colonisation', were well represented, as were those of the Kurds. Some constituent groups were nothing if not eclectic in their concerns – for instance, Helena Fjortoft reported that her Merseyside Council for Human Rights was currently interested in 'Fair Rates, Kidney machines, and the Death Sentence for Holding Bibles (in China)'.[121] The smaller organisations, therefore, relished the opportunity to air their particular concerns, while the larger ones saw the value in working together to achieve specific goals as well as, potentially, exercising more influence over government. This level of cooperation was only possible, however, because of the emphasis on freedom and flexibility. As Cecil Evans of the Quaker International Relations Committee warned Ennals in 1975, the network must not be a new bureaucracy: it existed to facilitate and not to control.[122]

Even so, there were some notes of controversy. For instance, in October 1975 Peter Burns of War on Want declined to sign a joint letter to the Prime Minister calling for ratification of the Human Rights Covenants on the grounds that, while the cause was 'no doubt worthy', it was hardly one of the 'practical issues' which his organisation now gave priority to.[123] More serious was the row that blew up in 1978 when the British Anti-Zionist Organisation (BAZO) joined the network and was said to be using the mailing list to distribute its bulletin. This was strongly criticised by the Board of Deputies and the Zionist Federation, but the small 'Bureau' that ran the network declined to take any action on grounds that membership was open to all groups that 'embrace[d] some aspect of human rights work'.[124] As BAZO expressed a concern for violations of human rights in the Middle East, it satisfied this criterion, and the fact that its policy on Zionism was contrary to that of the UNA was not enough to deny it membership. The only concession was that henceforward groups were instructed not to refer publicly to their membership of the network.[125]

The Human Rights Network was established with a core function of emphasising the 'inter-relatedness of human rights causes, and to identify the "common cause" aspect of efforts in the field'.[126] This gentle bringing together of quite disparate groups was characteristic of the period, both domestically (in the case of the network) and, increasingly, internationally. This greater international-mindedness was influenced by developments such as the Helsinki Accords, Britain's membership of the EEC and the greater willingness of the Labour government, in comparison to its predecessor, to discuss the significance of human rights for foreign policy and development.[127] Some British organisations subscribed in the late 1970s to the presciently titled 'Human Rights Internet', a US organisation which, by means of regular newsletters, filled the 'vacuum' that existed between different human rights groups, between activists and academics, and between human rights groups and policymakers.[128] Moreover, some members of the network were already organising on an international basis. For instance, the 'Campaign for Human Rights 78' was a 'pan-European' campaign with a London headquarters and offices in ten West European countries, based on pacifist and civil liberties organisations. It was dedicated to securing the appointment of a UN High Commissioner for Human Rights, a goal finally achieved in 1993.[129]

A parallel attempt was made to organise a loose network in the later 1970s amongst churches and religious denominations.[130] In 1975 two meetings were held at the London Ecumenical Centre with a view to creating an 'ad hoc liaison group' for Christians concerned with prisoners of conscience. The Chairman was Ernest Payne, a prominent Baptist with a long-standing interest in the treatment of Christians in the Soviet Union, and a Trustee of Amnesty's Prisoner of Conscience Fund. However, the driving force was the Rev. Paul Oestreicher, Chairman of the British Section of Amnesty (1974–79), and previously International Affairs Secretary of the British Council of Churches (BCC) with a special interest in Eastern Europe.[131] His goal was explicitly not to create a 'churches group for Amnesty', but rather to find a way of disseminating Amnesty's message across the many religious constituencies in Britain. In Payne's words, human rights were now 'a matter of basic concern to Christians'. The new group would 'enable the churches to make a more worthwhile contribution and may help to educate the Christian constituency'. The exploratory meetings were well attended, but when Oestreicher mentioned that the group would need a budget of £2000 many of the churches back-tracked or only offered nominal assistance. However, the initiative bore fruit in 1977 when Brian Duckworth of the BCC's Division of International Affairs convened an 'Informal Advisory Group on Human Rights' to run for three years, intended to offer a 'forum for debate, coordination (where needed) and expression of Christian conviction'. A leaflet prepared for the group made clear that 'human rights is a Christian concern': after all, Jesus was a refugee from a despotic government, a prisoner of conscience convicted on false testimony and the martyr of 'an occupying colonial power'.[132] Although religious groups remained reluctant to invest substantial resources, this episode demonstrates that by the late 1970s none disputed the centrality of human rights to their witness, and most were happy to work together in collaboration with groups such as Amnesty International.

In Britain, therefore, the human rights movement of the 1970s represented an eclectic mixture of religious, political and cultural strands.

Amnesty stood apart in terms of scale, resources and distinction, but there were also many medium-sized organisations pursuing specific missions, and there was no shortage of idiosyncratic one-man bands. The *Human Rights Handbook* used a term popularised by Alvin Toffler – an 'Adhocracy' – to describe the current state of play: the concept may have expressed hope in a new, non-bureaucratic way of doing business, or, conversely, alarm at an inability to organise the field. This ambiguity was, arguably, a source of weakness in the changed national and international politics of the next decade, but no individual or organisation was – it seemed – offering to provide leadership.

Conclusion: the Winds of History

The late 1970s offer a vantage point for assessing not only what had been achieved by the emerging human rights movement in Britain, but also its readiness for the challenges that lay ahead. There is no question that a process of transmutation had taken place, and was continuing to take place, during the postwar decades, whereby a mixture of beliefs, causes and personal empathies was slowly turning into something greater. Canon Collins once wrote that 'the lot of anyone who engages in causes' is that one follows another 'as night follows day',[1] but what had occurred in this case was rather less haphazard. Peter Archer argued that a transition was taking place from 'private conscience to world law',[2] while the Baptist David Russell, a pillar of the World Council of Churches, spoke of how his profound interest in religious liberty in the Soviet Union became an understanding that concern for human rights went beyond religious freedoms and expressed itself in a 'bewildering variety of ways'.[3] Many more examples can be drawn from the preceding chapters to show how an interest in, say, political imprisonment, colonial liberation or women's rights could evolve into a broader engagement with human rights, even if in some cases the process was incomplete, or had not even been started. Many politicians, trade unionists and religious leaders certainly remained happy to invoke the principle of human rights for the causes that they supported, while showing no interest in the equally deserving causes that they did not.

In 1979 Eric Baker's widow, Joyce, donated a tranche of her husband's papers to Amnesty's International Secretariat. In thanking her, the official responsible noted that 'I have spent most of today reading through the two files of 1960–61, it is all so amazing, isn't it?'[4] It is difficult to disagree. Looking at human rights activism across the postwar years, the distance travelled was, indeed, remarkable, and the events of 1961 were surely the turning point. The Universal Declaration of 1948 had not inspired a strong, united movement for human rights, partly due to the divisive impact of the Cold War. Instead, human rights activism was incubated during the 1950s, principally in campaigns over Africa and political prisoners in southern Europe, but lacked cohesion and focus. In 1961 Peter Benenson, who had navigated the campaigns and organisations of the 1950s, and learnt from his own failures, provided the vital spark. His Appeal for Amnesty served up, as he put it, a 'distillation of the world's conscience – a strong, rough and heady drink'.[5] It not only rallied support from across the diverse groups – legal, religious, political and humanitarian – that had previously taken an interest in human rights abuses, but also awakened interest amongst new constituencies. As Eric Baker noted in 1975, there was no doubt that Benenson was *the* founder of Amnesty. It was his idea as it was his energy and enthusiasm' which launched Amnesty so successfully.[6] However, Amnesty was by no means prefabricated: policies, strategies and institutions were developed on the hoof in response to its unanticipated success, and many ideas had to be abandoned or completely rethought along the way. Benenson himself fell victim to the crisis of 1966–67, but, as Baker noted in the same letter, Amnesty was not sustained by Benenson, or for that matter by MacBride or Baker, alone: 'any future account of the beginnings of Amnesty should do justice to the multitude of men and women who worked devotedly – and voluntarily – to start it off'. Despite continued internal ructions, by the 1970s Amnesty had come to define a new kind of human rights activism. It was effective, inspirational and a model for others. By the end of the decade Amnesty may have been the most significant actor in the 'field of human rights', but the field itself had become richer and more diverse as a result of its success.

An analysis of the progress that had been made during these years points to a complex set of factors at work. The ability of a few significant individuals to articulate new ideas and mobilise groups of volunteers was crucial, but timing and contingency were also important. In 1964, in the first flush of Amnesty's early success, Peter Benenson wrote that 'the movement has taken on a momentum which only happens when the wind of history fills out the sails of a small barque'.[7] This sounds trite, but it contains more than a kernel of truth: human rights activism can only succeed through a combination of good leadership, high levels of personal commitment at every level of the campaign or organisation, and favourable political, social and cultural conditions. Activists are never completely masters of their destiny, and Benenson's evocation of the impersonal forces driving change recalled a similar metaphor in a poem that Elwyn Jones composed during the Nuremberg trial, addressed to the defendants: 'You cast your bitter bread. It has returned on tides of justice . . . '.[8]

One point that this book has sought to demonstrate is the vital importance of different forms of leadership. Only visionary leaders can define a 'big problem'[9] and inspire others to act collectively in order to overcome it; while only those with superior managerial and diplomatic skills can successfully carry the work forwards and negotiate the 'crises of growth'. It is surely no coincidence that Danilo Dolci – whose own tribulations demonstrated this dilemma so clearly – meant so much to this generation of activists. Of the leaders discussed here, only Canon Collins was still in charge of his creation at the end of his career, and only Eric Baker combined these two principal types of leadership with any degree of success. Michael Scott spent a decade building a formidable reputation, and then threw it away by pursuing interests which others could not see the significance of and which brought ever-diminishing returns.[10] Peter Benenson – by far the most important individual catalyst in the growth of postwar human rights activism – was ultimately unable to match his ambition to the constraints of the organisations that he founded. These personal setbacks were often devastating for the individuals concerned, but should not be allowed to obscure the profound legacies left by their most creative periods of leadership. The Minority Rights Group has gone on to become a significant international player, even if it appears to have forgotten Michael Scott's crucial role in its conception.[11] Benenson was only in charge of Amnesty for a few years, but his influence has proved enduring. For instance, Dirk Börner's Secretary's report for 1975–76 celebrated Amnesty's 100,000 members spread across five continents. His comment that 'this large number of non-professionals has done more than any professional organisation could ever have hoped to achieve in 15 years' could hardly have been truer to Benenson's original vision.[12]

The activists who responded to these appeals form a fascinating and eclectic group. They were not collectively representative of any established political tradition, of either left or right, or any single religious congregation. These were not conventional radicals (not even the many students involved) and do not fit an image of the campaigning politics of the 1960s and 1970s as dominated by the left, just as the staid events of the UN's Human Rights Year in Britain do not sit easily with the clichés of '1968'. The interviews conducted in the early 1980s with Amnesty's founding volunteers indicate a group – often of women, sometimes marked by experiences of alienation or discrimination much earlier in their lives – for whom 'The Forgotten Prisoners' presented a challenge that they had not knowingly sought until that point. Such people were often drawn to human rights activism by a sense that it offered a direct, principled engagement with a cause, different from more mundane forms of voluntary work. As one leading local activist who conducted a survey of Amnesty's British members in 1967 commented: 'Many Groups – mine among them – have echoed the thought: Amnesty work attracted me just because there was no fund-raising attached to it'.[13] He added that he had now learnt the vital importance of more humdrum forms of activity.

For all the activists' diversity, however, two generalisations are worth making. First, they were primarily drawn from the middle class, and represented a recognisably middle-class form of organisation – marshalling professional expertise and authority, working through local committees and raising funds through coffee mornings, fetes and exhibitions. During the 1960s and 1970s the human rights movement developed alongside the flourishing of the middle class associated with university expansion, the growth of the public sector, the welfare state and the advent of new technologies, just as it also developed alongside middle-class enthusiasms such as international development and care for the environment. This does not mean that the working-class was absent from these initiatives, but the principal institutions of the working class – the trade unions – approached human rights activism (as opposed to the more overtly political NCCL, anti-apartheid movement or the Spanish Amnesty campaign) with marked suspicion. There was no British trade union leader, for instance, who expressed the same enthusiasm for Amnesty – or understanding of its goals – as readily as Victor Reuther had done.[14] A representative of Belfast Trades Council who attended a UNA branch garden party at the height of Human Rights Year found it unashamedly middle class and hoped that more working-class involvement might save the cause from the 'plodders and do-gooders'.[15]

Secondly, this activism represented a significant mobilisation of religious energies, one that was particularly striking during a period in which the churches generally felt that they were on the defensive. Indeed, the idea that one 'wind of history' was religious faith is at odds with a narrative of postwar secularisation, just as much as with a narrative of 1960s radicalism. Yet the evidence is compelling at many different levels. Clergymen such as Scott, Collins and Huddleston pulled the diverse threads of activism together in the 1950s, Archbishop Roberts provided an influential link to both the Catholic Church and pacifism in the 1960s and in the 1970s Paul Oestreicher effectively combined being a parish priest, ecumenical diplomat and Chairman of Amnesty's British Section. Even secular leaders such as Benenson and Baker were, as we have seen, profoundly motivated by both religious as well as political insights. One can also point to the significance attached to sites of worship by recurrent generations of activists – St Martin-in-the-Fields, for instance, was not just a convenient space in central London, but one imbued with a meaning of compassion and social engagement. Moreover, the support provided by churches and congregations was often crucial to the success of Human Rights Year and the founding of new Amnesty branches, or of local committees against torture. In 1980 the British Council of Churches nominated Fr O'Mahoney and his dedicated parishioners in the West Midlands for the Council of Europe's first human rights prize.[16] Finally, religious leaders were often the best placed to offer a critical – sometimes unwelcome – perspective on human rights activism. During the 1970s it was the World Council of Churches (and, indeed, the British Council of Churches) which spoke out about the deficiencies in human rights in Britain itself and the hypocrisy in Britain's relations with the Third World, or noted that the Helsinki Final Act did not only raise questions about human rights in the Soviet sphere.[17]

These activists did not spend much time discussing human rights law. If, as a UNA memorandum put it in the 1970s, 'Human Rights is both a slogan and a defined concept', one suspects that the first was the more important for activists.[18] Even so, some fixed points – above all, the Universal Declaration of 1948 – were vitally important to their ascent, like crampons for a mountaineer. By the 1970s many gay or feminist activists may well have come to feel disappointed by the Declaration's textual omissions, just as pacifists had decried the lack of reference to a right to conscientious objection in the 1950s. Ultimately, however, the Universal Declaration was – like Magna Carta – important to activists for what it represented rather than what it actually said: a solemn agreement, commanding broad international support. Close attention to the text of the Universal Declaration reached its peak in 1968, when beautifully bound copies were being displayed in British town halls 'like a war memorial'.[19] In the intervening decades those who cared about human rights had wanted to see the foundational documents such as the Universal Declaration, the covenants, the Genocide Convention and the ECHR ratified, implemented and activated. The task of realising the rich promise of these postwar documents seemed daunting when governments of both major parties were so prone to drag their feet. However, this balance between legalism and activism shifted markedly in the 1970s, as ratification was achieved and as activists came to realise that powerful new instruments could be created to address specific abuses such as torture, within an increasingly conducive international context.

The growth of human rights activism in Britain was greatly assisted by a generally favourable reception, whether by other non-governmental organisations, international institutions and churches or, more problematically, by governments and political parties. In the case of Amnesty, one reason for its rapid growth was precisely because it was so swiftly accepted and so widely welcomed. Less than three years after Amnesty's formation the Secretary of the 125-year old Anti-Slavery Society offered this glowing endorsement: 'We in this Society have a profound admiration for Amnesty International and have an excellent liaison with them which we value greatly'.[20] These groups were responding to Amnesty's freshness, dynamism and ability to articulate issues in a way that attracted the devoted support of activists and the interest of the general public. Only NGOs which felt directly threatened – such as the existing 'Amnesty' campaigns – were less forthright in their welcome. One particularly striking seal of approval came when, during Anthony Marreco's 1974 libel case over his work in Greece, Mr Justice Tugendhadt stated that Amnesty was 'an organisation of high integrity'.[21]

Inevitably, the British government's reception of human rights activism was more complex, as Michael Scott's work on South West Africa, Eileen Fletcher's intervention over Kenya, or Amnesty's over Aden and Northern Ireland all posed serious challenges to British policy. This was the kind of 'meddling' that government so detested, especially when it believed that – wittingly or not – it stood to benefit international communism. However, the crisis of 1966–67 over Aden and Rhodesia is striking as the one occasion of serious rupture between government and a human rights organisation – and even then the damage was contained and short-lived. Human rights activism might be irksome at times for government, but levels of discomfort were manageable in return for the perceived benefits. This was particularly evident during the 1974–79 Labour government, when there was a striking congruence between the views of Foreign Office ministers and human rights organisations, and a general appreciation within government that working with this emerging constituency would enhance Britain's role in the UN and the Commonwealth, especially over difficult issues such as apartheid. The British government's response was, therefore, relatively benign compared to the far more hostile and pernicious behaviour towards human rights organisations during the 1970s by some governments and intelligence agencies.[22]

Political parties faced a particular problem in responding to human rights activism because the demands of realpolitik meant that, however well intentioned, they could rarely deliver completely on a commitment. In 1964 Harold Wilson promised Peter Benenson that if Labour won the forthcoming election it would ratify the ECHR 'in full':[23] he duly secured the right of individual petition in 1966. However, while Wilson appears to have been sincere in wanting to make Labour 'the party of human rights',[24] his good intentions were overtaken by the Kenyan Asian crisis of the late 1960s, the new Northern Ireland 'Troubles' and the complex demands of late colonial conflicts. In the 1970 election Labour's manifesto could point to genuine achievements in the promotion of human rights, but ultimately this counted for less than the government's failure in handling the economy.[25] The Conservatives, meanwhile, made no pretence to be the 'party of human rights'. This began to change under Margaret Thatcher's leadership, with her enthusiastic support for the Soviet dissidents and the work of Keston College.[26] Thatcher was reasonably comfortable with a language of human rights, but this was a language of the new Cold War:[27] lambasting the Soviet Union for its treatment of dissidents and its invasion of Afghanistan, while restoring the British Ambassador to Chile. Domestically, she championed the right to equal access to the market, but not the right to strike, to join a union or to express one's sexuality.

Thatcher's divisive premiership was just one aspect of the changed environment for human rights activism in the 1980s, alongside the heightened superpower tensions and a growing sophistication on the part of NGOs in reaching mass audiences, typified by the Live Aid concerts of 13 July 1985. In 1980 the Chairman of Amnesty's British Section had hailed – somewhat regretfully – the coming 'age of massive growth, cinemascope publicity, world-encircling campaigns and awe-inspiring budgets'.[28] As the emphasis shifted to greater scale, professional marketing and the involvement of celebrities, Amnesty had its own contribution to make: whereas in the 1970s it had raised its public profile through a successful series of late-night satirical stage reviews in London, initiated by John Cleese, in 1988 leading rock musicians undertook a global tour to mark the fortieth anniversary of the Universal Declaration. In the course of the 1980s even small organisations such as Survival International found their fortunes – and capabilities – transformed by improved access to funds.[29]

Yet, in many respects the human rights movement in Britain met the challenges of the 1980s with the tools of the 1970s. The reactive 'adhocracy' identified by the *Human Rights Handbook* flourished, and new organisations continued to proliferate. Two new organisations were created little more than a month apart in 1986 – entitled 'Article 19' and 'Rights and Humanity' – to meet perceived international challenges related to censorship and development.[30] The tireless Martin Ennals, having retired from Amnesty, was closely involved in the creation of both Article 19 and another group, International Alert, which was set up in 1985 to campaign against genocide 'in the way that Amnesty International works for the release of prisoners of conscience'.[31] Northern Ireland was particularly fertile ground for new human rights organisations during the later 1980s.[32] Amnesty not only maintained its international growth and developed its existing work on torture, disappearance and extrajudicial killing,[33] but also broadened its remit to include campaigning against the death penalty. Within Britain, the Thatcher government's assault on the postwar settlement and workers' rights stimulated the resurgence of the NCCL, while Stonewall was set up in 1989 as a lobbying organisation for gay and lesbian rights, partly in response to oppressive legislation such as Section 28 of the Local Government Act.[34]

One important change during the 1980s, however, was that the artificial distinction between abuses of human rights (which happened abroad) and of civil liberties (which happened at home) became far less apparent. This was best represented by Charter 88, which drew its inspiration from both the struggle for political liberty within Britain *and* the Czech dissidents of Charter 77. Thatcher's authoritarian tendencies encouraged many progressives to look again at a written constitution or Bill of Rights (which, ironically, had a fleeting – and swiftly forgotten – mention in the 1979 Conservative manifesto). According to Charter 88's founding document: 'The time has come to demand political, civil and human rights in the United Kingdom'.[35] At the launch of the new organisation the barrister Geoffrey Robertson was quoted as saying that the only advances in civil liberties came from 'our commitments to the European Convention on Human Rights and to the Treaty of Rome'.[36] The activist was far from obsolete, but the 1980s marked a shift in emphasis from activism to institutions and legal defences. The era of professional international lobbying and the human rights lawyer was at hand.

Notes

PREFACE AND ACKNOWLEDGEMENTS

1. The conference was held at the University of the West of England, 18–20 July 1996. My paper was published as T. Buchanan, 'Receding Triumph: British Opposition to the Franco Regime, 1945–59', *Twentieth Century British History*, vol. 12, no. 2 (2001), 163–84.
2. T. Buchanan, '"The Truth Will Set You Free": the Making of Amnesty International', *Journal of Contemporary History*, vol. 37, no. 4 (2002), 575–97 and 'Amnesty International in Crisis, 1966–7', *Twentieth Century British History*, vol. 15, no. 3 (2004), 267–89.
3. Column by Chairman Jacques Berthoud in *British Amnesty*, August–September 1980.
4. International Institute of Social History, Amsterdam, Amnesty International, International Secretariat papers (IISH, AI IS), 1174, 17 October 1975, Baker to Mark Grantham.
5. Charles Foley, *Island in Revolt* (London: Longman's, 1962), pp. 125–7.
6. IISH, AI IS, 986, Peggy Crane interview transcript, 17 June 1985, pp. 7–8, p. 12. This interview formed part of an oral history project carried out during the early 1980s to mark Amnesty's twentieth anniversary. The interviewers were Andrew Blane and Priscilla Ellsworth.

INTRODUCTION

1. Peter Benenson papers (Amnesty International/AI), 'Community of Conscience', speech to Amnesty's German Section, 5 June 1976, p. 9).
2. The term 'human rights activist' was first used in *The Times* on 14 November 1972, and in *The Guardian* on 7 July 1975, in both cases referring to Soviet dissidents. For an example of use in a British context see Bishopsgate Institute, Index on Censorship papers, INDEX 20, Special meeting of Finance and Editorial Committee, 11 June 1980 (discussion of how to reach 'Human Rights Activists').
3. See below, pp. 26–7.
4. For a helpful snapshot of their range and variety from a contemporary source see M. Garling, *The Human Rights Handbook: A Guide to British and American International Human Rights Organisations* (London: Macmillan Press, 1979).
5. See below, p. 88.

6. London Metropolitan archives (LMA), National Council for Voluntary organisations papers (formerly the National Council of Social Service, NCSS), LMA/4016/IS/A/04/053.
7. University of Bristol Library, Special Collections, Bateman papers, Box N3/3, memorandum [1977] on 'The Origins of the Group'.
8. S. Hopgood, *Keepers of the Flame: Understanding Amnesty International* (Ithaca, NY & London: Cornell University Press, 2006), p. vii (my emphasis); see also S.-L. Hoffman, 'Introduction: Genealogies of Human Rights' in his edited collection, *Human Rights in the Twentieth Century* (Cambridge University Press, 2011), pp. 1–26.
9. IISH, AI IS, 977, 23 February 1983, Andrew Blane to 'Suriya and Thomas'.
10. The definition is from N. Crowson, M. Hilton and J. McKay, *NGOs in Contemporary Britain: Non-State Actors in Society and Politics since 1945* (Basingstoke: Palgrave Macmillan, 2009), pp. 3–4; see also M. Hilton, J. McKay, N. Crowson and J. Mouhot, *The Politics of Expertise: How NGOs Shaped Modern Britain* (Oxford University Press, 2013); M. Hilton et al., *A Historical Guide to NGOs in Britain: Charities, Civil Society and the Voluntary Sector since 1945* (Basingstoke: Palgrave Macmillan, 2012).
11. M. Hilton, 'Politics is Ordinary: Non-Governmental Organizations and Political Participation in Contemporary Britain', *Twentieth Century British History*, vol. 22, no. 2 (2011), 230–68.
12. Archivum Britannicum Societatis Iesu (henceforward Jesuits in Britain archives), London, Roberts papers, 19/5/1, report on Königswinter conference, 20–22 September 1963. There is a copy of *World Conscience* (10 December 1963) in IISH, AI IS, 997, and for its distribution see *The Oxford Times*, 10 December 1963, n.p.; see King's College London, Archives and Special Collections (KCL), League for Democracy in Greece papers (LDG), MGC CORRESP 1, Appeal for Amnesty, background notes.
13. J. Fletcher, 'A Quaker View of Conscience', *Reconciliation*, vol. 33, no. 9 (September 1956), part of a special edition on 'The Authority of Conscience'.
14. See below, p. 216.
15. University of Warwick, Modern Records Centre (MRC), Mss 292B/863/4, text of Reuther's lecture, 10 December 1967, 'Amnesty: Towards a World Conscience', p. 11.
16. Borthwick Institute, University of York, Duncan papers, 5.3, 3 June 1963, Benenson to Duncan.
17. See below, pp. 34–6.
18. London School of Economics and Political Science (LSE), Special Collections, UNA 4/8/1, Human Rights Committee, 7 January 1973, report by Keith Suter.
19. Bodleian Library, Oxford, Scott papers, Box 59, Cadogan to Scott, 26 September 1963; for Dolci see below, pp. 94–5.
20. Bodleian Library, Scott papers, Box 19, 2 November 1963, Astor to John Alexander Sinclair.
21. Bodleian Library, Scott papers, Box 79, 11 October 1951, Scott to Agatha Harrison (Scott was specifically referring to the failure of the Africa Relations Council to arouse public opinion in Britain).
22. Bodleian Library, Scott papers, Box 79, 5 April 1967, Benenson to Scott.

23. Library of the Society of Friends, Friends' House, London, FSC/KEN/6, 26 July 1956, anon to Paul Sturge.
24. See below, p. 109.
25. IISH, AI IS, 1017, 3 December 1962, Ennals to Benenson.
26. *Rights*, vol. 2, no. 5, interview with Scaffardi, pp. 5–6.
27. See below, p. 144.
28. P. Duff, *Left, Left, Left: A Personal Account of Six Protest Campaigns, 1945–65* (London: Allison & Busby, 1971), p. 14.
29. MRC, Gollancz papers, Mss 157/3/LB/2/1–63, 15 September 1965, Gollancz to Stuart Samuels.
30. MRC, Gollancz papers, Mss 157/3/AW/1/1–80, 19 June 1952, Gollancz to Leonard Behrens. He was referring to 'Save Europe Now'.
31. MRC, Gollancz papers, Mss 157/3/RHO/1/1–65; see also Bodleian, Violet Bonham Carter papers, Ms Bonham Carter 238. Collins had placed a misleading newspaper advert concerning prisoners in Rhodesia, without properly consulting his committee.
32. See below, p. 51.
33. W. Korey, *NGOs and the Universal Declaration of Human Rights: 'a Curious Grapevine'* (Basingstoke & New York: Macmillan, 1998), p. 167; The National Archives, Kew, London (TNA), KV2/4045; www.martinennalsaward.org/about-us/.
34. *El País* (Argentina), 23 March 2014, transcript of Tricia Feeney's interview with Martín Granovsky,
35. See Hopgood, *Keepers of the Flame*, pp. 120–35 for the tensions that this caused in the 1990s and early 2000s.
36. University of Bradford, Special Collections, Baker papers, 2/5, 12 January 1973, Morris to Sean MacBride.
37. Desmond was forced out by a 676–643 vote amongst members of the British Section (see the detailed report in *Sunday Times*, 22 March 1981, p. 2). Desmond was quoted as saying that his experience of the 'malevolent' people he encountered in Amnesty was worse than five years of house arrest in South Africa! The selection of the disgraced former Liberal Party leader Jeremy Thorpe as his eventual successor in February 1982 was even more ill-starred, as Thorpe was forced to withdraw in the face of internal opposition: M. Bloch, *Jeremy Thorpe* (London: Abacus, 2014), pp. 547–8.
38. C. Moores, 'The Progressive Professionals: The National Council for Civil Liberties and the Politics of Activism in the 1960s', *Twentieth Century British History*, vol. 20, no. 4 (2009), 541. For interesting records of discussions between the local groups and the NCCL officers see the reports of meetings of the NCCL Liaison Groups, 14 June and 15 November 1969, University of Bristol, Bateman papers, Box N 3/1.
39. AI British Section report for 1967/8, p. 2.
40. Jesuits in Britain archives, Roberts papers, 19/5/1, 23 June 1973, papers for British Section AGM.
41. The UNA was tasked in its founding 'objects' to 'defend human rights and freedoms' (LSE, UNA/3/1/1, minutes of first meeting, 7 June 1945, object ii (b)).

42. The phrase is Gilbert Murray's (see UNA, *International Outlook*, November 1946). The literature is currently far richer on the LNU than on the UNA: see D. Birn, *The League of Nations Union, 1918–1945* (Oxford University Press, 1981); H. McCarthy, *The British People and the League of Nations: Democracy, Citizenship and Internationalism, c. 1918–45* (Manchester University Press, 2011).

43. For LNU membership, see McCarthy, *The British People and the League*, p. 4; Birn, *League of Nations Union*, p. 93. For detailed membership information on the UNA's early years see LSE UNA/3/1/3, report of 11 November 1947; UNA, *Annual Report for 1976*.

44. I have been unable to find any complete records for SCESWUN. Some for the period 1957–62 have survived in the Anti-Slavery Society papers, Bodleian Library, Mss Brit Emp. S.22/G788 and G789. Norman Bentwich recalled that the aim of SCESWUN was 'gently to prod the offices of Government' (N. Bentwich, *My Seventy-Seven Years: an Account of My Life and Times, 1883–1960* (London: Routledge & Kegan Paul, 1962), p. 303).

45. LSE, UNA/3/1/2, Executive Committee minutes for 16 January 1947.

46. See in particular below, pp. 192–7.

47. Friends' House archives, Fletcher papers, 367/3/4, undated offprint from '*The War Resister*' of 'Seeds in Stony Soil' by Eileen Fletcher, with 'Editor's Page'.

48. University of Bradford Library, Baker papers, 2/7, Baker's progress report, 8 October 1975.

49. The best source on the Community is A. Muir, *Outside the Safe Place: An Oral History of the Early Years of the Iona Community* (Glasgow: Wild Goose, 2011): see also R. Ferguson, *Chasing the Wild Goose: the Story of the Iona Community* (London: Fount, 1988). The Community's journal *The Coracle* is also a valuable source.

50. R. Morton, *The Iona Community Story* (London: Lutterworth Press, 1957), p. 91.

51. R. Ferguson, *George MacLeod: Founder of the Iona Community* (London: Collins, 1990), pp. 369–71.

52. Speech in commemoration of Dowding in the Australian Parliament by Melissa Parke MP, 12 November 2008 (https://parlinfo.aph.gov.au/parlInf o/search/display/display.w3p;db=CHAMBER;id=chamber%2Fhansardr%2 F2008-11-12%2F0113;query=Id%3A%22chamber%2Fhansardr%2F2008 -11-12%2F0062%22); National Library of Scotland, Edinburgh (NLS), MacLeod papers, Acc 9084/313, 16 July 1958, Dowding to MacLeod.

53. London Metropolitan Archives (LMA), Board of Deputies papers, Acc 3121/E3/217, 8 April 1958, Edelman to Barnett Janner.

54. LMA, Board of Deputies papers, Acc 3121/E3/217, statement issued on 17 November 1963.

55. See P. Sands, *East West Street: on the Origins of Genocide and Crimes against Humanity* (London: Weidenfeld & Nicolson, 2016); H. Lauterpacht, *An International Bill of the Rights of Man* (New York: University of Columbia Press, 1945).

56. The Honorary Secretary was F. L. Brassloff of the World Jewish Congress (WJC). In October 1957 seven out of twenty-six members of the Working

Group were representatives of the Anglo-Jewish Association, the Board of Deputies or the WJC (list in Bodleian Library, Mss Brit Emp S.22/G788).

57. Manchester Archives, Bernard Langton papers, M784/7/12, report of conference, 24 July 1968.

58. *The Times*, 4 April 1970, p. 4; 17 April 1970, letter from Mark Benenson and Nelson Bengston. UN resolution 3379 was eventually revoked in 1991. For an account of the controversy over Amnesty's report, and its damaging effect on Amnesty's relations with Jewish activists, see J. Loeffler, *Rooted Cosmopolitans: Jews and Human Rights in the Twentieth Century* (New Haven: Yale University Press, 2018), pp. 276–88.

59. See M. Hurst, *British Human Rights Organisations and Soviet Dissent, 1965–1985* (London: Bloomsbury, 2016), ch. 3.

60. University of Bradford, Baker papers, 3/1, typescript of speech.

61. For Bonhoeffer see IISH, AI IS, 982, interview with Peter Benenson, 12 November 1983, p. 94. Linda Rabben's, *Fierce Legion of Friends: a History of Human Rights Campaigns and Campaigners* (Wyattsville, MD: Quixote Centre, 2002), traces a line of activism from anti-slavery to Amnesty, via the campaigns for Sacco and Vanzetti and the Rosenbergs. At the close of the 1968 UN Human Rights Year there was an exhibition of busts of 'Human Rights Champions' in the crypt of St Paul's Cathedral (see below, p. 181). A modern equivalent, the 'I Have a Dream' photographic exhibition in the Museum of Goteborg (May–October 2018), brought together a similarly eclectic collection of sometimes unlikely individuals.

62. P. Archer, 'Action by Unofficial Organizations on Human Rights' in E. Luard (ed.), *The International Protection of Human Rights* (London: Thames and Hudson, 1967), p. 162.

63. See Z. Elkins, T. Ginsburg and J. Melton, 'On the Influence of Magna Carta and Other Cultural Relics', *International Review of Law and Economics*, vol. 47, S (2016), 3–9; see also, R. V. Turner, *Magna Carta: Through the Ages* (London: Longman, 2003).

64. In her speech of 9 December 1948 to the UN General Assembly: (www .kentlaw.edu/faculty/bbrown/classes/HumanRightsSP10/CourseDocs/2Ele anorRoosevelt.pdf).

65. *UNESCO Courier*, iv, 12, December 1951, p. 15.

66. Nottinghamshire archives, DD/CR/59/1, May 1967, statement issued by the UK committee.

67. AI 'News Sheet for Groups', #9, June 1965.

68. According to its founders, Charter 88 was so named to dispute the complacency with which the tercentenary of the 'Glorious Revolution' of 1688 was being celebrated, to 'reassert a tradition of demands for constitutional reform in Britain', and to 'salute the courage' of Charter 77 and other Eastern European dissenters (*The Times*, 1 November 1968, p. 7; *The Guardian*, 30 November 1988, p. 11, see also p. 23).

69. TNA, FO371/178307, text of speech, 8 July 1964.

70. Winston Churchill, 'The Sinews of Peace (Iron Curtain Speech' (8 March 1946) *International Churchill Society*, https://winstonchurchill

.org/resources/speeches/1946–1963-elder-statesman/the-sinews-of-peace/.

71. J. Lindsay and E. Rickword (eds), *A Handbook of Freedom: a Record of English Democracy through Twelve Centuries* (London: Lawrence & Wishart, 1939), p. vii.

72. TNA, HO 45/25462, NCCL Declaration of 28 May 1935.

73. R. Kidd, *British Liberty in Danger: an Introduction to the Study of Civil Rights* (London: Lawrence & Wishart, 1940), esp. pp. 36–7. For the 1970s see below, p. 208.

74. See Bodleian Library, AAM 6, press conference of 24 November 1959 for the precedent of the 1791 sugar boycott invoked at the launch of boycott of South Africa. Connections between anti-slavery and human rights campaigning are frequently made in A. Hochschild, *Bury the Chains: The British Struggle to Abolish Slavery* (London: Macmillan, 2005); see also J. R. Oldfield, *Popular Politics and British Anti-Slavery: The Mobilisation of Public Opinion against the Slave Trade, 1787–1807* (Manchester University Press, 1995).

75. See J. R. Oldfield, *Chords of Freedom: Commemoration, Ritual and British Transatlantic Slavery* (Manchester University Press, 2007), pp. 92–107.

76. R. Bridges, *The Testament of Beauty* (Oxford: Clarendon Press, 1929), p. 146.

77. *The Times*, 25 April 1839, p. 3; *The Observer*, 2 June 1839, p. 2.

78. Bodleian Library, Mss Brit. Emp. s20/E2/E3, Anti-Slavery Society minutes for 24 February 1955.

79. See J. Heartfield, *The British and Foreign Anti-Slavery Society 1838–1956: A History* (London: Hurst & Company, 2016).

80. A. Ribi Forclaz, *Humanitarian Imperialism: The Politics of Anti-Slavery Activism, 1880–1940* (Oxford, Oxford University Press, 2015), see also S. Pennybacker, *From Scottsboro to Munich: Race and Political Culture in 1930s Britain* (Princeton, NJ: Princeton University Press, 2009), ch. 3 on Lady Simon.

81. E. Baughan, "Every Citizen of Empire Implored to Save the Children!' Empire, Internationalism and the Save the Children Fund in Inter-War Britain', *Historical Research*, vol. 86, no. 231 (2013), 116–37; R. Skinner and A. Lester, 'Humanitarianism and Empire: New Research Agendas', *The Journal of Imperial and Commonwealth History*, vol. 40, no. 5 (2012), 729–47.

82. In 1947 Elizabeth Allen of the NCCL was interviewed about its forthcoming international conference on human rights: she told the interviewer that there would be four commissions, including one on slavery which 'to our immense surprise had not been dealt with so far as a problem, by the United Nations'. Interviewer: 'Though it was dealt with, wasn't it, by the League of Nations?' Allen: 'Yes, you're quite right . . . ' (Hull History Centre, UDCL 77/4, text of BBC broadcast, undated). This began to change in 1956 when the UN passed a supplementary convention on the abolition of slavery, while still refusing to set up a committee of experts as the Society wished.

83. Bodleian Library, Mss. Brit. Emp. s 20/E2/23, Anti-Slavery Society minutes for 6 March and 2 April 1958.

84. IISH, AI IS, 1006, 4 August 1964, Benenson to MacBride.

85. See the helpful overview and critique in M. Barnett, *Empire of Humanity: A History of Humanitarianism* (Ithaca, NY: Cornell University Press, 2011)

86. M. Black, *A Cause for Our Times: Oxfam, the First 50 Years* (Oxford: Oxfam, 1992), pp. 1–40.

87. Both quotations are from T. Buchanan, 'Human Rights Campaigns in Modern Britain', in N. J. Crowson, *NGOs in Contemporary Britain: Non-State Actors in Society and Politics since 1945* (Basingstoke: Palgrave Macmillan, 2009), pp. 125 and 113.

88. M. Hilton, 'International Aid and Development NGOs in Britain and Human Rights since 1945', *Humanity: an International Journal of Human Rights, Humanitarianism, and Development*, vol. 3, no. 3 (2012), 449–65.

89. M. Luetchford and P. Burns, *Waging the War on Want: 50 Years of Campaigning against Global Poverty* (London: War on Want, 2003); there are numerous references in Hilton et al., *Politics of Expertise*; *Poverty and Power*, vol. 1, no. 1 (1978), article by A. Wilson, 1–2; see also the editorial in *LINKS* (Third World First), 5, 1978. Amnesty's British Section signed a formal agreement of cooperation with Third World First in 1973 (*British Amnesty*, 14, June 1973).

90. C. Fink, *Defending the Rights of Others: the Great Powers, the Jews, and International Minority Protection, 1878–1938* (Cambridge University Press, 2004).

91. D. Gorman, *The Emergence of International Society in the 1920* (Cambridge University Press, 2012); B. Matzger, 'Towards an International Human Rights Regime during the Inter-War Years: the League of Nations' Combat of Traffic in Women and Children', in K. Grant et al., *Beyond Sovereignty: Britain, Empire, and Transnationalism, c. 1880–1950* (Basingstoke: Palgrave Macmillan, 2007), pp. 54–79; D. Marshall, 'The Construction of Children as an Object of International Relations: the Declaration of Children's Rights and the Child Welfare Committee of League of Nations, 1900–1924', *The International Journal of Children's Rights*, vol. 7, no. 2 (1999), 103–48.

92. Birn, *League of Nations Union*, p. 2, citing *League of Nations Journal*, August 1919, p. 275.

93. *The League*, vol. II, 1, October 1919, p. 14, citing A. Simpson in the *Yorkshire Post*, 18 September 1919.

94. *The Times*, 24 February 1921, p. 6, advert for the Save the Children Fund.

95. F. S. Litten, 'The Noulens Affair', *The China Quarterly*, vol. 138 (1994), 492–512. Noulens was a pseudonym.

96. Author's interview with Benenson, 29 October 1997; IISH, AI IS, 982, Benenson interview, 12 November 1983, p. 1.

97. Friends' House archives, Fletcher papers, 367/6/5/1, 28 Dec. 1935, Elwyn Jones to Fletcher; F. Elwyn Jones, *In My Time: an Autobiography* (London: Weidenfeld and Nicolson, 1983); during World War II MI5 ruled that Elwyn Jones should not have access to secret information due to his links to the communists and his role in the defence of the Austrian socialists (see

TNA HS 9/808/4, minute of 5 February 1943 – I am grateful to Roderick Bailey for this information); IISH, AI IS, 986, 989 and 988 (interviews with Marlys Deeds, Norman Marsh and Christel Marsh).

98. *The Sunday Times Magazine*, 19 October 1975, p. 38.
99. See R. C. Cottrell, *Roger Nash Baldwin and the American Civil Liberties Union* (New York: Columbia University Press, 2000).
100. See below, pp. 99–103.
101. *New York Times*, 8 December 1948. William Korey claimed that it was 'not at all unlikely' that Roosevelt was thinking about the role of the NGOs when making this comment (Korey, *NGOs and the Universal Declaration of Human Rights*, p. 48). However, as Korey also shows in his book, the initial NGOs of 1945–46 were not specialists in human rights, but religious groups, professional associations or trade unions, such as the Federal Council of Churches, the American Jewish Committee and the Congress of Industrial Organisations.
102. William James, letter to Mrs Henry Whitman, 7 June 1899 (www .gutenberg.org/files/38091/38091-h/38091-h.htm); Baker's version was condensed: 'I am done with great things and big things, great organisations and big successes . . .', University of Bradford, Baker papers, 2/7, typescript dated 11 December 1963.
103. S.-L. Hoffman, 'Human Rights and History', *Past and Present*, vol. 232, no. 1 (August 2016), 279–310.
104. www.westminster-abbey.org/abbey-commemorations/commemorations/jo ost-de-blank/. I am grateful to the archivist of Westminster Abbey, Christine Reynolds, for her assistance on this point.
105. M. Mazower, 'The Strange Triumph of Human Rights, 1933–1950', *The Historical Journal*, vol. 47, no. 2 (2004), 379–98.
106. There was a 'British Non-Sectarian Anti-Nazi Council to Champion Human Rights', which called for an economic boycott of Nazi Germany. Few records survive, apart from a programme from a rally in Hyde Park, 27 October 1935, LMA/4457/01/001. It was presumably related to an American organisation of similar name, which campaigned for a boycott of German goods. Originally named the American League for the Defence of Jewish Rights, the new title was chosen to broaden the base of the campaign. See R. Hawkins, 'The Internal Politics of the Non-Sectarian Anti-Nazi League to Champion Human Rights, 1933–1939', *Management & Organizational History*, vol. 5, no. 2 (2010), 251–78.
107. For instance, John Eppstein referred to Catholics championing the 'natural, human rights of the non-European 'backward' races' (*Anti-Slavery Reporter*, October 1930). See also G. Padmore, *How Britain Rules Africa* (London: Wishart Books Ltd, 1936), p. 391.
108. See below, pp. 44–49.
109. J. Stephenson, 'Women's Rights', *British Amnesty*, December 1978.
110. The term 'human rights lawyer' was first used in *The Times* on 8 September 1983: in both the *Guardian* and the *New York Times* there were isolated uses in the 1970s, but the phrase only became widely used in the 1980s.

111. Article by T. Smythe in *Civil Liberties*, #7 (December 1972), 2–3.
112. J. Eppstein, *Defend These Human Rights: Each Man's Stake in the UN – a Catholic View* (New York: Catholic Social Guild, 1947), pp. 29–34. Eppstein was a British writer who worked for the LNU in the 1930s.
113. The literature on Britain's attitude to the ECHR is particularly rich: see A. W. B. Simpson, *Human Rights and the End of Empire: Britain and the Genesis of the European Convention* (Oxford University Press, 2001) and G. Marston, 'The United Kingdom's Part in the Preparation of the European Convention on Human Rights, 1950', *International and Comparative Law Quarterly*, vol. 42, no. 4 (1993), 796–826.
114. Peter Benenson papers (in private possession), 1 August 1963, Benenson to Christopher Barclay and 7 November [1962] Whitaker to Benenson.
115. *Hansard*, Parl. Debs, 25 May 1973, col. 923.
116. We first encounter this name in the latter stages of World War I when a group opposing conscription took the name 'National Council for Civil Liberties'. However, despite Kidd's interesting comment in 1939 that the NCCL had been 're-founded' in 1934 there is no evidence of any continuity between the two (MRC, TUC papers, Mss.292/860/3, NCCL circular, 15 September 1939).
117. Hull History Centre, UDCL 77/4, transcript of conference, 13 June 1947, p. 7. De Reeth was vice-chair of the International Association of Democratic Lawyers.
118. C. Moores, *Civil Liberties and Human Rights in Twentieth-Century Britain* (Cambridge University Press, 2017), p. 148.
119. *The Independent*, 16 October 2007 (cited in T. Buchanan, 'Human Rights Campaigns in Modern Britain', in Crowson, *NGOs in Modern Britain*, p. 125).
120. *Civil Liberties*, #7 (December 1972), 2–3.
121. University of Bristol, Bateman papers, Box N 3/1, 15 November 1969, report of second meeting of NCCL Liaison Groups, p. 2.

1 DAWN: 1934–1950

1. For an excellent recent overview and analysis of the NCCL's history see C. Moores, *Civil Liberties and Human Rights in Twentieth-Century Britain* (Cambridge University Press, 2017).
2. V. Brittain, *The Story of St Martin's: an Epic of London* (Bournemouth: Pardy and Son, 1951); esp. p. 32, which quotes the words spoken at Sheppard's funeral.
3. See below, pp. 105–06 and 112.
4. Hull History Centre, NCCL papers, UDCL 74/1, agenda for 22 February 1934 meeting.
5. TNA HO 45/25462, Kidd to the Secretary of the ILD, 19 February 1934 (my emphasis).
6. M. Pottle, 'Kidd, Ronald Hubert (1889–1942)', *Oxford Dictionary of National Biography (ODNB)*.

7. Hull, NCCL papers, UDCL 74/1, 15 March 1934.
8. B. Cox, *Civil Liberties in Britain* (Harmondsworth: Penguin, 1975), p. 30.
9. Hull History Centre, UDCL, 74/1, 3 October 1934, Kidd to F. W. Hirst of the National Liberal Federation; UDCL 74/2, 31 October 1935, Kidd to E. M. Forster.
10. Dingle Foot joined the Labour Party in 1956.
11. However, the Sedition Act remained on the statute books and was used in the 1970s against protestors calling for the withdrawal of British troops from Northern Ireland.
12. For Bing's later career see pp. 78–9.
13. Hull History Centre, UDCL 74/2, 10 January 1935, Kidd to E. M. Forster. Kidd was probably using exaggerated language as Forster had questioned whether the NCCL should intervene in Northern Ireland at all. Kidd was arguing that something dangerously new was happening, with implications for mainland Britain as well as Northern Ireland.
14. NCCL, *Report of a Commission of Enquiry into the Civil Authorities (Special Powers) Act in Northern Ireland, 1922 and 1933* (NCCL, 1936); for the later Troubles see below, pp. 171–5.
15. Kidd offered a sustained refutation of communist influence in a letter to Owen Rattenbury, 28 July 1941 (Hull History Centre, UDCL 32/8).
16. K. Morgan, *Labour Legends and Russian Gold: Bolshevism and the British Left, Part One* (London: Lawrence & Wishart, 2013), p. 265.
17. TNA, HO 45/25462, 17-page Special Branch report on Kidd, 12 November 1935. There *was* evidence that Kidd was a member of the FSU, an organisation with extremely close links to the Communist Party, in January 1933. Special Branch believed that Kidd had applied for Communist Party membership in 1934 but had been deemed more useful to the party as a non-member.
18. TNA, HO 45/24562, 19 February 1934, Kidd to Secretary of ILD. In *The National Council for Civil Liberties and the Policing of Interwar Politics: At Liberty to Protest* (Manchester University Press, 2012, p. 46), Janet Clark argues that Kidd was simply demarcating territory between the ILD and the NCCL. However, his message went further than this, and Kidd was at pains to make clear that the NCCL would not be an ideological embarrassment to the Communist Party. Kidd was aware that the American Council for Civil Liberties had 'deviated from the correct line and is a hindrance', and he reassured the ILD that the 'the comparatively limited scoop [*sic*] of our work would [not] give much chance to the "liberals" for deviation'. Moores, *Civil Liberties and Human Rights*, p. 52, broadly shares Clark's interpretation. See also the discussion in C. Moores, 'From Civil Liberties to Human Rights? British Civil Liberties Activism and Universal Human Rights', *Contemporary European History*, vol. 21, no. 2 (2012), 169–92, 179–181.
19. Hull History Centre, UDCL, 32/8, 25 June 1941, Kidd to Raymond Postgate.
20. Hull History Centre, UDCL 74/1, 16 October 1936, Kidd to Dingle Foot, and attached appeal letter.

21. Kidd, *British Liberty in Danger: an Introduction to the Study of Civil Rights* (London: Lawrence & Wishart, 1940), p. 258.
22. W. H. Thompson, *Civil Liberties* (London: V. Gollancz, 1938), p. 96.
23. F. Elwyn Jones, 'Liberty in Britain – Is It in Danger?', *The London Mercury*, vol. 39 no. 23 (December 1938), 165–70.
24. See T. Buchanan, 'Beyond Cable Street: New Approaches to the Historiography of Anti-Fascism in Britain', in H. Garcia et al., *Rethinking Anti-Fascism: History, Memory and Politics, 1922 to the Present* (New York: Berghahn Books, 2016), pp. 65–6.
25. TNA, KV2/3809, MI5 note, 4 July 1940.
26. TNA HO 4525462, report of 12 November 1935.
27. TNA, KV2/3593 (this file, on the NCCL lawyer Neil Lawson, uses the words 'fraction' and 'faction' interchangeably). See T. Buchanan, *East Wind: China and the British Left, 1925–1976* (Oxford University Press, 2012) for caucuses within the China Campaign Committee and other organisations in the 1930s, pp. 68–70.
28. J. Platts-Mills, *Muck, Silk and Socialism: Recollections of a Left-Wing Queen's Counsel* (Wedmore: Paper Publishing, 2001), p. 92. Cited in Moores, 'From Civil Liberties to Human Rights?', p. 180.
29. KCL, LDG papers, MGA CORRESP IV, D. N. Pritt file, 19 March 1946, Diana Pym to Pritt.
30. TNA, KV2/1062, Special Branch report, 29 September 1936; in his memoirs he wrote that he had not anticipated so much 'hullabaloo' in Britain about the case as 'I combined a lawyer's belief in the proper behaviour of Courts with a Socialist belief that a Socialist State would not try people unless there was a good case against them … ', *The Autobiography of D. N. Pritt, Part One, From Right to Left* (London: Lawrence & Wishart, 1965), p. 109.
31. J. Saville, *Memoirs from the Left* (London: Merlin, 2003), p. 77.
32. TNA, KV2/2159, Special Branch report, 29 April 1937.
33. Working Class Movement Library, Salford (WCML), Tuckett papers, Box 04, notebook, 'Letters from DNP during Nov 1941', emphasis in original. Tuckett's notebook is a valuable source, although in the absence of the original letters (presumably destroyed) is not clear exactly how much weight can be placed on it. It is also striking that Pritt was apparently writing to Tuckett many times a day without this correspondence (or the relationship) coming to the attention of MI5.
34. B. Dyson, *Liberty in Britain, 1934–1994: a Diamond Jubilee History of the National Council for Civil Liberties* (London: Civil Liberties Trust, 1994), p. 20.
35. TNA, HO 45/25464, 648.133/110, Special Branch report, 24 September 1940.
36. Hull History Centre, UDCL 32/8, 13 May 1941, Laski to Kidd; *Report of the Annual Conference of the Labour Party, 1941*, 2–4 June 1941, p. 119.
37. S. Scaffardi, *Fire under the Carpet: Working for Civil Liberties in the Thirties* (London: Lawrence & Wishart, 1986), p. 184.
38. TNA, KV2/1064, MI5 file note, 1 December 1941.

39. For a report see WCML, Tuckett papers, NCCL Misc 1941–1992 box. For other wartime initiatives see below, p. 37.
40. LSE, Fellowship of Reconciliation (FOR), London Union papers, FOR 10/4, minutes of civil liberties conference, 10 August 1944; MRC, Gollancz papers, Mss 157/3/CL/3/1–31, 26 July 1950, Violet Bonham Carter to Gollancz.
41. Hull History Centre, UDCL 332/1, Barry Cox, 'Synopsis for Book on Civil Liberties in Britain' (1970). Cox did not use this term in his *Civil Liberties in Britain*.
42. There is a good discussion of this episode in Moores, 'From Civil Liberties to Human Rights?', pp. 173–5.
43. Lord Ritchie-Calder, *On Human Rights: Inaugural Lecture Delivered on 7th December 1967 at Conway Hall, Red Lion Square, London W.C. 1; With Two Appendices Incorporating the Sankey Declaration of the Rights of Man (1940) and the Universal Declaration of Human Rights (1948)* (H. G. Wells Memorial Lectures) (H. G. Wells Society; Distributed by M. Katanka Ltd, 1968), p. 4. No study has yet been made of the international impact of the declaration, but see 'Mr Wells' Liberal Conception of War Aims', *Times of India*, 27 February 1940 for Wells's All-India broadcast. Ritchie Calder's diary contains some fascinating insights regarding international interest in the project: it offers the fullest and most revealing account of this episode (NLS Acc. 12533/12).
44. *Daily Herald*, 12 February 1940; H. G. Wells, *The New World Order: Whether It Is Attainable, How It Can Be Attained, and What Sort of World a World at Peace Will Have to Be* (London: Secker and Warburg, 1940).
45. League of Coloured Peoples (LOCP), *LCP Letter 6*, March 1940, pp. 729–30.
46. See pp. 44–5, and S. Moyn, *Christian Human Rights* (Philadelphia, PA: University of Pennsylvania Press, 2015).
47. Father Woodlock in *Daily Herald*, 1 March 1940, p. 8. There was an interesting discussion of Christian responses to Wells's Declaration, including comments from Karl Mannheim, at the seventh meeting of the Christian discussion group The Moot, 9–12 February 1940, Keith Clements (ed.), *The Moot Papers, 1938–1944* (London: T&T Clark, 2009), pp. 272–87.
48. Text in Raghavan Iyer (ed.), *The Moral and Political Writings of Mahatma Gandhi, Volume III* (Oxford University Press, 1987), p. 492.
49. H. G. Wells, 'Money, Ownership and You', *Daily Herald*, 11 February 1940.
50. 'Debate Adjourns', *Daily Herald*, 2 March 1940.
51. *New Statesman & Nation*, 16 March 1940, p. 358.
52. LSE, FOR London Union papers, FOR 10/4.
53. Bodleian Library, Sankey papers, Sankey M.Eng.hist. c. 518, 18 April 1940, Calder to Sankey.
54. C. R. Attlee, 'The Communists Have No Case', *Daily Herald*, 21 February 1940.
55. A term used by Wells himself (Bodleian Library, Sankey papers, M.Eng. hist. c. 518, drafting committee minutes, 6 April 1940). Cited in Moores, 'From Civil Liberties to Human Rights?', p. 175.

56. Bodleian Library, Mss Attlee Dep. 3, speech at Neath, 13 July 1941.
57. 'Critic', *New Statesman & Nation*, 8 November 1941.
58. There is a good discussion of the diplomacy in A. W. B. Simpson, *Human Rights and the End of Empire: Britain and the Genesis of the European Convention* (Oxford University Press, 2001), ch. 4; see also E. Borgwardt, *A New Deal for the World: America's Vision for Human Rights* (Cambridge, MA & London: Belknap Press of Harvard University Press, 2005).
59. Full text at www.nato.int/cps/en/natohq/official_texts_16912.htm?
60. LOCP *Newsletter*, September, October and November 1941.
61. LOCP *Newsletter*, August 1943.
62. S. Moyn, *The Last Utopia: Human Rights in History* (Cambridge, MA: Belknap Press of Harvard University Press, 2010), p. 89; J. Eckel, 'Human Rights and Decolonization: New Perspectives and Open Questions'. *Humanity: an International Journal of Human Rights, Humanitarianism, and Development*, vol. 1, no. 1 (2010), 111–35; pp. 114–15.
63. *Hansard*, 1 May 1953, col. 2514.
64. For the impact of the Atlantic Charter see F. Klose, *Human Rights in the Shadow of Colonial Violence: the Wars of Independence in Kenya and Algeria* (Philadelphia, PA: Pennsylvania University Press, 2013), ch. 2.
65. LOCP *Newsletter*, February 1943 and August 1944.
66. *Peace News*, March and April 1944. Douglas-Home was younger brother of the future Prime Minister Alec Douglas-Home. He was jailed for a year for refusing to participate in the assault on Le Havre in September 1944 (J. Tomes, 'William Douglas-Home', *ODNB*).
67. *Tribune*, 26 March 1943; British Library, sound archive, interview with Weight, especially Part 29 (https://sounds.bl.uk/Arts-literature-and-performance/Art/021M-C0466X0007XX-2900V0).
68. Hull History Centre, UDCL 266, resolution of 18 December 1944.
69. KCL, LDG papers, INFO III, 'December 1944' file, 7 December 1944, speaker notes.
70. Westminster Diocesan archives, Beales papers, Box 8, Joint Committee minutes, 23 October 1944.
71. KCL, LDG papers, MGA CORRESP 1, 10 May 1962, letter from Dimitrios Vlisidis.
72. WCML, Tuckett papers, Box 04.
73. Hull History Centre, UDCL 58/2, 7 September 1946, J. Beck to NCCL.
74. Hugh Brock, *Peace News*, 5 January 1962; 'Pacifist Portraits, No. 3', *Peace News*, 12 May 1950, p. 5.
75. Friends' House archives, Fletcher papers, 367/6/8, 4 March 1948, Corder Catchpool to Chuter Ede.
76. WCML, Tuckett papers, Box 04.
77. LMA, Board of Deputies papers, Acc 3121/E1/75/1, 27 October 1943, J. M. Rubens to Salamon; 25 October 1943, Elizabeth Allen to Salamon; Christ Church, Oxford, Driberg papers, R1. Driberg was elected for Maldon as an independent MP in 1942, and switched to Labour in 1945.

78. LMA, Board of Deputies papers, Acc. 3121, E1/75/2, undated, 'Terms of Co-operation'. The NCCL had estimated that the entire campaign would cost £5000.

79. LMA, Board of Deputies papers, Acc 3121/E1/75/1, 3 November 1943, Salomon to Rubens.

80. LMA, Board of Deputies papers, Acc 3121/E1/75/3, 14 October 1947, Allen to Salomon.

81. *Peace News*, 31 March 1944, p. 4.

82. Hull History Centre, UDCL 266, NCCL minutes, 15 February 1946; Manchester, LHAS&C, LP/ELEC/1945/1 for Pollard's election leaflet.

83. For a good account see M. A. Glendon, *A World Made New: Eleanor Roosevelt and the Universal Declaration of Human Rights* (New York: Random House, 2001).

84. UNESCO, *Human Rights: Comments and Interpretations* (London: Allan Wingate, 1949), pp. 191–2.

85. *The Listener*, 3 November 1949, pp. 747–8.

86. See M. Duranti, *The Conservative Human Rights Revolution: European Identity, Transnational Politics and the Origins of the European Convention* (Oxford University Press, 2017).

87. Denis Healey, 'What Happened at Strasbourg?', *Tribune*, 8 September 1950.

88. Simpson, *Human Rights and the End of Empire*, p. 741.

89. See M. Rask Madsen, 'From Cold War Instrument to Supreme European Court: the European Court of Human Rights at the Crossroads of International and National Law and Politics', *Law & Social Inquiry*, vol. 32, no. 1 (2007), 137–59.

90. 'There is much activity in the field of human rights' (Hull History Centre, UDCL 76/2, typescript on 'Human Rights' [1948]).

91. A. Ribi Forclaz, *Humanitarian Imperialism: The Politics of Anti-Slavery Activism, 1880–1940* (Oxford University Press, 2015), esp. ch. 2, pp. 46–76.

92. LSE, Haldane Society papers, HALDANE/37, 30 January 1946, Gardiner to 'Stephen'.

93. LSE, SLL papers, SLL/4/1. (To his annoyance, Bing had been inadvertently enrolled and subsequently excluded.)

94. Peter Benenson papers (in private possession), 7 July 1963, Benenson to Clara Urquhart.

95. There is a good account in Moores, *Civil Liberties and Human Rights*, pp. 88–90.

96. LSE, FOR 10/4, 10 July 1944, Forster to PPU.

97. 'The NCCL', *New Statesman*, 15 May 1948, and 'Civil Liberties', *New Statesman*, 29 May 1948 for the NCCL response.

98. Friends' House archives, Fletcher papers, 367/6/5/2, Forster to Fletcher, 23 April and 6 May 1948.

99. WCML, Tuckett papers, Box 04.

100. Hull History Centre, UDCL 77/4, transcript of international conference, comments by Professor E. Walker, pp. 34–6.

101. WCML, Tuckett papers, Box 04; according to Latimer's obituary he was in the process of leaving the Communist Party in 1947 and subsequently testified

against it (*Chicago Tribune*, 17 February 1985: articles.chicagotribune.com/1985-02-17/news/8501090867_1_small-businesses-civil-rights-public-utility-companies).

102. Hull History Centre, UDCL, 77/4, 'General Introduction on Human Rights in Great Britain and the Colonies'; Attlee speaking in Parliament, *The Guardian*, 19 January 1949, p. 6.

103. Hull History Centre, UDCL 77/4, paper by Marian Muszkat, p. 8.

104. Hull History Centre, UDCL 267, NCCL EC minutes, 13 June 1950.

105. Moores, *Civil Liberties and Human Rights*, p. 72.

106. Moyn, *The Last Utopia*, p. 47. See also Moores, *Civil Liberties and Human Rights*, ch. 2 for a discussion in relation to 1940s Britain.

107. J. Eppstein, *Defend These Human Rights* (New York: Catholic Social Guild, 1947). More generally see Moyn, *Christian Human Rights*.

108. J. B. Coates, 'Personalism', in *The People and Freedom News Sheet*, March 1949.

109. Sword of the Spirit, *Bulletin 49*, 3 September 1942.

110. WCML, NCCL papers, 'Recent publications' box, Report of London Black-Coated Workers' Conference, 18 February 1939.

111. For Harari see 'Manya Harari', entry in *ODNB* by P. J. V. Rolo, revised by M. C. Loughlin-Chow; M. J. Walsh, *From Sword to Ploughshare: Sword of the Spirit to Catholic Institute for International Relations, 1940–80* (London: Catholic Institute for International Relations, 1980), pp. 5–6, and 'Ecumenism in War-Time Britain: the Sword of the Spirit and Religion and Life, 1940–45 (Part 1)', *Heythrop Journal*, vol. 23, no. 3 (July 1982), 243–58; Mira Benenson was on the Executive Committee of Sword of the Spirit and wrote numerous articles on international relations in Catholic journals in the 1940s.

112. *Voyage: Bulletin of the British Council of Churches*, July/August 1972, p. 13.

113. See P. Betts, 'Religion, Science and Cold War Anti-Communism: the 1949 Cardinal Mindszenty Show Trial', in P. Betts and S. A. Smith (eds), *Science, Religion and Communism in Cold War Europe* (Basingstoke: Palgrave Macmillan, 2016).

114. This is covered extensively in *The Sword*, especially June 1948, 'The Human Rights Campaign'.

115. *The Sword*, February 1948, p. 3.

116. L. J. Collins, *Faith under Fire* (London: Frewin, 1966), p. 141.

117. Bodleian Library, Cripps papers, SC 20/2, 'Christian Action: Its Policy and Its Organisation' [1948–49], 'Draft progress report No. 2' and report of Caxton Hall meeting, 14 February 1949; Diana Collins, *Christian Action* (London: Gollancz, 1949), p. 123.

118. *Peace News*, 10 May 1940, p. 3.

119. Friends' House archives, Fletcher papers, 367/6/6, WRI to Fletcher, April 1947; see also IISH, WRI papers, file 155.

120. *The Friend*, 26 February 1954. For interesting recent research on this theme see Rachel M. Johnston-White, 'A New Primacy of Conscience? Conscientious Objection, French Catholicism and the State during the Algerian War', *Journal of Contemporary History*, vol. 54, no. 1 (January 2019), 112–38.

121. See *UNESCO Courier*, v: 11, November 1952, p. 13; UNA, *Annual Report* for 1951/1952, pp. 715–16. This also contains a photograph of the UNA shop, with a banner that reads 'Human Rights Campaign'.
122. *Observer*, 4 December 1949, p. 2.
123. *Peace News*, 15 August 1952, p. 3.
124. *Peace News*, 28 April 1950, p. 2.
125. See M. Scott, *A Time to Speak* (London: Faber and Faber, 1958); Scott's MI5 file is also a helpful source (TNA KV2/2052).
126. Bodleian Library, Scott papers, Box 15, typescript entitled 'Charity versus the Law', 1973, p. 2.
127. Bodleian Library, Scott papers, Box 88, 2 June 1975, Baldwin to Cyril Dunn. Baldwin wrote that Scott was 'as you say, a loner, never close friend to anybody I heard of. He seemed married to the cause of South Africa: he was the black man's white man'.
128. M. Benson, *A Far Cry* (London: Viking, 1989), pp. 63–4.
129. Bodleian Library, Scott papers, Box 29, contains details of Scott's intervention.
130. For example, see Scott, *Time to Speak*, p. 226.
131. *News Chronicle*, 29 November 1949. Scott's statement was published by the Union of Democratic Control (UDC) as M. Scott, *Shadow over Africa* (London: Union of Democratic Control, 1950). For Scott at the UN see W. Korey, *NGOs and the Universal Declaration of Human Rights: 'a Curious Grapevine'* (Basingstoke & New York: Macmillan, 1998), pp. 101–4.
132. Towards the end of his life, Scott would explain his aversion to intimate personal relationships as being due to abuse that he had suffered at school (A. Yates and L. Chester, *The Troublemaker: Michael Scott and His Lonely Struggle against Injustice* (London: Aurum Press, 2006), pp. 1–3; Benson, *A Far Cry*, p. 92).
133. TNA, KV2/2053, intercept dated 19 March 1951.
134. See R. Cockett, *David Astor and the Observer* (London: Deutsch, 1991); there is also a thorough biography by J. Lewis, *David Astor* (London: Jonathan Cape, 2016).
135. Yates and Chester, *Troublemaker*, p. 129.
136. Bodleian Library, Scott papers, Box 15, Astor to Scott (undated letter, postmarked 2 August 1950).
137. Bodleian Library, Scott papers, Box 15, Astor to Patrick Gordon-Walker, 7 July 1950.
138. Ibid.
139. MRC, Gollancz papers, Mss 157/3/WW/2/1–23, 3 July 1961, Muirhead to Gollancz.
140. Bodleian Library, Africa Bureau papers, Box 152, file 10, undated manuscript, Iona Community response to Scott.
141. Bodleian Library, Africa Bureau papers, Box 152, file 10, 13 September 1949, Fletcher to Maurice Webb.
142. Bodleian Library, Scott papers, Box 12, 28 June 1950, letter from Audrey Jupp (referring to the UDC leaflet *Shadow over Africa*).

143. Christchurch, Oxford, Driberg papers, S18, 30 December 1948, Citizen Films to Driberg.
144. F. Troup, *In Face of Fear: Michael Scott's Challenge to South Africa* (London: Faber and Faber, 1950).
145. Bodleian Library, Scott papers, Box 71, 24 October 1979, Jane Symonds to Scott.
146. Bodleian Library, Mss Huddleston, Box 4, 8 August 1961, Huddleston to Scott.
147. Scott, *Shadow over Africa*, Introduction by Driberg.
148. Bodleian Library, Mss Perham, 28/3, 30 June 1953, Perham to Scott.

2 AFRICA, DECOLONISATION AND HUMAN RIGHTS IN THE 1950s

1. R. Cockett, *David Astor and the Observer* (London: Deutsch, 1991), pp. 186–7.
2. W. A. Lewis, M. Scott, M. Wight and C. Legum, *Attitude to Africa* (Harmondsworth: Penguin, 1951), p. 106.
3. Bodleian Library, Mss Brit. Emp. s. 20/E2/23, Anti-Slavery Society minutes, 24 February 1955.
4. Peter Benenson papers (in private possession), 23 February 1955, memorandum of first meeting. See below, p. 88.
5. For the MCF see S. Howe, *Anticolonialism and British Politics, 1918–1964: the Left and the End of Empire, 1918–1964* (Oxford: Oxford University Press, 1993).
6. A. Yates and L. Chester, *The Troublemaker: Michael Scott and His Lonely Struggle against Injustice* (London: Aurum Press, 2006), p. 139; LHA&SC, Labour Party International Department papers, Box 129, 13 April 1957, Manchester and District Council for African Affairs to John Hatch; *Peace News*, 30 September 1955, p. 6 (re Sheffield).
7. Bodleian Library, Mss Brit Emp. 285, Box 9, File 7, December 1950, draft statement by UDC Executive Committee.
8. For a profile of Fox-Pitt see *Peace News*, 8 August 1958, p. 2.
9. *Peace News*, 15 December 1950, p. 6. He did admit to there being a 'good deal of largely submerged anti-Semitism' in Britain.
10. LSE, CEWC papers, files CEWC 362 and CEWC 363.
11. Bodleian Library, Africa Bureau papers, Box 271, File 1, 28 March 1959, Jane Symonds to Guy and Molly Clutton-Brock.
12. Borthwick Institute, University of York, Patrick Duncan papers, 5.45, 2 April 1957, Huddleston to Duncan.
13. Bodleian Library, Brit. Emp. s.19 D 10/5, file 4, 18 May 1953, Freda White to Greenidge.
14. Bodleian Library, Mss Afr. S. 1681, Box 16, file 6, 2 October 1956, Benson to Huddleston.
15. LHAS&C, LP ID, Box B57/2 contains extensive reports on the regional meetings.

16. Bodleian Library, Scott papers, Box 34, undated interview transcript with Richard Kershaw.

17. Although there were differences. In 1960, perhaps referring to Capricorn's white-settler supporters, the Africa Bureau's Jane Symonds noted that it reached 'a section of the community closed to us', Bodleian Library, Ranger papers, File AB, 24 October 1960, Symonds to Terence Ranger.

18. Lambeth Palace Archives, Fisher vol. 167, 7 June 1956, Henry Crookenden to the Archbishop of Canterbury; see also the critical article by Lord Lucan in *Venture*, February 1956, n.p.

19. School of Oriental and African Studies, London (SOAS), PPM56, Thomas Fox-Pitt papers, Box 3, 6/2/1, 23 July 1953, Collins to Fox-Pitt.

20. LH&ASC, Manchester, CP/CENT/PC/02/05, memorandum for Political Committee, June 1952; Westminster Archdiocese papers, London, Gri 2/75 14 February 1951, Cardinal Griffin to Rev. Clement Tigar; 17 October 1949, J. Eppstein to Griffin. For the MRA see below, p. 99.

21. Eileen Fletcher in *Peace News*, 4 May 1956; see also Fr Raymond Raynes' appeal to voters over British policy towards South Africa at the UN in T. Huddleston, L. J. Collins, R. Raynes and M. Scott. *Four Words on South Africa* (London: Christian Action, 1957), p. 18.

22. For a good account of the controversy see S. Williams, *Colour Bar: the Triumph of Seretse Khama and His Nation* (London: Allen Lane, 2006).

23. P. Benenson, *Gangrene* (London: Calderbooks, 1959), p. 38.

24. F. Brockway, *African Journeys* (London: Gollancz, 1955), p. 210; W. A. Lewis, *Attitude to Africa* (Harmondsworth: Penguin, 1959), p. 9.

25. Bodleian Library, Mss Huddleston 2, 30 September 1959, Huddleston to 'Vov' (Mrs Snell).

26. Bodleian Library, Africa Bureau papers, Box 32 file 7, flyer launching the SCAQ.

27. Bodleian Library, Africa Bureau papers, Box 32, file 7, 10 January 1953, Rev. Galbraith to Hemingford.

28. Bodleian Library, Mss Brit. Emp. S.19. D 10/9, file 3, 26 June 1952, Greenidge to Hemingford (?) For Greenidge see Forclaz, *Humanitarian Imperialism*, p. 204.

29. Bodleian Library, Mss Brit. Emp. S.19. D 10/5, file 4, 20 May 1953, Greenidge to Freda White; David Astor was in agreement, but warned against a 'partial betrayal' of the Hereros (Astor to Greenidge, 9 January 1952, Mss Brit. Emp. s.19. D 10/9, file 1).

30. Bodleian Library, Mss. Brit. Emp. s.20/E2/21, Anti-Slavery Society minutes for 2 April 1958.

31. Bodleian Library, Ms Castle 251, 3 March 1958, Castle to Mrs Johnson (in Salisbury).

32. *Peace News*, 8 February 1952, p. 1.

33. Bodleian Library, Mss Afr. S. 1681, Box 32, file 1, 4 October 1952, Mary Attlee to Michael Scott.

34. For archive material on Racial Unity see Christ Church, Driberg papers, R1/4; Bodleian Library, Africa Bureau papers, Box 32, file 1. The fullest

published account is in P. B. Rich, *Race and Empire in British Politics* (Cambridge University Press, 1986), pp. 176–80.

35. Bodleian Library, Africa Bureau papers, Box 32, file 1, Progress Report number 2.
36. Bodleian Library, Africa Bureau papers, Box 32, file 1, 7 July 1952, Turnbull to Scott.
37. LOCP *Newsletter*, August 1947, pp. 157–9.
38. For an excellent discussion see R. Skinner, 'The Moral Foundations of British Anti-Apartheid Activism, 1946–1960', *Journal of Southern African Studies*, vol. 35, no. 2 (June 2009), 399–416.
39. See Bodleian Library, Africa Bureau papers, Box 16, file 6.
40. Bodleian Library, Scott papers, Box 5, Bishop Anthony of Swaziland to Dunn, 26 August 1974, adding '. . . while Scott was a prophet who preferred [politics]'.
41. SOAS, Fox-Pitt papers, Box 3, 6/2/1, 23 July 1953, Collins to Fox-Pitt; Bodleian Library, Africa Bureau papers, Box 201, file 5, 5 December 1960, Astor to Collins.
42. Mary Benson later wrote a biography: *Tshekedi Khama* (London: Faber and Faber, 1960); Bodleian Library, Scott papers, Box 15, 7 July 1950, Astor to Gordon-Walker.
43. P. Chater, *Grass Roots: the Story of St Faith's Farm in Southern Rhodesia* (London: Hodder & Stoughton, 1962), p. 14, citing Scott's letter to the *Observer*.
44. Reginald Reynolds in *Peace News*, 23 September 1955.
45. See T. Ranger, *Writing Revolt: an Engagement with African Nationalism, 1957–1967* (Oxford: James Currey, 2013).
46. R/ Ferguson, *George MacLeod: Founder of the Iona Community* (London, Collins, 1990), p. 300.
47. S. Moyn, *The Last Utopia: Human Rights in History* (Cambridge, MA: Belknap Press of Harvard University Press, 2010), p. 114.
48. 'Human Rights Find a Champion', *Peace News*, 11 April 1952.
49. Hull History Centre, UDEV/1/60, MCF Annual Conference, 30 October 1955; this was to accord significantly higher prominence to human rights than its forerunner, COPAI, which in 1953 gave the application of the Universal Declaration as the ninth and final item in a list of demands, SOAS, Fox-Pitt papers, Box 3, 6/2/1.
50. *Peace News*, 14 June 1963, p. 3.
51. Bodleian Library, Mss Brit. Emp. S.19 D 10/11, 24 April 1959, Fox-Pitt to Hella Pick.
52. *Peace News*, 16 October 1959, p. 7.
53. Howe, *Anticolonialism,* p. 170; Bodleian Library, Africa Bureau papers, Box 17, file 14, 25 June 1952, Brockway to Scott.
54. Howe, *Anticolonialism,* p. 172.
55. T. Benn and R. Winstone, *Years of Hope: Diaries, Letters and Papers 1940–1962* (London: Hutchinson, 1994), p. 295 (entry for 19 December 1958).
56. LHAS&C, CPGB papers, CP/CENT/EC/03/04, meeting of 9–10 May 1953.

57. National Library of Wales, Elwyn Jones papers, I1, 21 May 1951, Audrey Jupp to Elwyn Jones.
58. MRC, Gollancz papers, Mss 157/3/CL/1, 18 June 1950, Baldwin to Gollancz.
59. J. Stonehouse, *Prohibited Immigrant* (London: Bodley Head, 1960); see also his contribution on Hola Camp in Benenson, *Gangrene*, pp. 127–56.
60. Benn, *Years of Hope*, p. 326 (16 March 1960).
61. *Peace News*, 17 January 1958, p. 2.
62. D. Anderson, 'Mau Mau in the High Court and the 'Lost' British Empire Archives: Colonial Conspiracy or Bureaucratic Bungle?' *The Journal of Imperial and Commonwealth History*, vol. 39, no. 5 (2011), 699–716. See also D. Anderson, *Histories of the Hanged: Britain's Dirty War in Kenya and the End of Empire* (London: Weidenfeld & Nicholson, 2005); C. Elkins, *Britain's Gulag: the Brutal End of Empire in Kenya* (London: Pimlico, 2005).
63. F. Klose, *Human Rights in the Shadow of Colonial Violence: the Wars of Independence in Kenya and Algeria* (Philadelphia, PA: University of Pennsylvania Press, 2013), p. 198; J. Eckel, 'Human Rights and Decolonization: New Perspectives and Open Questions', *Humanity: an International Journal of Human Rights, Humanitarianism, and Development*, vol. 1, no. 1 (Fall 2010), 125.
64. J. Lewis, 'Daddy Wouldn't Buy Me a Mau Mau: the British Popular Press and the Demoralisation of Empire', in E. S. Atieno Odhiambo and J. Londsdale (eds) *Mau Mau and Nationhood: Arms, Authority and Narration* (Oxford: James Currey, 2003).
65. SOAS, PPMS 6, Box 22, 6/10/3, 21 July 1953, Douglas Rogers to Fox-Pitt (my emphasis).
66. Bodleian Library, Mss. Brit. Emp. s. 527/8, *End of Empire* ITV transcripts, volume 1, fol.114.
67. Klose, *Human Rights*, p. 193; see the MI5 file on Koinange, TNA KV2/2535–2552.
68. Brockway, *African Journeys*, pp. 167–70. See also his *Why Mau Mau? An Analysis and a Remedy* (London: Congress of Peoples against Imperialism, 1953).
69. For his resignation see Bodleian Library, Young papers, Mss. Brit. Emp. S. 486, Box 5/3, Young to Baring, 14 December 1954.
70. For Castle see Bodleian Library, Mss Brit. Emp. S. 486, Box 5/1, Narrative (1969), p. 29; for Scott see ibid., Box 6, 1 June 1956, Young to Sir Frank Newsam.
71. See correspondence in Lambeth Palace archives, Fisher vol. 127. Trevor Huddleston, who was an old friend of Sir Evelyn Baring and his wife Lady Mary, shared Fisher's assessment of the Governor's religious devotion, at one point noting that turning 'the corner in Kenya' was 'a great triumph for [Baring's] sanity + wisdom + *faith*' (Bodleian, Mss Huddleston 2, 17 November 1954, Huddleston to Lady Mary Baring).
72. TNA, DO 35/5357; articles in *The Times of India*, 26 June 1953, 1 July, 14 July; P. Evans, *Law and Disorder; or, Scenes of Life in Kenya* (London: Secker & Warburg, 1956).

73. For a good recent analysis of her allegations and the government's response see K. Bruce-Lockhart, '"The Truth about Kenya": Connection and Contestation in the 1956 Kamiti Controversy', *Journal of World History*, vol. 26, no. 4 (December 2015), 815–38.

74. See her letter to *The Friend*, 17 October 1947.

75. Friends' House archives, FSC/KEN/6, file 4, 26 May 1956, Nairobi to R. Ede, 1 June 1956, R. Ede to E. Cleaver; File 7, Carter to P. Sturge.

76. Friends' House archives, FSC/KEN/6, file 1, Fletcher to Askwith, 1 July 1955.

77. Friends' House archives, FSC/KEN/6, file 5, 14 March 1956, Fletcher to Sturge. There is controversy over how far she made her complaints known at the time: at a private meeting she told the Anti-Slavery Society Executive Committee that she quit due to prison conditions and had protested about 'the brutalities committed by a warder', Bodleian Library, Mss Brit. Emp. s 20/E2/23, Anti-Slavery Society minutes, 29 May 1956, item 6284.

78. *Concord*, April 1956, pp. 29–30.

79. *Peace News*, 8 June 1956, pp. 1 and 8.

80. Friends' House archives, FSC/KEN/6, file 4, 15 June 1956, John Fletcher on 'Eileen Fletcher's Concern'.

81. *Concord*, April 1956.

82. Bodleian Library, Mss Brit. Emp. s 20/E2/23, Anti-Slavery Society minutes, 29 May 1956, item 6284.

83. See her letters to *The Friend*, 30 August 1957 and 31 June 1958.

84. The fullest account is in *Peace News*, 15 June 1956, p. 1.

85. SOAS, PPMS 6, Box 4, 7 March 1956 and 18 April 1956, Brockway to Fox-Pitt.

86. MRC, Mss 157/3/MC/1/1–20, Brockway to Gollancz, 15 March and 5 June 1956.

87. Hull History Centre, UDCL 51/8, 29 May 1957, Allen to Fletcher. An NCCL pamphlet issued at around the same under Fletcher's name (*Kenya Curtails Civil Liberties*) listed the rights currently limited under the Emergency and concluded with a section on 'Other human rights'.

88. *Hansard*, 27 July 1959, col. 237.

89. Death notice in *The Friend*, 27 August 1976.

90. Benenson, *Gangrene*, pp. 97–126; Peter Benenson papers (in private possession), Hilary Cartwright to Benenson, 26 April 1963 (Evans, who lived outside of Europe, offered to speak at an Amnesty conference in Germany, and said that he had been interested in Amnesty's work 'for some time').

91. Rich, *Race and Empire*, pp. 131–5.

92. Bodleian Library, Mss. Brit. Emp. 23, HI/15, Ernest Adkin to John Harris, 7 August 1930.

93. *The Friend*, 29 June 1956, p. 581.

94. Friends' House archives, Fletcher papers, 367/3/4, 9 June 1956, E. Fletcher to J. Fletcher.

95. Friends' House archives, Fletcher papers, 367/4/7, extracts from Collins' sermon, 7 September 1952.

96. Bodleian Library, Ms AAM 870, file 1, speech by Wilson, 17 March 1963; see LHAS&C, Labour Party International Department (ID), Box 127 for the International Department's notes for Wilson, as well as Wilson's text for a speech on 2 May in which he reflects on the response to it. In a letter to Ennals in ID Box 130, 2 May 1963 he reassured him that on this occasion 'I altered hardly a word and am proposing to stick to the speech as you drafted it'.
97. Friends' House archives, Fletcher papers, 367/4/7, extracts from Collins' sermon, 7 September 1952.
98. Saul Dubow, *Apartheid, 1948–1994* (Oxford University Press, 2014), provides an excellent overview.
99. Bodleian Library, Africa Bureau papers, Box 29, file 7, Christian Action circular, 8 January 1953, my emphasis.
100. There is a copy in the Labour Party files (LHAS&C, LP ID Box 127). The Charter was approved by a meeting of the ANC, the Indian Congress, the Coloured People's Organization and the Congress of Democrats
101. IISH, AI IS, 982, Peter Benenson essay, November 1983, p. 5; Lambeth Palace archives, Fisher vol. 193, *Christian Action News Sheet*, Easter 1957.
102. Bodleian Library, Africa Bureau papers, Box 190, file 2, 8 April 1958, Bishop Reeves to Scott.
103. See J. S. Peart-Binns, *Archbishop Joost de Blank: Scourge of Apartheid* (London: Muller, Blond and White, 1987).
104. Reeves published *Shooting at Sharpeville: the Agony of South Africa* (London: V. Gollancz, 1960). For the Circle see, for instance, Jesuit archives, Roberts papers, 19/6/3, Peter Benenson circular, 12 July 1963.
105. Huddleston, *Four Words*, p. 14.
106. Chater, *Grassroots*, pp. 14–15.
107. L. J. Collins, *Faith under Fire* (London: Frewin, 1966), p. 180.
108. Friends' House archives, Fletcher papers, 367/1/1, Fletcher to Paton, 25 November 1952.
109. Collins, *Faith under Fire*, pp. 188–90.
110. Friends' House archives, Race Relations Committee minutes, 5 November 1952.
111. Lambeth Palace archive, Mss 3299, report of Collins' speech at a Christian Action meeting on 'South Africa: A Challenge to the Conscience', 6 October 1954.
112. Lambeth Palace archives, Fisher vol. 193, *Christian Action News Sheet*, Easter 1957.
113. Christian Action Newsletter, September and December 1959.
114. See D. Herbstein, *White Lies: Canon Collins and the Secret War against Apartheid* (Cape Town: HSRC Press, 2004).
115. Huddleston, *Naught for Your Comfort* (London: Collins, 1956), p. 44.
116. Bodleian Library, Scott papers, Box 88, 19 September 1953, Huddleston to Benson.
117. Bodleian Library, Scott papers, Box 68, report of June 1956 meeting.
118. See especially C. Gurney, 'A Great Cause': The Origins of the Anti-Apartheid Movement, June 1959–June 1960 (London: AAM Archives

Committee, 1988) and R. Skinner, *The Foundations of Anti-Apartheid: Liberal Humanitarians and Transnational Activists in Britain and the United States, c.1919–64* (Basingstoke: Palgrave Macmillan, 2010).

119. See for instance, the comments at the NCCL AGM, 11 June 1960 (Bodleian Library, AAM 890); AAM 839, Labour Party 'Statement on South Africa', 23 March 1960.

120. TNA KV2/4045, cutting from *Reynolds News*, 7 February 1960 for interview with Martin Ennals, and intercepted conversation of 17 April 1961 between South African Communist Vella Pillay and Ros Ainslie.

121. Bodleian Library, AAM 6, Patrick van Rensburg memorandum for 24 November 1959 press conference.

122. Driberg papers, Christ Church, Oxford, S15, Labour Party, 'Africa Year 1960'.

123. Bodleian Library, Scott papers, Box 60, 3 August 1961, Scott's note for Gollancz on manuscript entitled "'Portugal and Its Empire – the Truth'".

124. Although see Benenson's *Gangrene*; Fox-Pitt left the Anti-Slavery Society to work with Algerian refugees.

125. Bodleian Library, Scott papers, Box 21, text of broadcast, 13 March 1957.

126. Hull History Centre, UDJU 2/1, minutes of emergency meeting of Executive Committee, 19 and 24 September 1957.

127. *Amnesty* 4, 9 Aug. 1961, p. 2. In 1973 Curle became the first Professor of Peace Studies at the University of Bradford.

128. IISH, AI IS, 984, Louis Blom-Cooper interview, 6 June 1984, pp. 11–16.

129. Bodleian Library, Mss Brit Emp s.19, D 10/12 file 2, 23 August 1960, Fox-Pitt to Michael Faber, notifying him that Banda was still a committee member and that the Anti-Slavery Society would not 'part with him' despite allegations concerning his behaviour.

130. *Peace News*, 5 December 1958, p. 7.

131. Christ Church, Oxford, Driberg papers, G3 (2), Driberg to Tom Sargant, 9 November 1961; Driberg to Nkrumah, 21 October 1963.

132. Churchill College, Cambridge, DGFT 5/26, letter of 18 November 1963. The other signatories were F. Elwyn Jones, John Stonehouse, the Liberal MP Donald Wade and Humphrey Berkeley, a liberal Conservative MP who joined Labour in 1970.

133. R. Burke, "'How Time Flies': Celebrating the Universal Declaration of Human Rights in the 1960s', *The International History Review*, vol. 38, no. 3 (2015), 10–12.

134. Churchill College, Cambridge, DGFT 8/5 and 8/7.

135. See Bing's MI5 files (TNA, KV2/3811 and 3812).

136. J. Platts-Mills, 'Geoffrey Henry Cecil Bing', *ODNB*, citing the *Times*, 25 April 1977; *Daily Mail*, 13 September 1957.

137. Christ Church, Oxford, Driberg papers, G3(2), 13 November 1961, Sargant to Driberg.

138. See G. Bing, *Reap the Whirlwind: An Account of Kwame Nkrumah's Ghana from 1950 to 1966* (London: MacGibbon & Kee, 1968).

139. Regent's Park, Oxford, E. A. Payne papers, 'Human Rights' box, 'AI Book Reviews', undated [1968].

140. Herbstein, *White Lies*, pp. 49–50.

141. Hull History Centre, UDJU 2/2, Report by Allott, January 1961 in Justice's Colonial Affairs Committee Minutes, esp. pp. 2 and 7.
142. Institute of Commonwealth Studies library (ICS), Senate House, London, ICS 28/11/A, Halpern papers, AI British Section, report for 1963–64; Bodleian Library, Africa Bureau papers, Box 16, file 8, 27 August 1963, Creech-Jones to Jane Symonds.
143. *Views*, 3, Autumn/Winter 1963, pp. 118–21.
144. ICS 28/11/A, Halpern papers, July 1964, 'News Sheet for Threes Groups', p. 2, comments by Dr K. A. Busia.
145. Bodleian Library, Scott papers, Box 28, 28 June 1960, memorandum of meeting; 1 December 1961, Scott to Brockway.
146. *The Observer*, 30 October 1960.
147. Bodleian Library, Scott papers, Box 19, 22 January 19, 'A Council for Human Rights (?)' [*sic*].

3 POLITICAL IMPRISONMENT AND HUMAN RIGHTS, 1945–1964

1. The following account is based on reports in *The Times*, 13 March, p. 11; 16 March, p. 8; 24 March, pp. 2, 6; and 18 April 1953, p. 3. For images of some of the other designs see *Peace News*, 4 December 1964, p. 7.
2. Scottish Museum of Modern Art, Edinburgh, RPA 0694, Penrose papers, Reg Butler file, Typescript for the 'Third Programme', 24 June 1953, pp. 1 and 4–5.
3. For the politics behind the competition see R. Burstow, 'The Limits of Modernist Art as a "Weapon of the Cold War": Reassessing the Unknown Patron of the Monument to the Unknown Political Prisoner', *Oxford Art Journal*, vol. 20, no. 1 (1997), 68–80. Burstow shows that the American billionaire John Hay Whitney was the secret patron, acting largely as a front for the CIA, and that the project was not completed because the CIA regarded the winning design as '"too ultra modern"'.
4. LMA, Board of Deputies papers, Acc 3121/E3/217, Report of Human Rights Working Group of SCESWUN, 21 October 1957; 24 October 1957, Barnett Janner to R. N. Carvalho, President of the AJA.
5. Peter Benenson papers (AI), Benenson's note, 'The Situation before 1961'.
6. Bodleian Library, Africa Bureau papers, Box 152, file 10, undated, Iona Community, response to a sermon by Michael Scott.
7. KCL, LDG papers, MGA CORRSP IV, R.W. Sorenson file, 14 May 1957, Sorenson to Diana Pym; Sorenson, 'Brief Report on My Visit to Athens, May 31st–June 2nd, 1961', p. 8.
8. LSE, HALDANE/41, Haldane Society minutes 13 November 1956 and 27 November 1956; *The Guardian*, 2 December 1956, letter from Chairman.
9. LSE, HALDANE/41, Haldane Society statement on the IADL, 6 November 1957.
10. LSE, HALDANE/41, Haldane Society minutes, 30 October 1952 and 22 April 1953.

11. LSE, HALDANE/41, Haldane Society minutes, 2 January 1957; 28 January and 11 February 1958.

12. For Benenson in Spain see LSE, SLL/1/1, minutes for 30 March 1953 and *Daily Worker*, 20 March, p. 1; 27 March, n.p.; and 30 March, p. 3; and 7 April, p. 2 and 20 April, p. 3, all 1953. See also T. Buchanan, 'Holding the Line: the Political Strategy of the International Brigade Association, 1939–1977', *Labour History Review*, vol. 66, no. 3 (Winter 2001), 294–312; R. Brown, 'The International Brigade Association and Political Prisoners in Franco's Spain', *Bulletin of the Marx Memorial Library*, vol. 136 (Autumn 2002), 4–26.

13. Westminster Diocesan archives, Sword of the Spirit papers, Box 6, File 7, 17 September 1948, Beales' draft script for BBC Home Service.

14. Westminster Diocesan Papers, Heenan papers, HE3/103, 25 June 1968, Heenan to the Apostolic Delegate.

15. LSE, SLL/6/27, 9 February 1954, SLL to G. R. Mitchison.

16. KCL, LDG papers, MGA CORRESP IV, 'Personalities' file, 21 July 1949, Pym to Sheppard (commenting on his publication, *Mindszenty and the Protestant Pastors: a Factual Account of the Famous Trials in Hungary and Bulgaria* (1949)).

17. E. Bone, *Seven Years Solitary* (London: Hamish Hamilton, 1957); P. Ignotus, *Political Prisoner* (London: Routledge and Kegan Paul, 1959). Ignotus spoke at the press conference when Amnesty was launched.

18. For Dery see *Manchester Guardian*, 26 September 1957, p. 11 for the appeal by Liberal leader Jo Grimond; there is a small amount of material on the British Tibor Dery Committee, established September 1957, in The Keep, Sussex, Benn Levy papers, 9/10 and 9/11.

19. Benenson cited these committees in 'The Forgotten Prisoners' (*Observer*, 28 May 1961) as proof that governments may relent when 'world opinion is concentrated on one weak spot'.

20. The best biographical source is the series of lengthy interviews conducted in 1983–84 for Amnesty's Oral History project, and Benenson's accompanying essay (IISH, AI IS, 982 and 983). James Loeffler's recent book *Rooted Cosmopolitans: Jews and Human Rights in the Twentieth Century* (New Haven: Yale University Press, 2018) provides a fascinating account of the period up until Benenson's departure from Amnesty in 1967, focusing on his complex relationship with his Jewish heritage. For an introductory biography see D. Winner, *Peter Benenson: the Lawyer Who Campaigned for Prisoners of Conscience and Created Amnesty International* (Watford: Exley, 1991).

21. Bodleian Library, Scott papers, Box 79, 21 March 1967, Benenson to Calvocoressi.

22. IISH, AI IS, 982, Benenson's 1983 essay, p. 2.

23. Hull History Centre, UDJU/11/64, 14 December 1956, Benenson's notes for Gardiner.

24. See C. Veliz, 'The True Genesis of Amnesty International', *Quadrant*, vol. 51, no. 5 (May 2007). Claudio Veliz had worked as a volunteer for the International Brigade Association in the early 1950s.

25. See F. Solomon and B. Litvinoff, *Baku to Baker Street: the Memoirs of Flora Solomon* (London: Collins, 1984).

26. The phrase 'the establishment' was popularised by the journalist Henry Fairlie in 1955.
27. H. Tennyson, *The Haunted Mind: an Autobiography* (London: A. Deutsch, 1984), esp. pp. 136–7.
28. Copies of election material in Peter Benenson papers (in private possession).
29. Peter Benenson papers (private possession), undated memorandum. Benenson's initiative appears to have built on an existing committee established by the lawyer Robert Pollard (9 February 1954, Pollard to Benenson), possibly in turn a remnant of the abortive civil rights organisation launched by Victor Gollancz with encouragement from Roger Baldwin in 1950 (see correspondence in MRC, Gollancz papers, Mss 157/3/CL).
30. Peter Benenson papers (in private possession), 29 July 1954, Benenson to A. B. McNulty (Council of Europe); draft letter to *The Times*, undated. McNulty had recommended that 'Human Rights' should be used in the title. It is not clear why his advice was rejected (McNulty to Benenson, 10 February 1955). IISH, AI IS, 982, Benenson interview 12 November 1983, p. 31.
31. Peter Benenson papers (in private possession), 23 February 1955, report of meeting at the House of Commons; Steven Jensen, *The Making of International Human Rights: the 1960s, Decolonization, and the Reconstruction of Global Values* (New York: Cambridge University Press, 2016), pp. 42–3.
32. Peter Benenson papers (in private possession), 24 September 1985, Benenson to Niall MacDermot (ICJ).
33. Hull History Centre, UDJU/1/1, typescript of Peter Benenson's remarks and report of meeting.
34. Technically, Justice appears to have disbanded at the moment of union with the ICJ, but the decision was immediately taken to retain the title of 'Justice'. Hull History Centre, UDJU/1/1, undated typescript.
35. Hull History Centre, UDJU 2/1, Council minutes, 27 March 1957.
36. Hull History Centre, UDJU 2/3, Council minutes, 15 January 1970.
37. See W. Goodhart and H. C. G. Matthew, 'Thomas Sargant', *ODNB* entry.
38. IISH, AI IS, 991, Tom Sargant interview, 22 June 1985, pp. 2–3; Peter Benenson papers (in private possession), 1956 diary, entries for 27 January, 25 February, and 30 May.
39. IISH, AI IS, 991, Tom Sargant interview, 21 June 1985, p. 31.
40. Hull History Centre, UDJU, 2/1, Minutes, 11 July 1957.
41. Hull History Centre, UDJU/11/31, Benenson's undated report on his visit to Hungary, funded by the ICJ.
42. Hull History Centre, UDJU 2/3, at the 3 July 1967 AGM, Shawcross said that Justice was 'almost entirely responsible' for the appointment of an Ombudsman.
43. Hull History Centre, UDJU 2/1, Council minutes, 26 June, 29 July 1958. See also Bodleian Library, S.22 G 802, report of meeting of 26 June 1958. Hoare's was also Amnesty International's bank.

44. Hull History Centre, UDJU 2/1, EC minutes, 17 May 1960; UDJU/1/2, 18 May 1960, Shawcross to Sargant ('people will think we are the Christian Action, the African Defence League or something of that kind').

45. Hull History Centre, UDJU/1/2, 19 June 1957, Benenson to Shawcross.

46. Hull History Centre, UDJU/1/2, Justice memorandum, undated.

47. Hull History Centre, UDJU/1/2, 30 April 1959, Shawcross to Sargant.

48. Hull History Centre, UDJU 2/1, EC 23 July 1959 and Council minutes, 12 October 1959. This principle was, of course, later adopted by Amnesty.

49. Peter Benenson papers (in private possession), 30 November 1957, Benenson to Marsh.

50. Hull History Centre, UDJU/1/1, 12 December 1957, notes for Chairman's speech to Justice AGM.

51. IISH, AI IS, 991, Tom Sargant interview, 21 June 1985, pp. 34–5 and p. 32.

52. IISH, AI IS, 989, Norman Marsh interview, June 1984, pp. 48–9.

53. Peter Benenson papers (in private possession), Benenson to Sargant (from Mondello), 28 March 1960, emphasis in original.

54. Peter Benenson papers (in private possession), Benenson to Sargant, 13 August 1961.

55. Benenson, *Persecution 1961* (Harmondsworth: Penguin, 1961), pp. 12 and 10.

56. P. Benenson, 'Amnesty looks East', *The Observer*, 17 June 1962.

57. For Cuba see Peter Benenson papers (private possession), Benenson to Lalive, 2 February 1960. He found his visit to Cuba 'extraordinarily interesting'.

58. Peter Benenson papers (AI), 10 July 1986, Benenson to Louise M. Badcock (whose sister had married Berger).

59. Peter Benenson papers (AI), 27 June 1963, background paper by Benenson for Amnesty. *Pacem in Terris* (11 April 1963) had stressed that 'A man who has fallen into error does not cease to be a man'.

60. University of Bradford, Baker papers, 1/B, August 1960 Baker manuscript on Christian pacifism; Benenson papers (in private possession), Baker to Benenson, 13 February 1960.

61. University of Bradford, Baker papers, 2/4, 12 March 1967, Vincent to Baker.

62. Peter Benenson papers (AI), Benenson's lecture on the 15th anniversary of Amnesty, 5 June 1976, p. 6. When I interviewed him on 29 October 1997, Benenson told me that he had noticed that torture generated newspaper coverage – and not for a 'very noble reason'.

63. Unpublished 'Dictionary of Quaker Biography', Friends House; Baker's CV in IISH, AI IS, 1280.

64. University of Bradford, Baker papers, 1/I, 22 June 1958, Baker to Tucker, p. 4; IISH, AI IS, 980, Joyce Baker interview, June 1983, pp. 21–3.

65. LSE, NPC 1/7, NPC Council minutes, 16 September 1954.

66. IISH, AI IS, 1005, Baker's speech to Eltham Group, 4 April 1962.

67. Friends' House archives, Fletcher papers, 367/1/3, Fletcher note, 1 December 1954.

68. LSE, NPC 1/8, NPC Council minutes, 9 October 1958.

69. M. Bess, *Realism, Utopia and the Mushroom Cloud: Four Activist Intellectuals and Their Strategies for Peace, 1945–1989* (Chicago University Press, 1993),

ch. 4, provides a succinct introduction to his life and work; see also J. McNeish, *Fire under the Ashes: the Life of Danilo Dolci* (London: Hodder & Stoughton, 1965) which is written from first-hand observation.

70. Faber's obituary in *The Guardian*, 20 May 2015.

71. University of Bradford, Baker papers, 1/I, Bulletin No. 1, May 1960. Apparently there had been 'hundreds of enquiries and donations' as a result of the review; *The Observer*, 4 October 1959, p. 25; NPC minutes 15 October 1959. The book was Dolci's *To Feed the Hungry: Enquiry in Palermo* (London: MacGibbon & Kee, 1959).

72. Peter Benenson papers (in private possession), 'Sunday Evening', Sargant to Benenson. The film was Stephen Peet's film *Murder by Neglect*, shown on BBC TV in March 1960, and partly written by Dolci.

73. LSE, NPC 1/8, NPC minutes, 13 March 1958.

74. *The Friend*, 31 July 1959, pp. 849–40 and 16 October 1959, pp. 1182–3; University of Bradford, Baker papers, 1/B, *The Christian Century*, 19 August 1959.

75. LMA, Muriel Smith papers, LMA/4196/09/003/02, Waller to Booker, 8 April 1960 and 11 May 1960.

76. LMA, Muriel Smith papers, LMA/4196/09/003/02, Booker to 'Mu' [Muriel], 23 October 1960, 3 March 1961 and 4 July 1961. Booker also published 'A Sicilian experiment' in *Community Development Bulletin*, vol. XIII (June 1962), 3.

77. *The Friend*, 26 February 1971, p. 234.

78. LSE, NPC 1/8, NPC minutes, 11 November 1957; see also University of Bradford, Baker papers, 1/H, NPC memo, 13 November 1957 re meeting with Benenson.

79. Peter Benenson papers (AI), typescript by Benenson, undated.

80. University of Bradford, Baker papers, 1/H, undated Baker memorandum, 'Cyprus: Interview with Sir Hugh Foot'. After Foot's 'introductory soliloquy . . . I turned the matter over to Peter Benenson . . . who conducted the majority of the interview'. In an interesting exchange many years later, Eric Baker sought to draw Caradon on how his experiences as an administrator in Mandatory Palestine had shaped his 'revulsion . . . towards the use of torture', IISH, AI IS, 1210, Baker to Caradon, 26 October 1973.

81. David French, *Fighting EOKA: The British Counter-Insurgency Campaign on Cyprus, 1955–1959* (Oxford University Press, 2015), p. 307. These figures are for 1 April 1955 to 31 December 1958.

82. University of Bradford, Baker papers, I/E, 1 October 1958, Kenneth Mackenzie, *Cyprus Mail*, to Baker.

83. For a helpful discussion of the work of the commission see B. Drohan, *Brutality in an Age of Human Rights: Activism and Counterinsurgency at the End of the British Empire* (Ithaca, NY & London: Cornell University Press, 2018), pp. 16–80.

84. P. Benenson, *Gangrene* (London: Calderbooks, 1959), p. 33.

85. IISH, AI IS, 982, Benenson's 1983 essay, p. 6 ('nice little practice'); NLW, Elwyn Jones papers, D15, Benenson's self-description in ICJ, 'The Hungarian Situation and the Rule of Law', 1957.

86. *Manchester Guardian,* 19 February 1957.
87. See Benenson's article in *Manchester Guardian,* 23 January 1957. Benenson hailed Radcliffe as 'one of the greatest constitutional lawyers this country has produced' (Churchill College, NBKR 4/150, 22 June 1958, Benenson to Philip Noel-Baker). Unpropitiously, Radcliffe was best known for his work on the Indian boundary committee at the time of partition.
88. S. L. Carruthers, *Winning Hearts and Minds: British Governments, the Media and Colonial Counter-Insurgency, 1944–1960* (London: Leicester University Press, 1995), p. 207.
89. TNA, FCO 141/4605, broadcast by Foley on CBS, 26 May 1955.
90. Churchill College, Cambridge, NBKR 4/157, 18 April 1958, Noel-Baker to Foley.
91. *Morning Star,* 12 June 1967, p. 5.
92. Bodleian Library, Ms Castle 10, diary of her visit: see, for instance, 21 September 1959, 'A hectic but enjoyable day. In the morning a swim with PB [Peter Benenson] at Kyrenia'.
93. TNA, FCO 141/4605, minute of 31 May 1957.
94. *Peace News,* 23 October 1964, p. 8.
95. KCL, LDG papers, MGA CHRON III, 17 October [1957?] Frank to Betty (Ambatielos); MGA INFO III, 7 October 1957, Betty to Frank (with pencil note of meeting).
96. University of Bradford, Baker papers, 1/E, 8 May 1959, Baker to Makarios. He had already contributed to a paper on Cyprus in 1955: Friends' House archives, Friends' Peace Committee minutes, 26 October 1955.
97. University of Bradford, Baker papers, 1/J, 22 June 1958, Baker to Tucker.
98. University of Bradford, Baker papers, IF, 8 May 1959, Baker to Makarios. The recommended reading was *The Quakers – Their Story and Method* by A. Neave Brayshaw, ch. 19; H. Loukes, *Friends Face Reality* (London, 1954), ch. 12, and a biography of the late Corder Catchpool – who had dedicated himself to Anglo-German reconciliation – to demonstrate the importance of individuals.
99. University of Bradford, Baker papers, 1H for Baker's notebook diaries of the two missions.
100. University of Bradford, Baker papers, 1/J, 22 June 1958, Baker to Tucker.
101. Hull History Centre, UDJU/1/2, 9 December 1959, Sargant to Shawcross.
102. There is a brief section of the Introduction to *Gangrene* devoted to Cyprus (pp. 15 and 31–6). Here Benenson noted that armed rebellion against British rule was 'scarcely surprising', criticised Makarios for failing to condemn EOKA violence and described the use of torture by the British authorities as counterproductive.
103. Peter Benenson papers (in private possession), Baker to Benenson, 17 March 1960.
104. *New World News,* 27, October–December 1962; Bodleian Library, MRA papers, 3/38, paper dated 23 July 1959, gives the inside story of the Cyprus settlement from an MRA perspective.
105. University of Bradford, Baker papers, 2/1, 4 March and 26 March 1960, Benenson to Baker.

106. University of Bradford, Baker papers, 2/1, 4 March 1960, Benenson to Baker.
107. G. Lean, *Frank Buchman: a Life* (London: Constable, 1985), pp. 238–9. Buchman made these ill-advised comments to the *New York World Telegram* on 24/25 August 1936, on his return from the Berlin Olympics.
108. University of Bradford, Baker papers, 1/H, diary of 1959 visit, meeting with Emin Bey and letter from Francis Golding; 1/I, 26 February 1959, Baker to Eric Tucker.
109. MRC, Mss.292B/949.5/3, I July 1963, 'Societies Opposing the Greek State Visit'.
110. The fullest account of these campaigns, albeit from an anti-communist perspective, is the memorandum entitled 'Campaign on Behalf of Spanish, Portuguese and Greek "Political" Prisoners and Exiles', May 1963 (MRC, TUC papers, Mss 292B/863/4).
111. Arguably, Benenson's original choice of title, 'Armistice', for a campaign culminating on 11 November 1961, was closer to his true ambition – to promote an armistice in the Cold War.
112. MRC, Mss 157/3/AS/1/1–23, 28 September 1959, Turner to Gollancz.
113. Public Record Office of Northern Ireland (PRONI), Belfast Trades Council papers, D1050/6/D/31 is an interesting source on this conference. See also *Daily Worker*, 9 March 1961, p. 1 and 8 May 1961, p. 3.
114. According to the source cited in note 110, the British committee was set up after a meeting of West European communist parties in November 1959, but the appeal was clearly already in circulation by that point. Interestingly, in September 1959 the fellow-travelling barrister John Platts-Mills, just back from visiting a trial in Spain, wrote to Lord Faringdon and Stephen Swingler (both veterans of the campaign to support the Spanish Republic during the Civil War) to propose a campaign for amnesty (Hull History Centre, UDPM 4/21, letters dated 9 September 1959). There is no indication that he was familiar with Turner's proposal. This suggests that if there was an international meeting in November it was responding to pressures from activists, as well as possibly the recent success of the campaign for Manolis Glezos, which had led to a reduction of his sentence (*Daily Worker*, 23 July 1959, p. 1). For Richard Turner's report for the IBA see LSE, HALDANE/37, 24 June 1958; also copy in Benenson papers (private possession).
115. *Daily Worker*, 14 December 1959, p. 1; *Guardian*, 15 December 1959, p. 2. Thorpe apart, Liberals were divided over the campaign's communist affiliations: the Liberal International and Bertrand Russell boycotted the March 1961 conference, but the former Liberal Party leader Clement Davies still chose to attend (NLW, Davies papers, G/12/2 and G/12/4; Churchill College, NBKR/9/10/1, Derek Mirfin to Noel-Baker.)
116. The best source on the Spanish Amnesty campaign is the collection of Eileen Turner's papers in the Marx Memorial Library, London (MML). This collection includes a helpful memoir by the lawyer Stephen Sedley, who was personally involved at the time, written in June 2015. For the Portuguese Amnesty committee a series of five campaign bulletins survives in the Bodleian (January 1963–July 1964); beyond that there is little apart

from a few newspaper articles and circulars. See for instance the letters from the secretary, Helen Ward, in *Peace News*, 12 June 1964 and 9 October 1964. For its launch see Jesuit archives, Archbishop Roberts papers, 19/5/2, undated announcement of the launch of the 'British Committee for Portuguese Amnesty'. The best account of the Greek Amnesty campaign is the TUC memorandum of 16 May 1963, 'The Campaign in Britain for an Amnesty for "Political" Prisoners and Exiles' (MRC, Mss 292B/949.5/3). The leading figures were the Labour MP Marcus Lipton and lawyer Benedict Birnberg, secretary of the Haldane Society; KCL, LDG papers, MGA CHRON IV, 15 October 1962, preparatory committee for a European conference.

117. Jesuits in Britain archives, Roberts papers, 19/5/1, 1 April 1964, N. Adler, Southport Amnesty International group to Roberts.
118. AI papers, 3 December 1963, Turner to Albert Lodge.
119. Peter Benenson papers (in private possession), 29 June 1963, Albert Lodge to Benenson.
120. See, for example, Marcos Ana, Vidal de Nicolas, and Agustin Ibarrola, *From Burgos Jail: Poems and Drawings* (London: Appeal for Amnesty in Spain, April 1964).
121. MRC, Mss 157/3/AS/1/1–23, 19 October 1959 Turner to Gollancz, replying to his letter of 30 September 1959.
122. This was even more apparent with the rival Labour-supported Council for Freedom in Portugal and Colonies. The Council intended 'to work with those in Portugal and her colonies who are struggling for freedom, independence and human rights', and was supported by long-standing critics of colonialism such as Anthony Wedgwood Benn and Dorothy Woodman.
123. *Daily Worker*, 13 August 1959.
124. Hull History Centre, UDEV/1/81, text of speech by Evans to the conference.
125. Human Rights Year *Newsletter*, 1, October 1967, article by Burns.
126. LSE, Ernest Davies papers, 3/25, Minutes of first meeting, 2 February 1959, attended by Benenson.
127. *Amnesty Newsletter*, 11, 15 November 1961, Ernest Davies, 'Franco's Persecution of the Basques' describes his attendance at a trial of Basque nationalists. For the context see T. Buchanan, 'Receding Triumph: British Opposition to the Franco Regime, 1945–59', *Twentieth Century British History*, vol. 12, no. 2 (2001), 163–84.
128. LHAS&C, Labour Party archives, SDDC Box, 1960 correspondence, 10 March 1960, Benenson to John Clark.
129. Peter Benenson papers (in private possession), 24 June 1959, Benenson to Lalive; see Benenson, 'The Forgotten Prisoners'; Benenson, *Persecution 1961*, pp. 123–34; MRC, Mss 292B/946/8. According to David Ennals, Amat attributed his release to pressure from the SDDFC (7 June 1961, Ennals to Mrs Kolarz).
130. *Observer Weekend Review*, 28 May 1961.
131. KCL, LDG papers, MGA CORRESP I, 29 May 1961, Ambatielos to Baker; the *Manchester Guardian* of the same date had announced her participation.

132. Peter Benenson papers (in private possession), 8 July 1958, Benenson to Digges. Benenson later said that he did not think that attending trials was very effective, and that it was better to send out money and parcels (author's interview with Peter Benenson, Oxford, 29 October 1997).

4 THE EARLY YEARS OF AMNESTY INTERNATIONAL, 1961–1964

1. IISH, AI IS, 1008, 13 January 1961, Benenson to Baker.
2. There are interviews with David Astor and Louis Blom-Cooper in the AI archives which cover this period (IISH, AI IS, 979 and 984). There are a few other hints of prior conversations. James Loeffler notes that Benenson met Maurice Perlzweig of the World Jewish Congress, his old mentor from Eton, in London prior to the launch and discussed the idea for what became 'Amnesty' (Loeffler, *Rooted Cosmopolitans: Jews and Human Rights in the Twentieth Century* (New Haven: Yale University Press, 2018), pp. 214–17). Recalling this meeting in an interview recorded on 12 November 1981, Perlzweig said that he had 'planted the seed' for Amnesty. He also mentioned that Benenson had spoken to the former British diplomat John Alexander-Sinclair before contacting him ('The Reminiscences of Dr. Maurice L. Perlzweig', www.columbia.edu/cu/libraries/inside/ccoh_as sets/ccoh_4074305_transcript.pdf, pp. 370–3; for Alexander-Sinclair see below pp. 145–6). Tom Sargant recalled Benenson typing up three sheets of paper and saying 'Tom, here's my new movement', but gave no indication as to the date (IISH, AI IS, Sargant interview, 22 June 1985, p. 38).
3. IISH, AI IS, 982, interview with Peter Benenson, 12 November 1983, p. 28; IISH, AI IS, 1163, 26 March 1960, Benenson to Baker. However, in a letter to Hugh Gaitskell of 14 June 1961 Benenson still referred to his 'socialist convictions', IISH, AI IS, 1023.
4. Peter Benenson papers (AI), typescript, 14 February 1986, p. 7.
5. IISH, AI IS, 982, Benenson interview, 12 November 1983, p. 49.
6. Peter Benenson papers (in private possession), Peter to Margaret Benenson, 14 June 1960; Gilmour to Benenson, 27 August 1960.
7. Amnesty International website, www.amnesty.org/en/who-we-are/.
8. I first pointed out this discrepancy in my article '"The Truth Will Set You Free": the Making of Amnesty International', and my sceptical conclusions about this incident (which remain provisional given that one cannot prove a negative) have not been challenged since. I have only found one occasion on which Benenson was directly asked about the details of his story, when the American writer Howard Blue told him that 'I really think that I need it straight from you' – no reply is recorded (Peter Benenson, AI papers, 26 February 1974, Blue to Benenson). Bill Shipsey supports my conclusions in his article 'The "Toast to Freedom" that Led to Amnesty International' (*Huffington Post* blog, 22 September 2011, www.huffingtonpost.com/bill-shipsey/th e-toast-to-freedom-that_b_976849.html). Instead, on the basis of some confusion over dates in Benenson's various accounts, Shipsey argues

that Benenson may well have been influenced by an article in the *Times* on 19 December 1961. However, Benenson only made one reference to 19 December, and this may have been a simple mistake on his part. Moreover, the two convicted people mentioned in this article cannot be seen as models for the story subsequently told by Benenson: they were found guilty of 'subversive activities' and 'crimes against the state', do not appear to have been students, and at least one was a communist.

9. See *New Statesman*, 2 March 1957. Gerald Gardiner recalled this episode in Churchill College, GARD 10, 2 June 1981, Gardiner to Dr J. A. Veiga-Pires.

10. P. Benenson, 'The Lusiad of the *Santa Maria*', *Spectator*, 3 February 1961, pp. 139–40. Although the article was inspired by the hijacking of a passenger ship by opponents of the regime on 23 January 1961, it shows that Benenson already had a very good understanding of the situation in Portugal.

11. *Africa Events*, July/August 1986, p. 100 (my emphasis).

12. Jesuits in Britain, archives, Archbishop Roberts papers, 19/5/3, 29 July 1963, Benenson to Roberts, including Benenson's draft for the competition.

13. The text for the article was checked by the International Press Institute, and 'some of the wording actually comes from [its Director] Jim Rose' (IISH, AI IS, 1018, 9 May 1961, Benenson to Pringle). It was illustrated by cartoonist Haro Hodson, IISH, AI IS, 1010, 11 February 1965, Lodge to Hodson.

14. IISH, AI IS, 1296, 21 July 1967, Benenson to Baker: by 'box and cox' Benenson meant that while one was travelling the other would be in charge; IISH, AI IS, 982, Benenson essay, 1983, p. 8.

15. *The Friend*, 18 October 1963, p. 1204.

16. *The Friend*, 'Quakerism in the 1960s', Parts I–IV, 29 April, 6 May, 13 May and 20 May 1960.

17. IISH, AI IS, 982, interview with Benenson, 12 November 1983, p. 70. This change clearly happened at an early point, as by 4 February 1961 Benenson was writing to his publisher on paper headed 'Appeal for Amnesty – 1861–1961 – Appel pour l'Amnistie'. At the foot of the letter was a quotation from John 8:32, 'and the truth will set you free – et la verité vous libera'. Benenson would later refer to this as the 'motto of the campaign', which he had removed from the writing paper as 'it may not be generally understood' (University of Bristol, Penguin Archives, DM1107/S200, Benenson to Charles Clark; AI papers, 5 June 1961, 'First Notes on Organisation').

18. IISH, AI IS, 982, Benenson interview, p. 77; author's interview with Peter Benenson 29 October 1997.

19. IISH, AI IS, 1163, 15 January 1961, Baker to Benenson, and reply, 18 January 1961.

20. IISH, AI IS, 1163, 11 April 1961, Baker to Benenson, reply, 14 April 1961.

21. KCL, LDG papers, MGA CORRESP 1, Appeal for Amnesty, 1961, 'Background Notes'.

22. University of Bradford, Baker papers, 2/1, Benenson to Baker, 22 January 1961. There is a substantial file in the Penguin archives (see DM 1107/S200), although it sheds no light on the book's genesis. It is,

however, interesting to note that one of the senior editors, Dieter Pevsner, was the son of the architectural historian Nikolaus Pevsner, who would later put his name to an Amnesty appeal (*Guardian*, 24 July 1961, p. 8). Penguin had originally agreed to Benenson's proposal to publish two books, the second being putatively entitled 'The Rights of Free Men' and focusing on the Commonwealth. Peter Archer was scheduled to write the book, but it was postponed and never published as a Penguin Special. John Pringle of the *Guardian* joked that two books with Penguin were better than one with Collins (IISH, AI IS, 1018, Pringle to Benenson, 8 February 1961), suggesting that Collins – which Benenson had connections to through his aunt – was an alternative publisher.

23. *Observer Weekend Review*, 28 May 1961.
24. University of Bristol, Penguin archives, DM 1107/S200, undated editors' notes; 27 November 1961, Benenson to Charles Clark.
25. University of Bristol, Penguin archives, DM 1107/S200, 29 September 1961, Charles Clark to Lord Birkett.
26. I have only found the dummy-run and accompanying memorandum in the Penguin archive, DM 1107/S200.
27. Benenson, *Persecution 1961* (Harmondsworth: Penguin, 1961), p. 152.
28. Benenson outlined his ideas in IISH, AI IS, 1023, 5 June 1961, Benenson to Viscount Samuel. Only the 'Appeal to Pictorial Artists' was formally advertised, in *The Observer*, 4 June 1961, but Benenson told Melvin Lasky of the Congress for Cultural Freedom that the international appeal to musicians would be launched on 10 July in Bonn (IISH, AI IS papers, 1020, 22 June 1961, Benenson to Lasky).
29. University of Bradford, Baker papers, 2/1, 18 February 1961, Benenson to Baker.
30. Baker expressed it in these terms: 'The Temple itself [home to Benenson's chambers] is so near to Fleet Street and (in spirit) so near both to Parliament and the law, Amnesty was born at the focus of press, legal and parliamentary activity', IISH, AI IS, 1174, 17 October 1975, Baker to Mark Grantham.
31. KCL, MGA CORRESP 1, 28 June 1961, Benenson to Diana Pym.
32. Peter Calvocoressi to the author, 22 October 2002
33. Peter Benenson papers (in private possession), 21 January 1963, Benenson to unattributed (probably Kit Barclay of IRD).
34. IISH, AI IS, 985, Peggy Crane interview, 17 June 1985, p. 20.
35. Peter Benenson papers (in private possession), 13 December 1962, Benenson to Lt. Col. Twaddle.
36. IISH, AI IS, 1023, 30 May 1961, Gaitskell to Benenson.
37. MRC, Mss 292B/946/8, 25 May 1961, David Ennals to Mrs Kolarz; 26 May 1961 TUC International Department to K. Dallas, ICFTU.
38. IISH, AI IS, 1023, 20 June 1961, Derek Mirfin, Liberal International, to Benenson. For Macmillan see below, p. 137.
39. KCL, MGA INFO V, 1 August 1961, *Reynolds News* to Diana Pym. See the articles by George Pollock – 'from the files of Appeal for Amnesty' – in *Reynolds News* 16 July 1961 (on the Portuguese prisoner Francisco Miguel);

6 August 1961 (on the Latvian Fricis Menders) and 13 August 1961 (on Robert Sobukwe and Sharpeville).

40. IISH, AI IS, 1190, Policy Committee, 12 December 1961 (re USDAW); IISH, AI IS, 1163, 31 May 1961, Percy Bartlett, Embassies of Peace, to Baker; IISH, AI IS, 983, Benenson interview, 12 November 1983, p. 119.
41. University of Bradford, Baker papers, 2/1, 9 June 1961, William E. Barton (FSC) to Baker.
42. Friends' House archives, Friends' Peace Committee minutes, 5 April 1962.
43. IISH, AI IS, 1163, 6 June 1961, MacBride to Benenson.
44. Peter Benenson, 'Prisoners Remembered', *The Spectator*, 21 July 1961, p. 81; IISH, AI IS, 1029, script for 'Liberty to the Captives', BBC Home Service, 4 March 1962, p. 10.
45. IISH, AI IS, 1029, script for 'Liberty to the Captives'.
46. IISH, AI IS, 1020, 22 June 1961, Benenson to Melvin Lasky. The CCF – now seen as an archetypal anti-communist organisation of the Cold War – continued to work with Amnesty. For instance, in 1966 it supported an observer's visit to Mozambique (IISH, AI IS, 1293, 23 September 1966, Robert Swann to Hans Goran Franck).
47. University of Bradford, *Peace News* archive, PN 10/11, 'Background Notes'.
48. IISH, AI IS, 982, Benenson's 1983 essay, p. 9; IISH, AI IS, 982, Benenson interview, 12 November 1983, pp. 80–1.
49. Benenson in *Amnesty*, 14, 3 January 1962. The first formal mention is in an undated document, 'Notes on Organisation', which appears to have been published after the launch of the campaign. Here, 'Threes' groups are mentioned as the second of three initiatives, after an office for the employment of refugee prisoners. The Threes, which would be based on a specific locality, organisation or profession, would last for 'as long as the need exists', but would not form one of the two permanent elements.
50. 'World Conscience', University of Bristol, Penguin Archives, DM 1107/S200.
51. Appeal for Amnesty, 1961–2 Annual Report, p. 6.
52. 'The Forgotten', *Peace News*, 10 March 1961.
53. IISH, AI IS, 982, Benenson's 1983 essay, p. 10.
54. Westminster Diocesan Archives, Godfrey papers, GO2/133b, Benenson to Worlock, 31 July 1961, and reply, 5 August 1961.
55. IISH, AI IS, 1030, 21 June 1961, Hugh Samson to Benenson, and 13 September 1961 memorandum by John Pellow; IISH, AI IS, 982, Benenson's essay, 1983, p. 10.
56. In fact, right from the beginning Benenson appears to have been thinking about a longer-term campaign, as in the proposal for *Persecution 1961*, submitted to Penguin in February, he envisaged that the book's conclusion would deal with ideas for 'continuing the campaign in 1962' (University of Bristol, Penguin archive, DM 1107/S200, synopsis for 'Amnesty 1961'). For the agenda of the first international meeting see IISH, AI IS, 1.
57. IISH, AI IS, 1163, 9 August 1961, Benenson to Baker. See also the even more lurid memorandum of June 1961.
58. Peter Benenson papers (in private possession), 21 August 1961, Baker to Benenson. Benenson did not wholly abandon these ideas. For instance in

August 1962 he told MacBride that Amnesty had a role in developing the 'first European Party': 'we are the only people who can bring together the Catholic parties of Europe and the Labour Party on the one hand and the continental Socialists on the other. Indeed, if we stick to Human Rights as a basic platform, I think we can even bring in people like the Dutch Protestants and perhaps the English Tories . . .'. Peter Benenson papers (in private possession), 4 August 1962, Benenson to MacBride.

59. LMA, Cy Grant papers, LMA/4709/G/01/001, Benenson to Grant, 11 December 1961 – 'your part of the ceremony certainly caught the imagination of the television and press'. *Daily Mirror*, 11 December 1961.

60. The text is in *Amnesty*, 13, 13 December 1961.

61. Westminster Diocesan Archive, Godfrey papers, GO2/133b, 19 December 1961, Benenson to Worlock.

62. P. Benenson, 'The First Phase', in *Amnesty*, 14, 3 January 1962.

63. See *Observer*, 25 May 1986, p. 10.

64. Hull History Centre, UDPM 1/10, *Haldane Society Annual Report 1961*, p. 3.

65. See, for instance, a letter from John Fletcher, of 10 May 1960, in which he argued that if, in addition to raising money for the anti-apartheid movement in South Africa, a township or prison could be adopted by a group in Manchester or Leeds, 'this personal help of people actually knowing and writing to other people, would be quite a different type of help added to what exists now' (Friends House archives, 367/1/2, addressee unknown); 14 January 1960 letter from Richard Hauser about community 'activation' (Friends' House archives, 367/2/4/1); for Hauser see below, p. 221. See also a letter from Mrs A. Rosen to D. N. Pritt recommending a Society for the Prevention of Cruelty to Homo Sapiens (KCL, LDG papers, MGA CORRESP IV, Pritt file, letter dated 14 May 1963).

66. When the appeal ended Amnesty was known as 'AMNESTY: An International Movement for Freedom of Opinion and Religion', and from September 1962 as Amnesty International. To avoid confusion, in this chapter I will simply use the name Amnesty.

67. Peter Benenson papers (in private possession), 19 June 1962, Benenson to Lord Weidenfeld.

68. *AI Bulletin*, 2, May 1963.

69. Peter Benenson papers (AI), 10 December 1974, Benenson to Mrs Francoise Clark; 11 July 1991, Benenson to Marie Jose Protais.

70. IISH, AI IS, 987, transcript of interview with Sean MacBride, 8 June 1984, p. 47.

71. IISH, AI IS, 1028, 18 October 1961, Crane to Hilary Cartwright.

72. IISH, AI IS, 1190, minutes of first meeting of Policy Committee, 14 November 1961; IISH, AI IS, 1028, Elvin finally agreed in May 1962, if the committee 'really presses' (Elvin to Crane, 16 May 1962).

73. See below, p. 111.

74. 'News from the London Office', *Eustomy*, April 1965.

75. Peter Benenson papers (in private possession), 4 August 1963, Neville Vincent to Benenson; 4 July [1963], Urquhart to Benenson. It was, for

instance, Urquhart – who held no formal position in the organisation – who wrote to Martin Luther King to invite him to speak at Amnesty's Human Rights Day commemoration on his way back from the Nobel Peace Prize ceremony in Oslo: 2 November 1964, Urquhart to Martin Luther King, available online at www.thekingcenter.org/archive/document/letter-clara-urquhart-mlk.

76. For instance, Norman Marsh and his wife intended to give the proceeds from the sale of a Rembrandt print to Amnesty and other groups he was involved in (IISH, AI IS, 1006, 11 March 1963, Marsh to Mr Shins. Likewise, in 1967–68 a group of leading British members acted as guarantors for salaried posts (IISH, AI IS, 1177).

77. IISH, AI IS, 1190, policy committee minutes, 2 August 1962, Oxfam gave £250 for families in Portugal.

78. Peter Benenson papers (private possession), 21 August 1961, Baker to Benenson; E. Larsen, *Flame in Barbed Wire: The Story of Amnesty International* (London: F. Muller, 1978), p. 19; IISH, AI IS, 982, Benenson's 1983 essay, p. 12.

79. Keith Siviter and Tom Sargant both talk frankly openly about the Prisoners of Conscience Fund in their interviews (IISH, AI IS, 992 and 991): Tom Sargant, 21 June 1985, pp. 58–9, and Keith Siviter, 5 June 1984, pp. 17–20. In his interview (982) Benenson states that 'we siphoned [the fund] into administrative work, perhaps illegally, but it couldn't go for any political purpose . . . ' (12 November 1983, p. 133). The fund was first discussed at Policy Committee, 7 March 1962 (IISH, AI IS, 1190), but had been opened by Neville Vincent on 10 July 1961, IISH, AI IS, 1249, Vincent to Hoare & Co. (MRC, 292B/863/4, 'Amnesty: An International Movement for Freedom of Opinion and Religion', p. 2). In his interview (IISH, AI IS, 987), 8 June 1984, p. 2, MacBride claimed to have chaired the Fund from the start and said that in order to regularise it he had asked for a Trust Deed to be drawn up on 11 October 1962. Benenson hired accountants for the Fund shortly afterwards, IISH, AI IS, 1249, 25 May 1963, Benenson to F. Nicholson.

80. Bodleian Library, Scott papers, Box 79, 21 March 1967, Benenson to Peter Calvocoressi.

81. It was agreed at Amnesty's Second International Conference, Sisjele, Belgium, 28–30 September 1962, to launch a 'World Human Rights Fund' sponsored by Nobel laureates (report p. 6). Lambeth Palace archives, RAMSEY 31, correspondence; RAMSEY 151, 13 March 1969, M Ennals to Ramsey.). Peter Benenson papers (in private possession), 7 July 1963, Benenson to Urquhart (draft of the appeal); IISH, AI IS, 1253, paper presented at Bruges; IISH, AI IS, 167, 22 March 1967, finance committee minutes.

82. Benenson's 'First Notes on Organisation', 5 June 1961 (IISH, AI IS, 1000).

83. The authorship of the 'office paper' is not attributed, but it is essentially the same as 'A Report on the First Six Months', submitted by Benenson (University of Bradford, Baker papers, 2/1). Here he argued that 'there is no practical voluntary machine for the release' of prisoners, and that Amnesty should focus on threats of execution or torture. The local groups

should undertake fundraising and educational work, such as annual lectures to schools on 'Tolerance'.

84. Copy in Jesuits in Britain archives, Roberts papers, 19/5/4. This handbook is undated, but presumably is the same booklet referred to in Peter Benenson papers (in private possession), 28 May [1963], Bert Lodge to Benenson – 'it makes you want to rush out and get yourself a prisoner'.

85. IISH, AI IS, 1190, Policy Committee minutes for 5 April 1962, 5 July 1962 and 19 March 1963; 7 March 1962.

86. *Amnesty*, 2, 11 July 1961 and 3, 25 July 1961.

87. IISH, AI IS, 1005; and 999, 2 October 1962 meeting of London Threes Groups.

88. Jesuits in Britain archives, Roberts papers, 19/5/1, report of the AI Königswinter conference, 20–22 September 1963.

89. ICS, Halpern papers, ICS 28/11/A, AI British Section, 3rd Annual Report, June 1963–May 1964.

90. *Amnesty*, 8, 4 October 1961, focus on Margaret Archer; IISH, AI IS, 986, Marlys Deeds interview transcript, 19 June 1985.

91. IISH, AI IS, 990, Diana Redhouse interview, 4 June 1984, pp. 27–8.

92. KCL, LDG papers, MGA CORRESP 1, 27 May 1962, Charles Pledger, Eltham Group to Pym; IISH, AI IS, 994, Dorothy Warner interview, 18 June 1985, p. 13.

93. *Amnesty*, 2, 11 July 1961.

94. *Observer Weekend Review*, 28 May 1961.

95. *Amnesty*, 5, 23 August 1961; IISH, AI IS, 988, Christel Marsh interview, 7 November 1983, pp. 18–20. For PEN ('Poets, Essayists and Novelists') see R. A. Wilford, 'The PEN Club, 1930–50', *Journal of Contemporary History*, vol. 14, no. 1 (1979), 99–116, and *PEN News*.

96. *Amnesty*, 5, 23 Aug. 1961; IISH, AI IS, 1190, Policy Committee minutes, 14 November 1961.

97. Larsen, *Flame in Barbed Wire*, p. 27.

98. Peter Benenson papers (AI), 14 June 1961, Benenson to David Ennals.

99. *Amnesty*, 11, 15 November 1961; Westminster Diocesan Archives, GO2/133b, typescript for colloquy on 'The Boundaries of Freedom' sets out the original plans.

100. IISH, AI IS, 982, Peter Benenson interview transcript, 12 November 1983, p. 34. In practice, however, the roles were not so clearly defined – for instance, in 1963 Benenson appealed to the UNA for financial assistance to allow a former *Observer* journalist to attend the trial of Baha'is in Morocco (LSE, UNA/3/1/15, UNA EC minutes, 12 January 1963).

101. IISH, AI IS, 982, Benenson's 1983 essay, pp. 12 and 13.

102. IISH, AI IS, 982, Benenson's 1983 essay, p. 13; 'The Shame of Portugal', *The Spectator*, 13 April 1962,; 'Portugal: the Government on the Defensive', *Eustomy* 2, 1964; Lord Russell of Liverpool (not to be confused with Bertrand Russell) published interviews with many prisoners, often denying Amnesty's claims, in *Prisons and Prisoners in Portugal: An Independent Investigation* (London: Waterlow, 1963); Peter Benenson papers (in private possession), 9 July 1963, Benenson to Editor, *Daily Telegraph*.

103. Peter Benenson papers (AI), 19 December 1975, Benenson to F. Stepan; Jesuit archives, Roberts papers, 19/5/4, 27 November 1964, Benenson to Archbishop Roberts.
104. Peter Benenson papers (AI), 24 January 1965, Benenson to Mr Harding.
105. *The Friend*, 17 June 1966, p. 706.
106. *Amnesty*, 2, 11 July; *Amnesty*, 3, 25 July 1961. An employment bureau was also appointed under the social activist Donald Chesworth, but does not appear to have met (IISH, AI IS, 1034 and 1036).
107. KCL, LDG papers, MGA CORRESP 1, Pym to Baker, 25 June 1961; Benenson to Pym, 28 June 1961.
108. IISH, AI IS, 3, Amnesty's Second International Conference, Sisjele, Belgium, 28–30 September 1962, pp. 5–6.
109. *Amnesty*, 1, 27 June 1961.
110. Jesuits in Britain archives, Roberts papers, 19/5/4, 24 November 1961, Benenson to Roberts with notes for Human Rights Day; Westminster Diocesan Archives, Godfrey papers, GO2/133b, 2 October 1961, Benenson to Worlock.
111. S. Moyn, *Christian Human Rights* (Philadelphia, PA: University of Pennsylvania Press, 2015), p. 176; S. Hopgood, *Keepers of the Flame: Understanding Amnesty International* (Ithaca, NY: Cornell University Press, 2006), pp. 3 and 8. See also M. Mazower, *Governing the World: the History of an Idea* (London: Penguin, 2013), p. 326, 'If Amnesty International was a kind of church, with its own congregation, other groups emerged in the United States [such as Helsinki Watch/Human Rights Watch] that looked less like churches and more like lobbies . . . .'
112. Peter Benenson papers (in private possession), 9 July 1963, Benenson to Editor, *Daily Telegraph*; Westminster Diocesan Archives, GO2/133b, 24 March 1962 Archbishop Godfrey to the Apostolic Delegate. See E. T. Fagan, 'The International Secretariat of Lawyers of Pax Romana', in *The Catholic Lawyer*, vol. 11, no. 2 (Spring 1965) (https://scholarship .law.stjohns.edu/cgi/viewcontent.cgi?referer=https://www.google.com /&httpsredir=1&article=1535&context=tcl).
113. Jesuits in Britain archives, Roberts papers, 19/5/4, Sermon notes for human rights day.
114. Peter Benenson papers (AI), handwritten notes for 'Talk at Swansea 8. v.62'. It is not clear if the 'Six Catholic reasons' belong to the lecture notes. The other approaches were those of the lawyer, democrat, pragmatist and humanitarian.
115. Peter Benenson papers (AI), 'Community of Conscience', lecture by Benenson to mark Amnesty's fifteenth anniversary, Berlin, 5 June 1976, pp. 9–10.
116. Report in *Amnesty* 1, 27 June 1961; Westminster Diocesan Archives, GO2/ 133b, resumé of the Paris conference on religious persecution, 20 June 1961.
117. Jesuits in Britain archives, Roberts papers, 19/5/1, 'Amnesty and the Archbishop', *The Month*, May 1970, p. 286.
118. Peter Benenson papers (in private possession), 23 October 1962, Benenson to Urquhart. The sentence concludes: ' . . . and especially appropriate to me,

who like you, is a member of the race from which God chose the mother to His son'.

119. *Peace News*, 2 June 1961, p. 8.
120. This final point derives from IISH, AI IS, 991, interview with Tom Sargant, 22 June 1985, p. 51.
121. Peter Benenson papers (AI), 24 February 1986, Benenson to Janet Johnstone.
122. Jesuits in Britain archives, Roberts papers, 21/4/6, 'Archbishop T. D. Roberts, 1893–1976', Benenson's tribute at a Thanksgiving mass, 1 October 1976, p. 13; IISH, AI IS, 982, Benenson interview, 12 November 1983, note added on 28 February 1989, p. 51, Benenson says he first wrote to Roberts in 1961 as a result of this sermon. Although the correspondence between Baker and Benenson rarely touches on Quaker affairs, it seems unlikely that Baker (who had sent books on Quakerism to Makarios) would have missed the opportunity to inform Benenson about it.
123. See for instance the implied reprimand in Baker's letter to Benenson, 1 April 1962: 'As you have realised by now, mine is a slow and unsubtle mind which prefers to know the whole blunt truth about a situation' (Peter Benenson papers (in private possession)). University of Bradford, Baker papers, 2/1, has a slightly earlier (draft?) version dated 29 March in which Baker warns Benenson against 'economy of truth'. Peter Benenson papers (in private possession), 10 July 1963, Baker to Benenson.
124. For instance, Marlys Deeds said that he 'hadn't any warmth' (IISH, AI IS, Box 986, interview 19 June 1985, p. 45), and the point is made strikingly in Peter Archer's obituary notice in *British Amnesty*, July/August 1976. Peggy Crane described Baker as 'crushed into the background' by Benenson (IISH, AI IS, 985, interview 17 June 1985, p. 22).
125. IISH, AI IS, 982, Peter Benenson interview, 12 November 1983, p. 94; for St Francis, Peter Benenson papers (in private possession), 28 March 1960, Benenson to Sargant; for John XXIII, Westminster Diocesan Archives, Godfrey papers, GO2/133b, 31 July 1961, Benenson to Worlock.
126. *Amnesty*, 1, 27 June 1961, Benenson article on 'The Persecution of Protestants'; *The Times*, 'The Anglican Church', 21 June 1961.
127. *Amnesty*, 14, 3 January 1962, p. 8.
128. Peter Benenson papers (AI), Benenson's notes for a talk in Swansea, 8 May 1962.
129. Jesuits in Britain archives, Roberts papers, 19/5/1, 12 October 1968, C. B. Carty to Roberts; IISH, AI IS, 1005, minutes of meetings.
130. Regent's Park College, Payne papers, March 1976, 'Amnesty International – Human Rights and the British Churches', p. 3, note by Steven Duckworth, Prison Coordinator, Kensington Amnesty Group.
131. See Father P. O'Mahoney, *One Parish and Human Rights* (Catholic Truth Society pamphlet CTS S311, 1974?); *The Catholic Herald*, 12 November 1971, p. 4.
132. *Baptist Times*, 9 February 1976, n.p.
133. IISH, AI IS, 992, Siviter interview, 5 June 1984, p. 5.
134. IISH, AI IS, 1296, 21 July 1967, Benenson to Baker.

135. IISH, AI IS, 1009 and 1012. In his application to the Dean and Chapter of St Paul's, Benenson indicated that he would be willing to limit the service to Anglicans (1 July 1964).

136. IISH, AI IS, 1006, November 1965 circular by Lionel Elvin.

137. C. Brown, *The Death of Christian Britain: Understanding Secularisation 1800–2000*, 2nd ed. (London: Routledge, 2009), ch. 8; H. McLeod, *The Religious Crisis of the 1960s* (Oxford University Press, 2007); H. Mcleod, 'The Religious Crisis of the 1960s', *Journal of Modern European History*, vol. 3, no. 2 (2005), 205–30; for a critique see J. Garnett (ed.), *Redefining Christian Britain: Post-1945 Perspectives* (London: SCM Press, 2007). See also S. J. D. Green, *The Passing of Protestant England: Secularisation and Social Change, c.1920–1960* (Cambridge University Press, Cambridge, 2011), pp. 242–302.

138. See below, p. 216.

139. See below, p. 225.

140. University of Bradford, Baker papers, 2/1, 18 March 1961, Benenson to Baker ('The French are going to form a Committee, and the moving spirit is a lawyer called Louis Pettiti').

141. Peter Benenson papers (in private possession), 29 August 1961, Benenson (to Baker?). A short-lived Moscow group was, indeed, created in the mid-1970s (see below, p. 202).

142. Benenson did not include Baker amongst those who had attended the meeting when interviewed, but MacBride did in his tribute to Baker in *The Friend*, 20 August 1976.

143. IISH, AI IS, 1163, 6 June 1961, MacBride to Benenson, and reply of 9 June 1961.

144. Westminster Diocesan papers, GO2/133b, 31 July 1961, Benenson to Worlock.

145. *Amnesty*, 3, 25 July 1961.

146. *Amnesty*, 4, 9 August 1961.

147. IISH, AI IS, 1190, Policy Committee minutes, 3 May 1962; IISH, AI IS, 982, Benenson interview, 12 November 1983, p. 161.

148. S. Snyder, 'Exporting Amnesty International to the United States: Transatlantic Human Rights Activism in the 1960s', *Human Rights Quarterly*, vol. 34, no. 3 (2012), 779–99.

149. See B. Bouwman, 'Outraged, Yet Moderate and Impartial: the Rise of Amnesty International in the Netherlands in the 1960s and 1970s', *BMGN: Low Countries Historical Review*, vol. 132, no. 4 (2017), 53–74. For West Germany see L. Wildenthal, *The Language of Human Rights in West Germany* (Philadelphia: University of Pennsylvania Press, 2013), pp. 76–88.

150. IISH, AI IS, 983, interview with Benenson, 6 June 1984, p. 215; the name had already been agreed at a planning meeting in October 1961.

151. IISH, AI IS, 3, report on conference.

152. IISH, AI IS, 982, Benenson's 1983 essay, p. 18.

153. *Amnesty*, 14, January 1962, 'The First Phase'.

154. Peter Benenson papers (in private possession), 9 August 1961, Benenson to Baker.

155. *The Friend*, 18 October 1963, p. 1204.
156. Peter Benenson papers (in private possession), June 1962 correspondence with Lord Weidenfeld; 10 December 1959, Benenson to Lord Weidenfeld regarding a commitment to write a book on 'The State of Freedom'; Benenson papers (in private possession), 18 February 1963, Benenson to Hilary Cartwright.
157. Peter Benenson papers (in private possession), 9 November 1983, Benenson to Sargant (?); and 14 August 1961, Benenson to (unknown); 10 November 1962, Benenson to Shawcross.
158. Peter Benenson papers (in private possession), 26 July 1963, Benenson to Clara Urquhart.
159. Bodleian Library, Brit Emp S.19 D 10/17, Box 1, File 1, June 1964, Benenson was listed as a patron for the Association of Nazi Camp Survivors.
160. Bodleian Library, Mss Perham, 25/1. Meetings were held in London and Geneva, in June and July 1964.
161. Peter Benenson papers (in private possession), 19 June 1962. In a letter to Weidenfeld, Benenson expressed the hope that by the end of the year his roles in Justice and Amnesty would be 'largely supervisory'; Norman Marsh refers to Benenson's 'subsidiary ideas' in IISH, AI IS, 989, interview transcript, June 1984, p. 54. Clara Urquhart reminded Benenson that he had promised his wife that he would 'give up the Executive administration of AMNESTY by the end of the year' (Peter Benenson papers, in private possession, 12 October 1962, Urquhart to Benenson). In early 1965 Albert Lodge went as far as to organise a scrapbook to mark Benenson's imminent retirement after four years in post. He even commissioned an affectionate sketch by Haro Hodson of Benenson arriving at the Amnesty office 'in overcoat, harassed, scarf too long, hanging down, rather like [a] Northern comic arriving on stage, briefcase bulging ... ' (IISH, AI IS, 1010, 11 February 1965, Lodge to Hodson).

5 'THE CRISIS OF GROWTH': AMNESTY INTERNATIONAL 1964–1968

1. In 1967 MacBride investigated what had actually been agreed and decided that there was no evidence that Benenson had been appointed 'life President' as he was currently claiming (University of Bradford, Baker papers, 2/4, 1 February 1967, MacBride to Baker, Swann and Enthoven). See also IISH, AI IS, 1294, 27 December 1966, MacBride to Baker (citing the original resolution).
2. See the profile of Halpern in *Jewish Chronicle*, 'Incidentally' column, 2 October 1964.
3. See below, pp. 142–3.
4. IISH, AI IS, 1006, Halpern to Vincent, 20 October 1964.
5. ICS, Halpern papers, 28/11/E, 8 February 1965, Halpern to Neta Eran, and 28/11/E, 21 February 1965, Halpern to Yael Hirson; 28/12/A, 7 January 1965, Halpern to 'Fred'. Unfortunately, not all of Halpern's personal correspondence is available (although some details

are given in the handlist): I am grateful to Richard Temple and Mrs Sophie Halpern for their advice. See also IISH, AI IS, 1006, especially 19 October 1964, Halpern to Benenson.

6. Bodleian Library, Scott papers, Box 79, undated typescript, 'Du Cote de Chez Swann', p. 1; ibid., 'The Amnesty Take-Over Bid', undated, p. 3.

7. Bodleian Library, Scott papers, Box 79, 'Takeover', p. 3. For the discussion of the merits of the candidates see IISH, AI IS, 1006.

8. Bodleian Library, Scott papers, Box 79, 'Du Cote de Chez Swann'; 'Report on Certain Matters Affecting Amnesty, Presented to Sean MacBride by Peter Calvocoressi, March 1967' (hence 'Calvocoressi report'), p. 5.

9. For a fuller account see T. Buchanan, 'Amnesty International in Crisis, 1966–7', *Twentieth Century British History*, vol. 15, no. 3 (2004), 267–89. In the following section I have prioritised source material that I did not have access to at the time of writing the original article.

10. J. Grant, *Jack Grant's Story* (Guildford: Lutterworth Press, 1980), pp. 150–2.

11. In a tribute after Elwyn Jones's death in 1990, Benenson said that without his 'persistent support the operation would soon have been brought to its end' ('Fred Elwyn Jones' in Benenson papers (AI)). There is no trace of these activities in Elwyn Jones's papers or autobiography (*In My Time: an Autobiography* (London: Weidenfeld and Nicolson, 1983).

12. The operation was latterly run directly by the Christian Council, aided by volunteers on tourist visas.

13. See Buchanan, 'Amnesty International in Crisis'.

14. For a good recent account see B. Drohan, *Brutality in an Age of Human Rights: Activism and Counterinsurgency at the End of the British Empire* (Ithaca, NY & London: Cornell University Press, 2018), ch. 3.

15. AI British Section AGM report, 11 June 1966.

16. Bodleian Library, Scott papers, Box 79, 'Take-Over', p. 20.

17. Ibid., p. 27.

18. TNA, FO953/2506, 20 October 1966, Benenson to G. Brown.

19. 'Aden: Rastgeldi Report Vindicated', *AI Bulletin*, 18, February 1967; *Hansard*, 19 December 1966, col. 1007. The Justice Council minutes, 9 October 1963, p. 1, show that in 1963 both Bowen and Benenson were members of Justice's Finance and Membership Committee, Hull History Centre, UDJU 2/2. For the debate over the Bowen report see: S. Dingli, and C. Kennedy, 'The Aden Pivot? British Counter-Insurgency after Aden', *Civil Wars*, vol. 16, no. 1 (2014), 86–104, and H. Bennett, '"Detainees Are Always One's Achilles Heel": The Struggle over the Scrutiny of Detention and Interrogation in Aden, 1963–1967', *War in History*, vol. 23, no. 4 (2016), 457–88.

20. The main source is the correspondence in IISH, AI IS, 1032: see in particular the February 1967 memorandum by Stella Joyce. For Benenson's suspicions see IISH, AI IS, 1295, 9 January 1967, Benenson to Hoare's Bank (Amnesty's banker) and Bodleian Library, Scott papers, Box 79, 'The Amnesty Take-Over', pp. 7–11. Groth later alleged that he had been falsely accused of being a CIA spy by a Danish communist journalist (IISH, AI IS, 1033, 3 March 1967, Bent Knudsen to Amnesty).

21. University of Bradford, Baker papers, 2/4, draft letter to the press.
22. IISH, AI IS, 1295, MacBride's press release, 20 February 1967; Benenson to MacBride, 23 February 1967.
23. *Sunday Telegraph*, 5 March 1967, p. 13 (with Toynbee interview); *Sunday Times*, 5 March 1967, p. 1.
24. *Hansard*, 9 March 1967, col. 342.
25. *Guardian*, 6 March 1967, p. 16.
26. IISH, AI IS, 1293, MacBride's 'Chronological Table of Events', p. 12, and associated 'Interview Held in Geneva'.
27. IISH, AI IS, 1295, 15 February 1967, MacBride to Calvocoressi with his terms of reference.
28. IISH, AI IS, 39, for text of interviews; *The Times*, 13 March 1967, p. 4: Swann denied any knowledge of secret government funds and said that, while in Rhodesia, he was so busy doing relief work that there had been 'no time to think of where the money came from'. Calvocoressi predicted his departure in Bodleian Library, Scott papers, Box 79, Calvocoressi to Benenson, 19 April 1967. Less accurately, he predicted that MacBride would also go.
29. P. Calvocoressi, *Threading My Way* (London: Duckworth, 1994), p. 159. When I sent Calvocoressi an early draft of my article, drawing his attention to the declassified material from the National Archives, he replied as follows: 'My answer to your question of how much I knew of the events you narrate is "virtually nothing"' (Calvocoressi to the author, 12 July 2001).
30. IISH, AI IS, 1293, MacBride's chronological table of events, additional note for 6 February 1967; Calvocoressi report, pp. 8–9.
31. University of Bradford, Baker papers, 2/2, Baker to C. van der Vlies, 31 May 1967.
32. Calvocoressi report, p. 23.
33. IISH, AI IS, 1296, letters from Brian Horrocks 14 March 1967, AI Bristol Branch, 5 March 1967, and Irmgard Payne, Oxted AI group, 9 March 1967.
34. IISH, AI IS, 1265, circular by Tony Barton, May 1967.
35. British Section report, 1967/8, p. 4.
36. University of Bradford, Baker papers, 2/2, 31 May 1967, Baker to C. van der Vlies. Indeed, Baker took some comfort in the fact that Amnesty's 'crisis has made front page news in more than one country' as proof of the movement's success.
37. The Intel 68 of 1963 was cancelled. According to an internal FCO memorandum, FO Intel 11, 9 May 1967 had insisted that relations must be one 'of reserve' – a pen note added 'largely owing to their activities in connection with Aden at the end of 1966' (FCO 61/185, King to Morphet, undated [1968]).
38. University of Bradford, Baker papers, 2/2, 31 May 1967, Baker to C. van der Vlies, and 4 June 1967, reply.
39. Jesuits in Britain archives, Roberts papers, 19/5/1, 3 April 1967 and 13 April 1967, Justice T. C. Kingsmill Moore to Archbishop Roberts. O'Donovan had been secretary of the Section since 1963 and had visited East Germany on Amnesty's behalf in 1965 (*Irish Times*, 10 April 1967, p. 10 and 11 April 1967, p. 7).

40. University of Bradford, Baker papers, 2/4, 12 March 1967, Vincent to Baker; 2/1, 27 March 1962, Benenson to Baker.
41. As MacBride interpreted it, Wilson's willingness to meet Smith was the trigger for Benenson's attempt to repay the money.
42. IISH, AI IS, 1295, 9 January 1967, Benenson to Baker. This letter refers to a previous meeting between the two men on 5 January, of which there is a note in Baker's papers. According to this, Baker said that money from the groups for donation to Southern Rhodesia should still go there: Benenson 'said yes but he wasn't having it go through British Intelligence channels' (University of Bradford, Baker papers, 2/4, note of meeting on 5 January 1967).
43. University of Bradford, Baker papers, 2/4, Baker's notes, 2 March 1967.
44. IISH, AI IS, 1296, 'Private and Confidential Letter to All Members' from Eric Baker, 20 March 1967.
45. March 1966 IEC minutes, item 4a.
46. IISH, AI IS, 1296, 6 March 1967, Baker to AI members; undated draft, my emphasis.
47. IISH, AI IS, 1296, MacBride interview, 'not for publication before' 11 March 1967. My emphasis.
48. Bodleian Library, Scott papers, Box 79, 21 March 1967, Scott to Calvocoressi.
49. IISH, AI IS, 1296, 9 March 1967, Menuhin to Baker. At seminars at which I have spoken about Amnesty's crisis over the years, the argument of the greater good has often been strongly articulated in discussion.
50. TNA FCO 36/436, memorandum of meeting with George Thomson, 13 December 1968.
51. IISH, AI IS, 1296, 11 March 1967, MacBride interview.
52. Bodleian Library, Scott papers, Box 81, text for 'Persecution 1963', 8 December 1963; Scott papers, Box 42, 26 July 1965, Benenson to Scott greeting the latter on his return from India.
53. University of Bradford, Baker papers, 2/4, 9 January 1967, Benenson to Baker.
54. Bodleian Library, Scott papers, Box 79, Benenson to Scott, 21 March, 5 April and 30 April 1967.
55. These are the two accounts in the Bodleian Library, Scott papers, Box 79 ('Du Cote de Chez Swann' and 'Take-Over'). The two men were also brought together by one of the bizarre footnotes to this story: a letter from Benenson to President Kaunda of Zambia, dated 22 November 1966, which Benenson alleged was a forgery. In the letter, Benenson purported to warn Kaunda that human rights abuses in Zambia and other newly independent African states could alienate Western opinion and result in a 'new occupation of Africa'. Scott intervened personally with Kaunda, who now regarded the matter as closed. There is a copy of the letter in IISH, AI IS, 1313, 22 November 1966; Bodleian Library, Scott papers, Box 79, 11 April 1967, Kaunda to Benenson.
56. IISH, AI IS, 1023, 4 June 1961, Benenson to Philip Woodfield.
57. As the Amnesty crisis unfolded Benenson appealed to Jenkins 'because we have known each other personally, militarily and politically without

interruption since 1939 . . . ' (Jesuits in Britain archives, Roberts papers, 19/ 5/1). In his memoirs Jenkins barely mentions Benenson, referring to him only as an 'unusual Etonian' whom he had met at Balliol and Bletchley Park (*A Life at the Centre* (London: Macmillan, 1991), p. 31).

58. Churchill College, Cambridge, GARD 19, 1/4, text of speech, 19 January 1966.

59. Bodleian Library, Scott papers, Box 79, 'Take-Over', p. 16. The Lord Chancellor saw it slightly differently: 'Amnesty held the Swedish complaint as long as they could simply because Peter Benenson did not want to do anything to hurt a Labour Government' (TNA, PREM 13/1294, 4 November 1966, Gerald Gardiner to Prime Minister).

60. Marreco to the author, 31 October 2002.

61. Jesuits in Britain archives, Roberts papers, 19/5/4, Benenson to Roberts, 27 November 1964.

62. Peter Benenson papers (AI), 2 June 1961, Philip Woodfield to Benenson; IISH, AI IS, 1023, 4 June 1961, Benenson to Philip Woodfield. See also Peter Benenson papers (AI), Benenson to the Foreign Secretary, 5 June 1961.

63. See T. Shaw's article, 'The Information Research Department of the British Foreign Office and the Korean War, 1950–1953', *Journal of Contemporary History*, vol. 34, no. 2 (April 1999), 262–81 for a good introduction to its work.

64. TNA CAB/301/399, Lord Strang, 'A Report on the Unavowable Information Services of Her Majesty's Government Overseas', July 1963, pp. 17 and 21 (heavily redacted).

65. *The Guardian*, 23 July 2018, mentions Ampersand books. Cranston went on a mission for Amnesty to Romania in 1962.

66. TNA FO 1110/1475, 10 July 1965, Ariel Foundation to Foreign Office with confidential report; IISH, AI IS, 1022, 11 November 1961, Foley to Peggy Crane.

67. IISH, AI IS, 1190, Policy Committee 2 August 1962. However, Foley does not appear to have attended any meetings. For Benenson's suspicions see Bodleian Library, Scott papers, 'The Amnesty Take-Over', p. 1.

68. TNA, FO 371/189943, 4 February 1966, responding to a parliamentary question by Amnesty member Paul Rose, a briefing memorandum admitted that IRD 'maintain regular contact with Amnesty primarily for the exchange of information'.

69. Bodleian Library, Scott papers, Box 79, 'Take-Over', p. 3.

70. Benenson papers (in private possession), 15 August 1961, Benenson to Christopher Barclay.

71. Benenson papers (in private possession), Benenson to Barclay, 1 August 1963.

72. Bodleian Library, Scott papers, Box 79, 'Du Cote de Chez Swann', p. 2 (This title of this typescript is a pun on the first volume of Proust's *À la recherche du temps perdu*, 1909).

73. Peter Benenson papers (in private possession), Benenson's letter of 21 January 1963. Although the recipient is not specified, the contents indicate clearly that this was Christopher Barclay of IRD.

74. Bodleian Library, Scott papers, Box 79, 21 March 1967, Scott to Calvocoressi.
75. Bodleian Library, Scott papers, Box 79, 'Takeover', pp. 3–5, 'Du Cote de Chez Swann', p. 2. Andrew Roth obituary of Vernon, *Guardian*, 25 August 2000.
76. University of Bradford, Baker papers, 2/4, 29 November 1966, Swann to Benenson.
77. Bodleian Library, Scott papers, Box 79, 'Take-Over', p. 3. Benenson told Barclay that, after Halpern, Amnesty, 'once-bitten, would not advertise again but would make a private appointment'. When Benenson asked Barclay for a reference for Robert Swann he said 'no comment' – which Benenson took as evidence that the Foreign Office had no objection ('Du Cote de Chez Swann', p. 3).
78. University of Bradford, Baker papers, 2/4, Baker's notes of meeting with Benenson, 5 January 1967.
79. TNA FO 953/2506, 9 November 1966, W. Maitland to Permanent Under-Secretary (who signalled his disagreement).
80. TNA, DEFE 24.252, 12 December 1966, Brigadier Gibbon to Ministry of Defence.
81. Bodleian Library, Scott papers, Box 15, 24 June 1983, Astor to Scott.
82. Jesuits in Britain archives, Roberts papers, 19/5/1 for text of the appeal; *The Times*, 27 February 1967, p. 1.
83. NSA Briefing book #572, Document 2, CIA, Report, 'Counterterrorism in the Southern Cone', Secret, 9 May 1977, https://nsarchive.gwu.edu/b riefing-book/southern-cone/2016-12-14/operation-condor-officials-amnesty-international-targeted, document dated 9 May 1977; National Archives, NARA Record Number: 104–10225-10027; archives.gov. Page 14, www.archives.gov/files/research/jfk/releases/2018/104–10225-10027 .pdf#page=14 takes a close interest in Amnesty.
84. University of Bradford, Baker, 2/4, 7 December 1971, MacBride to Lothar Belcke. My emphasis. When interviewed by the Irish national broadcaster RTE a few weeks earlier he had denied that the British secret services had infiltrated Amnesty but said that it was 'always a danger' and that there was a 'British machine' at work (*The Irish Times*, 15 November 1971, p. 10). MacBride had written prior to the Calvocoressi report that 'I agree entirely as to the dangers of Secret Service infiltration', but that the facts must be established (University of Bradford, Baker papers, 2/4, MacBride to Arno Christensen, 1 February 1967).
85. Benenson papers (AI), Benenson to Richard Reoch, 6 December 1985. One of the best-known images of the massacre had also been used on the cover of *Persecution 1961*.
86. *The Guardian*, 30 May 1961.
87. IISH, AI IS, 1033, Mandela to Amnesty, 11 November 1962. Mandela sent an equally courteous letter to Christian Action (*Christian Action Newsletter*, February 1963).

88. C. J. Driver, *Patrick Duncan: South African and Pan-African* (Oxford: James Currey, 2000). In 1964 Duncan refused to help Amnesty investigate political imprisonment in Algeria, where he was currently working, as he was against political arrests 'except in the many cases where such arrests are necessary', although this does not appear to have affected the warmth of his relationship with Benenson (Borthwick Institute, Duncan papers, 5.3, 27 August 1964, Duncan to Mrs Teitelbaum).

89. See E. Larsen, *Flame in Barbed Wire: The Story of Amnesty International* (London: F. Muller, 1978), pp. 24–5. For the Oxted group see *Eustomy*, April 1965, 6.

90. IISH, AI IS, 1007, Eltham group minutes for 22 June 1964.

91. *The Guardian*, 15 June 1964, p. 3.

92. The principal source for the 'poll', appears to be Larsen, *Flame in Barbed Wire*, p. 24, and J. Power, *Against Oblivion, Amnesty International's Fight for Human Rights* (London: Fontana, 1981), p. 23, where Larsen refers to a poll producing an 'overwhelming majority' in favour of the status quo. See ICS, Halpern papers, 28/11/C, 'Violence and Racialism: a Report on the *Eustomy* Questionnaire', 26 September 1964. On the brink of taking office Halpern signalled his commitment to Amnesty's 'present limited, agreed aims' in an article under the pseudonym 'James Fairbairn', *New Statesman*, 23 September 1964.

93. Power, *Against Oblivion*, ch. 5, pp. 129–35.

94. MRC, Gollancz papers, Mss 157/3/AF/2/1/1–135, 19 May 1960, Urquhart to Gollancz; Benenson papers (in private possession), 4 January 1963, Urquhart to Benenson.

95. According to Urquhart, in 1963 Benenson was Tambo's first choice to lead a new organisation for political prisoners in South Africa: Benenson suggested Archbishop Roberts instead. Benenson papers (in private possession), 26 July 1963, Benenson to Urquhart; Jesuits in Britain archives, Roberts papers, 19/5/1, Benenson to Roberts.

96. Benenson papers (private possession), 23 October 1962, Urquhart to Benenson.

97. This was a compendium of short essays on non-violence by Dolci, Scott, Schweitzer and others (*A Matter of Life* (London: Cape, 1963). She edited a similar collection for Amnesty entitled *A Time to Keep Silence and a Time to Speak* (London: Amnesty International, 1962). Urquhart also paid the wages of Amnesty worker Iolanthe Elek.

98. The proposal was discussed – and politely turned down – at the SAFG sponsors' meeting; Bodleian, Africa Bureau papers, Box 205, File 3, 21 Nov. 1962; Benenson papers (in private possession), 12 October 1962, Urquhart's comments on Benenson's draft. For a different version of this scheme see Borthwick Institute, Duncan papers, 5.3, Benenson to Duncan, 9 August 1962.

99. Benenson papers (in private possession), Benenson to Urquhart 25 January 1964 and reply 27 January.

100. Larsen, *Flame in Barbed Wire*, pp. 25–6.

101. TNA, FO 953/2506 for copy of the report and annexes.
102. *The Spectator*, 11 September 1964, letter from Albert Lodge.
103. See TNA, CO 1048/570, Benenson to Lord Lansdowne, Colonial Secretary, 29 May 1963.
104. One official accused Cunningham of complicity in 100 deaths in the 'Bathurst Bay Ferry disaster of 1958', but I have been able to find no record of this event, which presumably refers to the modern Banjul in the Gambia (TNA, FO 953/2506, High Commission to Colonial Office, 19 October 1964). Clara Urquhart's original choice for the post had been Guy Clutton-Brock, IISH, AI IS, 1253, Urquhart to Benenson, 22 October 1963.
105. *Sunday Telegraph*, 5 March 1967, p. 13.
106. TNA CO 1048/570, 10 July 1964, Benenson to Nigel Fisher.
107. See Borthwick Institute, SRLA&WF papers, file 1, 29 May 1964, M. Haddon to Benenson, 8 February 1965, M. Haddon to Benenson; for Vodden see file 1, 8 September 1965, Benenson to Haddon; file 3 for Guy Clutton-Brock to M. Haddon, 4 January 1964.
108. Borthwick Institute, SRLA&WF papers, file 3, 11 January 1964, Clutton-Brock to Haddon.
109. Bodleian Library, Africa Bureau papers, Box 254, file 8, 22 November 1965, 'Inauguration of Association for Legal Action in Rhodesia'.
110. TNA, FO 371/190600; the letter was signed by John Foster, Benenson, Blom-Cooper and Vincent.
111. Bodleian Library, Africa Bureau, Box 254, File 8, has the minutes from 22 November 1965 to June 1966; Box 259, File 1 for other papers; Hull History Centre also has a file, with some overlap, but takes the minutes to October 1966.
112. Bodleian Library, Africa Bureau, Box 254, file 8, HRAS Rhodesia Committee, minutes for 23 December 1965.
113. Bodleian Library, Africa Bureau, Box 254, file 8, HRAS Rhodesia Committee, minutes for 30 December 1965.
114. Borthwick Institute, University of York, Lemkin papers, File 2, HRAS minutes, May 1966.
115. All in TNA, DO 207/63.
116. 'Amnesty and "Harry"', *Sunday Times*, 5 March 1967.
117. TNA, DO 207/63, report of 22 February 1966, p. 6.
118. Hull History Centre, DJU/11/56, HRAS minutes for 19 October 1966.
119. Hull History Centre, D JU/11/56, HRAS minutes for 14 September, 5 October and 19 October 1966. The Rhodesians were presumably representatives of the African nationalist organisation ZANU, which had sent a representative to the committee (see minutes for 13 July 1966).
120. Bodleian Library, Scott papers, Box 24, 18 July 1967, Stephanie Grant to Scott.
121. IISH, AI IS, 1273, 26 May 1970, British Section EC minutes; subsequent minutes refer to the winding up of the 'Human Rights Trust' and the splitting of £3000 between the Institute and Amnesty (IISH, AI IS, 1274, minutes for 15 October 1970 and 1 December 1970). The interview with

Keith Siviter confirms that this Human Rights Trust was in fact the HRAS money (IISH, AI IS, 992, 5 June 1984, p. 17).

122. IISH, AI IS, 1167, 22 March 1967, Finance Committee minutes; IISH, AI IS, 1256, undated paper on 'Relief Accounts' (1973?).

123. IISH, AI IS, 1254, 21 January 1970, Ennals to Bernard Sheridan. Sheridan – a lawyer who was now Secretary at War on Want – had worked with Benenson in the HRAS.

124. University of Bradford, Baker papers, 2/1, Baker to C. van der Vlies, 31 May 1967. The Amnesty launch papers emphasised that it would 'avoid formal committees' in order to be 'speedy, and relatively efficient' (KCL, LDG papers, MGA CORRESP 1).

125. David Boulton, 'Amnesty: Not Quite Clean Enough', *New Statesman*, 17 March 1967, p. 353.

126. Although it flared up again in the mid-1970s; see below, p. 213.

127. The title of this section is from the Regent's Park College, Oxford, Payne papers, Human Rights box, title of the first section of AI British Section report, 1967–8.

128. University of Bradford, Baker papers, 2/2, 31 May 1967, Baker to C. van der Vlies; 9 June 1967 Baker to Goran Claesson; no date [*c.* July 1967] Baker to Goran Claesson.

129. University of Bradford, Baker papers, 2/2, undated [25 April 1967], draft message. This was the result of a working party on finances set up at Elsinore.

130. University of Bradford, Baker papers, 2/2, 21 May 1967, van der Vlies to Baker; British Section report 1967/8; in the summer and autumn of 1967 the British Section gave £1000 and a loan of £3000, in addition to £3570 in subscriptions, to the International Secretariat (IS).

131. Bodleian Library, Scott papers, Box 2, 15 April 1967, MacBride to Scott.

132. University of Bradford, Baker papers, 2/2, 10 June 1967, Baker to Hans-Goran Franck.

133. AI British Section report, 1967–8.

134. The details of the appointment are in IISH, AI IS, 1177.

135. Peter Benenson, 'Human Rights Day: No Abatement of Violence', *The Scotsman*, 10 December 1964.

136. *Daily Worker*, 22 June 1968.

137. Power, *Against Oblivion*, pp. 31–2.

138. S. Jensen, *The Making of International Human Rights: the 1960s, Decolonization, and the Reconstruction of Global Values* (New York: Cambridge University Press, 2016), pp. 198–9, has a good discussion of the meeting.

139. IISH, AI IS, 1293, IEC minutes, 1 September 1966.

140. *Amnesty International Review*, 25, November 1968. Ennals in *Amnesty International Annual Report* for 1968–9.

141. Benenson papers (AI), 10 December 1974, Benenson to Mrs Francoise Clark.

142. *British Amnesty News*, June 1971; Jesuits in Britain archives, Roberts papers, 19/6/2, Benenson signed Archbishop Roberts' menu; intriguingly, the seating plan shows that Benenson was flanked by his wife Margaret and Marna Glyn – Swann sat six spaces away (IISH, AI IS, 1275).

143. P. Benenson, *The Other Face* (The Pauper's Press, Oxford, 1977).
144. Peter Benenson papers (AI), 12 March 1979, Benenson to Mark Benenson.
145. Calvocoressi report, p. 22.
146. Bodleian Library, Scott papers, Box 79, 30 April 1967, Benenson to Scott; Box 2, 21 July 1967, Benenson to MacBride; IISH, AI IS, 1009, 21 July 1967, Benenson to Baker.

6 1968: THE UN YEAR FOR HUMAN RIGHTS

1. S. Jensen, *The Making of International Human Rights: the 1960s, Decolonization, and the Reconstruction of Global Values* (New York: Cambridge University Press, 2016).
2. R. Burke, 'From Individual Rights to National Development: The First UN International Conference on Human Rights, Tehran, 1968', *Journal of World History*, vol. 19, no. 3 (2008), 275–96, and '"How Time Flies": Celebrating the Universal Declaration of Human Rights in the 1960s', *The International History Review*, vol. 38, no. 3 (2015), 13–21.
3. Jesuits in Britain archives, Roberts papers, 19/5/1, 23 June 1968, AGM of British Section; minutes of same meeting in Hull History Centre, UDCL 608/5, p. 2; IISH, AI IS, 996, MacBride to Eric Baker, 30 May 1968.
4. *AI Review*, 24 August 1968.
5. *Toward an NGO Strategy for the Advancement of Human Rights* (Conference report, 1968), p. 1. I am grateful to Steven Jensen for directing me to this document.
6. Burke, 'Celebrating the Universal Declaration', pp. 20–1.
7. KCL, LDG papers, INFO XVI, 'universities' file, Betty Ambatielos to Marion Sarafis, 15 February 1968.
8. J. Becket, *Barbarism in Greece: a Young American Lawyer's Inquiry into the Use of Torture in Contemporary Greece, with Case Histories and Documents* (New York: Walker, 1970), p. x.
9. See L. Heerten, *The Biafran War and Postcolonial Humanitarianism: Spectacles of Suffering* (Cambridge University Press, 2017).
10. Bodleian Library, Oxfam papers, DR/2/3/4/4, report of AI observer in Jakarta, 9–16 April 1966, pp. 5–6.
11. *Peace News*, 15 November 1968, p. 5.
12. Chapter title in T. Garton Ash, *The Uses of Adversity: Essays on the Fate of Central Europe* (Cambridge: Granta, 1989).
13. Hull History Centre, UDJU 2/2, 6 April 1965, memorandum by Secretary.
14. N. H. Twitchell, *The Politics of the Rope: the Campaign to Abolish Capital Punishment in Britain, 1955–1969* (Bury St Edmunds: Arena, 2012).
15. H. Wilson, *The New Britain: Labour's Plan* (Harmondsworth: Penguin, 1964), pp. 88–9 (speech of 20 April 1964).
16. Draft message in TNA FO371/183652.
17. *Labour Party Conference Report*, 1 October 1968, p. 169.
18. *Tribune*, 1968; speech by Gerry Fitt reported in the *Oxford Times*, 6 December 1968.

19. *Labour Party Conference Report*, 1970, p. 170; see also Wilson's comments in a speech that 'the battle against racialism knows no limits . . . Its boundaries are not the civic limits of Birmingham or Bradford or Wilverhampton [*sic*]. They extend to Africa – south of the Zambesi as well as north of the Zambesi . . .', *Birmingham Post*, 6 May 1968.

20. Bow Group pamphlet, *Coloured Peoples in Britain*, by Anthony McGowan, 1952, p. 4, and memorandum on *Coloured Peoples in Britain*, 1958, pp. 1–2, copies in Bodleian Library, Howe papers, Ms Howe Dep. 107.

21. PEP, *Racial Discrimination in Britain* (London: PEP, 1967).

22. *New Statesman*, 'When Labour Played the Racist Card', 22 January 1999, contains a good summary of the Cabinet discussions.

23. *Birmingham Post*, 6 May 1968.

24. Copy of the 4 March 1968 circular in Birmingham Library, IWA papers, Mss 2141, A/4/6.

25. *Peace News*, 1 March 1968, no. 1.

26. *Observer Review*, 3 March 1968; Unattributed cutting, 'A Question of Integration', 9 February 1968, in MRC, Mss 292B/805.9/5; Indian Workers' Association papers, Library of Birmingham, Mss 2141 A/1/2, notes for meeting with David Ennals, 1 October 1967.

27. MRC, Mss 292B/805.9/6, 14 June 1968, TUC International Department to Mr Baker; *The Guardian*, 1 November 1968, p. 22.

28. B. W. Heineman, *The Politics of the Powerless: a Study of the Campaign Against Racial Discrimination* (Oxford University Press, 1972); D. Hiro and S. Fay, 'Race Relations', *Sunday Times*, 29 October 1967 gives a helpful overview of the organisations and personalities. One of CARD's stated aims was for the British government to ratify the Universal Declaration of Human Rights – presumably a reference to the Covenants (*The Friend*, 5 February 1965, p. 131).

29. Borthwick Institute, York, SRLA&WF papers, File 1, 23 January 1963, J. Symonds to M. Haddon.

30. Nottinghamshire Archives, DD/CR/59/1, 8 July 1967, 'Equal Rights for Women in Britain' by Mrs M. K. Baxter.

31. Ibid., p. 1.

32. *Guardian*, 13 December 1968, p. 3. The UNA's Field Officer during Human Rights Year, Keith Dowding, reported that local committees were neglecting women's rights and saw it as a 'subject for academic discussion', Bodleian Library, Anti-Slavery Society, S.22 G881 4R, File B, EC minutes for 24 July 1968.

33. Nottinghamshire Archives, DD/CR/59/1, May 1967, UK Committee circular.

34. *Peace News*, 24 March 1967, p. 2.

35. Birmingham Library, Mss 2141, A/4/1, 29 July 1969, circular letter from Charles Parker, organising a meeting on Travellers in the West Midlands; *Peace News*, 5 April 1968, p. 12. See also NCCL 1972 Annual Report.

36. When moving the bill the Liberal MP Eric Lubbock, later Lord Avebury, stated that it dealt 'with the problem of gipsies and other travellers'. Bodleian Library, Anti-Slavery Society, S.22 G881, File B, February 1968 NCCL briefing.

37. Nottinghamshire Archives, DD/CR/59/1, Preparatory Committee minutes for 22 June and 26 July 1967. Ironically, Balloon Woods became the site of a notorious modernist housing development, built in 1970 and demolished in 1984.

38. The official brochure, *Human Rights* (London: Central Office of Information, 1967), features Magna Carta prominently on p. 7.

39. LSE, UNA papers, UNA 3/1/19, minutes for 30 March 1968.

40. TNA, FO371/189943, minutes of meeting of 5 May 1966.

41. ICS, Halpern papers, ICS 28/13/B, memorial service, Westminster Abbey, 26 January 1968. In 1970 a white Rhodesian woman who had adopted a black African baby was awarded £2000 to study race relations in Rhodesia (*The Guardian*, 27 June 1970).

42. *Peace News*, 15 December 1967, pp. 1, 12; Bodleian Library, Anti-Slavery Society, S.22 G881, File A, address by Calder to the HRY committee, 8 June 1967; File B, Ballot papers for new chair.

43. Bodleian Library, Anti-Slavery Society, S.22 G881, File A, circular for publication in *New World*, July 1967.

44. *New World*, January 1968, p. 3: the conventions were for the elimination of all forms of Racial Discrimination, and two ILO conventions concerning discrimination in employment.

45. LMA, Board of Deputies papers, Acc 3121/E4/311, Evans circular, 26 April 1968 (emphasis in original).

46. LSE, UNA 3/1/18, minutes for 6 January 1968.

47. Bodleian Library, Anti-Slavery Society, S.22 G881 4R, File A, Executive Committee minutes for 4 May 1967; and 30 November 1967.

48. Bodleian Library, Anti-Slavery Society, S.22 G881, File B, EC minutes, 30 October 1968.

49. Manchester Archives, Bernard Langton papers, M784/7/12, 'Human Rights: A Service', October 1967, devised by Rev. Arthur Peacock (Unitarian General Assembly and Free Christian Churches); 'Sermon Notes for Human Rights Day – 10 December 1967', Rev. T. Corbishley; see also Jesuits in Britain Archives, Corbishley papers, SJ/53/8/7.

50. Bodleian Library, Anti-Slavery Society, S.22 G881, File B, 12 December 1967, Working Group on Women's Rights, p. 3 and 24 July 1968, EC minutes; *New World*, December 1968, p. 5.

51. *New World*, January 1968, p. 3; TNA FCO 61/183, Prime Minister's draft message; Lambeth Palace archives, Ramsey 116, full text of Ramsey sermon.

52. *Peace News*, 19 January 1968, p. 10; *The Guardian*, 3 January 1968, p. 12; *Morning Star*, 3 January 1968, p. 1.

53. TNA FCO 61/185, 2 July 1968, memorandum by P. Gore-Booth. See Arthur Hearnden, *Red Robert: Life of Robert Birley* (London: Hamish Hamilton, 1984).

54. Bodleian Library, Anti-Slavery Society, S.22 G881, File B, EC minutes 27 February and 14 March 1968; LMA, Board of Deputies papers, Acc 3121/E4/810, copy of prior letter sent by the officers to Harold Wilson, 23 February 1968.

55. Bodleian Library, Anti-Slavery Society, S.22 G881, File B, 29 April 1968, Birley to Powell.
56. Bodleian Library, Anti-Slavery Society, S.22 G881, File B, EC minutes 24 July 1968. He also reported a lack of awareness of the extent of exploitation of women over unequal pay.
57. Bodleian Library, Anti-Slavery Society, S.22 G881, File B, The text was agreed at the 15 January 1969 meeting.
58. TNA FO371/189944, 30 December 1966, J. E. Powell-Jones to A. E. Coles.
59. TNA FCO 61/183, 30 November 1967, J. E. Tyrer memorandum.
60. Bodleian Library, Anti-Slavery Society, S.22 G881, File B, minutes of 30 October 1968.
61. Bodleian Library, Anti-Slavery Society, S.22 G881, File A, Steering committee, 22 December 1967; File B, Dependent Territories Working Party, 26 March 1968 and 25 October 1968. Ten thousand copies were originally printed – the remainder were given to the anti-apartheid movement.
62. Nottinghamshire Archives, DD/CR/59/1, 8 July 1967, Evans to committees.
63. LHASC, CP/LON/BRA/16/8, 11 January 1968, Cox to Chris Birch, Fulham.
64. *Morning Star* articles, 2 January, 3 January and 4 January 1968. However, the subsequent debate in the *Morning Star* about the latest trials of Soviet writers showed how far the party still had to travel (see 13, 19 and 30 January 1968).
65. *Sanity*, January 1968, p. 3.
66. Nottinghamshire Archives, DD/CR/59/1, Evans briefing session, 2 December 1967.
67. *Peace News*, 12 August 1966, p. 1.
68. *The Guardian*, 13 December 1968, p. 3.
69. LSE, UNA 14/2/1, February 1967, 'Human Rights in Britain', proposal for a survey; Bodleian Library, Anti-Slavery Society, S.22 G881, File A, Steering Committee, 22 December 1967 and Executive Committee, 11 January 1968.
70. *Civil Liberties 1969*, Introduction (annual report of the NCCL).
71. *New World*, July 1967, p. 5.
72. MRC Mss 16B/HR/1/1–7, H. Klade to Evans; MRC, Mss 292B/866(1), note on Evans' letter of 23 May 1967, 21 July 1967 memorandum and 22 July 1968, note.
73. Bodleian Library, Anti-Slavery papers, S.19D 10/21, File 2, 18 April 1967, Montgomery to Jan Papanek; File A, 20 December 1966, J. Alexander-Sinclair to chair.
74. TNA, FCO 61/179, for a list of sixty-seven organisations, 1 June 1967.
75. LMA, Acc 3121/C11/9/5/2, 12 December 1954, Janner to Lauterpacht.
76. Manchester Archives, Soroptimist papers, G/SIG/2/12, Executive Committee minutes, 26 October 1969; LSE/UNA/14/1/1, 15 November 1973, Soroptimists to UNA.
77. Jesuits in Britain archives, Roberts papers, 19/5/1, 10 November 1967, Baker circular. In fact, there was no evidence of a rise in membership due to the year (see British Section Report for 1967–68).

78. AI *Annual Report*, 1968–69.
79. Jesuits in Britain archives, Roberts papers, 19/5/1, Programme for conference, 22 June 1968.
80. *Civil Liberty*, December 1967.
81. Hull History Centre, UDCL 271, July 1967, 'Memorandum on Human Rights Year'.
82. Bodleian Library, Anti-Slavery Society, S.22 G881, File A, 15 November 1967, reports of Working Groups.
83. For the activities in Wales see *New World*, August 1966, p. 10; August 1967, p. 13; February 1968, p. 12; and January 1969, p. 5.
84. Some papers survive in West Yorkshire Archives, Bradford, 49D79/5/2/1.
85. For instance, *New World*, May 1968, p. 12, lists considerable activity in Hillingdon but there is no record of a committee there.
86. Nottinghamshire Archives, DD CR 59/2, 6 July 1967, Taylor to Sheila Parkes; 26 September 1967, Taylor to Gordon Evans.
87. 'Human Rights: "We Should Be Ashamed", Says Mayor', *Oxford Times*, 26 January 1968, citing Lord Mayor Frank Pickstock. The anti-racist group JACARI and Michael and Ann Dummetts' Committee for Racial Integration were both Oxford-based. Luard had recently edited *The International Protection of Human Rights* (London: Thames and Hudson, 1967). For the Oxford context see S. Tuck, *The Night Malcolm X Spoke at the Oxford Union: a Transatlantic Story of Antiracial Protest* (Berkeley: University of California Press, 2014).
88. LSE, UNA 3/1/18, UNA EC minutes 29 April 1967; LHAS&C, CP/LON/BRA/16/8, 12 January 1968, Stephens to Birch; Bodleian Library, Anti-Slavery Society, S.22 G881, File A, on 9 January 1968 only forty-nine were listed.
89. Hull History Centre, UDCL 608/8, 18 June 1968, Smythe to Evans.
90. Notts Archives, DD/CR/59/1, April 1967 memorandum from UK Human Rights Year Committee entitled 'Local Human Rights Committees: Suggestions for Their Formation and Programmes'.
91. Nottinghamshire Archives, DD CR 59/1, undated paper on 'Human Rights Year'.
92. Bodleian Library, Anti-Slavery Society, S.22 G881, File A, April 1967 document.
93. Nottinghamshire Archives, DD/CR/59/1, 1 November 1967, Nottingham committee circular.
94. West Yorkshire Archives, Bradford, 49D79/5/2/1, Yorkshire committee circular [December 1967].
95. Holborn Library, Camden Borough GPC minutes, 31 January 1968. KCL, LDG papers, MGA CHRON XI, *Bulletin* of the North London Group for the Restoration of Democracy in Greece, 2, December/January 1968.
96. Nottinghamshire Archives, DD/CR/59/1, undated [1967], 'Notes on Fund-Raising'. The pub crawl was a surprisingly effective tool – Camden International Voluntary Service raised £40 (*North London Press*, 10 May 1968).

97. Nottinghamshire Archives, DD/CR/59/2, 2 May 1968, Taylor to Guy Dauncey; DD/CR/59/2, 10 June 1968, Evans to Taylor.
98. Nottinghamshire Archives, DD/CR/59/2, 2 May 1968, Taylor to R. McLeish.
99. Holborn Library, Camden Borough GPC minutes, 1 November 1967 and 31 January 1968. In the event, Camden did not make this a condition, but did carry out a survey of the 162 agencies in the Borough: 151 agencies signed a written assurance of no racial discrimination and only 5 refused.
100. Nottinghamshire Archives, DD/CR/59/2, 3 April 1968, Taylor to Collins quoting a letter from Evans about the ceremony at Tunbridge Wells; DD/CR/59/2, Vicki Chadwick of Tunbridge UNA told Taylor that the book cost £60 (equivalent to almost £1000 in 2018), but other quotes had been in the region of £200, Chadwick to Taylor 26 October 1968.
101. Nottinghamshire Archives DD CR 59/1, April 1967, UKCIHYR, 'Local Human Rights Committees: Suggestions for Their Formation and Programmes'; D CR/59/1, 2 December 1967, Evans briefing.
102. New World, Sept. 1968, p. 10 (and photograph in December 1968, p. 10).
103. Nottinghamshire Archives, DD CR/59/1, UK Committee 'Suggestions' for local committees, April 1967.
104. 'Human Rights Sermon at Cowley', Oxford Times, 10 May 1968.
105. Nottinghamshire Archives, DD CR/59/1, UK Committee circular, May 1967.
106. Nottinghamshire Archives, DD/CR/59/1, report on 2 December 1967 briefing session.
107. Nottinghamshire Archives, DD CR/59/1, 25 May 1967, minutes of Nottinghamshire HRY Preparatory Committee, as in the April 1967 'Suggestions'.
108. Nottinghamshire Archives, DD CR/59/1, Presentation speech by Mr R. P. Collins, 6 January 1969.
109. TNA FCO 61/178, March 1967 circular.
110. TNA FCO 61/181, Taylor to Evans 26 September 1967; Preparatory Committee, 26 July 1967.
111. Nottinghamshire Archives, DD CR/59/1, Sermon by Rev. Wood, 10 December 1967.
112. New World, January 1969, p. 5.
113. New World, Sept. 1968, p. 16 (for Yorkshire) and February 1969, p. 5 (for Evans).
114. Nottinghamshire Archives, DD CR/59/1, speech by Collins, 6 January [1969]; New World, February 1969, p. 5.
115. New World, January 1969, p. 12.
116. P. Rose, Backbencher's Dilemma (London: Frederick Muller, 1981), pp. 178–85.
117. ICJ report, Human Rights in Northern Ireland. Reprint from the Review of the International Commission of Jurists, Geneva, June 1969, p. 1.
118. Belfast Newsletter, 22 January 1968, p. 4; see the two articles by C. Rynder, 'Sheelagh Murnaghan and the Struggle for Human Rights in Northern

Ireland', *Irish Studies Review*, vol. 14, no. 4 (2006), 447–63; and 'Sheelagh Murnaghan and the Ulster Liberal Party', *Journal of Liberal History*, vol. 71 (Summer 2011), 14–20. See *Northern Ireland Parliament, Commons Debates*, vol. 68 (30 January 1968), 573–605, for Murnaghan's speech and responses to it.

119. Cited in CSJ, *The Plain Truth*, 2nd ed. (Castlefields, Dungannon: Campaign for Social Justice, 1969).

120. H. Wilson, *The Labour Government 1964–70: A Personal Record* (London: Weidenfeld & Nicolson, 1971), p. 672; P. Rose, *How the Troubles Came to Northern Ireland* (Basingstoke: Macmillan, 2000), p. 179. Rose provides a very helpful political overview.

121. See M. Mulholland, *Northern Ireland at the Crossroads: Ulster Unionism in the O'Neill Years, 1960–9* (Basingstoke: Macmillan, 2000).

122. Northern Ireland Civil Rights Association, '*We Shall Overcome*': the History of the Struggle for Civil Rights in Northern Ireland, 1968–78 (Belfast: NICRA, 1978) and B. Purdie, *Politics in the Streets, the Origins of the Civil Rights Movement in Northern Ireland* (Belfast: Blackstaff, 1990).

123. A. Currie, *All Hell Will Break Loose* (Dublin: O'Brien Press, 2004); for new political forces see S. Prince, *Northern Ireland's '68: Civil Rights, Global Revolt and the Origins of the Troubles* (Dublin: Irish Academic Press, 2007).

124. Hull History Centre, UDCL 270, NCCL minutes for 11 October 1962; further inquiries were discussed in 1949 (Hull History Centre, UDCL, 267, minutes for 24 March 1949).

125. C. Moores, *Civil Liberties and Human Rights in Twentieth-Century Britain* (*Cambridge University Press*, 2017), pp. 171–3; *Peace News*, 17 January 1969, p. 5.

126. IISH, AI IS, 1031, 18 March 1961, Baker to Benenson, citing Mrs Turtle in Lisburn, Northern Ireland.

127. IISH, AI IS, 1027, 3 January 1962 Faulkner to Benenson and Baker.

128. AI papers, 3 November 1962, Benenson to MacBride; *Belfast Telegraph*, 27 March 1968, p. 6.

129. University of Bradford, Baker papers, 2/4, 2 October 1968, Justice T. E. Kingsmill Moore to Baker; see also MRC, Mss 292B/863/4, AI British Section, Annual meeting of Threes Groups, 23 June 1968. There is a brief account of the meeting in IISH, AI IS, 1273, 16 June 1970, Marreco to Baker. In ibid., British Section EC minutes, 30 June 1970 it was reported that the Belfast Section had closed.

130. See *Northern Ireland Parliament, Commons Debates*, vol. 68, 30 January 1968, 588–91 for a speech by Miss Bessie Machonachie, who was invited to join the committee in October 1966.

131. PRONI, D4201/B/3/1–25, UNA Belfast EC minutes for 15 May 1967; PRONI, D4201/B/2, 14 October 1968, statement by UNA Belfast Branch; *New World*, November 1967, p. 1 and May 1968, p. 12.

132. PRONI, D4201/B/2, 4 August 1967, Brian Walker to Denis Barritt, and reply 14 August 1967.

133. D. P. Barritt and C. F. Carter, *The Northern Ireland Problem: a Study in Group Relations* (Oxford University Press, 1962); see also D. P. Barritt and

A. Booth, *Orange and Green: a Quaker Study of Community Relations in Northern Ireland* (Sedbergh, UK: Northern Friends Peace Board, 1972).

134. *New World*, November 1969, p. 13.
135. Bodleian Library, Anti-Slavery Society, S.22 G881, File B, UK committee EC minutes, 30 October 1968. *Irish Times*, 25 October 1968, p. 16; *New World*, November 1968, p. 5, similar statement of 14 October 1968 by Belfast EC of UNA. I have not been able to find a full copy of the Human Rights Year Committee text.
136. Bodleian Library, Anti-Slavery Society, S.22 G881, File B, UK committee EC minutes, 27 November 1968.
137. LSE UNA/3/1/19, EC minutes, 16 November 1968.
138. 'March for Civil Rights for the Northern Irish', *Oxford Times*, 6 December 1968.
139. *Irish Times*, 27 August 1968, p. 1 and 10 October 1968, p. 13.
140. *Peace News*, 17 January 1969, p. 5.
141. *Irish Times*, 7 December 1968; *New World*, January 1969, p. 12, report by Harry Barton.
142. KCL, 1992/KFL/F28, 23 August 1968, Alexander-Sinclair to Evans.
143. Bodleian Library, Anti-Slavery Society papers, S.22 G 994, memorandum by Marreco [1969].
144. *The Guardian*, 11 December 1973, p. 13, article about Granada TV programmes during the Campaign for the Abolition of Torture. For Kewley see her *ODNB* entry by Anthony Hayward (2016).
145. Bodleian Library, Ms Eng.c.4658, File 1: a file note makes clear that John Alexander took the surname Alexander-Sinclair to avoid being confused with another employee.
146. The sources are copies of Alexander-Sinclair's CV in Bodleian Library, Scott papers, Box 19 and Bodleian Library, Ms. Eng. C. 4658, and *The Times* obituary (4 November 1988). His papers in the Bodleian Library only cover his years working with the UN and its agencies. File 1, 22 April 1955, Alexander to G. van Heuven Goedhart.
147. Bodleian Library, Anti-Slavery Society, S.22 G881, File B, 25 April 1968, EC minutes; Hull History Centre, UDCL 608/8.
148. Bodleian Library, Anti-Slavery Society, S.22 G881, File B, EC minutes 15 January 1969: even the Institute was only agreed to with five in favour and four abstentions.
149. Hull History Centre, UDCL, 608/8, 18 June 1968, Smythe to Gordon Evans.
150. Hull History Centre, UDCL 608/8, 3 March 1972, memorandum by Smythe.
151. Ibid.; Hull History Centre, UDCL/271, NCCL minutes 14 March 1968.
152. Hull History Centre, UDCL, 608/8, 3 March 1972 memorandum.
153. *New World*, November 1967, p. 1 and September 1969, p. 7.
154. TNA FCO 61/179, 23 July 1967, Evans to Coles gives a blow-by-blow account. Evans later retracted his resignation, and Alexander-Sinclair was brought in (from outside the UNA) to support him.

155. LSE, UNA 4/8/1, minutes for first meeting of the UNA Human Rights Committee, 27 March 1969. It is not wholly clear from the report, but it appears that this money came from the UK HRY committee.

156. See www.echr.coe.int/Documents/Anni_Book_Chapter10_ENG.pdf, for an appreciation of McNulty by Hans Christian Krüger. See also Borthwick Institute, Capricorn Africa papers, File 9, 3 June 1953, Stirling to McNulty.

157. KCL, 1992/KFL/F28, 3 April 1969, Alexander-Sinclair to Kimber.

158. Bodleian Library, Anti-Slavery Society, S.22 G881, File J, catalogue of the exhibition's subjects and artists. There were fifty-four exhibits in all, with some subjects covered twice.

7 TORTURE STATES: 1967–1975

1. J. Becket, *Barbarism in Greece: a Young American Lawyer's Inquiry into the Use of Torture in Contemporary Greece, with Case Histories and Documents* (New York: Walker, 1970), p. 2.

2. See *Peace News*, 16 February 1968, p. 3, with drawings by Bernard Power-Canavan; LHAS&C, CSC/21/1, CSC pamphlet entitled 'Deport the Chilean Ambassador', with Sheila Cassidy's sketch of a victim, tied to a bed and tortured with electric shocks; Amnesty International, *Where Is William Beausire? Disappearance in Chile* (1981), carries similarly graphic images of torture, pp. 9–13.

3. Needham Research Institute, Cambridge, SCC 2/373/10, Needham to G. Kitson-Clark. Needham was following Amnesty's campaign against torture closely: see also the report of his speech to the Cambridge Amnesty group in April 1974, *British Amnesty*, April/May 1974.

4. B. Dickson, *The European Convention on Human Rights and the Conflict in Northern Ireland* (Oxford University Press, 2010), pp. 149–51.

5. *Hansard*, 25 November 1974, col. 35.

6. Justice could not reach a consensus over internment, while the UNA Human Rights Committee wanted to condemn it but was overruled by the Executive Committee. Hull History Centre, UDJU 2/3, Executive Committee minutes, 22 September 1971 and Council minutes, 13 October 1971; LSE, UNA 4/8/1, Human Rights Committee minutes 30 September 1971, 3 November 1971 and 13 December 1971.

7. University of Bradford, Baker papers, 2/7, undated 'Progress Report' on the CAT [1975].

8. Amnesty International, *Report on Torture* (London: Duckworth, 1973), p. 17.

9. Foreword to British Amnesty Section, *Epidemic: Torture* (British Amnesty, 1973).

10. E. Baker, 'What Do We Mean By Torture?', *Baptist Times*, 9 February 1976.

11. *NCCL Annual Report*, 1974, p. 3; *NCCL Annual Report*, 1974–75, p. 3.

12. AI *Annual Report*, 1972–73, pp. 3–4.

13. E. Pedaliu, 'Human Rights and International Security: the International Community and the Greek Dictators', *International History Review*, vol. 38, no. 5 (2016), 1014–39.

14. *The Times*, 26 June 1968, p. 8; according to a later clarification Wilson had been meaning to use the only marginally less powerful adjective 'barbarous' (*The Times*, 4 July 1968, p. 4).
15. See Pedaliu, 'Human Rights and International Security' and E. Pedaliu, 'Human Rights and Foreign Policy: Wilson and the Greek Dictators, 1967–70', *Diplomacy and Statecraft*, vol. 18, no. 1 (2007), 185–214.
16. As Cedric Thornberry argued in *The Guardian*, 24 November 1967.
17. *The Guardian*, 21 October 1967. Thornberry (1936–2014) was born in Northern Ireland and called to the Bar in 1959. For most of his career he was a prominent academic at the LSE, and from 1978 held a series of prominent positions at the UN (obituary in *The Guardian* by Martti Ahrtisaari, 1 June 2014). He was shortlisted to be Amnesty Secretary General in 1968 (see below, p. 150).
18. *The Guardian*, 24 November 1967, pp. 1, 15.
19. This was explicitly stated in Eric Baker's formal 'Order of Mission' of 29 December 1967, IISH, AI IS, 1179.
20. IISH, AI IS, 1179, 2 August 1967, Marreco to Baker; 7 August 1967, Elizabeth Gordon to Bent Knudsen; IISH, AI IS, 1180, 4 March 1968, Baker to European National Sections.
21. Anthony Marreco to the author, 31 October 2002.
22. MRC, Mss 292B/863/4, Amnesty International, Report of the Annual General Meeting of the British Section, 23 June 1968.
23. AI *Annual Report*, 1966–67, p. 5.
24. Becket, *Barbarism in Greece*, p. xi. AI *Annual Report*, 1967–68, p. 4, 'The Greek Mission'. There was no mention of torture in the background briefing for the mission IISH, AI IS, 1179, notes by Martin Enthoven, 28 December 1967. Becket's statement takes precedence over a misleading comment in Amnesty's later publication *Torture in Greece: the First Torturers' Trial 1975* (London: Amnesty International, 1977): 'In response [to torture allegations in November 1967] Amnesty International dispatched American lawyer James Becket and British lawyer Anthony Marreco to Greece in late December 1967 to investigate the torture allegations as well as to determine the extent and implementation of a much publicised Christmas amnesty for political prisoners.'
25. AI, *Situation in Greece: Report by Amnesty International*, 27 January 1968. My emphasis.
26. *Torture of Political Prisoners in Greece: A Second Report by Amnesty International* (London: Amnesty International Publications, 6 April 1968). Marreco was supported in Greece by the researcher Denis Geoghegan (*AI British Section Report*, 1967–68). *Irish Times*, 29 June 1968, p. 5.
27. Churchill College, NBKR 4/354, typescript by F. Noel-Baker, 'Greece since the Revolution'; *Hansard*, 11 April 1968; K. Young, *The Greek Passion: a Study in People and Politics* (London: J. M. Dent, 1969), pp. 433–4; for the legal action see *Morning Star*, 26 July 1974 and *The Times*, 26 July 1974, p. 4.
28. Jesuits in Britain archives, Roberts papers, 19/5/1, AI British Section AGM, 23 June 1968.

29. See A. H. Robertson and J. G. Merrills. *Human Rights in the World: an Introduction to the Study of the International Protection of Human Rights*, 4th ed. (Manchester University Press, 1996), pp. 136–7.

30. B. Keys, 'Anti-Torture Politics: Amnesty International, the Greek Junta, and the Origins of the Human Rights "Boom" in the United States', in A. Irive, P. Goedde and W. I. Hitchcock (eds), *The Human Rights Revolution: an International History* (Oxford University Press, 2012), pp. 201–21.

31. IISH, AI IS, 1180, February 1968 'Brief', probably for Denis Geoghegan. A circular by Eric Baker of 4 March 1968 also referred to the islands as the 'all-important question'.

32. Amnesty's report on *Chile* (London: Amnesty International Publications, 1974), p. 31 claimed that between 5000 and 30,000 were killed in the coup; *The Guardian*, 14 December 2016, article by E. MacAskill and J. Franklin.

33. LHAS&C, Hart papers, 4/6, Amnesty International paper, November 1973, 'Refugees in Chile'.

34. Amnesty International, *Annual Report* for 1973–74, p. 8.

35. The CSC was formed by Liberation (the recently renamed Movement for Colonial Freedom) alongside the existing Association for British–Chilean Friendship (see A. Jones, *No Truck with the Chilean Junta! Trade Union Internationalism, Australia and Britain, 1973–1980* (ANU Press, 2014), pp. 25–37). For other recent contributions on the impact of the coup in Britain see S. Hirsch, 'The United Kingdom: Competing Conceptions of Internationalism' and J. Eckel, 'Allende's Shadow: Leftist Furor and Human Rights: The Pinochet Dictatorship in International Politics', both in K. Christiaens, Idesbald Goddeeris and Magaly Rodríguez Garciá (eds), *European Solidarity with Chile: 1970s–1980s* (Frankfurt am Main: Peter Lang, 2014). See also C. Moores, 'Solidarity for Chile, Transnational Activism and the Evolution of Human Rights', *Moving the Social: Journal of Social History and the History of Social Movements*, vol. 57 (2017), 115–36.

36. See M. Gatehouse, 'Chile: the First Dictatorship of Globalisation', *Red Pepper*, 9 September 2013, www.redpepper.org.uk/chile-the-first-dictatorship-of-globalisation.

37. University of Bradford, Harold Blakemore papers, Chile, September 1973 file, Amnesty International, 'Violence, Torture and Detention in Chile', 10 October 1973, copy in Bradford. According to a handwritten note by Gatehouse: 'This is a report I wrote for Amnesty'. See also the anonymous article in *Morning Star*, 6 November 1973.

38. LHAS&C Hart papers, 4/7, 28 December 1973, Wendy Tyndale to Judith Hart; 12 February 1974 CSC circular.

39. LHAS&C, Hart papers, 4/7, undated circular announcing formation of the CCHR.

40. LHAS&C, Hart papers, 4/11, undated report [1974].

41. LHAS&C, Hart papers, 4/11, undated CCHR circular. The Peace Committee was closed by the Chilean government in November 1975.

42. LHAS&C Hart papers, 4/11, correspondence and report from Tyndale.

43. LHAS&C, Hart papers, 4/7, report of meeting, 12 February 1974.

44. Hull History Centre, Platts-Mills papers, UDPM 2/12, CCHR minutes, 2 July 1976.

45. See Amnesty International, *Chile: An Amnesty International Report* (London: Amnesty International Publications, 1974).

46. LHAS&C, CSC papers, 21/2, 20 January 1976, Amnesty International's text of Cassidy's statement given in Geneva to the UN Ad Hoc Working Group of the Commission on Human Rights, 19 January 1976.

47. LHAS&C, CSC papers, 21/2, 15 January 1976, Gatehouse to Ben Ford, MP.

48. LHAS&C, CSC papers, 21/2, CSC Local Committees Newsletter, 17, 4 January 1976.

49. Hirsch, 'The United Kingdom', p. 153. The case of William Beausire, a 'disappeared' Chilean with British citizenship, was doggedly pursued for many years by Amnesty activists Helen Bamber and Dick Barbor-Might. However, it failed to achieve the impact of the Cassidy case in Britain, mainly because Beausire was probably murdered soon after he was seized in 1974 and did not live to bear witness (N. Belton, *The Good Listener: Helen Bamber, a Life against Cruelty* (London: Weidenfeld & Nicolson, 1998), pp. 221–7.

50. LHAS&C, CSC papers, 21/2, 15 January 1976, Gatehouse to Ben Ford MP.

51. AI *Annual Report*, 1974–75, pp. 116–17.

52. 'AI Spanish Mission Says Torture Used against Basque Detainees', *British Amnesty*, November/December 1975; *Report of an Amnesty International Mission to Spain* (1975), Amnesty International; IISH, AI IS, 1203, May 1972, 'Torture Report: a Background Paper'.

53. For material on the campaign see University of Bradford, Baker papers, 2/3. *British Amnesty News*, 3 July 1971. Regent's Park College, Oxford, Payne papers, Human Rights Box, 'The 2(.5)% Holiday Tax Call', August 1969.

54. IISH, AI IS, 1273, British Section EC minutes, 29 April 1970 and 30 June 1970.

55. For the campaign see KCL, LDG papers, bulletins in CHRON XI file; memorandum in CHRON IX, GCAD '1970' file.

56. *British Amnesty News*, 3 July 1971.

57. W. Paynter in the *Morning Star*, 20 December 1973.

58. IISH, AI IS, 7, memorandum by Eva Blumenau, September 1966.

59. LHAS&C, Labour Party International Department files, B43/4, 'Suggestions for Tribunal'.

60. LHAS&C, Labour Party International Department files, B43/4, 20 August 1973, Jokel to Jack Jones.

61. LHAS&C, Bob Edwards papers, BE 5/6, 9 July 1975, Edwards to Jack Jones.

62. See A. M. Clark, *Diplomacy of Conscience: Amnesty International and Changing Human Rights Norms* (Princeton University Press, 2001), pp. 37–69.

63. *British Amnesty*, January 1973.

64. Clark, *Diplomacy of Conscience* attributes the campaign to Amnesty's IEC 'under Sean MacBride and Eric Baker's leadership', p. 44; Samuel Moyn writes that MacBride won the Nobel Prize for the CAT, but it is not

mentioned in the citation and he made only one brief reference to torture in his acceptance speech (Moyn, *Human Rights and the Uses of History* (London: Verso, 2014), p. 103).

65. Peter Benenson papers (AI), 'Community of Conscience', Berlin, 5 June 1976, pp. 6–7.
66. *The Friend*, 16 July 1965, p. 843; AI British Section AGM report 16 June 1965.
67. University of Bradford, Baker papers, 2/7, handwritten notes, 11 December 1965. The phrase 'ancient evil' was not included in the typescript.
68. 'What Do We Mean by Torture?', *Baptist Times*, 9 February 1976.
69. University of Bradford, Baker papers, 2/7, typescript, April 1968, p. 7.
70. *AIR* 24, Aug. 1968, for Baker's article, abstracted from his paper. University of Bradford, Baker papers, 3/2 has a copy of the paper for the conference and records some of the discussion – Baker's is the only named voice. There is a full account in *AIR (Amnesty International Review)*, 25 November 1968, pp. 2–4. See also, IISH, AI IS, 8 and 1202.
71. IISH, AI IS, 1274, AI International Council meeting, 25–27 September 1970.
72. University of Bradford, Baker papers, 2/7, Baker's speaker's notes for CAT, p. 8; 'What Do We Mean by Torture?', *Baptist Times*, 9 February 1976.
73. *The Friend*, 31 July 1970, pp. 891–2; *Life* magazine (July 17, 1970).
74. University of Bradford, Baker papers 3/1, Meeting for Sufferings, 3 April 1971, Minute 2.
75. *The Friend*, 26 November 1971, p. 1432 and 31 March 1972, pp. 393–3.
76. E. Baker, 'So Many of Our Ideals Have Died', *Baptist Times*, 26 February 1976.
77. IISH, AI IS, 1215 for a report of the November meeting; University of Bradford, Baker papers, 3/1, Baker to Friends, 20 June 1972; 2/5 MacBride to Director General, UNESCO, 22 November 1972.
78. University of Bradford, Baker papers, 3/1, Baker to Friends, 20 June 1972.
79. Amnesty International, *Report on Torture* (London: Duckworth, 1973); a first draft was presented by Baker in May 1972, see IISH, AI IS1203, 'AI Torture Report: a Background Paper' and cover note, 8 May 1972); much of the published report was drafted by James Becket and his sister Elise Becket-Smith, IISH, AI IS, 1233, CAT subcommittee minutes, 6 April 1973.
80. IISH, AI IS, 1211 for the Dutch section's detailed evaluation of its own campaign.
81. *The Friend*, 26 October 1973, p. 1281.
82. *The Friend*, 12 October 1973, pp. 1228/9, on separate seminars for lawyers and doctors.
83. For good accounts of the conference and the Granada TV programmes about torture shown at it see *The Guardian*, 11 December 1973, p. 13.
84. *The Friend*, 11 January 1974, pp. 31–2. For Baker's links to Dolci see above, pp. 74–6. University of Bradford, Baker papers, 3/1, June 1974, 'The part the Friends can play in the CAT'. Dolci's poem is in IISH, AI IS, 972.

85. IISH, AI IS, 1211, 20 December 1973, circular from Ennals to National Sections.
86. IISH, AI IS, 1213, January 1976, meeting of 10–11 April 1976, Appendix II: 'The Role of C. A. T. in Amnesty International'.
87. *British Amnesty*, July/August 1976.
88. University of Bradford, Baker papers, 2/7, 5 February 1973, minute of meeting; *The Friend*, 12 October 1973, pp. 1228–9, described the seminar as being under Quaker auspices; see also IISH, AI IS, 1204, CAT subcommittee minutes, 13 December 1972; IISH, AI IS, 1277, CAT subcommittee minutes for 10 January, 14 February and 15 March 1973.
89. *The Friend*, 16 February 1973, pp. 199–200, re Jean Edwards and the Farnham group. She and her husband Derek (British Section Vice-Chair) had set up the group (see *British Amnesty*, September/October 1974).
90. KCL, LDG papers, INFO XIV, 'Torture' file, 17 December 1973 circular.
91. University of Bradford, Baker papers, 2/5, 2 January 1973, MacBride to Martin Enthoven. Likewise, as early as 1971 Martin Ennals had noted apropos torture that 'the support of the Quakers is very important': IISH, AI IS, 1214, 6 April 1971, Ennals to Baker.
92. *The Friend*, 4 July 1975, p. 753; 24 October 1975, p. 1214.
93. *The Friend*, 30 August 1974, pp. 1024–6 and 1042.
94. University of Bradford, Baker 3/2, 31 August 1975, Baker to Gerald Priestman.
95. University of Bradford Baker papers 3/1, 21 October 1974, Baker to Sidney Greaves.
96. University of Bradford, Baker papers 3/1, 'A Quaker Concern for the Abolition of Torture' (March 1973). For encouragement of prayer see University of Bradford, Baker papers, 3/2, 18 December 1975, Baker to Mr Locks.
97. *The Friend*, 19 November 1971, p. 1402.
98. *British Amnesty*, February/March 1974.
99. University of Bradford, Baker papers, 2/4, Benenson to Baker, 15 December 1972. Benenson added that he believed that torture was greatly diminished compared with a century ago when it was 'almost universal'.
100. University of Bradford, Baker papers, 3/1, 11 November 1974, L. Hugh Doncaster, clerk of the Worcestershire and Shropshire meeting to Baker.
101. The heading of this section, 'Dissent as Disease' comes from the title of an article on the case of Natalia Gorbanevskaya in *The Guardian*, 16 February 1972.
102. *AIR* 24 April 1968. For a thorough account of the Soviet abuse of psychiatry see M. Hurst, *British Human Rights Organisations* and Soviet Dissent, 1965–1985 (London: Bloomsbury, 2016), chs. 1 and 2.
103. *AI Report*, 1971–72, p. 43.
104. Garling, *The Human Rights Handbook*, p. 124.
105. See C. Mee, *The Internment of Soviet Dissenters in Mental Hospitals* (Cambridge: J. Arliss, 1971).
106. Amnesty International, *Report on Torture* (1973), p. 188; Amnesty International, *Prisoners of Conscience in the USSR: Their Treatment and*

Conditions (London: Amnesty International Publications, 1975), pp. 101–36; this quote p. 119.

107. LSE, UNA 14/2/4, record of General Council decision.
108. LSE, UNA/28/1/6: these meetings were on 12 May and 30 November 1976.
109. AI Report, 1974–75, p. 118. The two key texts, both by S. Bloch and P. Reddaway: *Psychiatric Terror: How Soviet Psychiatry Is Used to Suppress Dissent* (New York: Basic Books, 1977) and *Soviet Psychiatric Abuse: the Shadow over World Psychiatry* (London: V. Gollancz, 1984).
110. Troublingly for many activists, Scientologists were prominent campaigners in this area from an early stage and supported a British 'Citizens' Commission on Human Rights: Psychiatric Violations'. See correspondence from 1973 in University of Bristol, Bateman papers, Box N 3/1, and discussion over whether to work with the Scientologists.
111. Cited in *Asylum Magazine*, [2017], 'Professor Alec Jenner, 1927–2014' (https://asylummagazine.org/2014/06/professor-alec-jenner-1927-2014//).
112. *The Guardian*, 24 January 1972, p. 11.
113. According to Garling, *The Human Rights Handbook*, p. 128, the group's first newsletter (June 1977) also detailed abuses in Romania, East Germany, Argentina, Chile and South Africa.
114. University of Bradford, Baker papers, 2/4, Benenson to MacBride, 16 December 1966. Benenson added that he may yet write the 'British sequel'. Manya Harari set up the publishers Harvill in 1946, which became a subsidiary of Collins in 1954, and published many Russian authors. Benenson actually told MacBride that *Ward 7* was 'translated into English by my aunt', but this attribution is not made elsewhere.
115. The title of *Ward 7* itself refers to Chekhov's short story about a Russian mental hospital, 'Ward No. 6' (1892).
116. *The Guardian*, 9 October 1965, p. 14.
117. *The Guardian*, 13 May 1965, p. 10 and 6 October 1965, p. 12.
118. Hurst, *British Human Rights Organisations*, ch. 5 gives a good account of the 'chaos and stress' (p. 152) amongst Amnesty researchers on the USSR in the 1960s.
119. This was an Amnesty International publication, 1970–84.
120. See correspondence in Bodleian Library, MS Bonham Carter, 174.
121. M. Bourdeaux, in *AIR*, February 1968. See also his book, *Religious Ferment in Russia: Protestant Opposition to Soviet Policy* (Basingstoke: Macmillan, 1968).
122. IISH, AI IS, 1005, meeting of AI Eltham Group, 25 February 1963, comments by Roger Burke (Amnesty's General Secretary). In 1963 Peter Benenson told Andrew Martin that as many as 40 per cent of these executed for economic offences were identifiable as Jews. However, he went on, Amnesty doubted that this was due to a 'calculated policy of 'liquidating' Jews', but rather an indication that Jews were being scapegoated as a result of local anti-Semitic pressures on prosecuting authorities (AI papers, Benenson to Martin, 5 July 1963).

123. *AI Report* 1969–70, pp. 18–19 and 1970–71, pp. 58–9; the *AI Report* for 1966–67 stated that most imprisoned Jews were guilty of '"economic offences"' against strict anti-capitalist laws.

124. *British Amnesty*, August 1973; Hurst, *British Human Rights Organisations*, ch. 3 for 'the 35s'.

125. *British Amnesty*, November/December 1974.

126. *AI Report*, 1969–70, p. 19. Block and Reddaway, in *Psychiatric Terror*, identified this prisoner as Bukovsky, p. 76.

127. A. Wynn, *Notes of a Non-Conspirator: Working with Russian Dissidents* (London: Andre Deutsch, 1987), pp. 34–8.

128. *The Guardian*, 28 January 1977, p. 22.

129. *The Guardian*, 1 June 1971, p. 1.

130. These were published as P. Reddaway and J. Telesin, *Uncensored Russia: the Human Rights Movement in the Soviet Union: the Annotated Text of the Unofficial Moscow Journal A Chronicle of Current Events* (Nos. 1–11) (London: Cape, 1972).

131. *Guardian*, 24 January 1972, p. 11.

132. See Bloch and Reddaway, *The Shadow over World Psychiatry*.

133. See B. Nathans, 'Soviet Human Rights Activists to Amnesty International', www.geschichte-menschenrechte.de/en/hauptnavigation/schluesseltexte/so viet-human-rights-activists-to-amnesty-international/?type=98765.

134. S. B. Snyder, *Human Rights Activism and the End of the Cold War: a Transnational History of the Helsinki Network* (Cambridge University Press, 2011).

135. *The Times*, 4 April 1970, p. 4.

136. 'Some abuses of human rights are so flagrant, so egregious, and so offensive by any national or cultural standard, that we will always be justified in opposing and deterring them' (M. Thatcher, *The Path to Power* (London: HarperCollins, 1995), p. 529).

137. See Belton, *The Good Listener*. Bamber had come to appreciate the link between medicine and human rights when working as secretary to the doctor Maurice Pappworth, who campaigned in the 1960s against the use of humans in medical trials (p. 208).

138. Peter Benenson papers (AI), 'Community of Conscience', Berlin, 5 June 1976, pp. 7–8.

8   'ALL THINGS COME TO THOSE WHO WAIT': THE LATER 1970s

1. *The Times*, 11 October 1977, p. 15.

2. See C. McKeown, *The Passion of Peace* (Belfast: Blackstaff Press, 1984), pp. 238–44.

3. AI *Annual Report*, 1978, pp. 1–5; AI *Annual Report*, 1975–76, p. 6, uses block graphs to illustrate growth in membership and budget.

4. The handbook was commissioned by the Writers and Scholars Educational Trust, a branch of WSI, and published by Macmillan. The list of British agencies was compiled in September 1977, and

some European and American names were then added to make the book more 'international', Bishopsgate Institute, Index/21, WSI minutes for 13 March 1978.

5. S. Moyn, *The Last Utopia: Human Rights in History* (Cambridge, MA: Belknap Press of Harvard University Press, 2010), p. 3.
6. Cited in D. Sargent, 'Oasis in the Desert? America's Human Rights Rediscovery', in J. Eckel and S. Moyn, *The Breakthrough: Human Rights in the 1970s* (Philadelphia: University of Pennsylvania Press, 2014), p. 129.
7. *Les Prix Nobel, 1977* (1977) (unpaginated).
8. J. Eckel, 'Explaining the Human Rights Revolution of the 1970s', in Eckel and Moyn, *Breakthrough*, p. 254; Eckel cited by Moyn, the *Last Utopia*, pp. 146–7.
9. LMA/4016/IS/A/04/053, 15 October 1977 memorandum; Bishopsgate Institute, INDEX/20, Council minutes, 21 January 1976.
10. *British Amnesty*, October 1978.
11. *Links* (Third World First journal), 1977.
12. LMA/4016/IS/A/04/053, 15 October 1977 memorandum.
13. LMA/4016/IS/A/04/053, 23 March 1978, Owen to Hinton.
14. M. Garling, *The Human Rights Handbook: a Guide to British and American International Human Rights Organisations* (London: Macmillan Press, 1979), p. 1.
15. *The Times*, 10 December 1977, p. 14; see *The Times*, 29 March 1976, p. 7 for his first 'Prisoner of Conscience' column.
16. *The Friend*, 7 December 1973, pp. 1465–6. Evans was International Secretary of the Friends' Peace and International Relations Committee.
17. *New World*, 'Whose Human Rights?', November–December 1973.
18. *Hansard*, 25 May 1973, cols. 924–5.
19. *British Amnesty*, July 1974.
20. Oxfam 'advert in *The Friend*, December 1971, pp. 1526–7; Minority Rights Group' advert in *New World*, October 1975.
21. Amnesty International, *Torture in Greece: the First Torturers' Trial 1975* (London: Amnesty International, 1977); *British Amnesty*, July 1973.
22. S. B. Snyder, *Human Rights Activism and the End of the Cold War: a Transnational History of the Helsinki Network* (Cambridge University Press, 2011), pp. 7–8.
23. *British Amnesty*, August 1973.
24. Hull History Centre, UDCL/335/1, 25 July 1973, Loney to Berger; 13 December 1973, Loney to Sicco Mansholt.
25. MRC, Mss 296D/866/2, 6 October 1977, J. Monks to G. Bish. For the wider debate see *Civil Liberty*, vol. 42, no. 2 (April 1976), 'Do We Need a Bill of Rights?'
26. LSE, UNA 14/4/2, 25 May 1976, Archer to Frank Field.
27. IISH, AI IS, 1177, 30 November 1967, Eva Blumenau to MacBride.
28. *British Amnesty*, Feb/March 1980, profile of Lord Avebury. There is reference to an earlier parliamentary group in 1966, chaired by Benenson's friend Ian Gilmour MP (AI British Section, Report of AGM, Bristol, 11 June 1966). This initial committee appears to have lapsed by May 1969, when the

question was posed as to whether it could be revived at the British Section's Executive Committee, 1 May 1969 (IISH, AI IS, 1269).

29. *Observer Magazine*, 23 May 1971, pp. 25–9; AI *Annual Report* for 1971–72, pp. 14–15; Regent's Park College, Payne papers, 'Human Rights' box, 23 May 1972, Ennals to Payne, indicates that this was £15,000 per annum for five years from 1971; AI British Section report, 1967–68, p. 4 refers to earlier grants from the same source.

30. Bodleian Library, Scott papers, Box 82, 1 June 1976, Astor to Roland Oliver; 19 January 1976 Ben Whitaker memorandum prepared for meeting with Ford Foundation.

31. M. Luetchford and P. Burns, *Waging the War on Want: 50 Years of Campaigning against Global Poverty* (London: War on Want, 2003), p. 75. Bodleian Library, Huddleston papers, Box 50, 18 December 1972, circular from Victor Powell, outgoing General Secretary, War on Want.

32. The CHE was initially the Homosexual Law Reform Society. For a good overview see M. Waites, 'Lesbian, Gay and Bisexual NGOs in Britain: Past, Present and Future', in N. Crowson, M. Hilton, and J. McKay, *NGOs in Contemporary Britain: Non-State Actors in Society and Politics since 1945* (Basingstoke: Palgrave Macmillan, 2009), pp. 95–112.

33. For instance, *Spare Rib*, January 1973, pp. 30–1, and August 1975.

34. C. Moores, *Civil Liberties and Human Rights in Twentieth-Century Britain* (Cambridge University Press, 2017), pp. 187–209.

35. *British Amnesty*, February 1978 ('A Case of Conscience' by Steve Whaley); see also August 1978 and October/November 1979.

36. *British Amnesty*, October 1978.

37. *British Amnesty*, April 1979 and June/July 1979.

38. See *The Times*, 12 October and 24 October 1978, letters from Brian Crozier; *The Free Nation*, 29 September–13 October 1978, p. 3.

39. Interview with Joseph in *British Amnesty*, October 1978; Joseph's papers in the Bodleian Library, KJ 8/22, show that Amnesty's British Section approached Thatcher directly in 1977.

40. Hartley Shawcross, who had recently stepped down as chair of Justice, had also become disenchanted with the civil liberties organisations in the 1970s. He accused the NCCL of only caring for the liberties of those accused of a crime (Hull History Centre, UDJU/1/2, Shawcross to Tony Smythe, 28 November 1972).

41. *The Free Nation*, 27 October—9 November 1978, 'The New Pope's Stand on Human Rights'.

42. An article by J. Eckel offers an excellent analysis of how this growth was achieved ('The International League for the Rights of Man, Amnesty International, and the Changing Fate of Human Rights Activism from the 1940s through the 1970s', *Humanity: an International Journal of Human Rights, Humanitarianism, and Development*, vol. 4, no. 2 (2013), 183–214.

43. AI *Annual Report*, 1973–74, p. 8; AI *Annual Report*, 1975–76, p. 22.

44. IISH, AI IS, 1172, Baker to Kevin [White], 15 June 1974.

45. *The Irish Times*, 23 November 1971, p. 15.

46. IISH, AI IS, 1181, 1 November 1969, Marreco to Baker.

47. University of Bradford, Baker papers, 2/5, 6 July 1973, Ennals to MacBride; letter to the author from Anthony Marreco, 31 October 2002; in an exasperated letter to Ennals of 18 October 1971 MacBride listed all of his promptings on Northern Ireland, '*not one*' of which had been replied to (IISH, AI IS, 1183).

48. As Treasurer Marreco had set up an Amnesty International Development Inc. (AID Inc.) in the United States in 1970, which was totally separate from Amnesty International and which could send funds to families of Greek prisoners. This was strongly opposed by AI USA (Bodleian Library, Spender papers, MS Spender 74, 4 October 1971, Spender to Michael Scammell (WSI); see also IISH, AI IS, 48). After his resignation Marreco offered AID Inc. as an alternative to Amnesty, true to its original values, *Irish Times*, 23 November 1971, p. 15.

49. University of Bradford, Baker papers, 2/5, 12 July MacBride to Baker, complaining about Zeman's 'Cold War language'; 20 September 1972, MacBride to Baker about the new Treasurer.

50. IISH, AI IS, 1269, 23 April 1969, Gordon Smith to Marreco.

51. IISH, AI IS, 1255, 26 January 1974, Marsh to MacBride.

52. See correspondence in University of Bradford, Baker papers, 2/5.

53. IISH, AI IS, 1276, draft chairman's report for British Section, 1970–71.

54. The committee was set up in 1968 after British peace protestors occupied the Greek Embassy and were controversially refused prisoner of conscience status.

55. HAPOTOC stood for 'Help a Prisoner and Outlaw Torture Organizing Committee'.; *The Guardian*, 15 September 1975, p. 11. See also *Workers Press*, 13 September 1975, pp. 10-11, and Amnesty's press release, 19 September 1975 (Peter Benenson papers (AI)).

56. MRC, Mss 292B/863/4, minutes of AI British Section AGM, 23 June 1968.

57. *British Amnesty*, January/February 1975.

58. Jesuits in Britain archives, Roberts papers, 19/6/2, British Section AGM, 1975.

59. Patricia Feeney, paper for Seminario Solidaridad Internacional, Buenos Aires, 7–8 March 2007, p. 1.

60. AI *Annual Report*, 1971–72, p. 5; *British Amnesty* September/October 1974 for a similar comment by the Vice-Chair of the British Section; *British Amnesty News*, 3 July 1971.

61. *British Amnesty*, July/August 1974.

62. AI *Annual Report*, 1972–73, pp. 12–13; 1973–74, pp. 10–11.

63. Moyn, *Last Utopia*, p. 149; B. Keys, *Reclaiming American Virtue: The Human Rights Revolution of the 1970s* (Cambridge, MA: Harvard University Press, 2014); S. Snyder, 'Exporting Amnesty International to the United States: Transatlantic Human Rights Activism in the 1960s', *Human Rights Quarterly*, vol. 34, no. 3 (August 2012), 779–99.

64. Keys, *Reclaiming American Virtue*, p. 187; Moyn reports growth to 90,000 by the end of the decade, *Last Utopia*, p. 146.

65. AI *Annual Report*, 1977, p. 11; 1975–76, p. 10.

66. *British Amnesty*, April–May 1974. By 1979 the Director of British Amnesty was referring to 'what used to be called the "Threes Principle"' (*British Amnesty*, April 1978).

67. IISH, AI IS, 1272, 15 February 1970, Baker to Bruce Findlow.

68. AI *Annual Report*, 1968–69, p. 4.

69. *British Amnesty*, July 1973.

70. *British Amnesty*, September/October 1975 (with accompanying letter from Oestreicher and Simpson); November/December 1976; June 1978; February 1979.

71. Figures given in C. Rootes, 'Environmental NGOs and the Environmental Movement in England', in Crowson et al., *NGOs in Contemporary Britain*, p. 212.

72. *British Amnesty*, October/November 1979.

73. S.-L. Hoffman, 'Human Rights and History', *Past & Present*, vol. 232, no. 1 (August 2016), 279–310.

74. *The Observer*, 16 October 1977, p. 4.

75. *British Amnesty*, January 1973, March/April 1973.

76. Series of articles by A. Bristow in *British Amnesty*, June 1978; October 1978, December 1978, February 1979, April 1979, June/July 1979.

77. AI London Region, *Report on Case Work*, March 1979, pp. xxvii–xxix.

78. *The Times*, 2 June 1972, p. 4.

79. Luetchford and Burns, *Waging the War on Want*, p. 75.

80. Bishopsgate Institute, INDEX 20, Minutes of Council, 21 January 1976; *British Amnesty*, February 1979.

81. M. Scammell, 'How Index on Censorship Started', in G. Theiner (ed.), *They Shoot Writers, Don't They?* (London: Faber and Faber, 1984), p. 21.

82. Copy in Bodleian Library, Ms Spender 74.

83. Bishopsgate Institute, Index 3, 'I regard you as the founding father of Index', Hugh Lunghi to Crankshaw, 13 October 1980.

84. Bishopsgate Institute, INDEX 19, undated memorandum from Crankshaw, attached to his letter of 3 June 1969 to Leonard Wolfson.

85. Bishopsgate Institute, INDEX 3, 1 November 1974, Crankshaw to Scammell. But see also INDEX 19, April 1970, Crankshaw to Wolfson: 'there is a strong Jewish angle to this affair, but it cannot be specifically Jewish'.

86. Bodleian Library, Ms Spender 74, WSI, *Aims*.

87. Bishopsgate Institute, INDEX 19, 10 December 1968, Crankshaw to Astor; INDEX 13, 24 October 1975, David Kessler to Lois Sieff.

88. Bishopsgate Institute, INDEX 3, 27 March 1979, Scammell to Crankshaw.

89. *The New Yorker*, 18 August 1975, pp. 21–3; Bishopsgate Institute, Index 21, WSI minutes, June 1977.

90. In the discussions prior to the launch of Index the decision had been taken – after significant disagreements – that the WSI should not take up the case of the countercultural magazine *Oz*, which was being prosecuted for obscenity (INDEX 20, Editorial Committee, 16 January 1976, and Executive Committee, 21 January 1976.

91. See above, p. 80; none of this early history is mentioned in the MRG's brief online publication, *40 Years Protecting Minorities, 1969–2009*, minorityrights .org/wp-content/uploads/2015/12/MRG-AR09-ARTWORK-Proof-lo-2 .pdf.

92. Bodleian Library, Scott papers, Box 82, Scott's undated memo on 'Rights of Man in Minorities and Nationalities' (undated, March 1968?). Scott sent a copy to Peter Benenson: he was sympathetic, but sceptical about Scott's call for an international organisation for minorities (Scott papers, Box 9, Benenson to Scott, 3 April 1967).

93. Bodleian Library, Scott papers, Box 43, 24 November 1977, Astor to Richard Kershaw.

94. See Bodleian Library, Scott papers, Box 44, Dinah Brook to Council members, 13 June 1969; for the origins of Survival International see R. Hanbury-Tenison, *Worlds Apart: an Explorer's Life* (London: Arrow, 1991).

95. An evaluation of MRG's work carried out in 1974 by Edward Mortimer gives a good assessment of the reception of the reports (Bodleian Library, Scott papers, Box 44).

96. Bodleian Library, Scott papers, Box 82, 17 January 1977, Astor to Keith Kyle (draft).

97. Bodleian Library, Scott papers, Box 44, memorandum by Ben Whitaker, September 1971.

98. Bodleian Library, Scott papers, Box 44, Scott's memorandum, 1 October 1975.

99. Bodleian Library, Scott papers, Box 5a, Scott to Cyril Dunn, 9 October 1976.

100. Bodleian Library, Scott papers, Box 44, Scott and Astor to Kessler, 7 November 1977.

101. Bodleian Library, Scott papers, Box 79, 28 June 1982, Scott to the Ferrys.

102. *Human Rights Handbook*, p. 16; Bodleian, Scott papers, Box 44, undated Student Press Service syndicated interview with Whitaker; Box 44, memorandum by Whitaker, September 1971.

103. Bodleian Library, Scott papers, Box 44, MRG minutes, 27 November 1973.

104. IISH, AI IS, 986, interview with Marlys Deeds, 17 June 1985, pp. 68–70.

105. *The Guardian*, 19 December 1958, p. 2. The typescript of Hauser's interview with Theodore Roszak, editor of *Peace News* 1964–65, is a good source on the Centre for Group Studies (Bradford, *Peace News* archive, 10/161).

106. R. Hauser and H. Menuhin, *The Fraternal Society* (London: Bodley Head, 1962), pp. 7–11; see also IISH, AI IS, 1176, 1961 report of the Institute for Group and Society Development.

107. *The Friend*, 16 May 1969, pp. 591–2; Churchill College, DGFT 8/19, 'Kathleen' to Dingle Foot, 2 July 1970.

108. Friends' House Archives, 367/2/4/1, 14 January 1960, Hauser to Francis Jude. Hauser was paraphrasing Neville Chamberlain's infamous broadcast on the Sudetenland crisis in 1938.

109. University of Bradford, Baker papers, 1/O, February 1975 CHHR memorandum; Bodleian Library, Scott papers, Box 35, 20 December 1976, Hauser and Lee to Scott; LSE, UNA 28/2/17
110. Bodleian Library, Scott papers, Box 66, 1975 CHHR memorandum. Only one scheme was specifically identified – a Local Community Activation project in Pimlico and Islington.
111. Jesuits in Britain archives, Roberts papers, SJ/13/12/3.
112. LSE, UNA 28/2/9, 1979 CHHR report. It should be noted that Ceauşescu had been courted by the West and made a state visit to Britain in 1978.
113. Jesuit archives, Roberts papers, SJ/13/12/3, 29 January 1975, Hauser to Roberts.
114. LSE, UNA 4/8/1, UNA minutes, 24 June 1971.
115. See UNESCO, *Human Rights: Comments and Interpretations* (London: Allan Wingate, 1949), and above, p. 35
116. *The Human Rights Handbook*, p. 5.
117. LSE, UNA 4/8/1, report by Suter, January 1973.
118. LSE, UNA 14/1/1, 30 October 1975, Cecil Evans to Martin Ennals.
119. LSE, UNA 14/2/4, Evans to Levin, 12 December 1975.
120. LMA/4016/IS/A/04/053, 1 September 1977 memorandum by Bill Seary.
121. LMA/4016/IS/A/04/053, minutes for 18 October 1977.
122. LSE, UNA 14/1/1, 30 October 1975, Evans to Ennals.
123. LSE, UNA 14/1/1, 16 October 1975, Burns to Leah Levin.
124. LSE, UNA/14/1/1, undated draft memorandum, 'Operation of the Human Rights Network in the UK', p. 2.
125. LSE, UNA/4/1/1, 21 December 1978, Michael Fidler, Board of Deputies to Rev. Harding, Director of UNA, and undated reply; 16 February 1979, Harding to Fidler.
126. LSE, UNA/14/1/1, undated draft memorandum, 'Operation of the Human Rights Network in the UK', p. 5.
127. LSE/UNA/4/8/2, UNA HRC minutes, 28 June 1977, report on 'completely informal' seminar on human rights organised by the Foreign and Commonwealth Office.
128. *Human Rights Handbook*, pp. 204–5.
129. CHR '78 news sheet, December 1977. The British offices were provided by the PPU (England) and the Scottish Council for Civil Liberties, but the campaign was slow to develop in Britain (for details see IISH, WRI papers file 150).
130. The best source for this initiative is Regent's Park College, Payne papers, Human Rights Box, Amnesty file.
131. For Oestreicher's biography see British Section, 1974 AGM, candidates' notes. See also his pamphlet *Thirty Years of Human Rights* (British Churches' Advisory Forum on Human Rights and the Christian Institute Fund Trustees, 1980).
132. Regent's Park College, Russell papers, Box 5, 'Consider Jesus … Human Rights Is a Christian Concern' (undated).

CONCLUSION: THE WINDS OF HISTORY

1. L. J. Collins, *Faith under Fire* (London: Frewin, 1966), p. 353.
2. P. Archer, *Human Rights*, Fabian research series 274 (London: Fabian Society, 1969), pp. 22–3.
3. Regent's Park College, Russell papers, Box 3, Russell's undated notes for a speech moving the resolution to set up the Advisory Forum on human rights at the BCC, 13 April 1977.
4. IISH, AI IS, 1280, [illegible] to Joyce Baker.
5. P. Benenson, 'Political Dissent in Developing Countries', *Views*, vol. 3 (Autumn/Winter 1963), 118–21.
6. IISH, AI IS, 1174, 17 October 1975, Baker to Mark Grantham.
7. Benenson, 'Human Rights Day: No Abatement of Violence', *The Scotsman*, 10 December 1964.
8. F. Elwyn-Jones, *In My Time: an Autobiography* (London: Weidenfeld and Nicolson, 1983), p. 111.
9. See above, p. 5.
10. During the 1970s he devoted much time to the case of the Rhodesian refugee Didymus Mutasa, which he wrongly hoped would force Britain to intervene in the conflict, and his allegations of corruption in relief work for Bangladesh, an issue which did little more than sour his relations with Huddleston (see Bodleian Library, Mss Huddleston, Box 19).
11. MRG, *40 Years Protecting Minorities, 1969–2009*, minorityrights.org/wp-content/uploads/2015/12/MRG-AR09-ARTWORK-Proof-lo-2.pdf.
12. AI *Annual Report*, 1975–76, p. 7.
13. IISH, AI IS, 1265, circular by Tony Barton of West Bristol AI, May 1967.
14. See above, p. 4.
15. PRONI, D 1050/6/E/16, 25 July 1968, report by A. Lightbody.
16. *British Amnesty*, August–September 1980.
17. *Voyage*, January/February 1975, p. 7, 'W.C.C. Consultation on Human Rights'; the B. C. C. assembly, 28–30 October 1974, concluded that any call by the British churches for human rights in Eastern Europe would 'rightly be judged in terms of their commitment to the full implementation of human rights in the UK' (ibid., p. 13).
18. LSE, UNA 14/2/2, undated, application entitled 'Human Rights research programme'.
19. See above, p. 169.
20. Bodleian Library, Anti-Slavery Society, S.19 D 10/16, File 5, Secretary to Mr Woodall, 30 March 1964.
21. *The Times*, 26 July 1974, p. 4.
22. See above, p. 141.
23. IISH, AI IS, 1253, 21 September 1964, Benenson to Father Pire.
24. See above, p. 156.
25. 'Today as often in the past the extension of human rights has had to wait for a Labour Government', *Labour Party 1970 Manifesto*, p. 4.

26. M. Hurst, *British Human Rights Organisations and Soviet Dissent, 1965–1985* (London: Bloomsbury, 2016), p. 138; *The Guardian*, 28 January 1977, p. 22.
27. See Thatcher, *Path to Power*, pp. 527–30.
28. Jacques Berthoud in *British Amnesty*, February/March 1980.
29. R. Hanbury-Tenison, *Worlds Apart: an Explorer's Life* (London: Arrow, 1991), p. 282.
30. *The Times*, 31 October 1986, p. 9 and 10 December 1986, p. 7.
31. *The Guardian*, 23 April 1985, p. 8.
32. L. Selden and T. Kierans, *Irish Human Rights Handbook: a Guide to Nongovernmental Organisations* (Dublin: Oak Tree Press, 1994). For an interesting analysis of the rise of rights discourse in Northern Ireland see J. Curtis, *Human Rights as War by Other Means: Peace Politics in Northern Ireland* (Philadelphia: University of Pennsylvania Press, 2014).
33. A. M. Clark, *Diplomacy of Conscience: Amnesty International and Changing Human Rights Norms* (Princeton University Press, 2001), chs. 3–5.
34. Section 28, which banned local authorities from promoting homosexuality, was a private member's amendment supported by the government passed in 1988.
35. *The Guardian*, 30 November 1988, advert for Charter 88, p. 11.
36. *The Guardian*, 30 November 1988, p. 7. For the importance of legal activism in the 1980s see M. Rask Madsen, 'France, the United Kingdom and the "Boomerang" of Human Rights, 1945–2000', in S. Halliday and P. Schmidt, *Human Rights Brought Home: Socio-Legal Perspectives on Human Rights in the National Context* (Oxford: Hart, 2004), pp. 57–71.

Bibliography

Primary Archive Sources

Amnesty International (Easton Street, London)

Amnesty International
Peter Benenson

Archivum Britannicum Societatis Iesu (Jesuits in Britain archives),
Mount Street, London

Father Thomas Corbishley
Archbishop Roberts

Bishopsgate Institute, London

Index on Censorship
Shelter

Bodleian Library, Oxford

Commonwealth and African Collections

Africa Bureau
Anti-Apartheid Movement
Anti-Slavery Society
End of Empire transcripts (ITV)
Fabian Colonial Bureau
Bishop Trevor Huddleston
Margery Perham
Prof. Terence Ranger
Rev. Michael Scott
Arthur Young

Modern Political Manuscripts

John Alexander-Sinclair
Clement Attlee (Earl Attlee)
Violet Bonham Carter
Barbara Castle (Baroness Castle)
Sir Stafford Cripps
Anthony Greenwood
Geoffrey Howe (Lord Howe)
Harold Macmillan (Earl Macmillan)
Moral Re-Armament
Oxfam
Lord Sankey
Stephen Spender
Harold Wilson (Lord Wilson)

Borthwick Institute, University of York

Capricorn Africa Society
Patrick Duncan
James Lemkin
Southern Rhodesia Legal Aid and Welfare Fund

Camden Local Studies and Archive Centre, Holborn Library

Camden Borough Council

Christ Church, Oxford

Tom Driberg

Churchill College, Cambridge

Fenner Brockway
Dingle Foot
Gerald Gardiner
John Hynd
Philip Noel-Baker

Hull History Centre

Justice
National Council for Civil Liberties

Robin Page Arnot
John Platts-Mills
Stanley Evans

Institute of Commonwealth Studies, Senate House, London

Jack Halpern
Colin Legum

International Institute of Social History, Amsterdam

Amnesty International, International Secretariat
War Resistance International

The Keep, Brighton

Benn Levy

King's College, London

British Institute of Human Rights
League for Democracy in Greece

Labour History Museum, Manchester

Chile Solidarity Campaign
Communist Party of Great Britain
Bob Edwards
Judith Hart
Labour Party

Lambeth Palace Archives, London

Archbishop Coggan
Canon John Collins
Archbishop Fisher
Archbishop Ramsey

The Library of Birmingham

Indian Workers Association

Library of the Society of Friends, Friends' House, Euston

John Fletcher
Friends' Peace Committee
Friends' Service Council (Kenya)

London Metropolitan Archives

Board of Deputies of British Jews
Cy Grant
National Council for Social Service
Muriel Smith

LSE Special Collections

Council for Education in World Citizenship
Fellowship of Reconciliation
Haldane Society
National Peace Council
Society of Labour Lawyers
United Nations Association

Marx Memorial Library, London

International Brigade Memorial Archive
Eileen Turner (Appeal for Amnesty in Spain)

Modern Records Centre, University of Warwick

Victor Gollancz
Howard League for Penal Reform
Clive Jenkins
Margaret Staunton
Trades Union Congress

The National Archives, Kew

Foreign Office/Foreign and Colonial Office (after 1968)
Home Office
MI5 (KV2 series) files on Neil Lawson, Michael Scott, Kwame Nkrumah,
    D. N. Pritt, Thomas Hodgkin, Basil Davidson, Fenner Brockway, Peter
    Koinange, Cheddi and Janet Jagan, Geoffrey Bing, David and Martin Ennals,
    Ambrose Applebe, W. H. Thompson, Dudley Collard, Kenelm Digby
Metropolitan Police

National Library of Scotland, Edinburgh

Lord Ritchie-Calder
George MacLeod/Iona Community
Scottish Council for Civil Liberties

National Library of Wales, Aberystwyth

Clement Davies
Lord Elwyn Jones

Nottinghamshire Archives

1968: UN Year for Human Rights

Private Papers

Peter Benenson (in the possession of Natasha Benenson)

Public Record Office of Northern Ireland, Belfast

Denis Barritt
Belfast Trades Council

School of Oriental and African Studies, London

Movement for Colonial Freedom
Thomas Fox-Pitt

Regent's Park College, Oxford, Park Library

Ernest Payne
David Russell

University of Bradford Library, Special Collections

Eric Baker
Harold Blakemore
Peace News papers

University of Bristol, Special Collections

Don Bateman

Penguin Archive

Westminster Diocesan Archives

ACF Beales
Cardinal Griffin
Cardinal Hinsley

Newspapers and Journals

Amnesty International, *Annual Reports*, 1962–79
Anti-Slavery Reporter
British Amnesty, 1973–80
The Free Nation, 1976–79
The Friend, 1945–76
League of Coloured Peoples Letter/News Letter, 1939–48
New World (UNA)
Peace News, 1940–70
The People and Freedom News Sheet, 1940–49
Sword of the Spirit/The Sword, 1940–54

Published Sources: Books and Pamphlets

Amnesty International, *Amnesty International, 1961–1976: a Chronology* (London: Amnesty International Publications, 1976).
Amnesty International, *Chile* (London: Amnesty International Publications, 1974).
Amnesty International, *Prisoners of Conscience in the USSR: Their Treatment and Conditions* (London: Amnesty International Publications, 1975).
Amnesty International, *Report on Torture* (London: Duckworth, 1973).
Amnesty International, *A Time to Keep Silence and a Time to Speak* (London: Amnesty International, 1962).
Amnesty International, *Torture in Greece: the First Torturers' Trial 1975* (London: Amnesty International, 1977).
Amnesty International, *Torture of Political Prisoners in Greece: a Second Report by Amnesty International* (London: Amnesty International Publications, 6 April 1968).
Ana, M., de Nicolas, V., & Ibarrola, A., *From Burgos Jail: Poems and Drawings* (London: Appeal for Amnesty in Spain, April 1964).
Anderson, D., *Histories of the Hanged: Britain's Dirty War in Kenya and the End of Empire* (London: Weidenfeld & Nicholson, 2005).
Archer, P., *Human Rights*, Research series 274 (London, Fabian Society, 1969).
Archer, P., & Reay, H. W. M., *Freedom at Stake* (London: Bodley Head, 1966).
Barnett, M., *Empire of Humanity: a History of Humanitarianism* (Ithaca, New York: Cornell University Press, 2011).

Barritt, D. P., & Booth, A., *Orange and Green: a Quaker Study of Community Relations in Northern Ireland* (Sedbergh, UK: Northern Friends Peace Board, 1972).

Barritt, D. P., & Carter, C. F. *The Northern Ireland Problem: a Study in Group Relations* (Oxford University Press, 1962).

Becket, J., *Barbarism in Greece: a Young American Lawyer's Inquiry into the Use of Torture in Contemporary Greece, with Case Histories and Documents* (New York: Walker, 1970).

Beeson, T., *Britain Today and Tomorrow* (London: Fount Paperbacks, 1978).

Beeson, T., *Discretion and Valour: Religious Conditions in Russia and Eastern Europe* (London: Collins, 1974).

Bell, G., *Christianity and World Order* (Harmondsworth: Penguin, 1941).

Belton, N., *The Good Listener: Helen Bamber, a Life against Cruelty* (London: Weidenfeld & Nicolson, 1998).

Benn, T., & Winstone, R., *Years of Hope: Diaries, Letters and Papers 1940–1962* (London: Hutchinson, 1994).

Benenson, P., *Gangrene* (London: Calderbooks, 1959).

Benenson, P., *The Other Face* (Oxford: The Pauper's Press, 1977).

Benenson, P., *Persecution 1961* (Harmondsworth: Penguin, 1961).

Bennett, H., *Fighting the Mau Mau: The British Army and Counter-Insurgency in the Kenya Emergency* (Cambridge University Press, 2013).

Benson, M., *A Far Cry* (London: Viking, 1989).

Benson, M., *Tshekedi Khama* (London: Faber and Faber, 1960).

Bentwich, N., *My Seventy-Seven Years: an Account of My Life and Times, 1883–1960* (London: Routledge & Kegan Paul, 1962).

Bess, M., *Realism, Utopia, and the Mushroom Cloud: Four Activist Intellectuals and Their Strategies for Peace, 1945–1989* (University of Chicago Press, 1993).

Bing, G., *Reap the Whirlwind: an Account of Kwame Nkrumah's Ghana from 1950 to 1966* (London: MacGibbon & Kee, 1968).

Birn, D., *The League of Nations Union, 1918–1945* (Oxford University Press, 1981).

Black, M., *A Cause for Our Times: Oxfam: the First 50 Years* (Oxford: Oxfam, 1992).

Bloch, M., *Jeremy Thorpe* (London: Abacus, 2014).

Bloch, S., & Reddaway, P., *Psychiatric Terror: How Soviet Psychiatry Is Used to Suppress Dissent* (New York: Basic Books, 1977).

Bloch, S., & Reddaway, P., *Soviet Psychiatric Abuse: the Shadow over World Psychiatry* (London: V. Gollancz, 1984).

Borgwardt, E., *A New Deal for the World: America's Vision for Human Rights* (Cambridge, MA & London: Belknap Press of Harvard University Press, 2005).

Bone, E., *Seven Years Solitary* (London: Hamish Hamilton, 1957).

Bottome, P., *Our New Order – or Hitler's? A Selection of Speeches by Winston Churchill, the Archbishop of Canterbury, Anthony Eden [and Others]* (Harmondsworth: Penguin, 1943).

Bourdeaux, M., *Religious Ferment in Russia: Protestant Opposition to Soviet Policy* (Basingstoke: Macmillan, 1968).

Box, M., & Gardiner, G., *Rebel Advocate: a Biography of Gerald Gardiner* (London: Victor Gollancz, 1983).

Bridges, R., *The Testament of Beauty* (Oxford: Clarendon Press, 1929).

Brittain, V., *The Story of St. Martin's: an Epic of London* (Bournemouth: Pardy and Son, 1951).

British Amnesty Section, *Epidemic: Torture* (British Amnesty, 1973).

Brockway, F., *African Journeys* (London: Gollancz, 1955).

Brockway, F., *Why Mau Mau? An Analysis and a Remedy* (London: Congress of Peoples against Imperialism, 1953).

Brockway, F., *Towards Tomorrow: the Autobiography of Fenner Brockway* (London: Hart-Davis, MacGibbon, 1977).

Brown, C., *The Death of Christian Britain: Understanding Secularisation 1800–2000* (London: Routledge, 2009).

Buchanan, T., *East Wind: China and the British Left* (Oxford University Press, 2012).

Burke, R., *Decolonization and the Evolution of International Human Rights* (Philadelphia: University of Pennsylvania Press, 2010).

Calvocoressi, P., *Threading My Way* (London: Duckworth, 1994).

Campaign for Social Justice, *The Plain Truth*, 2nd ed. (Castlefields, Dungannan: Campaign for Social Justice, 1969).

Carruthers, S., *Winning Hearts and Minds: British Governments, the Media and Colonial Counter-Insurgency, 1944–1960* (London: Leicester University Press, 1995).

Cassidy, S., *Audacity to Believe* (London: Collins, 1997).

Chater, P., *Grass Roots: the Story of St Faith's Farm in Southern Rhodesia* (London: Hodder & Stoughton, 1962).

Christiaens, K., Goddeeris, I., & Rodríguez Garciá, M. (eds), *European Solidarity with Chile: 1970s–1980s* (Frankfurt am Main: Peter Lang, 2014).

Clark, A. M., *Diplomacy of Conscience: Amnesty International and Changing Human Rights Norms* (Princeton University Press, 2001).

Clark, J., *The National Council for Civil Liberties and the Policing of Interwar Politics: At Liberty to Protest* (Manchester University Press, 2012).

Clements, K., ed., *The Moot Papers, 1938–1944* (London: T&T Clark, 2009).

Cockett, R., *David Astor and the Observer* (London: Deutsch, 1991).

Collins, D., *Christian Action* (London: Gollancz, 1949).

Collins, D., *Partners in Protest: Life with Canon Collins* (London: Gollancz, 1992).

Collins, L. J., *Faith under Fire* (London: Frewin, 1966).

Constantine, L., *Colour Bar* (London: Stanley Paul, 1954).

Cottrell, R., *Roger Nash Baldwin and the American Civil Liberties Union* (New York: Columbia University Press, 2000).

Cox, B., *Civil Liberties in Britain* (Harmondsworth, Middlesex: Penguin, 1975).

Cranston, M., *Human Rights To-Day* (London: Ampersand books, 1962).

Crowson, N., Hilton, M., & McKay, J., *NGOs in Contemporary Britain: Non-State Actors in Society and Politics since 1945* (Basingstoke: Palgrave Macmillan, 2009).

Currie, A., *All Hell Will Break Loose* (Dublin: O'Brien Press, 2004).

Curtis, J., *Human Rights as War by Other Means: Peace Politics in Northern Ireland* (Philadelphia: University of Pennsylvania Press, 2014).

Curtis, J., *The Land of Liberty* (London: Secker and Warburg, 1938).

Denniston, R., *Trevor Huddleston: A Life* (Basingstoke: Macmillan, 1999).

Dickson, B., *The European Convention on Human Rights and the Conflict in Northern Ireland* (Oxford University Press, 2010).

Dolci, D., *To Feed the Hungry: Enquiry in Palermo* (London: MacGibbon & Kee, 1959).

Driver, C. J., *Patrick Duncan: South African and Pan-African* (Oxford: James Currey, 2000).

Drohan, B., *Brutality in an Age of Human Rights: Activism and Counterinsurgency at the End of the British Empire* (Ithaca, NY & London: Cornell University Press, 2018).

Dubow, S., *Apartheid, 1948–1994* (Oxford University Press, 2014).

Duff, P., *Left, Left, Left: A Personal Account of Six Protest Campaigns, 1945–65* (London: Allison & Busby, 1971).

Duranti, M., *The Conservative Human Rights Revolution: European Identity, Transnational Politics, and the Origins of the European Convention* (Oxford University Press, 2017).

Dyson, B., *Liberty in Britain 1934–1994: a Diamond Jubilee History of the National Council for Civil Liberties* (London: Civil Liberties Trust, 1995).

Eckel, J., & Moyn, S., *The Breakthrough: Human Rights in the 1970s* (Philadelphia: University of Pennsylvania Press), 2014.

Elkins, C., *Britain's Gulag: the Brutal End of Empire in Kenya* (London: Pimlico, 2005).

Elwyn-Jones, F., *In My Time: an Autobiography* (London: Weidenfeld and Nicolson, 1983).

Eppstein, J., *Defend These Human Rights: Each Man's Stake in the UN – a Catholic View* (New York: Catholic Social Guild, 1947).

Evans, P., *Law and Disorder; or, Scenes of Life in Kenya* (London: Secker & Warburg, 1956).

Ferguson, R., *Chasing the Wild Goose: the Story of the Iona Community* (London: Fount, 1988).

Ferguson, R., *George MacLeod: Founder of the Iona Community* (London: Collins, 1990).

Fernández Soriano, V., *Le fusil et l'olivier: Les droits de l'Homme en Europe face aux dictatures méditerranéennes (1949–1977)* (Brussels: Éditions de l'Université de Bruxelles, 2015).

Field, F., *Sixty Years of UNA-UK* (London: United Nations Association of Great Britain and Northern Ireland, 2006) www.una.org.uk/sites/default/files/60%20Years%20of%20UNA-UK_0.pdf.

Fink, C., *Defending the Rights of Others: the Great Powers, the Jews, and International Minority Protection, 1878–1938* (Cambridge University Press, 2004).

Foley, C., *Island in Revolt* (London: Longman's, 1962)

French, D., *Fighting EOKA: the British Counter-Insurgency Campaign on Cyprus, 1955–1959* (Oxford University Press, 2015).

Garling, M., *The Human Rights Handbook: a Guide to British and American International Human Rights Organisations* (London: Macmillan Press, 1979).

Garnett, J. (ed.), *Redefining Christian Britain: Post-1945 Perspectives* (London: SCM Press, 2007).

Garton Ash, T., *The Uses of Adversity: Essays on the Fate of Central Europe* (Cambridge: Granta, 1989).

Glendon, M. A., *A World Made New: Eleanor Roosevelt and the Universal Declaration of Human Rights* (New York: Random House, 2001).

Gollancz, V., *Our Threatened Values* (London: Victor Gollancz, 1946).

Gorman, D., *The Emergence of International Society in the 1920s* (Cambridge University Press, 2012).

Grant, J., *Jack Grant's Story* (Guildford: Lutterworth Press, 1980).

Grubb, K., *Crypts of Power: an Autobiography* (London: Hodder & Stoughton, 1971).

Gurney, C., '*A Great Cause': the Origins of the Anti-Apartheid Movement, June 1959–June 1960* (London: AAM Archives Committee, 1988).

Halliday, S., & Schmidt, P., *Human Rights Brought Home: Socio-Legal Perspectives on Human Rights in the National Context* (Oxford: Hart, 2004).

Hanbury-Tenison, R., *Worlds Apart: an Explorer's Life* (London: Arrow, 1991).

Hauser, R., & Menuhin, H., *The Fraternal Society* (London: Bodley Head, 1962).

Hearnden, H., *Red Robert: Life of Robert Birley* (London: Hamish Hamilton, 1984).

Heartfield, J., *The British and Foreign Anti-Slavery Society 1838–1956: a History* (London: Hurst & Company, 2016).

Heineman, B. W., *The Politics of the Powerless: a Study of the Campaign Against Racial Discrimination* (Oxford University Press, 1972).

Heerten, L., *The Biafran War and Postcolonial Humanitarianism: Spectacles of Suffering* (Cambridge University Press, 2017).

Herbstein, D., *White Lies: Canon Collins and the Secret War against Apartheid* (Cape Town: HSRC Press, 2004).

Hilton, M., Crowson, N., Mouhot, J., & McKay, J., *A Historical Guide to NGOs in Britain: Charities, Civil Society and the Voluntary Sector since 1945* (Basingstoke: Palgrave Macmillan, 2012).

Hilton, M., McKay, J., Crowson, N., & Mouhot, J., *The Politics of Expertise: How NGOs Shaped Modern Britain* (Oxford University Press, 2013).

Hochschild, A., *Bury the Chains: the British Struggle to Abolish Slavery* (London: Macmillan, 2005).

Hoffmann, S.-L., *Human Rights in the Twentieth Century* (Cambridge University Press, 2011).

Hopgood, S., *Keepers of the Flame: Understanding Amnesty International* (Ithaca, NY & London: Cornell University Press, 2006).

Howe, S. *Anticolonialism in British Politics: the Left and the End of Empire, 1918–1964* (Oxford: Oxford University Press, 1993).

Huddleston, T., *Naught for Your Comfort* (London: Collins, 1956).

Huddleston, T., Collins, L. J., Raynes, R. & Scott, M., *Four Words on South Africa* (London: Christian Action, 1957).

Hurn, D. A., *Archbishop Roberts S. J.: His Life and Writings* (London: Darton, Longman & Todd, 1966).

Hurst, M., *British Human Rights Organisations and Soviet Dissent, 1965–1985* (London: Bloomsbury, 2016).

Ignotus, P., *Political Prisoner* (London: Routledge and Kegan Paul, 1959).

Iriye, A., Goedde, P., & Hitchcock, W., *The Human Rights Revolution: an International History* (Oxford University Press, 2012).

Ishay, M., *The History of Human Rights: From Ancient Times to the Globalization Era* (Berkeley: University of California Press, 2004).

Iyer, Raghavan (ed.), *The Moral and Political Writings of Mahatma Gandhi, Volume III* (Oxford University Press, 1987).

Jenkins, R., *A Life at the Centre* (London: Macmillan, 1991).

Jensen, S., *The Making of International Human Rights: the 1960s, Decolonization, and the Reconstruction of Global Values* (New York: Cambridge University Press, 2016).

Jones, A., *No Truck with the Chilean Junta! Trade Union Internationalism, Australia and Britain, 1973–1980* (Canberra: ANU Press, 2014).

Kariuki, J. M., *'Mau Mau' Detainee: the Account by a Kenya African of His Experiences in Detention Camps, 1953–1960* (Oxford University Press, 1963).

Keck, M., & Sikkin, K., *Activists beyond Borders: Advocacy Networks in International Politics* (Ithaca, NY: Cornell University Press, 1998).

Keys, B., *Reclaiming American Virtue: The Human Rights Revolution of the 1970s* (Cambridge, MA: Harvard University Press, 2014).

Kidd, R., *British Liberty in Danger: an Introduction to the Study of Civil Rights* (London: Lawrence & Wishart, 1940).

Klose, F., *Human Rights in the Shadow of Colonial Violence: the Wars of Independence in Kenya and Algeria* (Philadelphia: University of Pennsylvania Press, 2013).

Korey, W., *NGOs and the Universal Declaration of Human Rights: 'a Curious Grapevine'* (Basingstoke & New York: Macmillan, 1998).

Larsen, E., *A Flame in Barbed Wire: the Story of Amnesty International* (London: F. Muller, 1978).

Laski, H., *The Rights of Man* (London: Macmillan, 1940).

Lauterpacht, H., *An International Bill of the Rights of Man* (New York: University of Columbia Press, 1945).

Lauterpacht, H., *An International Bill of the Rights of Man*, with an introduction by Philippe Sands, ed. (Oxford University Press, 2013).

Lean, G., *Frank Buchman: a Life* (London: Constable, 1985).

Lewis, J., *David Astor* (London: Jonathan Cape, 2016).

Lewis, W. A., Scott, M., Wight, M., & Legum, C., *Attitude to Africa* (Harmondsworth: Penguin, 1951).

Lilly, M., *The National Council for Civil Liberties: the First Fifty Years* (London: Macmillan, 1984).

Lindsay, J., & Rickword, E. (eds), *A Handbook of Freedom: a Record of English Democracy through Twelve Centuries* (London: Lawrence & Wishart, 1939).

Lodge, T., *Sharpeville: an Apartheid Massacre and Its Consequences* (Oxford University Press, 2011).

Loeffler, J. B., *Rooted Cosmopolitans: Jews and Human Rights in the Twentieth Century* (New Haven: Yale University Press, 2018).

Luetchford, M., & P. Burns, *Waging the War on Want: 50 Years of Campaigning against Global Poverty* (London: War on Want, 2003).

McCarthy, H., *The British People and the League of Nations: Democracy, Citizenship and Internationalism, c.1918–45* (Manchester University Press, 2011).

McCluskey, C., *Up Off Their Knees: a Commentary on the Civil Rights Movement in Northern Ireland* (Galway: Conn McCluskey and Associates, 1989).

McGowan, A., *Coloured Peoples in Britain* (London: Bow Group, 1952).

McLeod, H., *The Religious Crisis of the 1960s* (Oxford University Press, 2007).

McNeish, J., *Fire under the Ashes: the Life of Danilo Dolci* (London: Hodder & Stoughton, 1965).

Mazower, M. *Governing the World: the History of an Idea* (London: Penguin, 2013).

Mazower, M., *No Enchanted Palace: the End of Empire and the Ideological Origins of the United Nations* (Princeton University Press, 2009).

McKeown, C., *The Passion of Peace* (Belfast: Blackstaff Press, 1984).

Mee, C., *The Internment of Soviet Dissenters in Mental Hospitals* (Cambridge: J. Arliss, 1971).

Moores, C., *Civil Liberties and Human Rights in Twentieth-Century Britain* (Cambridge University Press, 2017).

Morgan, K., *Labour Legends and Russian Gold: Bolshevism and the British Left, Part One* (London: Lawrence & Wishart, 2013).

Morton, R., *The Iona Community Story* (London: Lutterworth Press, 1957).

Moyn, S., *Christian Human Rights* (Philadelphia: University of Pennsylvania Press, 2015).

Moyn, S., *Human Rights and the Uses of History* (London: Verso, 2014).

Moyn, S., *The Last Utopia: Human Rights in History* (Cambridge, MA: Belknap Press of Harvard University Press, 2010).

Muir, A., *Outside the Safe Place: an Oral History of the Early Years of the Iona Community* (Glasgow: Wild Goose, 2011).

Mulholland, M., *Northern Ireland at the Crossroads: Ulster Unionism in the O'Neill Years, 1960–9* (Basingstoke: Macmillan, 2000).

Neier, A., *The International Human Rights Movement: a History* (Princeton University Press, 2012).

NCCL, *Report of a Commission of Enquiry into the Civil Authorities (Special Powers) Act in Northern Ireland, 1922 and 1933* (n.p.: NCCL, 1936).

Northern Ireland Civil Rights Association, '*We Shall Overcome': the History of the Struggle for Civil Rights in Northern Ireland, 1968–78* (Belfast: NICRA, 1978).

Northern Ireland Parliament, Commons Debates, vol. 68 (30 January 1968).

Oldfield, J. R., *Chords of Freedom: Commemoration, Ritual and British Transatlantic Slavery* (Manchester University Press, 2007).

Oldfield, J. R., *Popular Politics and British Anti-Slavery: the Mobilisation of Public Opinion against the Slave Trade, 1787–1807* (Manchester University Press, 1995).

Owen, D., *Human Rights* (London: J. Cape, 1978).

Padmore, G., *How Britain Rules Africa* (London: Wishart Books Ltd, 1936).

Peart-Binns, J., *Archbishop Joost de Blank: Scourge of Apartheid* (London: Muller, Blond & White, 1987).

Pennybacker, S. D., *From Scottsboro to Munich: Race and Political Culture in 1930s Britain* (Princeton University Press, 2009).

PEP, *Racial Discrimination in Britain* (London: PEP, 1967).

Platts-Mills, J., *Muck, Silk and Socialism: Recollections of a Left-Wing Queen's Counsel* (Wedmore: Paper Publishing, 2002).

Plesch, D., *Human Rights after Hitler: the Lost History of Prosecuting Axis War Crimes* (Washington DC: Georgetown University Press, 2017).

Power, J., *Against Oblivion: Amnesty International's Fight for Human Rights* (London: Fontana, 1981).

Prince, S., *Northern Ireland's '68: Civil Rights, Global Revolt and the Origins of the Troubles* (Dublin: Irish Academic Press, 2007).

Pritt, D. N., *The Autobiography of D. N. Pritt, Part One, From Right to Left* (London: Lawrence & Wishart, 1965).

Purdie, B., *Politics in the Streets, the Origins of the Civil Rights Movement in Northern Ireland* (Belfast: Blackstaff, 1990).

Rabben, L., *Fierce Legion of Friends: a History of Human Rights Campaigns and Campaigners* (Wyattsville MD: Quixote Centre, 2002).

Ranger, T., *Writing Revolt: an Engagement with African Nationalism, 1957–1967* (Oxford: James Currey, 2013).

Reddaway, P., & J. Telesin. *Uncensored Russia: the Human Rights Movement in the Soviet Union: the Annotated Text of the Unofficial Moscow Journal A Chronicle of Current Events (Nos. 1–11)* (London: Cape, 1972).

Reeves, R. A., *Shooting at Sharpeville: the Agony of South Africa* (London: V. Gollancz, 1960).

Ribi Forclaz, A., *Humanitarian Imperialism: the Politics of Anti-Slavery Activism, 1880–1940* (Oxford University Press, 2015).

Ritchie-Calder, P., *On Human Rights: Inaugural Lecture Delivered on 7th December 1967 at Conway Hall, Red Lion Square, London W.C. 1; With Two Appendices Incorporating the Sankey Declaration of the Rights of Man (1940) and the Universal Declaration of Human Rights (1948) (H. G. Wells Memorial Lectures)* (H. G. Wells Society; Distributed by M. Katanka Ltd, 1968).

Robertson, A. H., & Merrills, J. G, *Human Rights in the World: an Introduction to the Study of the International Protection of Human Rights*, 4th ed. (Manchester University Press, 1996).

Rose, P., *Backbencher's Dilemma* (London: Frederick Muller, 1981).

Rose, P., *How the Troubles Came to Northern Ireland* (Basingstoke: Macmillan, 2000).

Russell of Liverpool, Lord, *Prisons and Prisoners in Portugal: an Independent Investigation* (London: Waterlow, 1963).

Rich, P. B., *Race and Empire in British Politics* (Cambridge University Press, 1986).

Sands, P., *East West Street: on the Origins of Genocide and Crimes against Humanity* (London: Weidenfeld & Nicolson, 2016).

Sargant, T., *These Things Shall Be* (London: W. Heinemann Ltd., 1941).

Saville, J., *Memoirs from the Left* (London: Merlin, 2003).

Scaffardi, S., *Fire under the Carpet: Working for Civil Liberties in the Thirties* (London: Lawrence & Wishart, 1986).

Scarry, E., *The Body in Pain: the Making and Unmaking of the World* (Oxford University Press, 1985).

Scott, M., *Shadow over Africa* (London: Union of Democratic Control, 1950).

Scott, M., *A Time to Speak* (London: Faber and Faber, 1958).

Selden, L., & Kierans, T., *Irish Human Rights Handbook: a Guide to Nongovernmental Organisations* (Dublin: Oak Tree Press, 1994).

Sellars, K., *The Rise and Rise of Human Rights* (Stroud: Sutton, 2002).

Simpson, A. W. B., *Human Rights and the End of Empire: Britain and the Genesis of the European Convention* (Oxford University Press, 2001).

Skinner, R., *The Foundations of Anti-Apartheid: Liberal Humanitarians and Transnational Activists in Britain and the United States, c.1919–64* (Basingstoke: Palgrave Macmillan, 2010).

Snyder, S. B., *Human Rights Activism and the End of the Cold War: a Transnational History of the Helsinki Network* (Cambridge University Press, 2011).

Solomon, F., & Litvinoff, B., *Baku to Baker Street: the Memoirs of Flora Solomon* (London: Collins, 1984).

Stonehouse, J., *Prohibited Immigrant* (London: Bodley Head, 1960).

Tennyson, H., *The Haunted Mind: an Autobiography* (London: A. Deutsch, 1984).

Thatcher, M., *The Path to Power* (London: HarperCollins, 1995).

Theiner, G. (ed.), *They Shoot Writers, Don't They?* (London: Faber and Faber, 1984).

Thompson, W. H., *Civil Liberties* (London: V. Gollancz, 1938).

Tolley, H. B., *The International Commission of Jurists: Global Advocates for Human Rights* (Philadelphia: University of Pennsylvania Press, 1994).

Troup, F., *In Face of Fear: Michael Scott's Challenge to South Africa* (London: Faber and Faber, 1950).

Tuck, S., *The Night Malcolm X Spoke at the Oxford Union: a Transatlantic Story of Antiracial Protest* (Berkeley: University of California Press, 2014).

Turner, R. V., *Magna Carta: Through the Ages* (London: Longman, 2003).

Twitchell, N. H., *The Politics of the Rope: the Campaign to Abolish Capital Punishment in Britain, 1955–1969* (Bury St Edmunds: Arena, 2012).

UNESCO, *Human Rights: Comments and Interpretations* (London: Allan Wingate, 1949).

Vidal-Naquet, P., *Torture: Cancer of Democracy, France and Algeria, 1954–62* (Harmondsworth: Penguin, 1963).

Walsh, M., *From Sword to Ploughshare: Sword of the Spirit to Catholic Institute for International Relations 1940–1980* (London: Catholic Institute for International Relations, 1980).

Watts, M., *P.E.N. the Early Years, 1921–1926* (London: Archive Press, 1971).

Weeramantry, L., *The International Commission of Jurists: the Pioneering Years* (The Hague & London: Kluwer Law International, 2000).

Wells, H. G., *The New World Order: Whether It Is Attainable, How It Can Be Attained, and What Sort of World a World at Peace Will Have to Be* (London: Secker and Warburg, 1940).

Wildenthal, L., *The Language of Human Rights in West Germany* (Philadelphia: University of Pennsylvania Press, 2013).

Williams, S., *Colour Bar: the Triumph of Seretse Khama and His Nation* (London: Allen Lane, 2006).

Wilson, H., *The Labour Government 1964–70: a Personal Record* (London: Weidenfeld & Nicolson, 1971).

Wilson, H., *The New Britain: Labour's Plan* (Harmondsworth: Penguin, 1964).

Winner, D., *Peter Benenson: the Lawyer Who Campaigned for Prisoners of Conscience and Created Amnesty International* (Watford: Exley, 1991).

Winter, J., *Dreams of Peace and Freedom: Utopian Moments in the Twentieth Century* (New Haven: Yale University Press, 2006).

Wynn, A., *Notes of a Non-Conspirator: Working with Russian Dissidents* (London: Andre Deutsch, 1987).

Yates, A., & Chester, L., *The Troublemaker: Michael Scott and His Lonely Struggle against Injustice* (London: Aurum Press, 2006).

Young, K., *The Greek Passion: a Study in People and Politics* (London: J. M. Dent, 1969).

Articles and Book Chapters

Anderson, D., 'Mau Mau in the High Court and the 'Lost' British Empire Archives: Colonial Conspiracy or Bureaucratic Bungle?' *The Journal of Imperial and Commonwealth History*, vol. 39, no. 5 (2011), 699–716.

Archer, P., 'Action by Unofficial Organizations on Human Rights', in E. Luard (ed.), *The International Protection of Human Rights* (London: Thames and Hudson, 1967).

Baughan, E., '"Every Citizen of Empire Implored to Save the Children!" Empire, Internationalism and the Save the Children Fund in Inter-War Britain', *Historical Research*, vol. 86, no. 231 (2013), 116–37.

Benenson, P. 'Political Dissent in Developing Countries', *Views*, vol. 3 (Autumn/Winter 1963), 118–21.

Bennett, H., '"Detainees Are Always One's Achilles Heel": The Struggle over the Scrutiny of Detention and Interrogation in Aden, 1963–1967', *War in History*, vol. 23, no. 4 (2016), 457–88.

Betts, P., 'Religion, Science and Cold War Anti-Communism: the 1949 Cardinal Mindszenty Show Trial', in P. Betts and S. Smith, "(eds)" *Science, Religion and Communism in Cold War Europe* (Basingstoke: Palgrave Macmillan, 2016), 275–307.

Bouwman, B., 'Outraged, Yet Moderate and Impartial: the Rise of Amnesty International in the Netherlands in the 1960s and 1970s', *BMGN: Low Countries Historical Review*, vol. 132, no. 4 (2017), 53–74.

Bradley, M. P., 'American Vernaculars: the United States and the Global Human Rights Imagination', *Diplomatic History*, vol. 38, no. 1 (2014), 1–21.

Brown, R., 'The International Brigade Association and Political Prisoners in Franco's Spain', *Bulletin of the Marx Memorial Library*, vol. 136 (Autumn 2002), 4–26.

Bruce-Lockhart, K., '"The Truth about Kenya": Connection and Contestation in the 1956 Kamiti Controversy', *Journal of World History*, vol. 26, no. 4 (December 2015), 815–38.

Buchanan, T., 'Amnesty International in Crisis, 1966–7', *Twentieth Century British History*, vol. 15, no. 3 (2004), 267–89.

Buchanan, T., 'Beyond Cable Street: New Approaches to the Historiography of Anti-Fascism in Britain', in H. Garcia, M. Yusta, X. Tabet and C. Climaco "(eds)",

Rethinking Anti-Fascism: History, Memory and Politics, 1922 to the Present (New York: Berghahn Books, 2016), 61–75.

Buchanan, T., 'Holding the Line: the Political Strategy of the International Brigade Association, 1939–1977', *Labour History Review*, vol. 66, no. 3 (Winter 2001), 294–312.

Buchanan, T., 'Human Rights Campaigns in Modern Britain', in N. J. Crowson, M. Hilton, & J. McKay, "(eds)" *NGOs in Contemporary Britain: Non-State Actors in Society and Politics since 1945* (Basingstoke: Palgrave Macmillan, 2009), 113–28.

Buchanan, T., 'Human Rights, the Memory of War and the Making of a "European" identity, 1945–75', in M. Conway and K. K. Patel (eds), *Europeanization in the Twentieth Century: Historical Approaches* (Basingstoke: Palgrave Macmillan, 2010), 157–71.

Buchanan, T., 'Receding Triumph: British Opposition to the Franco Regime, 1945–59', *Twentieth Century British History*, vol. 12, no. 2 (2001), 163–84.

Buchanan, T., '"The Truth Will Set You Free": the Making of Amnesty International', *Journal of Contemporary History*, vol. 37, no. 4 (2002), 575–97.

Burke, R., '"How Time Flies': Celebrating the Universal Declaration of Human Rights in the 1960s". *The International History Review*, 38(3), 2015, 1–27.

Burke, R., 'From Individual Rights to National Development: the First UN International Conference on Human Rights, Tehran, 1968', *Journal of World History*, vol. 19, no. 3 (2008), 275–96.

Burstow, R., 'The Limits of Modernist Art as a "Weapon of the Cold War": Reassessing the Unknown Patron of the Monument to the Unknown Political Prisoner', *Oxford Art Journal*, vol. 20, no. 1 (1997), 68–80.

Clark, J., 'Sincere and Reasonable Men? The Origins of the National Council for Civil Liberties', *Twentieth Century British History*, vol. 20, no. 4 (2009), 513–37.

Dean, D., 'The Race Relations Policy of the First Wilson Government', *Twentieth Century British History*, vol. 11, no. 3 (2000), 259–83.

Dingli, S., & C. Kennedy, 'The Aden Pivot? British Counter-Insurgency after Aden', *Civil Wars*, vol. 16, no. 1 (2014), 86–104.

Eckel, J., 'Human Rights and Decolonization: New Perspectives and Open Questions', *Humanity: an International Journal of Human Rights, Humanitarianism, and Development*, vol. 1, no. 1 (Fall 2010), 111–35.

Eckel, J., 'The International League for the Rights of Man, Amnesty International, and the Changing Fate of Human Rights Activism from the 1940s through the 1970s', *Humanity: an International Journal of Human Rights, Humanitarianism, and Development*, vol. 4, no. 2 (2013), 183–214.

Elkins, Z., Ginsburg, T., & Melton, J., 'On the Influence of Magna Carta and Other Cultural Relics', *International Review of Law and Economics*, vol. 47, S (2016), 3–9.

Fagan, E. T., 'The International Secretariat of Lawyers of Pax Romana', *The Catholic Lawyer*, vol. 11, no. 2 (Spring 1965)(https://scholarship.law.stjohns.edu/cgi/viewcontent.cgi?referer=https://www.google.com/&httpsredir=1&article=1535&context=tcl)

Fernández Soriano, V., 'Facing the Greek Junta: the European Community, the Council of Europe and the Rise of Human-Rights Politics in Europe', *European Review of History: Revue Européenne D'histoire*, vol. 24, no. 3 (2017), 358–76.

Fletcher, J., 'A Quaker View of Conscience', *Reconciliation*, vol. 33, no. 9 (September 1956), part of a special edition on 'The Authority of Conscience'.

Gatehouse, M., 'Chile: the First Dictatorship of Globalisation', *Red Pepper* (9 September 2013), www.redpepper.org.uk/chile-the-first-dictatorship-of-globalisation.

Hawkins, R., 'The Internal Politics of the Non-Sectarian Anti-Nazi League to Champion Human Rights, 1933–1939', *Management & Organizational History*, vol. 5, no. 2 (2010), 251–78.

Hilton, M., 'International Aid and Development NGOs in Britain and Human Rights since 1945', *Humanity: an International Journal of Human Rights, Humanitarianism, and Development*, vol. 3, no. 3 (2012), 449–72.

Hilton, M., 'Politics is Ordinary: Non-Governmental Organizations and Political Participation in Contemporary Britain', *Twentieth Century British History*, vol. 22, no. 2 (2011), 230–68.

Hoffmann, S.-L., 'Human Rights and History', *Past & Present*, vol. 232, no. 1 (August 2016), 279–310.

Johnston-White, R. M., 'A New Primacy of Conscience? Conscientious Objection, French Catholicism and the State during the Algerian War', *Journal of Contemporary History*, vol. 54, no. 1 (January 2019), 112–38.

Keys, B., 'Anti-Torture Politics: Amnesty International, the Greek Junta and the Origins of the Human Rights "Boom" in the United States', in A. Iriye, P. Goedde, & W. I. Hitchcock (eds), *Human Rights Revolution* 201–21.

Lewis, J., "Daddy Wouldn't Buy Me a Mau Mau: the British Popular Press and the Demoralisation of Empire", in E. S. Atieno Odhiambo & J. Londsdale (eds), *Mau Mau and Nationhood: Arms, Authority and Narration* (Oxford: James Currey, 2003).

Litten, F. S., 'The Noulens Affair', *The China Quarterly*, vol. 138 (1994), 492–512.

Loeffler, J., 'The Particularist Pursuit of American Universalism: the American Jewish Committee's 1944 "Declaration on Human Rights"', *Journal of Contemporary History*, vol. 50, no. 2 (2015), 274–95.

Madsen, M. R., 'France, the United Kingdom and the "Boomerang" of the Internationalisation of Human Rights (1945–2000)"', in Halliday & Schmidt, *Human Rights Brought Home: Socio-Legal Perspectives on Human Rights in the National Context*.

Madsen, M. R., 'From Cold War Instrument to Supreme European Court: the European Court of Human Rights at the Crossroads of International and National Law and Politics', *Law and Social Inquiry*, vol. 32, no. 1 (2007), 137–59.

Marshall, D., 'The Construction of Children as an Object of International Relations: the Declaration of Children's Rights and the Child Welfare Committee of League of Nations, 1900—1924', *The International Journal of Children's Rights*, vol. 7, no. 2 (1999), 103–48.

Marston, G., 'The United Kingdom's Part in the Preparation of the European Convention on Human Rights, 1950', *International and Comparative Law Quarterly*, vol. 42, no. 4 (1993), 796–826.

Matzger, B., 'Towards an International Human Rights Regime during the Inter-War Years: the League of Nations' Combat of Traffic in Women and Children', in K. Grant, P. Levine, & F. Trentmann (eds), *Beyond Sovereignty: Britain, Empire, and Transnationalism, c. 1880–1950* (Basingstoke: Palgrave Macmillan, 2007).

Mazower, M., 'The Strange Triumph of Human Rights, 1933–1950', *The Historical Journal*, vol. 47, no. 2 (2004), 379–98.

McLeod, H., 'The Religious Crisis of the 1960s', *Journal of Modern European History*, vol. 3, no. 2 (2005), 205–30.

Moores, C., 'From Civil Liberties to Human Rights? British Civil Liberties Activism and Universal Human Rights', *Contemporary European History*, vol. 21, no. 2 (2012), 169–92.

Moores, C., 'The Progressive Professionals: the National Council for Civil Liberties and the Politics of Activism in the 1960s', *Twentieth Century British History*, vol. 2, no. 4 (2009), 538–60.

Moores, C., 'Solidarity for Chile, Transnational Activism and the Evolution of Human Rights', *Moving the Social: Journal of Social History and the History of Social Movements*, vol. 51 (2017), 115–36.

Nathans, B., 'Soviet Human Rights Activists to Amnesty International', *Quellen zur Geschichte der Menschenrechte* (n.d.) www.geschichte-menschenrechte.de/en/hauptnavigation/schluesseltexte/soviet-human-rights-activists-to-amnesty-international/?type=98765.

O'Mahoney, Father P., *One Parish and Human Rights*, Pamphlet CTS S311 (London: Catholic Truth Society, 1974?).

Pedaliu, E., 'Human Rights and Foreign Policy: Wilson and the Greek Dictators, 1967–1970', *Diplomacy & Statecraft*, vol. 18, no. 1 (2007), 185–214.

Pedaliu, E., 'Human Rights and International Security: the International Community and the Greek Dictators', *The International History Review*, vol. 38, no. 5 (2016), 1014–39.

Rynder, C., 'Sheelagh Murnaghan and the Struggle for Human Rights in Northern Ireland', *Irish Studies Review*, vol. 14, no. 4 (2006), 447–63.

Rynder, C., 'Sheelagh Murnaghan and the Ulster Liberal Party', *Journal of Liberal History*, vol. 71 (Summer 2011), 14–20.

Shaw, T., 'The Information Research Department of the British Foreign Office and the Korean War, 1950–1953', *Journal of Contemporary History*, vol. 34, no. 2 (April 1999), 263–81.

Skinner, R., 'The Moral Foundations of British Anti-Apartheid Activism, 1946–1960', *Journal of Southern African Studies*, vol. 35, no. 2 (2009), 399–416.

Skinner, R., & Lester, A., 'Humanitarianism and Empire: New Research Agendas', *The Journal of Imperial and Commonwealth History*, vol. 40, no. 5 (2012), 729–47.

Snyder, S. B., 'Exporting Amnesty International to the United States: Transatlantic Human Rights Activism in the 1960s', *Human Rights Quarterly*, vol. 34, no. 3 (August 2012), 779–99.

Veliz, C., 'The True Genesis of Amnesty International', *Quadrant*, vol. 51, no. 5 (May 2007), 11–22.

Walsh, M., 'Ecumenism in War-Time Britain: the Sword of the Spirit and "Religion and Life", 1940–45', Parts 1 and 2, *Heythrop Journal*, vol. 23, no. 3 (1982), 243–58 and vol. 23, no. 4, 477–94.

Wilford, R. A., 'The PEN Club, 1930–50', *Journal of Contemporary History*, vol. 14, no. 1 (1979), 99–116.

Film

Rogan , J. R. (dir.). *Amnesty! When They Are All Free* (Films of Record, Rogan Productions UK, 2011).

Index